Hamlet's Arab Journey

translation

T R A N S N A T I O N

SERIES EDITOR **EMILY APTER**

A list of titles in the series appears at the back of the book.

Margaret Litvin

HAMLET'S ARAB JOURNEY

Shakespeare's Prince and Nasser's Ghost

Princeton University Press   Princeton and Oxford

Published by Princeton University Press, 41 William Street,
Princeton, New Jersey 08540
In the United Kingdom: Princeton University Press,
6 Oxford Street, Woodstock, Oxfordshire OX20 1TW
press.princeton.edu

Library of Congress Cataloging-in-Publication Data
Litvin, Margaret, 1974–
Hamlet's Arab journey : Shakespeare's prince and Nasser's ghost / Margaret Litvin.
p. cm. — (Translation/transnation)
Includes bibliographical references and index.
ISBN 978-0-691-13780-3 (alk. paper)
1. Shakespeare, William, 1564–1616. Hamlet. 2. Shakespeare, William, 1564–1616—Appreciation—Arab countries. 3. Shakespeare, William, 1564–1616—Translations into Arabic—History and criticism. 4. Hamlet (Legendary character) 5. Heroes in literature. 6. Politics in literature. 7. Egypt—Civilization—English influences. 8. Arabic drama—Egypt—History and criticism. 9. Arabic drama—20th century—History and criticism. I. Title. II. Series.
PR2807.L63 2011
822.3'3—dc22 2011005331

British Library Cataloging-in-Publication Data is available

This book has been composed in Adobe Caslon Pro

Printed on acid-free paper. ∞

Printed in the United States of America

10 9 8 7 6 5 4 3 2 1

For Gary and Maria Litvin

CONTENTS

ILLUSTRATIONS

Figures

Tables

PREFACE AND ACKNOWLEDGMENTS

Hamlet is a wonderful gathering place for an intercultural conversation. Almost everyone has something to say about it, and what they say tends to be almost directly about themselves. Critics have long known that "every nation beholds its visage in Shakespeare's mirror,"[1] that *Hamlet* in particular has "attracted autobiography,"[2] and that the play is "a mirror in which every man has seen his own face."[3] As Jan Kott has said: Hamlet reads to himself, but every generation puts a different book in his hand.[4]

When I first read *Hamlet* as an American high school student, I found it quite obviously a play about individual consciousness. Hamlet's character dwarfs the plot. He loathes the petty intrigues and vendettas of a phony court. He feels burdened not only by his embarrassing mother and stepfather but by the very flesh (be it solid or sullied) that houses and limits him.[5] His closest literary relative is either Stephen Daedalus or Holden Caulfield.

The *Hamlet* I studied as an undergraduate sharpened but basically confirmed this early reading. I saw that each of the play's three older male characters (the Ghost, Claudius, and Polonius) has a script in which he wants to cast Hamlet, a theatrical use to which he would put him. But Hamlet strives to fight off these secondhand scripts; his consuming desire is to direct a production of his own.[6] The struggle over who will define Hamlet's character, who will write the script he must read, provides the play's sustaining tension.

I was surprised, then, when Soviet-émigré relatives and friends started telling me that for them *Hamlet* is just as obviously a play about justice. They had come to know *Hamlet* in the Russia of the late 1960s and 70s, where the individual's struggle for autonomy was understood in relation to the political demands of a totalitarian state. In this context Nietzsche's quarrel with Coleridge (does Hamlet think "too much" or "too well"?) hardly mattered.[7] The emphasis was not on "thinking too precisely" but on "th' oppressor's wrong . . . the law's delay, the insolence of office, and the scorn/ that patient merit of th' unworthy takes."[8] Hamlet's dilemma was not individual but social and political: how to preserve dignity and human decency in his relationships against a background of surveillance, humiliation, and lies.[9]

It became clear that our respective "communities of interpretation" had shaped our readings of the play.[10] Versions of "my" reading echo from T. S. Eliot to Harold Bloom. It has even been said that "*Hamlet,* the first great story in Europe of a young man growing up, in a sense originates the *Bildungsroman.*"[11] Meanwhile, versions of my friends' reading resonate in the work of such Soviet writers, directors, and balladeers as Boris Pasternak, Grigori Kozintsev, and Vladimir Vysotsky.[12] Our Hamlets, having grown up in different societies, are different men.

The Hamlets one meets in Arab countries are different again. They grew up playing with many of their cousins from the United States, Western and Eastern Europe, and the Soviet Union, but they are marked by distinctive experiences and concerns. At first glance, an Anglo-American reader may find them exotic. (And in case you don't, I have added an epilogue about why that might be.) Crucially, however, their distinctive traits arose over time and in response to events; they can be explained and discussed. Members of different interpretive communities cannot immediately borrow each other's eyes—that would make us members of the same community—but we can learn to wear each other's reading glasses. And through hours of patient conversation, we can come to understand the histories that helped to grind the lenses.

It is a great pleasure to thank the people who have pursued this conversation about Arab *Hamlets* with me over the past ten years. My first debt is to my University of Chicago dissertation committee: Joel Kraemer, David Bevington, Paul Friedrich, and Farouk Mustafa. Their four very different perspectives created the kaleidoscopic dialogue in which the project began to take shape. Their support and criticism have been invaluable; and Farouk's implausible dictum that "every Arab intellectual is a mixture of Hamlet, Jesus Christ, and Don Quixote" turns out to be largely true.

I am grateful to several other friends and interlocutors at Chicago: Aditya Adarkar, Nadia Abu El-Haj, Daniel Doneson, Leon Kass, Jonathan Lear, Mark Lilla, Patchen Markell, W. Flagg Miller, Glenn Most, Nathan Tarcov, and Lisa Wedeen.

In Cairo, several scholars welcomed my research and went out of their way to assist. Professors Abbas Al-Tonsi, Mohamed Enani, Mahmoud El Lozy, Sameh Mahran, Nehad Selaiha, and the late Fatma Moussa Mahmoud provided materials, recollections, and encouragement.

I have been fortunate to be in personal contact with many of the playwrights whose work this study describes. Mahmoud Aboudoma in Alexandria, Hani Afifi in Cairo, Jawad al-Assadi in Beirut, Sulayman Al-Bassam in Kuwait, Monadhil Daood in Baghdad, Nader Omran in Amman, and Mohamed Sobhi in Cairo promptly and generously provided scripts and/or videos and made themselves available for discussion. Peter Clark kindly shared his unpublished translation of Hakim Marzougui's *Ismail/Hamlet.*

For two years of wonderful discussions while revising the manuscript at the Whitney Humanities Center at Yale I am grateful to Maria Rosa Menocal, Norma Thompson, and friends including Mark Bauer, Shameem Black, Emily Coates, Bryan Garsten, Scott Newstok, Joseph Roach, Kathryn Slanski, and Roy Tsao. Lawrence Manley encouraged me to get involved in the Shakespeare Association of America, sparking many fruitful conversations. In this context I especially want to thank Michael Bristol, Thomas Cartelli, Mustapha Fahmi, Alexander C. Y. Huang, Peter Kanelos, Ania Loomba, Alfredo Michel Modenessi, Rahul Sapra, Jyostna Singh, Gary Taylor, and Ayanna Thompson.

While wrapping up this book I have enjoyed the great company and incredibly wide-ranging expertise of my colleagues in the Department of Modern Languages and Comparative Literature at Boston University. Kheireddine Djamel Bekkai, Sarah Frederick, Abigail Gillman, Giselle Khoury, Roberta Micallef, Katherine O'Connor, Peter Schwartz, Sunil Sharma, Keith Vincent, and Cathy Yeh have been partners in happily distracting conversations. Susan Jackson has been a real mentor. William Waters has been an energetic supporter and an inspiring example; I hope this book is up to his standards.

For opportunities to present drafts and for valuable comments on individual sections or chapters, I thank Ziad Adwan, Osama Abi-Mershed, Dina Amin, Lina Bernstein, Marvin Carlson, Rafik Darragi, Peter Donaldson, Ferial Ghazoul, Beatrice Gruendler, Waïl Hassan, Graham Holderness, Yvette Khoury, Hala Khamis Nassar, Said Samir, Greta Scharnweber, Zahr Said Stauffer, Shawkat Toorawa, Jessica Winegar, and Edward Ziter. Members of Chicago's Political Theory Workshop responded constructively to an early draft of chapter 1. For feedback on other sections I am grateful to scholars at the American Comparative Literature Association, the American Society for Theatre Research, the Middle East Studies Association, and the World Shakespeare Congress.

I am beholden to friends who have let me go on and on about my "*Hawāmlit,*" often pitching in with references and insights: these include Amahl Bishara, Sebaie El-Sayyed, Sameh Fekry Hanna, Lital Levy, Farouk Mustafa, Sonali Pahwa, and Mohamed Shoair. Hazem Azmy has offered advice on everything from directors' contact information to word choice. Robyn Creswell read the penultimate draft and offered many helpful and provocative suggestions. And I am privileged to enjoy the friendship and acuity of Ewa Atanassow, Anya Bernstein, Mira Bernstein, Rivi Handler-Spitz, Jennifer Rubinstein, Rachel Trousdale, and Ebru Turan.

The U.S. Department of Education made possible my year at the Center for Arabic Study Abroad in Cairo. The late Evelyn Stefansson Nef and the John M. Olin, Lynde and Harry Bradley, and Andrew W. Mellon foundations generously supported research, writing, and postdoctoral work. Robert Pippin, as chair of the University of Chicago's Committee on Social Thought, offered encouragement and helped secure funding at a crucial stage. William Waters and Virginia Sapiro nominated me for a Peter Paul Career Development Professorship at Boston University; I am grateful to them and to Peter Paul for facilitating the tranquil completion of this book.

Earlier versions of some of these arguments appeared in *Critical Survey,* the *Journal of Arabic Literature,* and *Shakespeare Yearbook.* I am grateful for permission to expand on them here. For permission to reproduce illustrations I thank Hani Afifi, Sulayman Al-Bassam, Monadhil Daood, Mahmoud El Lozy, Nader Omran, the Associated Press, Lenfilm Studios, and MISR Film International.

Fred Appel at Princeton University Press saw this project's potential from the beginning and helped greatly to make the book a reality; his patience and literary acumen have been a blessing. I am grateful to Muhsin al-Musawi and Marilyn Booth, whose comments for the Press helped sharpen and deepen my argument. Emily Apter heroically read the manuscript at a difficult time. Diana Goovaerts provided able editorial assistance. Shawn Provencal helped extract film stills, and Dimitri Karetnikov advised on illustrations. Kathleen Cioffi skilfully shepherded the book through production; Kate Babbitt's copy editing was intelligent and speedy. David Karjala helped proofread the transliterations; the errors that have crept in are surely mine.

It remains to thank my family. Enduring several years of Hamlet-themed delay jokes, they have contributed countless small efforts to help me sit and write. I am grateful to Valentin Litvin (for sharing his reminiscences of studying Shakespeare with Alexander Anikst); Ann Garden (for timely child care help); Aaron Litvin and Ana Paula Hirano Litvin (for being nearby when needed); and Gary and Maria Litvin (for everything). My husband, Ken Garden, inspires me with his intelligence and conscientiousness; his daily encouragement and insight have improved this book and everything I do. And the joy of spending time with Henry and Esther Garden has motivated me to complete this project. Now that they can both walk and talk, I look forward to many more journeys together.

NOTE ON TRANSLITERATION AND TRANSLATION

Any system of rendering Arabic words and names in Latin script must strike some balance between scholarly thoroughness and accessibility to the general reader. These systems move in and out of fashion. Currently, the trend among American scholars of Arabic is toward eliminating diacritical marks; meanwhile, the texting generation of Arabs is moving toward greater precision through such devices as the use of numerals to represent Arabic letters (e.g., 3 for ع , 7 for the back-of-the-throat "h" sound ح, and 9 for ق).

This book addresses readers fluent in Arabic, readers with no Arabic whatsoever, and the growing group in between: those students and scholars who have learned some Arabic but not enough to reconstruct a word without the assistance of diacritical marks. This latter group needs some help (as Hamlet might put it) telling a ح from a ه. In transliterating Arabic words and phrases I have therefore adopted a modified version of the International Journal of Middle East Studies system, not only representing the voiced pharyngeal fricatives and glottal stops (ʿ for ع; ' for medial and final hamza) but also including underdots for the ح (ḥ) and the emphatic consonants ص (ṣ), ض (ḍ), ط (ṭ), and ظ (ẓ), and macrons to mark the long vowels ا, و , and ي. The long vowels are usually pronounced as follows: ā = *ah* as in *man* or *father* (depending on the word); *ū* = *uu* as in *mood,* and *ī* = *ee* as in *bee*.

For personal names I have adopted a different approach. My book aims to make the intellectuals I discuss more accessible and less exotic for the Anglophone reading public. Many of these people are writing today: you can find their words and plays, in Arabic and/or English, through sites such as Facebook, Arabic Google, YouTube, and Wikipedia. To facilitate Internet and library catalog searches in both Arabic and English, I have given a systematic transliteration with diacritics in parentheses after the first reference; thereafter, I have used the author's own preferred English form or the one that occurs most frequently. Thus: Gamal Abdel Nasser (Jamāl ʿAbd al-Nāṣir); Tawfiq al-Hakim (Tawfīq al-Ḥakīm); Mahmoud Aboudoma (Maḥmūd Abū Dūmā); Hakim Marzougui (ʿAbd al-Ḥakīm al-Marzūqī); Sadiq Jalal al-Azm (Ṣādiq Jalāl al-ʿAẓm). Both forms appear in the index; the bibliography uses the fully transliterated form, except where the publication cited is in English. Transliterations within English quoted passages have been left as they are; names within Arabic quotations have been transliterated with diacritical marks. Except where otherwise noted, all translations from Arabic, French, and Russian are my own.

Hamlet's Arab Journey

INTRODUCTION

Between acts 4 and 5 of Shakespeare's tragedy, Hamlet is sent on a journey. He encounters pirates, passes from one vessel to another, and rediscovers a skill that he had almost forgotten he possessed. Critics have debated exactly how Hamlet's journey transforms him, but he returns aged and different. Having been momentarily beside himself, he appears re-centered, self-confident, perhaps more kingly. The ghosts and doubts of the early acts are forgotten. He stands at Ophelia's graveside and declares: "This is I, / Hamlet the Dane."[1]

This book follows *Hamlet* through the post-1952 Arab world. Here, too, is a Hamlet sent abroad, passed from one vessel to another, pirated, driven to re-writing, pressed to display character traits his close associates may not have known him to possess. He, too, returns from his travels deepened, complicated, and yet brought into clearer focus. To trace his journey is to see Hamlet splinter and be reconstituted; serve as a mask, a megaphone, and a measuring stick; and tell a story as revealing of his hosts' identities as of his own.

The Arab Hamlet will lead us through the tangled corridors of contemporary political debate, behind the loudspeakers of Nasser's revolutionary Egypt, and into the experimental theatres of post-1967 Egypt, Syria, Jordan, and Iraq. He will speak in different voices: secular and Islamist, shrill and playful, heroic and ironic. Sometimes he may get tipsy and stutter—or forget his lines altogether—but this, too, is part of his character, and he will remain a good guide. We know Hamlet well (or think we do); his unexpected words and silences can help illuminate some aspects of Arab literary and political culture, and also, like the best instances of cultural exchange, of our own interpretive habits and assumptions.

Why follow Hamlet, in particular, through the Arab world? That so many people there have things to say about him would be reason enough. Liberals, nationalists, and Islamists have enlisted Hamlet for their causes. Directors and playwrights have invited him into their work. Preachers, polemicists, filmmakers, novelists, poets, memoirists—no matter how public or private the message, Arab writers have drafted and redrafted Hamlet to help them express it.

But the ubiquity of the Arab Hamlet is not the only reason we should attend to him. He also has something interesting to say. To put it, for the moment, very simply: Hamlet's central concern is the problem of historical agency. He asks what it means "to be" rather than "not to be" in a world where "the time is out of joint" and one's very existence as a historical actor is threatened. He thus encapsulates a debate coeval with and largely constitutive of modern Arab identity: the problem of self-determination and authenticity. Following Hamlet's Arab journey, then, helps clarify one of the most central and widely misunderstood preoccupations of modern Arab politics.

The Arab Hamlet can contribute to literary studies as well. His multilayered history helps suggest a new analytical frame for scholarship on literary reception and appropriation: a frame that breaks out of the binary categories (influencer/influencee, colonizer/colonized, and, more recently, Arabs/West) that have shaped the study of postcolonial literatures. The binarism has been much criticized, but it is still with us. As teachers, we often find it easy and fruitful to show our students Text B and ask how it mimics and revises Text A—or, barely better, how it reflects Context X. In organizing its 2007 Complete Works Festival in Stratford-upon-Avon, the Royal Shakespeare Company followed the same logic, billing the Arabic and Indian performances, among others, as "responses" to the mainstream shows.[2] Some postcolonial "responders"—such as Sudanese novelist Tayeb Salih (al-Ṭayyib Ṣāliḥ)—have been well served by these labels. But to describe a broader range of interesting work and to serve the timely project of reinserting Arabic literature into world literature, it is useful to broaden the frame.

I have termed my new approach the "global kaleidoscope." For *Hamlet* did not arrive in the Arab world only or mainly through Britain's colonization of Egypt. Nor was Shakespeare's work first packaged as a single colonially imposed authoritative set of texts. Instead, as I will show, Arab audiences came to know Shakespeare through a kaleidoscopic array of performances, texts, and criticism from many directions: not just the "original" British source culture but also French, Italian, American, Soviet, and Eastern European literary and dramatic traditions, which at times were more influential than Britain's. Examining how Arabs got their *Hamlet* and what they have done with it over several generations can point the way to a more fruitful understanding of international Shakespeare appropriation and, in general, of international literary encounters.

Moving between these two main concerns, literary appropriation and moral/political agency, let me quickly map the terrain I hope to cover in this book.

"When Shakespeare Travels Abroad"

The paradox of *Hamlet* appropriation is already apparent in Shakespeare's text. Hamlet spends the whole play trying to resist appropriations, misrepresentations, or simplifications of his character. He refuses to be summarized: his speech quibbles and equivocates, maddening those who would "pluck out the heart of [his] mystery" or "sound [him] from [his] lowest note to the top of [his] compass."[3] From his first appearance, when he claims that outward forms cannot "denote [him] truly" because he has "that within which passes show,"[4] to his dying moment, when he wants Horatio to stay behind and tell *his* story, he always insists he is misunderstood. Yet his puns, riddles, and moods deter no one. Almost all the major and minor characters (including Fortinbras and the gravediggers) offer a theory of what Hamlet is "about."[5] No one can sound him (in either sense), but everyone keeps trying.

The same drama has played out among readers and audiences worldwide. Hamlet's first three lines are puns, challenging the very idea of translatability.[6] Yet *Hamlet* is one of Shakespeare's most often translated plays; in many languages (including Arabic and Russian) it is *the* most translated. Despite his resistance or because of it, Hamlet is one of the most intensely appropriated literary characters of all time.[7] There are wilting Romantic Hamlets, nationalist hero Hamlets, humanist dissident Hamlets, Puritan Hamlets, disenchanted philosopher Hamlets, existentialist Hamlets, *yeshiva-bokher* Hamlets,[8] and so on.

Scholars have followed the translators and adapters. Hundreds of studies have documented Shakespeare's global reach; many have focused on Prince Hamlet's naturalization as a Victorian Englishman, a German, a Russian or Soviet, a Lithuanian, or a mid-century Pole. At the present writing, the University of Chicago library catalog lists 110 works whose titles begin with "Shakespeare in . . ."—excluding copies of the 1998 film *Shakespeare in Love*. "Hamlet in . . ." covers another ten.[9]

The field of Shakespeare studies has opened up to international perspectives over the past thirty-five years.[10] Non-Anglophone Shakespeare really entered the scholarly mainstream in the 1990s, when several lines of academic inquiry converged. Translation theorists found in Shakespeare's plays a convenient (because widely known and prestigious) test case.[11] Scholars in performance studies, having noted how sharply local context could influence a play's staging and interpretation, saw a need to account for "intercultural" performances of Shakespeare in various languages and locales.[12] Marxist scholars became interested in the fetishization of Shakespeare as a British cultural icon which, in turn, was used to confer cultural legitimacy on the project of capitalist empire-building.[13] Scholars of postcolonial drama and literature began to explore how the periphery responded.[14]

All this scholarship developed quickly and with a great sense of urgency. For instance, the editor of the groundbreaking collection *Foreign Shakespeare* announced in 1993 that "we have not even begun to develop a theory of cultural exchange that might help us understand what happens when Shakespeare travels abroad" and proclaimed that this was "the most important task Shakespeareans face . . . much more important than linguistic analysis, textual examination, psychological assessments, historical research, or any of the Anglo-centered occupations scholars have traditionally valued and perpetuated."[15]

Yet hundreds of articles, monographs, conferences, and edited volumes later, such a "theory of cultural exchange" is still lacking. There exists no accepted method or theory to explain where and how Shakespeare's plays and other prestigious European texts are appropriated: who tends to deploy them, in what circumstances, for what ends, and whether some texts (such as *Hamlet*) lend themselves to different agendas than others.[16]

That mine is the first book-length analysis of Arab *Hamlets* is no surprise; we can look to the familiar disciplinary cleavages. Specialists in world Shakespeare appropriation, typically based in English or comparative literature departments, tend to lack Arabic language skills. Meanwhile, Arab and western scholars of Arabic literature have opted to spend their limited time exploring the vast terrain of Arabic literature "proper" rather than such hybrid (and "inauthentic"?) phenomena as Arab Shakespeare. They have perhaps felt that appropriation studies are a luxury, to be taken seriously only when enough of the basic research has been done.

The topic has been left to Arab scholars of English literature, and there, too, it has remained marginal. Several Arab students in U.S. and British graduate programs have written useful dissertations on Arabic translations or productions of Shakespeare, but none has led to a book.[17] The fine insights generated by theatre criticism have not been generalized.[18] Scholars in the English departments of Arab universities, facing a relative dearth of adequate Arabic-language studies of Shakespeare, have often felt their first priority was to write for their own students.[19] When well-placed Arab literary scholars in the West (such as Oxford's M. M. Badawi) have occasionally brought "Arab Shakespeare" to their colleagues' attention, they have presented it almost as a novelty, not hesitating to draw easy laughs with the old joke that Shakespeare was really a crypto-Arab, "Shaykh Zubayr."[20]

More significant is the lack of a convincing framework for a study like mine. The paradigm of literary influence, a mainstay of comparative literary studies, has been useful but inadequate: it overprivileges the influencer and limits the agency of the influencee. It thus neglects to ask why different writers take different things from Shakespeare and bring different things to him (and why many writers familiar with Shakespeare choose not to appropriate his texts at all). But subsequent explanations, despite their authors' professed desire to "provincialize Europe,"[21] have not moved past the basic idea of a binary relationship between original texts and rewritings.

One attempt is the model of "postcolonial rewriting," which stresses the agency (and the often transgressive intent) of the rewriter. This model serves very well for cases in which nationalist writers in the colonies straightforwardly "write back" to the metropole[22]—for example, Martinican poet Aimé Césaire's *Une Tempête* (1968), and, in a different way, *The Tragedy of Cleopatra* (1927) by Egyptian poet Ahmed Shawqi (Aḥmad Shawqī).[23] However, the postcolonial model has two well-known flaws. First, it reinscribes the same conceptual dichotomy that it aims to critique (albeit while drawing attention to it, at least).[24] Second, and more damaging, it is helpless before the many cases where the local text or performance that borrows from Shakespeare "is not anti-colonial," does not seek to subvert anything in particular, and "is actually not interested in Shakespeare at all, except as a suitably weighty means through which it can negotiate its own future, shake off its own cramps, revise its own traditions, and expand its own performative styles."[25]

When the former colonizer is not the implicit addressee, who is? If Shakespeare appropriation is not an "aggressive binary action," then what is it about?[26] Recently the twin concepts of "global" and "local" Shakespeare appear to be replacing "postcolonialism" as the *mots clefs*—but so far without unlocking new insights about who tends to borrow what from whom, when, and why. Tired with all these, some talented scholars have called for "more supple and comprehensive theories of cross-cultural Shakespeare encounters."[27] They have meanwhile returned to the working notion that what shapes a community's engagement with a foreign text are the specific talents and circumstances of local theatre-makers and their audiences.[28] This approach has produced some rich and sensitive scholarship, but it hardly helps chart a direction for future work.

The Global Kaleidoscope

This book proposes a model of literary appropriation that I call the "global kaleidoscope." As I argue in chapter 3, each rereading and rewriting is created in active dialogue with a diverse array of readings that precede and surround it. Contextual factors help condition both the way an Arab appropriator receives and interprets *Hamlet* and, later, the shape of the new version he or she ultimately produces. (My model is itself in dialogue with Bakhtin's "dialogical" speech appropriated from a web of previous speech, H. R. Jauss's idea of a dialectical question-answer relationship between context and text, and Paul Friedrich's notion of a "parallax" in which the gifted individual language user negotiates and in turn helps reshape surrounding norms of grammar and culture.)[29]

The first phase to notice is the reception. Many studies assume a simple one-on-one relationship between an "original" text and its (obedient or subversive) rewriter. But this assumption is unrealistic. Arab writers do not first encounter *Hamlet* just by sitting down and reading it. In general, the reception of a prestigious foreign literary work rarely entails a tabula rasa, a direct unmediated experience of an authoritative original. Instead, the would-be appropriator typically receives a text through a historically determined kaleidoscope of *indirect* experiences: some combination of the films, performances, conversations, articles, abridgments, translations, and other materials that happen to be available, along with or before the text itself. These materials come from multiple cultural traditions (not just the "original" source culture) and arrive in various languages. Their assortment and relative significance depends on the society's current circumstances: international alignments, social tensions, cultural fashions, and so forth. They offer distinct and even conflicting interpretations from which the receiver must synthesize or choose.

This indeterminacy confers a limited freedom. The appropriator is free to choose his or her influences, but only from the options made available by the kaleidoscope configuration of the day. (It is similar to the way we speak of a musical group's "influences": there is a sense of freely choosing, albeit from a limited sphere of options, what to be influenced by.)

After forming a coherent idea of the received text, the appropriator must decide whether and how to redeploy it for an artistic and/or polemical purpose: poetic meditation, literal reproduction, political allegory, parody, quotation or allusion, or sloganization. This is another moment of free decision within a limited sphere of options. The new interpretation cannot be wholly arbitrary but is conditioned partly by the surrounding conversations about art, culture, politics, and, of course, Shakespeare.[30] So while open to imaginative play, the choice is also circumscribed by audience considerations: what would make sense lexically, resonate culturally, and pay off politically. Each generation's reception and reinterpretation then becomes part of the kaleidoscope for the generation that follows.

Recognizing this global kaleidoscope does not lead to any predictive claims about the purpose of rewriting a respected literary work or the direction such a rewriting might take. Instead, its main virtue is to provide a method (a set of questions) through which to consider the individual appropriator's political, artistic, and philosophical situation and concerns. In particular, it draws attention to the great variety of actual sources through which an appropriator acquires a "source" text. It points out that every rewriting occurs in dialogue with a wide range of competing interpretations and with the "horizon of expectations" of the rewriter's own audience. Thus this approach can help us extricate studies of literary appropriation from the vexed and self-reproducing dichotomy variously termed dominant/subversive, original/rewriting, Empire/colony, center/periphery, and West/East.

The case of Arab *Hamlet* appropriation illustrates the usefulness of the global kaleidoscope approach. For one thing, the Arab *Hamlet* differs somewhat from the cases of Arab *Antony and Cleopatra, Othello,* and *The Merchant of Venice,* which have all, for obvious reasons of plot, attracted more explicitly anticolonial rewritings.[31] (However, a large number of *Othello* offshoots have instead raised other concerns, such as gender violence.)[32] *Hamlet* is also not part of a second group of Shakespeare plays, those in which scholars have identified elements of Arab or Middle Eastern origin.[33] It heads the third and largest group of Shakespeare plays, those for which most Arab readers and writers have not raised the issue of Occidental or Oriental roots at all.[34] Other major plays in this group are *King Lear, Julius Caesar,* and *Richard III*—also, incidentally, plays that feature autocracies and their problems. Already this shows the futility of trying to generalize about the way Shakespeare will function in a given cultural context. Different plays, due to their particular resonances with local circumstances, are perceived and deployed very differently.

Further, *Hamlet*'s reception history contravenes the postcolonial model. As we will see, British models were important but not decisive. Certainly there were British schools with required English classes; schoolchildren read abridgments (such as Charles and Mary Lamb's *Tales from Shakespeare*) in both English and Arabic. But the earliest Arabic Shakespeare adaptations, written by

Syro-Lebanese immigrants who knew French better than English, reflected mainly French Neoclassical theatre conventions and the tastes of Cairo's emerging middle class. At every moment, the geopolitical configuration helped determine which cultural models seemed most attractive. There were Italian acting styles, French and British traveling productions, Arab and international literary criticism, and, still later, American and Soviet productions and films. Arab students who pursued advanced degrees abroad (in Paris, Rome, London, Moscow, Sofia, Berlin, Prague, and Budapest or in various American cities) also returned with books and ideas. Thus, influential readings of Shakespeare came from Britain but also from France, Italy, Germany, the Soviet Union, the United States, and Eastern Europe. This was especially true of *Hamlet* because it obsessed so much of Europe and Russia throughout the nineteenth and twentieth centuries.

Moreover, as the global kaleidoscope model would predict, younger Arab *Hamlet* appropriators have also responded to the interpretations of their elders. Each generation's political and cultural context includes the preceding Arab versions. Thus (to glance briefly at examples we will later examine in detail): Syrian director Riad Ismat's (Riyāḍ ʿIṣmat, b. 1947) freedom-fighter Hamlet, presented at a Damascus high school in 1973, responded in part to Jan Kott's *Shakespeare Our Contemporary* and other Eastern European models of Shakespeare interpretation. Ismat's production helped inspire Syrian playwright Mamduh Adwan (Mamdūḥ ʿAdwān) to write his 1976 play *Hamlet Wakes Up Late,* whose ineffectual protagonist satirizes glorified revolutionary portrayals like Ismat's. Adwan's satire was in turn invoked by later pundits writing for Syrian and pan-Arab audiences, including Sadiq Jalal al-Azm, who in a 2000 column urges his Arab readers not to oversleep and let "the Fortinbrases of this world . . . win the day and have the final say."[35] And so on. To understand any of these borrowings, we need to hear the conversation in which they all participate. Simply taking one of these Syrian works and comparing it one-to-one with Shakespeare's *Hamlet* would fall far short of explaining what it means.

Hamlet and Political Agency

The main theme of the Arab *Hamlet* conversation, already evident in the three Syrian examples sketched above, is political agency: the desire to determine one's own fate, to be an actor in history rather than a victim of it, "to be" rather than "not to be." In the Arab context, such agency is usually imagined as collective. In political debate Hamlet's main contribution has been a slogan—"Shall we be or not be?"—an urgent, collective call to arms. In the Arab theatre, the archetypal Hamlet is a decisive political actor, a seeker of justice and righter of wrongs. One observer has summarized him as "a romantic hero who sets out to fight corruption, and dies for the cause of justice."[36] But it turns out that this archetypal Hamlet lasted less than a decade on the Arab stage. His style of political agency, then, is not the only style worth considering.

So let us listen to the conversation. First, let us explore how speakers of Arabic have chosen to "voice" the lexeme "Hamlet."[37] These voicings have developed over time; several factors (political pressures, available models, gifted individual speakers, etc.) have shaped the social grammar that circumscribes acceptable new voicings. Then let us analyze Hamlet's function diachronically: the changing addressees, tone, and rhetorical goals. My book approaches these two sets of questions in turn. The first chapter presents, basically, a phrasebook: a synchronic ordinary-language study of the way "Hamlet" works in today's Arab political lexicon. The second focuses on the dramatic imagination of Egyptian leader Gamal Abdel Nasser (Jamāl ʿAbd al-Nāṣir; 1918–70), whose personality and policies did the most to shape the figure I will call the Arab Hero Hamlet. The rest of the book traces the stage history of this heroic Hamlet: his origins in a global kaleidoscope of Shakespeare versions, his brief heyday in the 1970s Arab theatre, and the long ironic afterlife that kept him in circulation for the following thirty years.

Chapter 1 explores Hamlet's meaning in today's Arabic political vocabulary. Hamlet has been invoked in reference to nearly every major and minor political crisis touching the Arab world in the past decade. Analyzing his function in recent polemical writings such as newspaper columns, speeches, and sermons, I show how Arab writers read "to be or not to be" not as a meditation on the individual's place in the world but as an argument about collective political identity. Hamlet comes to represent a group: the Arab and/or Muslim community. (Some writers try to conflate the two.) Because "the time is out of joint," the group's continuous collective identity is under threat. Its existence is menaced at the very moment at which it comes into being. Other themes from *Hamlet*—words/deeds, sleep/waking, madness/wholeness—help reinforce the urgency of the crisis. However, these cries of outrage and alarm are not the only approach to the issue of historical agency. As a counterpoint I offer an instance of *Hamlet* rewriting by the important Palestinian-Iraqi writer Jabra Ibrahim Jabra (Jabrā Ibrāhīm Jabrā). Jabra's protagonist Walid Masoud constitutes himself through "words, words, words," pointing the way toward the more complex understandings of agency seen in the following chapters.

Turning to the stage history, we will find that Hamlet's link to political agency has remained remarkably stable across five decades. In different periods, however, writers and directors have used Hamlet to pursue quite different types of agency, and in different ways. Their preoccupations with *Hamlet* fall into four main phases: international standards (1952–64), psychological depth (1964–67), political agitation (1970–75), and intertextual dramatic irony (1976–2002). Because Arab theatre people see their work as necessarily political and because *Hamlet* is read as a political play, these phases have largely corresponded to the prevailing political moods in the region: euphoric pride after the Egyptian Revolution of 1952; soul-searching and impatience for progress in the mid-1960s; anger and defiance after the disastrous June War of 1967 and Nasser's death in 1970; and a mixture of cynicism and nostalgia since the mid-1970s, as stale autocracies spread through the region and stifled its dreams of national awakening.

Our journey begins in Egypt in 1952. As chapter 2 explains, much of what matters for Arab *Hamlet* appropriation in the postcolonial period—the international sources, the way they were absorbed, and the concerns they help express—was shaped by the legacy of Gamal Abdel Nasser. Nasser's geopolitical and cultural priorities made a range of *Hamlet*s available and conditioned how intellectuals received them. Beyond this, from the moment in 1954 when he declared to his people, "All of you are Gamal Abdel Nasser," the Egyptian leader personally embodied his country's identity and acted out its drama of historical agency. Beyond Egypt's borders, he became (like his radio station) "the voice of the Arabs." His defeat in the 1967 war and his death in 1970 meant a promise broken and an inheritance withdrawn. The problem of how to mourn him would create a hunger for the very works of art, including Shakespeare adaptations, that his policies had helped import.

Chapter 3 presents the global kaleidoscope theory as a much-needed revision to the Prospero-and-Caliban model of postcolonial rewriting. To this end, I summarize the actual kaleidoscope of *Hamlet*s available to Egyptian theatre professionals and audiences by 1964. The powerful but atypical reminiscences of Arab students who suffered under British schoolmasters (here represented by filmmaker Youssef Chahine and critic Edward Said) tend to obscure the broader origins of Arab Shakespeare. In fact, these origins were varied; different sources gained importance in different periods. Nineteenth-century French sources, including the hitherto-unidentified version from which Tanyus ʿAbdu (Ṭānyūs ʿAbduh) cribbed the earliest surviving Arabic *Hamlet* (1901), helped plant the seeds of a decisive, heroic Hamlet in pursuit of justice. Direct-from-English translations, with a greater commitment to treating Shakespeare's plays as written texts, became part of the kaleidoscope by the 1930s, as did German-inspired Romantic readings of Hamlet's introspective depths. A transformative addition was Grigori Kozintsev's edgy and politically allusive

Hamlet film (1964), which became a Cairo sensation, although it was not imitated until the 1970s. At the juncture of these competing approaches, we will consider a high-profile Egyptian production of *Hamlet* in 1964–65: an effort to mediate between the British and Soviet readings of *Hamlet* and a bid to claim Egypt's place on the world stage by showing mastery of the "world classics."

Chapter 4 examines a related bid for political agency (1964–67): the pursuit of interiorized subjectivity as proof of moral personhood. As the Egyptian theatre grew more ambitious, playwrights strove to create dramatic exemplars of authentic Arab political action. This in turn required characters who were "deep" enough to qualify as fully fledged moral subjects and hence modern political agents. Here Hamlet was still the gold standard. Looking at two landmark plays in which critics have heard Hamletian echoes, *Sulayman of Aleppo* by Alfred Farag (Alfrīd Faraj) and *The Tragedy of Al-Hallaj* by Salah Abdel Sabur (Ṣalāḥ ʿAbd al-Ṣabūr), I argue that the "Hamletization" of their Muslim protagonists is neither subversive in spirit nor driven by any desire to seize mastery of a colonizer's text. Rather, Hamlet serves as a model and even an emblem of psychological interiority. But because both Farag's seminarian and Abdel Sabur's Sufi were read as brave opponents of a tyrannical regime, these two Muslim heroes helped cement the link in the Arab audience's imagination between Hamlet and the theme of earthly justice.

Such appeals for recognition largely stopped after the Arab defeat by Israel in the June War of 1967. (The defeat also ended Egypt's unquestioned dominance of Arab culture. Therefore, starting in this period, we will begin to look at plays from Syria, Jordan, and elsewhere.) Chapter 5 begins with the cultural impact of the June War and its coda, Nasser's death in 1970. As we will see, the defeat fundamentally altered Arab conceptions of political theatre's role. A well-developed high culture was no longer considered enough to guarantee the world's respect. Psychological interiority was irrelevant: what mattered was not deserving agentive power but seizing it. Disillusioned with their regimes, dramatists stopped addressing subtly allegorical plays to the government; instead, they appealed directly to audiences, trying to rouse them to participate in political life. Analyzing two early 1970s *Hamlet* adaptations from Egypt and Syria, we will see how the 1970s Hamlet became a Che Guevara in doublet and hose. Guilt and sadness over his father's death only sharpened his anger; his fierce pursuit of justice left no room for introspection or doubt.

But this agitprop effort, too, quickly hit a dead end. Rejecting activist theatre, the Egyptian, Syrian, and Iraqi dramatists of the past thirty-five years have instead deployed Hamlet for dramatic irony. Chapter 6 examines six Arab *Hamlet* offshoot plays performed between 1976 and 2002. The most recent of these plays, written in English, stands on the margins of the Arab *Hamlet* tradition. But the rest, aware of their predecessors' heroic Hamlet, turn him into a foil for their own pointedly inarticulate and ineffectual protagonists. These new antiheroes are "not Prince Hamlet, nor were meant to be"; most lack even the eloquence of a Prufrock.[38] Meanwhile Claudius becomes a protean and all-powerful force who dominates the play; the ghost of Nasserism, discredited but not replaced, settles into the role of Hamlet's father's ghost. These bitter, often hilarious plays criticize the political situation, but they are at their best in mocking allegorical political theatre. The only real political agency available, they suggest, is the power to set oneself above one's circumstances through ironic laughter.

These plays highlight Hamlet's work as a political rewriter, one of the important themes *Hamlet* has offered Arab dramatists in recent years. For although he preaches against ad-libbing and clowning,[39] Hamlet is not averse to adapting a foreign play when the need arises. When "benetted round with villainies,"[40] he is quick to turn a trope into a trap. Hamlet's timely staging of *The Murder of Gonzago,* "the image of a murder done in Vienna,"[41] has provided first a model and more recently an anti-model to politically engaged Arab playwrights and directors.

As we will see, by 1990 the obvious failure of political drama on Hamlet's terms—its failure, that is, to spark concrete change in Arab regimes or societies—had pushed some younger Arab playwrights away from Hamlet's instrumental view of political theatre. In a comic or ironic mode, their work dramatized its own inefficacy as political art. Thus their Hamlets came to resemble the dreamy hesitators of the Anglo-American tradition, but carrying a different valence resulting from their particular historical trajectory. With their unavenged fathers and their betrayed revolutionary convictions, these Hamlets were not simply unheroic but post-heroic. Whether they will again find their voice in response to changing political circumstances in Egypt and elsewhere in the region remains to be seen.

1

HAMLET IN THE DAILY DISCOURSE OF ARAB IDENTITY

For educated English speakers, quoting Shakespeare is a natural and effective way to make a point. Shakespeare's works are "misread and misquoted in support of any and every position" in European and American political debate, because "who better than Shakespeare serves as secular scripture in our world today?"[1] As R. A. Foakes puts it:

> In the English-speaking world William Shakespeare and his works have an extraordinary status. . . . [His] cultural authority has paradoxically ensured that Shakespeare has been democratized as a representative consciousness, whose works embody in memorable language much of the wisdom of our civilization. Passages from his plays and poems are frequently cited in all sorts of contexts to support legal or political arguments, validate advertisements, justify prejudices, and generally sanction a whole range of beliefs and opinions.[2]

Less well known is that Shakespeare's plays hold this quasi-sacred status in the Arab world as well. As early as the 1930s, Lebanese writer Mikhail Naimy (Mikhaīl Nuʿayma) declared, "Shakespeare remains a Kaʿba to which we make pilgrimage and a Qibla to which we turn in prayer."[3] More recently, a columnist in the pan-Arab daily *Al-Hayat* complained that Arab unity had become just like Shakespeare: "[E]veryone swears by it (*al-kull yastashhid bihā*) . . . be it to the point or not."[4] Speakers cite chapter and verse, regardless of how well or badly they know the texts. Whether the target audience is Arab, western, or mixed, Shakespeare is both a staple of daily speech and a rhetorical trump card.

The 2006 "cartoon controversy" illustrates this phenomenon. In January 2006, tempers flared over a Danish newspaper's decision months earlier to run a series of cartoons caricaturing the Prophet Muhammad.[5] Around the world, thousands of commentators felt called either to defend freedom of speech or to lambaste European insensitivity to Muslims. Predictably, dozens of western polemicists lifted a phrase from *Hamlet* to do it. "Something is rotten *outside* the state of Denmark," proclaimed European, American, and Arab writers appalled at the violence of some Arab and Muslim responses.[6] "Buy Danish—Nothing Rotten in the State of Denmark!" urged a Belgian newspaper supporting a solidarity campaign.[7] "Rotten Judgment in the State of Denmark," countered a Danish-born political scientist.[8]

If they had noticed, these commentators might have been surprised to see Arab and Muslim editorialists on the other side of the issue paying them back in the same cultural currency. The quotation "Something Is Rotten in the State of Denmark" headlined an article decrying European double standards on religious taboos in the English-language, Saudi-based *Arab News*.[9] A writer in the Saudi daily *Al-Riyadh* quoted the phrase in an Arabic column on prejudice against Islam, adding, "And we affirm that the rot is still present in Denmark and several other European countries."[10] And a Jordanian blogger gloated: "Something Is Rotten in the State of Denmark . . . and it could be smell of rotting Danish products as a result of the most recently implemented boycotts."[11]

For weeks, commentators on both sides of the issue used the shared idiom of Shakespeare to hurl insults across an increasingly real-looking cultural divide. No one saw any irony in such uses of *Hamlet*. Unlike Danish havarti cheese, Shakespeare is globalized and naturalized, perceived in the Middle East as a long-ago-successful transplant from Europe rather than as a threatening import. The Denmark quotation seems to have occurred to each writer independently. Some simply wanted to look clever. Others may have realized that invoking Shakespeare, the crown jewel of western civilization, would boost their authority in defending (or questioning) "western values." In most cases the Shakespeare allusion was not explained; readers were expected to recognize it.[12] A month into the controversy, an Internet search combining the terms "something is rotten," "Denmark," and "cartoons" yielded 18,200 hits in English alone.[13]

The rhetorical step to *Hamlet* from a controversy involving Denmark may seem obvious.[14] Yet the play also recurs in intra-Arab discussions of other events. It is cited more often than any other Shakespeare play (*Julius Caesar* and *The Merchant of Venice* are distant seconds) and probably more than any other literary text at all.[15] During nearly every major and minor political crisis touching the Arab world in the past decade, fairly mainstream Arab commentators have expressed their opinions using *Hamlet*. There are examples referring to September 11, 2001, and its aftermath; the capture of deposed Iraqi dictator Saddam Hussein (2003);[16] the killing of Dutch filmmaker Theo Van Gogh (2004);[17] Syria's military withdrawal from Lebanon (2005);[18] Iraq's 2005 constitutional referendum and parliamentary elections (2005);[19] FIFA soccer;[20] Arabs' relationship to U.S. president Barack Obama (2009);[21] and antigovernment protests in Tehran (2009).[22] *Hamlet* has been invoked in reference to more general issues as well: economic development,[23] globalization,[24] women's rights,[25] the future of Iraq,[26] Egyptian democracy (or nondemocracy),[27] the Battle of Badr (624 CE),[28] the Palestine question,[29] the role of Arabs (or Muslims) in the world,[30] and the viability of "the Arab system."[31] These uses range from simple catchphrases to thoughtful, sustained engagements with Shakespeare's text.

It is not only western-educated Europhile intellectuals who cite *Hamlet* in Arabic. The play is invoked by religious as well as secular figures; by liberals, nationalists, and Islamists; by critics who write in obscure journals; and by cultural authorities who publish in major pan-Arab newspapers or command large satellite television audiences. These speakers may have very little in common besides their use of *Hamlet*; when they meet, they may not be on speaking terms. For example, Egyptian-born Islamist Shaykh Yusuf al-Qaradawi (Yūsuf al-Qaraḍāwī) and Syrian secularist Sadiq Jalal al-Azm (Ṣādiq Jalāl al-ʿAẓm) represent nearly opposite ends of the Arab religio-political spectrum; the confrontation between the two in a late-1990s television debate represented a serious challenge to al-Qaradawi's authority that made him appear unusually defensive and weak.[32] Yet we will shortly see published examples of each of these two men citing *Hamlet* to argue about the Arabs' or Muslims' place in history. In fact, the two use the play to raise quite similar alarms about the future: Can the Arabs (in al-Azm's case) or the Muslims (in al-Qaradawi's) seize their collective destiny or will they be doomed, like Hamlet, to watch Fortinbras capture the day?

My first aim in this chapter is not to explain *why* all these Arab speakers invoke *Hamlet* for political debate (that is partly a historical question for later chapters) but to make sense of *how* they do so. As we shall see, Arab polemical uses of *Hamlet* fall into a strikingly simple pattern: *Hamlet* is most often invoked to argue about a perceived existential threat to a valued collective identity. This pattern tends to draw on four basic themes: nonbeing versus being, madness versus wholeness, sleep versus waking, and talk versus action. Each of these themes hangs on certain key lines from Shakespeare's play; each also resonates with Arab political debates going back at least to the nineteenth century. These polemical deployments of *Hamlet* are built on both a meaningful relationship with Shakespeare's text and a consistent reading of Arab history.

However, such an "ordinary-language" analysis of *Hamlet* use will take us only so far. By focusing on sloganized political rhetoric, it leaves aside much of what Shakespeare's *Hamlet* has offered Arab writers in the past half-century. Our contemporary polemicists tend to emphasize identity and collective fate but overlook Hamlet's tireless writing, rewriting, acting, and directing—activities whose centrality in *Hamlet* has not escaped Arab adapters. Thus they stress Hamlet's predicament (the danger of erasure from history) but largely ignore the strategies and effects of his response. An analysis of their rhetoric therefore fails to account for the appropriations of *Hamlet* we will encounter in the next five chapters, all of which engage with the play's literary and theatrical dimensions, sometimes in self-consciously metatheatrical ways. To point the way toward some of these issues, I will conclude this chapter by highlighting how one important writer, Jabra Ibrahim Jabra, uses *Hamlet* to meditate on the possibilities of words and rewriting.

"Time Out of Joint": Coming to Terms with History

It is not difficult to find affinities between Shakespeare's Hamlet and the archetypal Islamist revolutionary of the past fifty years.[33] Like a young *salafī*, Hamlet loathes drinking (he calls it "swinish"), rails against unchastity, and believes that a "dram of evil" is enough to contaminate a whole person or even nation, however "noble" the remainder.[34] His distrust of social conventions and appearances ("I know not 'seems'"), of unregulated natural and social processes ("things rank and gross in nature"), and particularly things of the flesh (e.g., "O shame, where is thy blush?") suggests a puritanism that wishes nature could be restricted by divine law.[35] He invokes heavenly rewards and the power of prayer, choosing not to kill the kneeling Claudius lest he send him to heaven.[36] He contemplates suicide and finds it theologically incorrect, yet he embraces martyrdom.[37]

However, there is a deeper and more fruitful point of contact between Hamlet and (our stock picture of) the contemporary Islamist: their politics. Both act in ways that respond, albeit sometimes irrationally, to a sense of disempowerment stemming from a profound historical dislocation. Margreta de Grazia has recently drawn attention to the original sin of "dispossession" at the core of Shakespeare's play: a land usurped, an inheritance denied.[38] Hamlet, let down by the system of elective monarchy, would win a democratic election if he could hold one.[39] He faces a ruthless autocratic regime whose informers penetrate even the closest personal relationships (e.g., his relationship with Ophelia). Although allowed to read and talk all he wants, he is soon spied on, locked out of political power, exiled, and nearly executed through a conspiracy between a corrupt monarchy at home and pliant allies abroad.[40] Surrounded by political as well as moral corruption, he is moved to equate the two.

Hamlet's dispossession is part of a larger historical rupture: "the time" itself is "out of joint."[41] Critics, both in the then-Socialist bloc and in the West, have long noted that *Hamlet* is set at a turning point. Whether one understands the juncture as a transition from medieval chivalric heroism to modern individual moralism,[42] from a hauntingly undead Catholicism to an enforced Protestantism,[43] or even from a feudal society to bourgeois commercialism and Renaissance humanism,[44] Hamlet straddles a cultural shift in which the social and moral system has given way before there is anything solid to replace it. James Shapiro has argued that *Hamlet* responds to some historical and cultural anxieties of Shakespeare's own time: the irrelevance of chivalry, the uncertain wars in Ireland, and the looming question of who would succeed Queen Elizabeth:

> There's a sense in *Hamlet* no less than in the [late Elizabethan] culture at large of a sea change, of a world that is dead but not yet buried. . . . Acting as if one still lived in the world of Hamlet's heroic father—where it was possible to win fame through martial feats—was no longer possible. But how to act in the world that had replaced it was not clear, and was part of Hamlet's dilemma.[45]

An aura of nostalgia and loss thus pervades the play.[46] Things have come loose from their moorings. The old moral and political order is gone, but instead of a new one Hamlet finds only "an unweeded garden" (too much nature) or "a prison" (too much culture) run by a fraudulent crew of usurpers, impostors, bawds, sycophants, and spies. Friends deceive; fathers "loose" their daughters.[47] Relationships are unstable.[48] Words are not to be trusted, either. When his father's ghost reappears, Hamlet does not even know by what name or title to call it.[49] While Hamlet is particularly attuned to it, other characters confirm that the malaise affects the kingdom as a whole, not only the melancholy prince. It is Horatio who foresees "some strange eruption to our state," Marcellus who declares that "something is rotten."[50] Even Claudius fully expects Fortinbras to consider Denmark "disjoint and out of frame."[51]

Against this fractured background Hamlet struggles to find an authentic and appropriate way to behave. We can see his struggle as an effort to take ownership of his future: to establish his autonomy, to write his own lines instead of speaking from a script written by others. Seeing through the self-serving platitudes of the new "common" sense, Hamlet seeks a "particular" way of being. To his mother's admonition ("Thou know'st 'tis common: all that lives must die") he responds with withering sarcasm: "Ay madam, it is *common*."[52] Resisting the various roles thrust upon him by the play's older characters, he seeks instead a part that can "denote [him] truly."[53] Perhaps it is precisely this striving for self-definition that has made Hamlet appear to embody such a distinctly modern concept of the self.[54]

Collective Identity under Threat

In modern Arab political discourse (of which Islamist discourse is just one strand), Hamlet's concerns with agency and authenticity are expanded beyond the individual. Now it is the nation or community struggling to establish its autonomy, write its own lines, and shape its own destiny against the background of a great historical shift or crisis rooted in an act of violent usurpation. While extending Hamlet's concerns, such citations do not pervert them. Collectivizing Hamlet's dilemma simply carries it into the rhetorical mode of nineteenth- and twentieth-century nationalist discourse.

The text that Arab polemicists most often cite from *Hamlet* is the "to be or not to be" soliloquy, often called "the monologue of Being" (*mūnūlūj al-kaynūna*). But they tend to quote Hamlet's question in the plural: "Shall we be or not be?" (*nakūn aw lā nakūn*).[55] This rendition takes a liberty offered by the Arabic language. Since Arabic has no infinitive form ("to be," "être," "быть"), there is no way to ask "to be or not to be" without identifying who is doing the being. Each translator is forced to choose a pronoun.[56] But why choose "we"? None of the major literary translations of *Hamlet* in Arabic render "to be or not to be" in the plural.[57] Arab actors do not play it in the plural. Only in its life as a political slogan does Hamlet's question have this form.

The link between Hamlet and the Arabs depends on the widely accepted idea that the Arab world (as a whole) is living through a period of painful transition. Both the transition and the pain are usually blamed on the bulldozer force of western-driven modernity. In contrast with the one-time shock typically described by writers in other colonized societies,[58] Arab writers can choose from a long series of historical ruptures. Some date the start of the "out-of-joint time" as far back as the fifteenth-century loss of Muslim Spain; more typical proposed dates are 1798 (Napoleon's expedition to Egypt), 1948 (the founding of Israel), 1967 (the June War), 1991 (the first Gulf War, in which some Arab nations fought against others), or even 2001 (the start of the U.S.-led "war on terror"). Whatever the specific events, the trope remains similar. Confrontations between tradition and modernity and between East and West are among the "perennial themes" in Arabic literature.[59] The collision is seen to produce a radical historical rupture. The rupture in turn leads to an existential crisis, putting the very grounds of a continuous collective identity into question.[60] The question of "to be or not to be" is thus raised, over and over again, in every generation.

As a brief illustration of this view of history, let us look at part of an essay by Edward Said, "Arabic Prose and Prose Fiction after 1948." For reasons having to do with his own history and the history of the Arab novel, Said chooses 1948 as his archetypal traumatic moment, yet he acknowledges that there are others. Seeking to explain the twin senses of disappointment and urgency hovering over modern Arabic prose, he invokes the influential book, *Maʿnā al-Nakba* (*The Meaning of the Disaster*) by Constantine Zurayk (Qusṭanṭīn Zurayq). Zurayk is credited with coining the term *nakba,* now the accepted Arabic term for the Israeli victory and Palestinian dispossession of 1948. As Said stresses, the word means not only "catastrophe" or "calamity" but also "veering off course":

> [The events of] 1948 put forward a monumental enigma, an existential mutation for which Arab history was unprepared. . . . No concept seemed large enough, no language precise enough to take in the common fate. . . . The magnitude of such events is indicated, I think, in one of the words most usually employed to describe them, the Arabic word *nakba.* Its most celebrated use is in the name of Constantine Zurayk's 1948 book, *Maʿna al-nakba* [The meaning of the disaster];[61] yet even in Zurayk's work, which advances an interpretation of the Zionist victory as a challenge to the whole of Arab modernity, another of the meanings of *nakba* is in play. The word suggests in its root that affliction or disaster is somehow brought about by, and hence linked by necessity to, deviation, a veering out of course, a serious deflection away from a forward path. . . . The development of Zurayk's argu-

> ment in his book led him, as it was to lead many other writers since 1948, to interpret *al-nakba* as a rupture of the most profound sort. . . . [T]he disaster caused a rift to appear between the Arabs and the very possibility of their historical continuity as a people. So strong was the deflection, or the deviation, from the Arabs' persistence in time up to 1948, that the issue for the Arabs became whether what was "natural" to them—their continued national duration in history—would be possible at all.[62]

In other words, the deviation is so sharp that it raises the "to be or not to be" question: "the issue" of "whether . . . continued national duration in history would be possible." Said finds in Zurayk's formulation of this rift an "interesting paradox" that "would inform Arab writing thereafter." The dislocation, he says, threatens the grounds of Arab collective identity *at the very moment* when that identity is finally about to come into existence:

> So from the perspective of the past, the Arabs would seem to have swerved from the path toward national identity, union, and so on; from the perspective of the future, the disaster raised the specter of national fragmentation or extinction. The paradox is that both of these observations hold, so that at the intersection of past and future stands the disaster, which on the one hand reveals the deviation from *what has yet to happen* (a unified, collective Arab identity) and on the other reveals the possibility of *what may happen* (Arab extinction as a cultural or national unit). The true force then of Zurayk's book is that it made clear the problem of the *present,* a problematic site of contemporaneity, occupied and blocked from the Arabs.[63]

Finally, the ruptured past and threatened future combine to create an out-of-joint present that calls for urgent, collective action: "For the Arabs to act knowingly was to *create* the present, and this was a battle of restoring historical continuity, healing a rupture, and—most important—forging a historical possibility."[64]

Although the reference to a particular historical process would seem to prohibit it, the trope of calamity/rupture/deviation can float like any signifier. The loss of Palestine gains typological resonance from earlier events seen as similar and resonates typologically through later events. As Said and many others have noted, "[T]he effects of the war of 1967 predictably were to recall 1948."[65] More recent traumas have elicited traumatic memories as well: for instance, the Iraq war begun in 2003 has been variously imagined as a reenactment of Napoleon's expedition to Egypt (1798), the Mongol invasion of Baghdad (1258), and the Crusades.

"Something Existentially Meaningful"

The events and aftermath of September 11, perceived as another such critical juncture, elicited a fair amount of Hamlet-based discourse about Arab and Muslim identity. One example is a highly stylized, half-hidden invocation of Shakespeare's text by the Qatar-based "global mufti," Shaykh Yusuf al-Qaradawi. Al-Qaradawi is "easily the best-known if not the most popular Muslim preacher-scholar-activist of the early 21st century."[66] Imprisoned and then released in Egypt in the 1950s, he moved to Qatar in the early 1960s and has built a constituency among Muslims seeking to reconcile their religious beliefs and the demands of modernity. He preaches weekly to sizable television and Internet audiences all over the Muslim world and until recently headed the influential website IslamOnline; his poetry is often quoted as well.[67] His public pronouncements urge Muslims to behave rationally and with dignity; for example, he has called for nonviolent "logical and controlled anger" about the Danish Muhammad cartoons, avoidance of sectarian strife between Sunni and Shiʿa Muslims in Iraq (who should instead join forces against their foreign occupiers), and dialogue between Muslims and rational rulers, Christians, and rational secularists.[68]

In this vein, one of al-Qaradawi's first articles after the terrorist attack of September 11, 2001, calls for a "dialogue between Islam and Christianity" leading to joint action against atheism and terrorism. This dialogue, al-Qaradawi writes, is a matter of Muslims' very survival as a religious community:

> I do not exaggerate when I tell you that our personal credibility as believers, and as religious and spiritual leaders, is also at a crossroads. The efficacy and importance of our existence and our efforts [*wujūdinā wa-juhūdinā*] is now being tested more than at any time in the past. The world is awaiting, from us, something commensurate with the extent of our moral influence. I assure you that we are in a moment that resembles, to some extent, the saying of the one who says, "to

> be or not to be" [*qawl al-qā'il, akūn aw lā akūn*]. Either we do something existentially meaningful [*shay' lahu ma'nā wujūdī*] to take part in guiding events in a direction consistent with the spirit of the principles from which we trace ourselves—either this, or we will turn the page of neglect and oblivion on ourselves . . . perhaps forever.[69]

Invoked in the third paragraph of a lengthy article, Hamlet serves to draw readers in. He appears in Islamic garb, masked as "the one who says" and surrounded with Islamic moral vocabulary. Al-Qaradawi makes no extensive argument about Shakespeare's text, saying only that the post-9/11 Muslim predicament resembles Hamlet's "to some extent." Yet the invocation would not strike his audience as a stretch. It draws on a preexisting cluster of associations in Arab readers' minds that link Hamlet with a moral imperative for "existentially meaningful" action. If al-Qaradawi were questioned about the precise content of his analogy, he might say that Hamlet's mission to unseat his usurping uncle parallels "to some extent" the need for moderate Islamists to speak out against Osama bin Laden's usurpation of their moral mantle.[70] He might mention that Hamlet, caught in a time of transition between value systems, is called upon to enact a traditional deed in a fully conscious ("existentially meaningful") modern way. Most likely, however, he would simply invoke a general idea of Hamlet: a character caught in life-or-death circumstances requiring him to seize his destiny in his hands. In Arab and Muslim political rhetoric, this is the paradigmatic meaning of Hamlet.

But why must the destiny always be *collective*? Unlike many other writers, al-Qaradawi quotes Hamlet's question in the singular: "Shall I be or shall I not be?" His meaning, however, is clearly plural. (The rest of his article is shaped by the recurring phrase "we, we the Muslims.") He addresses all like-minded Muslim leaders and through them the Muslim community as a whole. The "neglect and oblivion" of which al-Qaradawi warns would threaten the community, not its individual members. "Not to be" would mean the weakening or fragmentation of the community, the dissolution of its collective identity, its marginalization or erasure from the book of history.

This, too, is typical of Arabic *Hamlet* rhetoric. In the overwhelming majority of citations, Hamlet's concern with individual decision making is played down. There is no private anguish over what is "nobler in the mind," no issue of when or why a man might "himself his quietus make."[71] Instead the first line becomes a plea for collective self-identification and action, an urgent call to arms. The rest of the soliloquy is quoted selectively, if at all.

"Shall We Be or Not Be?": Personifying the Group

Here one might be tempted to argue that in Arabic the pluralized, sloganized form of Hamlet's question has taken on a life of its own as a dead metaphor no longer meaningfully associated with Shakespeare's text at all. In some cases this is true: the slogan "*nakūn aw lā nakūn*" ("Shall we be or not be") simply serves as a rallying cry within an existing culture of unanimity, a shorthand for an already understood moral imperative. As such it has been very useful to Arab politicians, in contexts such as this 1983 interview by reporter Ghassan Bishara with Palestinian leader Yasser Arafat:

> Bishara: What can rescue the Palestinian issue from the present stalemate?
> Arafat: A unified Arab stand.
> Bishara: How likely is that to happen?
> Arafat: Simply, Arab leaders should rise to their historic, national responsibilities. It is a simple question for the Arab nation: "To be or not to be."[72]

However, the most adept speakers sometimes do retain an overt link to *Hamlet.* Besides recruiting Shakespeare (and his massive symbolic capital) to their cause, it lets them draw on further aspects of Hamlet's character and fate: the threat of madness, the obsession with words, the danger of sleep and dreaming. An even more basic rhetorical payoff comes from the fact that Hamlet is a single character made to stand in for an entire group: the Arabs, the Muslims, the Lebanese, the Shiʿa Iraqis, and so forth. Statements such as "Hamlet is like us" or "We are like Hamlet" or "Arabs are the Hamlet of the twentieth century" accomplish a valuable unifying purpose aside from any content they convey.

"We Are That Hamlet, Driven to Madness"

To take an example from Egypt: the Egyptian social service entrepreneur and media personality Mustafa Mahmud (Muṣṭafā Maḥmūd; 1921–2009), whose Islamist rhetoric aimed to bridge the languages of reason and revelation, referred frequently to *Hamlet.*[73] While often perfunctory, his citations sometimes grow into a full-fledged argument that the internal disorder in Hamlet's mind threatens the Arab-Muslim community as well. This community, Mahmud implies, is an individual writ large. If Hamlet's madness is a kind of psychological disharmony or strife, then its communal expression is private interest, which also leads to internal (political) division and hesitation.

A major thrust of his rhetoric is the effort to conflate Arab identity with

Muslim identity, to suggest that the two categories are or should be the same. He and other Islamist writers often deliberately use the terms *Arab* and *Muslim* interchangeably. They seek to gloss over two facts they find inconvenient: that the great majority of the world's Muslims are not Arab (many more are South Asian, Sub-Saharan African, Iranian, Turkish, etc., with the biggest single Muslim population being in Indonesia) and that there are significant native populations of Christians in several Arab countries (including Egypt, Sudan, Lebanon, Iraq, and Syria).[74]

Mahmud spells out his critique in a 1999 column, titled "Nakūn aw Lā Nakūn," purporting to explain Arab-Muslim inaction on behalf of the oppressed Chechens and Palestinians:

> Proclamations issue from the Arab nations, timidly; then for one reason or another they don't join together; then they announce a serious study of the matter at the coming meeting, as though they were camels lost in the wilderness. And this even though they speak one language and believe in one religion and one God and one goal. . . . Is it the fault of the leaders or the peoples? Or is it backwardness? Is it a lack of consciousness [*ʿadam al-waʿī*], or is it all of these reasons together and still others that we do not know? And will Israel find a nicer opportunity than this one to stretch out in its chaise longue and relax in its greatness?
>
> The Arabs don't join together for a simple reason: they are in confrontation with Israel, but, despite this, they're unable to take the decision to confront it jointly. And the reason is clear: such a decision will bring heavy commitments which they fear and on which they differ like night and day. But it's fate [*al-qadr*]. It's our fate, gentlemen, and there's no escaping it. The truth which has cornered us and which we can't evade. It's the Shakespearean predicament, as Hamlet put it: "to be or not to be." And we are that Hamlet whom the situation will drive to madness.
>
> But Hamlet was torn apart [*yatamazzaq*] between his love for his mother and his hatred for his uncle, who poisoned his father. And a mother is an awesome thing: how could he take the life of the one who gave him life? We, however, are in a different predicament. We fight over worldly trifles [*al-dunyā*]. Some seek these trifles at any price, even at the price

> of evading responsibility, or betraying principle . . . and others look upward, to the great Lord from whom we came, and want to satisfy this Great One even at the price of their lives. The question is a question of faith and unbelief, and that is the whole spirit of Islam.[75]

Mahmud's Shakespeare allusion makes a rhetorical bid to meld the Arab Muslim political community into a single moral being; he moves smoothly from "the Arab countries" to "the spirit of Islam." The suggestion that "we are that Hamlet" helps incorporate Mahmud's readers into a single political community, with Hamlet as its representative. A familiar move in western as well as Arab political thought, this community-as-man equation works here to emphasize the dangers of dissent.[76] To function well, Mahmud implies, the "body" politic must have a single head. Moreover, for Mahmud, as for other speakers who follow the same line, unanimity is more than an instrumental advantage: it is an existential imperative.[77] Without making an explicit argument, Mahmud's rhetoric implies that individuals must subordinate their private concerns to the identity of the group or the group will be "torn apart." Because the group is figured as a moral person with a distinct life and destiny (rather than, say, a convenient association between freely contracting self-interested individuals), such tearing can be presented as destructive of an almost mystical identity: a communal soul. Fragmentation (e.g., liberal individualism) is thus condemned from various angles: in Marxist terms as "private interest"; in Islamic terms as *fitna,* "worldly temptation" leading to "internal strife."[78]

An added twist is Mahmud's feint toward a *distinction* between Arabs/Muslims and Hamlet. He recognizes that Hamlet's case is specific: "But Hamlet was torn apart between his love for his mother and his hatred for his uncle." This preempts any readers inclined to question his analogy. However, the case turns out to be worse than these readers thought. Whereas Mahmud's Hamlet is at least torn between competing principles (revenge versus filial love for his mother), the Arabs who choose their private interests over the Chechen or Palestinian cause have no principled excuse at all. They are simply evading responsibility, betraying their identity, and violating "the whole spirit of Islam." Their selfishness tears the community apart, pulling it toward madness and disintegration.

"To Die, to Sleep"

Mahmud's reference to an Arab-Muslim "lack of consciousness" *(ʿadam al-waʿī)* opens another line of comparison to Hamlet. "Consciousness" in Arab political rhetoric connotes awakeness, accurate self-perception, and active participation in the events that shape one's destiny. Its opposite is a dream or trance whose victim floats obliviously on the current of history. Drawing a contrast between consciousness/activism/progress on the one hand and sleep/dreaming/trance/oblivion on the other hand can help rouse an audience to action.

The hope that Arabs (and later, Muslims) would "awaken" from their long historical "unconsciousness" has been voiced ever since Arab thinkers perceived a lag between their societies and European modernity in the mid-nineteenth century.[79] Early twentieth-century writers strove to ignite an intellectual *nahḍa* (literally: awakening, renaissance) and a nationalist "Arab Awakening."[80] More recent writers have mocked or eulogized those early dreams of awakening. Tawfiq al-Hakim's (Tawfīq al-Ḥakīm) 1974 memoir (to be discussed in chapter 2) chronicles his "return of consciousness" after nearly two decades in a Nasserist ideological trance.[81] Twenty-five years later, Fouad Ajami's *Dream Palace of the Arabs* (its title an ironic reference to T. E. Lawrence) mourns what he calls the "intellectual edifice of secular nationalism and modernity" built by Arab men and women of his generation, a fond dream preempted by the twin nightmares of dictatorship and theocratic movements.[82] Whatever the ideological perspective, the message remains remarkably consistent: it is time to wake up, for we have slept and dreamed long enough.

Arabs' self-condemnation as unproductive dreamers has been made to resonate with *Hamlet.* Drawing on the already established analogy between Hamlet and the Arabs, many speakers turn Hamlet's desire "to die, to sleep" from a meditation to a term of abuse, from a "consummation devoutly to be wish'd"[83] into a great political mistake and historical danger. The Arabs' centuries-long slumber, these critics charge, has all but killed their political power. The inaction that Hamlet ascribes to "conscience" (consciousness) or "thinking too precisely on th' event," these polemicists blame on a *lack* of penetrating insight, a failure to grasp the real situation and its stakes. Theirs is not a protagonist who thinks too much; rather, he is asleep on the job. To use *Hamlet* in this way requires ignoring the second half of Hamlet's soliloquy, but it is frequently done. Syrian dramatist Mamduh Adwan's 1976 play *Hamlet Wakes Up Late* (to be discussed in chapter 6) is a typical, if unusually emphatic and well-executed, example. Adwan's late-waking protagonist confronts a brutal political order run by killers, cynics, and spies. He slowly grasps the injustice around him—but his awakening, pointedly, comes too late to have any effect.[84] Adwan's title has acquired proverbial status, at least among a certain group of leftist Syrian intellectuals.[85]

Syrian philosophy professor and secularist Sadiq Jalal al-Azm has elaborated a critique of Arab "unconsciousness" on several occasions. (This critique fits into an argument he has been making since 1967 about a lack of "self-criticism" in Arab public discourse.)[86] Inspired to some extent by Adwan's play, which he cites, al-Azm floats the idea of a late-waking Hamlet in a 2000 column titled "Owning the Future: Modern Arabs and Hamlet":

> Modern Arabs are truly the Hamlet of the 20th century. Like the endlessly celebrated prince, they seem able continually to join the underlying passion of the elemental to the brooding intellectuality of the cerebral to the lyrical sensitivity of the poetic but only to end up in unrelieved tragedy. The tragedy consists of unending hesitations, procrastinations, oscillations and waverings between the old and the new, between *asalah* and *muʿasarah* (authenticity and contemporaneity), between *turath* and *tajdid* (heritage and renewal), between *huwiyyah* and *hadathah* (identity and modernity), between religions and secularity.
>
> In this way, the 21st century can only belong to the conquering Fortinbrases of this world and never to the Hamlets hung up on interminably rehearsing that classic—but now totally depassé—European *pièce* called *La Querelle des Ancients et des Modernes.* No wonder, then, to quote Shakespeare's most famous drama, that "the times seem out of joint" for the Arabs and "something looks rotten in their state." No wonder as well if they keep wondering, like the fabled Prince of Denmark himself and with as much tragic intensity, "whether they are the authors of their woes or there is a divinity that shapes their ends."[87]
>
> This analogy leads me to dig deeper inside ourselves and to think that for us Arabs to own our future, to hold ourselves responsible for it, we have to come to terms with a certain image of ourselves buried very deeply in our collective subconscious. What I mean is the following: As Arab and Muslims (and I use Muslim here in the purely historical, cultural, and civilizational sense) we continue deep down to image and imagine ourselves as conquerors, history-makers, pace-setters, pioneers, and leaders of world-historical proportions.[88]

Criticizing Arab nationalism as well as Islamism as desperate chimeras, al-Azm seeks to correct what he calls the Arabs' (and the Muslims') unrealistic image of themselves. His recent writings in both Arabic and English return frequently to the analogy with *Hamlet,* linking the grievance of usurpation—for the Arabs feel that their rightful "position of world-historical leadership and its glories was somehow usurped from us by modern Europe"—with the melancholy and perplexity that result. His language is that of psychoanalysis: "narcissistic wounds," "inferiority complexes,"[89] "huge compensatory delusions" that are "buried very deeply in our collective subconscious."[90] Against this crippling dream or fantasy he offers a stiff dose of historical realism: "Modernity is basically a European invention. . . . There is no running away from the fact that the Arabs were dragged kicking and screaming into modernity, on the one hand, and modernity was forced on them by superior might, efficiency, and performance, on the other."[91]

Like Yusuf al-Qaradawi and Mustafa Mahmud, then, al-Azm calls on Arabs (and Muslims) to wake up and accept the reality of their place in the world. He diagnoses a "cultural schizophrenia,"[92] a type of madness brought on by the misunderstanding of their own identity and mission, and he links this madness to historical irrelevance: unless it is corrected, "the Fortinbrases of this world will win the day and have the final say."[93] The Arabs, unable to take ownership of their own future, will forever be doomed to read from scripts written by others.[94] (Recall al-Qaradawi's quite similar warning that "we will turn the page of neglect and oblivion on ourselves, perhaps forever.") Thus the two Islamists and the secularist invoke *Hamlet* to advance diametrically opposed arguments, but using very similar rhetorical strategies.

The Discourse of Perpetual Crisis

Whatever the threat du jour, the discourse of existential crisis appears to be perpetual. One reason is that writers have every incentive to invoke it. Precisely by portraying modern Arab identity in crisis, the narrative of repeated trauma helps constitute and reproduce that identity. Advocates for a wide range of causes find it rhetorically effective to describe Arab destiny in this paradoxical way: at the mercy of history and yet facing an urgent moment of decision. (Edward Said glumly identifies this paradox as "one that turns the Arab into a world-historical individual because of his specialized talent for ineptitude.")[95] As long as this trope remains useful, there is no reason to expect the Hamlet analogy, with its rhetoric of being/nonbeing and waking/sleeping, to lose its appeal.

Another reason why the notion of crisis persists is that each rearrangement of power actually *has* been ushered in with violent conquest and is thus associated with a sense of injustice, usurpation, and trampled innocence. To be consoled and move on, as the westernizing al-Azm and some western observers recommend, would strike many Arab readers as a self-betrayal. Even the suggestion is offensive: it sounds like an attempt to legitimize the violence and hide (rather than heal) the wound. Here Hamlet's situation resonates again. As Alexander Welsh explains:

> Young Hamlet suffers lectures on the propriety of mourning *from the very two persons who have offended him*: words of characteristic matter-of-factness from his mother and more studied advice on "mourning duties" from his uncle. The most troubling aspect of this advice is its undeniable appropriateness. Mourning is the means of overcoming a loss. It is a process that pulls two ways, toward remembrance and forgetting, and is a remembering in order to forget—a process that has some unknown optimum time for completion. Hamlet is not yet ready to forgo mourning, as he makes plain; *and the man urging him to put an end to it will turn out to be a murderer.*[96]

The "appropriate" advice is offensive, yet to reject it puts one into rebellion against the facts. It then becomes urgently necessary to change those facts—which deepens the sense of crisis. Barring the lucky appearance of a ghost with an actionable conspiracy story (which is Welsh's point about Hamlet and revenge), one has few legitimate options. Learning to swim in the "sea of troubles" is, for moral reasons, ruled out; one can only "take up arms" against it, through words if necessary.

For politically committed Arab writers, then, the challenge has been how to find some middle ground between "to be" and "not to be": how to maintain some sort of ambivalent relationship with the injustices of the past (short of accepting them) while working energetically to forge a plausible present and future. Leaving behind the easy rewards of sloganeering, the Arab Shakespeare adapters considered in the rest of this book have sought to do just that.

"Words, Words, Words": Forging an Identity

How can rewriting *Hamlet* help a writer forge an ethical and political identity? *In Search of Walid Masoud,* a 1978 novel by Palestinian/Iraqi writer Jabra Ibrahim Jabra (1920–94), provides one kind of answer.[97] Like Jabra's other major novel, *The Ship* (1973), *The Search for Walid Masoud* abounds in allusions to *Hamlet.*[98] Several important scenes involve Masoud's conversations with his friends about the play. At key moments in his life, *Hamlet* seems to serve as a kind of spiritual lodestar, helping Masoud navigate a course between complacency and despair.[99]

There is evidence that the play occupied a similar place for Jabra himself. Born to a Syrian Orthodox Christian family in Bethlehem in 1920, Jabra studied at Cambridge and later at Harvard, established a life in Baghdad after 1948, and became one of Iraq's leading artists, literary and art critics, and writers.[100] His work has been central to Shakespeare reception in the Arab world. After he translated *Hamlet* (1960), Jabra also published translations with scholarly introductions of *King Lear* (1968), *Coriolanus* (1974), *Othello* (1978), *Macbeth* (1979), *The Tempest* (1979), *Twelfth Night* (1989), and forty of the sonnets.[101] He also translated major works of Shakespeare criticism, including Jan Kott's *Shakespeare Our Contemporary,* John Dover Wilson's *What Happens in "Hamlet,"* and Janette Dillon's *Shakespeare and the Solitary Man.*[102] He was deeply marked by Shakespeare's language; in his essay "Shakespeare and I" (in English), Jabra describes his dream, while still a student at the Arab College of Jerusalem, of tackling "the impossible task of making Arabic versions of Shakespeare which carried the same verbal charge, the same evocative imagery and sustained metaphors, the same diversity of rhythm, tone, eloquence, word-play, etc."[103]

Jabra's nonfiction writing reveals a very personal engagement with *Hamlet* in particular. The much-quoted introduction to his *Hamlet* translation, an essay titled "Between Absurdity and the Necessity of Action," summarizes recent western *Hamlet* scholarship but also proposes a reading of the prince as a humanistic figure who, like Jesus Christ, is driven to martyrdom for his love of humanity:

> And when he [Hamlet] approaches his inevitable destruction, he shows us little by little an abundant breadth of soul amid the riddles of life surrounding us. And when the end comes within sight, a deluge of love bursts in our hearts as tears for this one who seems as though he died to redeem us, as though he loved us just as he loved Ophelia and as he loved his friend Horatio.[104]

In *The Search for Walid Masoud,* the character Walid Masoud, like his author a Palestinian living in Baghdad, plays multiple roles (banker, writer, lover, father, polemicist, supporter of the Palestinian cause) but is not summed up by any of them. He disappears one night, abandoning his car in the Iraqi desert en route to Syria with a mysterious cassette tape in a recorder inside. The novel begins with his hypercultured friends in Baghdad listening to the tape. The rest of the book is a modernist mystery story made up of shards and fragments: childhood memories from Masoud's autobiography, extracts from his scattered papers, the recollections of his friends and lovers, and an account of his son Marwan's death in an attack on an Israeli village just over the Lebanese border. Although no one knows precisely where Masoud has gone, it is strongly implied that he has gone to Lebanon to join the Palestinian resistance.

Like Palestine itself, Walid Masoud is both absent and overdetermined: a canvas onto which the book's other characters project their memories, anxieties, and desires. Yet he rewrites himself continuously, displaying heroic agency as he eludes the categories others prepare for him. (His disappearance, presumably into the world of direct political action represented by the resistance movement, is only the final, most radical such act of rewriting.) In one of the novel's central scenes, his former lover Wisal Raouf recalls how Masoud celebrated the transformative power of words, consciously and playfully bending a famous line from *Hamlet*:

> "Words, words, words . . ." He whispered into my ear between the strands of my hair. He'd been hugging me from behind, but now turned me around to face him. "What a crafty devil Shakespeare is!" he said, looking straight into my eyes. "He makes Hamlet say that, and many people imagine that what he's saying is 'Void, void, void!' For some people that may well be true: people deficient in language, people with speech impediments, parrots. But Shakespeare's al-Mutanabbi's brother; they're both masters of words.[105] What Shakespeare wants to do is make Hamlet scream in the face of all the parrots of this world: 'Words, words, words!' The most wonderful thing God's given to man! Just imagine if someone like al-Mutanabbi was in love with you. What would he be saying? The words would come pouring out of his mouth and hands; he'd clean them and polish them, and then apply them to everything to be found in life in return for some pearls just like these dinars, 'shadows scurrying away from the fingertips' as he himself puts it. Words are everything. In the long run, words are all that's left of any-

> thing; if there are no words left, there's nothing. Intrigue, folly, murder, they're all in words; hatred, tedium, suicide, moonlit nights, sleepless nights, nights that refuse to come to an end, nights that melt into a sweet, passionate embrace. Words. They may be: 'No, no,' or 'Yes, yes,' or even mewing and purring. If a woman has al-Mutanabbi's gifts, then she can rob him of his sleep, not just through pain and torment, but, more, through sheer elation as his body's ripped apart with wicked delights. There are silent heroes, Wisal, and others who talk. I'm aware of that. There are silent and articulate scoundrels, too. Some are dead through silence, others through speaking; some can signify by talking, others can't even utter a coherent phrase. I realize all that, too. But words ... those who control words flagellate themselves with the bewitching sounds of letters; they adore the vibrations in the throat. When words of love are no longer to be heard on lovers' lips, doesn't the love itself disappear as well? Words are everything."[106]

Jabra's protagonist denies any simple opposition between words and deeds. Being articulate, for him, gives power over destiny. In one sense this interpretation itself represents an act of will, a "strong misreading" or rewriting of both Shakespeare's text and the dominant Arab consensus on its meaning, which he aptly sums up as "Void, void, void."[107] Shakespeare's Hamlet explicitly labels "words" as womanish and weak, the opposite of manly and effective deeds. He not only mocks Polonius with the contrast between "words" and "matter"[108] but later berates himself for speaking (and in a feminized and lower-class manner) when he should act instead: "But I . . . must like a whore unpack my heart with words / And fall a-cursing like a very drab, a scullion! Fie upon't! Foh!"[109]

But Jabra's Masoud, in this passage and others, takes a more writerly view. For him, "words are everything," and "in the long run, words are all that's left of anything." Artful language use is an index of masculine potency; it is no accident that Masoud's rhapsody about words occurs in the context of a sex scene. There is evidence that Jabra shares his protagonist's optimism. Elsewhere, he quotes Nikos Kazantzakis: "Words! Words! What salvation without them?"[110]

In denying young Hamlet's narrow dichotomy between words and deeds, Jabra picks up on a deeper theme running through Shakespeare's play. Being a "crafty devil" is useful. Words can produce results in the world. Speaking, writing, and rewriting can allow the writer to embrace his own history and integrate it into that of his time. They can help him become an integrated character and also an effective political actor—to overcome the crisis of threatened identity and find a credible way "to be."

"The Play's the Thing"

Effective rewriting may require compromise. For young Hamlet, who seeks to write his own script in a world destabilized by his father's death, success begins when he abandons the discourse of authentic identity. After trying in vain to find a language that will "denote [him] truly" and then to remake himself as a tabula rasa,[111] Hamlet finally comes to terms with his richly tainted history. Its "baser matter," he finds, is not a betrayal of his authentic identity but a valuable resource.[112] This acceptance guides him to an effective political identity: a rewriter of plays, a forger of documents, and the rightful heir of a king.[113]

The Shakespeare appropriators considered in the rest of this book are neither polemicists, like Sadiq al-Azm or Mustafa Mahmud, nor highbrow novelists, like Jabra. They are theatre people: stage adapters, playwrights, and/or directors. Their rhetorical registers lie somewhere on the (huge) spectrum between televised polemic and modernist fiction, appealing to a public set of ideals but intervening in a singular artistic voice. Their dilemma, too, is how to produce dramatic writing that makes effective use of a compromised history.

As it happens, nearly all of them are men. Perhaps this is because the discourse around *Hamlet* is so thoroughly gendered; Hamlet's *ʿajz* (the Arabic word means sexual impotence as well as political helplessness) is invoked even more commonly than the tropes of madness and sleep. Jabra's striking reversal of this commonplace, crediting precisely Hamlet's words for his heroic potency and agency, plays off his readers' assumption that political paralysis is a kind of failure of masculinity.[114] A few of the texts we will examine, from Salah Abdel Sabur's *Tragedy of Al-Hallaj* to Mahmoud Aboudoma's *Dance of the Scorpions,* include no female characters at all; several others minimize (or ironically maximize, to highlight the male characters' passivity) the roles of Gertrude and Ophelia. Female writers and directors have simply chosen other texts; it is their male colleagues who have engaged most intensely with Hamlet's words and silences.[115]

To understand their work will require a closer look at the Egyptian Revolution of 1952 and its leader, Gamal Abdel Nasser. For if "to be or not to be" is the defining slogan of Arab politics, as I have argued here, then Nasser is the figure most deeply and persistently associated with that slogan. The Arab *Hamlet* tradition, with its emphasis on collective political agency, responds directly to

Nasser's anticolonial revolution and the hopes it first inspired and then disappointed. The time has been most painfully "out of joint" in the ideological vacuum left by Nasser's 1970 death; the crisis of whether "to be or not to be" has arisen most sharply after the failure of Arab nationalism. This is true not only for Egyptians but for the generation of Arabs all over the Near East who spent their youth listening to Nasser's radio broadcasts and sharing his dreams.

2

NASSER'S DRAMATIC IMAGINATION, 1952–64

On April 23, 1964, Egyptian president Gamal Abdel Nasser stood in Tahrir Square (from *taḥrīr*, or liberation) in Sanaa, Yemen.[1] His anti-colonial revolution was twelve years old. Cracks had appeared in its domestic and international image, but there was still cause for pride. Land had been redistributed, university attendance had nearly quadrupled,[2] and intellectuals were following the doings of countless new government-run periodicals and book series[3] and over a dozen new theatre companies.[4] In foreign policy, Nasser's Cold War "positive neutrality" had borne real fruit. With Soviet assistance, the first phase of the Aswan High Dam project was almost finished; in less than a month, Soviet premier Nikita Khrushchev would travel to Egypt for the inaugural ceremony.

Nasser could also still claim progress on the pan-Arab front. Although Egypt's short-lived union with Syria (1958–61) had collapsed and Egypt alone now bore the name United Arab Republic, Nasser had found a face-saving regional cause in Yemen, where he had offered Egyptian help to republicans in a civil war against Saudi-supported royalists. By 1964 there were nearly 50,000 Egyptian troops in Yemen,[5] and the war was a tangible reminder of Nasser's pan-Arab commitment. Nasser told a cheering crowd in Sanaa on April 23 that when he saw the Egyptians fighting alongside their Yemeni brothers, he "felt that Arab unity is an actual reality, with no need for written documents because it has been written in blood, and with no need for constitutions to announce it because it has been announced by your martyrdom and your self-sacrifice."[6]

April 23, 1964, was a day for big speeches in the Shakespeare world as well. The 400th anniversary of William Shakespeare's traditional birthdate inspired a burst of activity on five continents, including conferences, publications, and stage and film productions. Arab scholars and theatre people took part in such activities with enthusiasm and new self-confidence. The Cultural Department of the Cairo-based Arab League was wrapping up a ten-year project (1955–65) to translate Shakespeare's complete works into Arabic. The new and influential Egyptian monthly magazine *al-Masraḥ* (Theatre), founded in 1964, devoted its entire fourth issue to articles on Shakespeare.[7] Essays on Arab Shakespeare reception appeared in several local and international journals.[8] Capping the quadricentennial celebrations, Egyptian director al-Sayyid Bidayr (al-Sayyid Bidayr) was assigned to stage *Hamlet* at Cairo's Royal Opera House with the World Theatre Company, one of several new state-funded troupes.[9] Though free from political content, his production sent a political message to the world: Egypt, culturally speaking, had arrived.

It was a heady time. In the maelstrom of Nasser's revolution, ideas and cultural energies aligned in ways that may seem, from today's perspective, difficult to recapture. These overlapping contexts—the Cold War, anticolonialism, the Egyptian Revolution, and, indirectly, the growth of and resistance to Soviet power in Eastern Europe—were decisive in shaping the history of Arab appropriation of *Hamlet.* They created the conditions for the development of a figure I call the Arab Hero Hamlet: Shakespeare's Hamlet understood as a visionary activist, a fighter for justice brutally martyred by an oppressive regime. This archetype, directly at first and later ironically through parody, would dominate Arab readings of *Hamlet* for the rest of the century.

To understand the appeal of this heroic Hamlet, we must cast ourselves back through time, striving to recover the horizon of expectations of mid-twentieth-century Arab writers and theatregoers.[10] In particular, we must try to grasp what it meant for them to live through Nasser's revolution, either actively as Egyptians or vicariously as observers from the Arab sidelines. More than an "intercultural" grasp of any peculiarly Arab cultural system, then, our reconstruction demands an effort of sympathetic *historical* imagination. (In this sense, all reception studies are intercultural.)

If we hope to reconstruct the political and psychological circumstances in which the Arab Hero Hamlet took shape, the first task is to understand the role of Gamal Abdel Nasser. He is one of the central figures in the historical imagination of the modern Arab Near East. To an even greater extent, Nasser underlies and enables the region's *Hamlet* tradition. As we will see, the heroic Hamlet was largely a product of Nasser's revolution and the way that revolution was lived out: through Ministry of Culture policies that valorized the theatre as a political outlet, through an intolerance for dissent that drove political critique into Aesopian guises, through foreign policy decisions that brought new exposure to Soviet and Eastern European cultural models, and through a pan-Arab outlook that broadcast Egyptian culture to the rest of the Arab world. The heroic reading of *Hamlet* was also partly shaped by the tone of Nasser's public conversation with the Egyptian people, which for a time made them feel that they were intimately involved in fateful decisions about heroism and pragmatism, ends and means, power and justice.

Although this chapter will focus on Egypt, it will become clear that the cultural impact of Nasser's policies and personality extended to other Arab countries as well. The effect was especially pronounced in Syria, whose government merged with Egypt's for three years (1958–61), and in Iraq, whose military rulers flirted with unification in 1958 and again in 1963.[11] Elsewhere, too, pan-Arabist sentiment amplified the effect of shared political experiences. While Egypt should not be taken as a synecdoche for the postcolonial Arab world, Nasser often inspired the populace even in those Arab countries whose regimes feared and hated him. "There was no one of comparable stature in any other Arab country," Derek Hopwood notes, and "other Arab leaders, until his death in 1970, had to act very much under his shade."[12] The most significant Egyptian cultural trends before 1967 thus resonated, albeit in locally conditioned ways, throughout the Arab Near East.

Revolutionary Drama

Let us start with a biographical fact. All the Arab playwrights and directors of the 1960s and 1970s (and nearly half of those writing in the 1980s and 1990s) were old enough to remember the Egyptian revolution of July 1952: a series of events more dramatic, in a way, than anything the region's stages could offer. The coup proceeded with astonishing speed: while Cairo slept during the night of July 23, a group of junior army officers took command of military headquarters and broadcasting stations. Four days later, the king had abdicated and sailed for Italy.

Nasser and his military colleagues, the Free Officers, had a strong instinct for drama. Good storytelling and "not a small amount of clever extemporaneous acting"[13] helped cover for their lack of political experience and build a convincing revolution out of their hurriedly executed coup. Their clever use of spectacle quelled popular sympathy for the ousted King Farouk (r. 1936–52), whose personal hedonism was seen as going hand in hand with his dependence on Britain:

> The ease with which the army seized power reinforced a vision of a decadent monarch and scurrilous political elite. When the Cinema Metro, a Cairo movie palace and target of arsonists during antiforeign riots in January 1952, reopened after the coup, it screened *Quo Vadis* as its first feature. Few could miss the parallels between the Emperor Nero and the ill-fated [King] Farouk, or the Roman patriarchs and Egypt's pashas. A media barrage of exposés and a series of show trials reinforced images of the "nights of Farouk."[14]

When the Free Officers defied expectations after the July 23 coup by refusing to return to the barracks, the theatre of politics helped them distance themselves from the partisan strife (*ḥizbiyya*) that had marred Egypt's parliamentary system since the 1930s. In September 1953 they launched the Revolutionary Tribunal, a military court for officials of the old regime, and broadcast its proceedings on the radio. This running drama featured fine performances by the Free Officers and some of those accused. One of the Free Officers gave a "stinging imitation of a [Wafd] party leader insisting he be allowed to kiss the monarch's hand."[15] Men accustomed to wealth and power were made to grovel and incriminate each other. As playwright Tawfiq al-Hakim (1898–1987) recalls, the court "stripped them absolutely of their dignity and made them stand before it and before the people naked, weak, frightened and greedy. . . . The revolutionary officers pointed them out and said to the people, 'These are those who used to rule you.'"[16] More than any arguments or information that came to light, what the audience remembered was the exhilarating (or terrifying) surrealism of the scene. Farouk Mustafa calls attention to

> the sometimes theatrical methods with which the July 1952 Revolution sought to discredit the *ancien régime*: for instance, the Revolution Tribunal sessions presided over by Gamal Salem which were broadcast live over the radio and which provided tremendous entertainment for the people in a mock-tragic mode: "tragic" because they were multiple depictions of "the fall of a prince," and "mock" because the emphasis was not so much on the heroic traits prior to the fall (otherwise the effort would have backfired and gained sympathy for the defendants) . . . [as] on the failings, which belonged more to the comic mode.[17]

Nasser's own preferred genre, however, was historical epic rather than comedy. Biographers have noted the extent to which his political imagination had been formed by literature and drama. As a boy he cared little for schoolwork but read extensively: biographies of groundbreaking personalities including Churchill, Bismarck, and Voltaire but also contemporary Arabic novels and plays. He was reportedly most influenced by Tawfiq al-Hakim's melodramatic novel *Return of the Spirit*, with its passages of dialogue written in Egyptian colloquial Arabic and its message that the Egyptians "lack only one thing . . . they lack that man in whom all their feelings and desires will be represented, and who will be for them a symbol of their objective."[18]

Anti-British sentiment colored all his readings. In January 1935, at al-Nahḍa School in Cairo, then-sixteen-year-old Gamal took the stage in the title role of *Julius Caesar*.[19] With education minister Naguib al-Hilali (Najīb al-Hilālī) in attendance (the Revolution would later unseat him as prime minister), Nasser played the Roman dictator as "the archetype of the popular hero, liberator of the masses, 'victor over Great Britain,' assassinated as though by accident."[20] A playbill from the show describes Caesar as "the hero of popular liberation."[21] (This approach reverses the more typical anticolonial/liberationist reading of *Julius Caesar*, which tends to identify with Brutus.)[22]

Biographers tell that Nasser's postal clerk father, seeing his son about to fall under Brutus's dagger, "all but leaped forward to rescue him."[23] The anecdote highlights the family's discomfort with the habitus of theatre—part of the mythology that was later constructed around Nasser's humble origins. But stage combat was likely not his father's greatest worry. As a high school student, young Gamal had already shown a penchant for both public speaking and real danger. In Alexandria, he had spent a night in jail after getting caught up in a demonstration of the ultranationalist group Young Egypt (which he supported but never joined).[24] In Cairo, jeopardizing his grades, he became a student activist and "led demonstrations from the Nahda Secondary School," shouting for "complete independence."[25] In November 1935, his forehead was grazed by a police bullet during an anti-British street demonstration, and police gunfire killed two of his friends.[26]

As he became an army officer and then an instructor at the Royal Military Academy, Nasser's self-understanding remained profoundly literary.[27] He helped found the Free Officers, a secret group dedicated more to a romantic ideal of "positive action" than to any particular ideology or even strategy. "Our life was, during this period, like an exciting detective story," he later wrote.[28] The Free Officers' early tactics (political assassination) were soon repudiated, but not their understanding of modern Egyptian history as a narrative that called for a heroic historical actor/agent. As Nasser later wrote, defending the army's intervention in politics: "I can say now that we did not ourselves define *the role given us to play*; it was the history of our country which *cast us in that role*."[29]

The July 1952 coup gave an outlet to both the revolutionary and the Caesar within Nasser. A shadowy background figure at first, Nasser gradually began to sideline his colleagues on the Egyptian Revolutionary Command Council. By 1954, stepping out from behind President Muhammad Naguib, the better-known and initially more charismatic figure, Nasser began to portray himself as an embodiment of Egypt, both its simple son and the realization of its historical hopes. His romance with the Egyptian people can be dated to October 26, 1954, with the brilliant speech he improvised in Alexandria's Manshiya Square just after surviving an assassination attempt by the Muslim Brotherhood:

> I am Gamal Abdel Nasser, from you and for you. My blood is from you and my blood is for you, and I will live until I die struggling for your cause and working for your sake, for your freedom and your dignity. . . . If Gamal Abdel Nasser should die, I will not die—for all of you are Gamal Abdel Nasser. Egypt's well-being is linked not to Gamal Abdel Nasser but to you and your struggle.[30]

As he rose to prominence, drama was never far from Nasser's mind. His spontaneous bravado at Manshiya perhaps echoed Julius Caesar's: "I rather tell thee what is to be feared / Than what I fear; for always I am Caesar."[31] His short book The *Philosophy of the Revolution,* published in September 1954 and quickly adopted as the official history of the July 1952 movement, binds its political and strategic analysis with theatre metaphors.[32] Its most-often-quoted passage (in English as well as inside Egypt) is Nasser's argument that Egypt deserves a central role on the world stage. After describing Egypt's unique location between three circles—the Middle East, Africa, and the Islamic world—he remarks:

> I do not know why I recall, whenever I reach this point in my recollections as I meditate alone in my room, a famous tale by a great Italian poet, Luigi Pirandello—*Six Characters in Search of Actors* [*sic*].[33] The pages of history are full of heroes who created for themselves roles of glorious valor which they played at decisive moments. Likewise the pages of history

> are also full of heroic and glorious roles which never found heroes to perform them. For some reason it seems to me that within the Arab circle there is a role, wandering aimlessly in search of a hero. And I do not know why it seems to me that this role, exhausted by its wanderings, has at last settled down, tired and weary, near the borders of our country and is beckoning to us to move, to take up its lines, to put on its costume, since no one else is qualified to play it.[34]

Nasser's choice to cite Pirandello's play, of which he later admitted having read "only the title" (and he garbled even that) was itself a dramatic flourish.[35] His manifesto's dedication to playwright Tawfiq al-Hakim (author of *Return of the Spirit*) was another.[36] If Egypt was to become the "hero" of a historical drama, the agent to actually perform on its behalf would be Nasser himself. Even backstage, the Free Officers saw themselves as creative directors and stars of a drama that they could rewrite at will. When they decided to oust President Naguib in November 1954, they reportedly invoked another al-Hakim work, the play *Pygmalion*.[37]

Nasser's narrative self-presentation developed into a powerful personality cult. By the late 1950s, Nasser was widely represented as a charismatic leader. His voice and portrait were reproduced in countless contexts in Egypt and beyond, resonating with different audiences in at least three distinct ways.

For Egyptians, Nasser represented Egyptian authenticity. On the radio, he enthralled audiences with his performances of their favorite stock character—that of *ibn al-balad,* or "son of the land."[38] His speeches, often departing from his prepared texts, incorporated *baladī* (folk or even folksy) colloquialism and humor. His photographs, which hung in nearly "every government office, store, schoolroom, and business," tended to inspire feelings of "familiarity rather than fear or hero worship."[39] Populist art, from musical ballads to comic books, stressed the intensity of Nasser's unmediated emotional connection with the Egyptian masses.[40] He represented (and helped constitute as a political unit) these masses; they lived vicariously as historical agents through him.

Non-Egyptian Arabs were a slightly different audience. For them, Nasser became "the iconic Arab ruler," the "hero of the Arab nation."[41] Nasser was larger than life, a conduit of historical agency through the grand aspirations he voiced rather than the ordinariness he embodied. On the day of the July 1958 Iraqi revolution, one historian writes, "crowds in Baghdad could be heard chanting 'We are your soldiers, Gamal Abd al-Nasser' over the radio."[42] Karbala-born playwright Jawad al-Assadi (b. 1947) recalls a childhood in which his whole secular Shiʿa family fell under Nasser's spell. Al-Assadi (whose play *Forget Hamlet* will be examined in chapter 6) believes that not only his political ideals but his early notions of theatre were shaped by "the *character* of Nasser: Gamal Abdel Nasser as a human being, a patriot, and a nationalist. He influenced all of us—an influence that was not only political. He had an emotional influence. I remember when Nasser gave a speech we would feel exceptionally moved."[43]

During the period 1953 to 1967 this "emotional influence" was beamed out to an increasingly wide Arab audience. Nasser's personal magnetism and political ambition fed each other. The Ṣawt al-ʿArab (Voice of the Arabs) radio station, launched in July 1953, soon became one of his chief regional propaganda tools. It broadcast in Arabic twenty-two hours per day, as his government boasted, "on tremendously strong broadcasting apparatus [able to] reach from the Atlantic Ocean to the Arab Gulf."[44] Newly available transistor radios brought the message into remote villages and humble homes. With its "habit of addressing Arab populations over the heads of their established rulers," the station made "the voice of the Nasser regime" central to the newly emerging sense of pan-Arab identity.[45]

A third audience, consisting of western policymakers and analysts, seems to have been most impressed with Nasser's self-dramatizing rhetoric and the "matinee idol or Valentino image" that he somehow acquired.[46] Western observers saw him as "that dashing, handsome officer who was transforming an ancient society by the sheer force of his personality, his daring, and his informal but earnest rhetoric."[47] Their accounts of the Nasser years tend to echo Nasser's theatre metaphors. The most perceptive ones do it consciously. For instance, Peter Mansfield concludes his 1969 study *Nasser's Egypt:*

> We know from *The Philosophy of the Revolution* that [Nasser] foresaw with extraordinary clarity from the earliest days of the Revolution, and perhaps before, the role that Egypt's strategic position gave it the chance to play in the world provided it could find a leader. Aided by a few devoted lieutenants, he has succeeded in hauling the Egyptian people on to the world stage by the scruff of their necks to play the role. Most of them still suffer from stage fright.[48]

The stage metaphor is so apt that even recent biographers find themselves borrowing it. "Global conflict *projected his voice onto the world stage,*" writes Anne Alexander, referring to Nasser's star turn alongside China's Zhou Enlai, Yugoslavia's Tito, and Indonesia's Sukarno at the 1955 Bandung Conference of Asian and African states.[49] Joel Gordon stresses that Nasser's charisma was deliberately constructed (he was initially awkward and even timid in public) but no less real for that. Being elected president in early 1956, Gordon writes, "officially ended [Nasser's] long journey *from the wings, on to center stage* and into the hearts of the masses."[50] Analyzing Nasser's leadership in this way—as a performance for several different audiences—helps capture both the excitement of his revolutionary effort and the contradictions that hobbled it.

Tawfiq al-Hakim's memoir of the period, *ʿAwdat al-Waʿī* (The Return of Consciousness, 1974), blames precisely Nasser's showmanship for the revolution's failure. His little book, its title a bitter retort to his earlier *Return of the Spirit,* argues that Nasser had no gift for practical politics. Instead he governed his people by mesmerizing them, creating spectacles of strength and military preparedness no more solid than theatrical décor. Stagecraft took the place of statecraft. Unfortunately, al-Hakim claims, this politics of appearance suited the enemy: Nasser "was a man who wanted peace and bluffed war; whereas Israel wanted war and bluffed peace."[51]

The publication of al-Hakim's memoir four years after Nasser's death opened the floodgates for former allies, rivals, and opponents to reassess Nasser's legacy.[52] It also sparked a controversy over its author's sudden turn against a regime he had always supported and under which he had prospered.[53] But few questioned the highly theatrical terms in which al-Hakim, with his playwright's sensitivity, described Nasser's "bewitching" effect on the Egyptian people:

> Whatever the fact, those glowing images [*ṣuwar*] of the accomplishments of the revolution made out of us instruments of the broad propaganda apparatus [*ajhizat al-diʿāya al-wāsiʿa*] with its drums, its horns, its odes, its songs and its films. We saw ourselves as a major industrial state, a leader of the world in industrial reform, and the strongest striking force in the Middle East. The face of the idolized leader [*wajh al-zaʿīm al-maʿbūd*], which filled the television screen and loomed at us from the podia of pavilions and of auditoria, related these tales [*ḥikāyāt*] to us for long hours and explained to us how we had been before and what we had now become. No one argued, checked, verified or commented. We could not help but believe, and burn our hands with applause.[54]

Al-Hakim's prose captures the dreamlike mutual ventriloquism of the relationship. In his account, media mix and overlap as audiences turn into noisy "instruments" and then back into passive applauding believers. The leader's disembodied "face" tells stories as though on its own initiative. Al-Hakim's syntax (in Arabic, the last three sentences quoted above are one) creates the sensation of an ongoing monologue that provides no opportunity to interrupt.[55]

The degree to which Nasser's "face" dominated Egyptian and Arab stages, screens, podiums, and loudspeakers would have a fateful effect on Arab art as well as politics. Audiences internalized the syllogism "Nasser is the sole authority; Nasser is represented everywhere." Its converse was that nearly every ruler or authority figure depicted on stage or film, regardless of context or period, was assumed to represent Nasser. Theatre critics saw Nasser's features in sultans, drug lords, railroad stationmasters, honey-tongued charlatans, and mythical kings.[56] Even a cruel lover could stand in for him. As anthropologist Virginia Danielson has observed, when popular Egyptian singer Umm Kulthūm sang the climactic line, "Give me my liberty, untie my hands," her "lyrics generalized easily from amorous situations to other social and even political situations that engendered frustration, pain, and waiting. Thus the line . . . was linked by listeners variously to the struggles of the Palestinians and Arabs against the West and of Egyptian citizens against ʿAbd al-Nāṣir's oppressions."[57]

Similar readings-*à-clef* occur in many autocracies and nearly all regimes built on the cult of personality. There were precedents in Egypt, too. In 1947, King Farouk's government banned films that made "direct allusions to titles, ranks, or decorations" and "went so far as to outlaw the depiction of historical personages and any historical depiction of resistance to foreign occupation, even in pharaonic dress."[58] Even earlier, Khedive Ismail (r. 1863–79), builder of the Royal Opera House in Cairo and the first state patron of modern Arabic theatre, had censored certain stage productions that cast long-ago or faraway rulers in an unfavorable light.[59]

But what is unusual about Nasser's case is the genuine warmth of the relationship between art and the regime. Since his high school performance as Caesar, Nasser had respected the theatre. As an adult politician his theatre metaphors were no accident: he coveted center stage, the defining monologue, the starring role. And playwrights, in turn, coveted the revolution's ear: first as coauthors, later as friendly critics, and finally as radical critics whose raison d'être still depended on the interpretive attentions of their keenest audience, the state censor.

Theatre Joins the Battle

In the exhilarating confusion of the mid-1950s, dramatists readily accepted the new government's invitation to participate in shaping a new Egypt. Many were eager to play their own historic role, that of mediators between the revolution and society. Supportive playwrights and directors felt called to educate the populace and build a progressive national consciousness. They sought to mediate in the other direction as well, conveying the people's concerns to those in power. And, of course, they tried to channel the moments of headiest nationalism, in which no mediation was believed necessary: the theatre became a festival of national unity in which the auditorium was as lively as the stage.

The most intense such moment came during the Suez Crisis of 1956. After Nasser announced the nationalization of the Suez Canal, Egypt's army and popular militias in Cairo and the Canal Zone cities mobilized against a ferocious Anglo-French invasion. Meanwhile the National Theatre, under the new leadership of Free Officer Ahmed Hamroush (Aḥmad Ḥamrūsh), hurriedly assembled a "nationalist play" and threw open its doors to a new public.[60] Hamroush recalls:

> Starting at noon, masses of people began to pour into the doorway at the Ezbekiya Theatre. They cut off the flow of traffic in ʿAtaba Square. We called in the police to help organize the entrance, but the pressure of the people was stronger. Some people entered the theatre who had never entered it before: men in *galabiyyas,* barefoot people, a man who had lost his leg and was leaning on a crutch. Women wrapped from head to toe in *milayas,* some of them carrying small children. And with them were school students and Azhar students and many members of the popular resistance, wearing khaki. These were new scenes [*maẓāhir jadīda*] in our theatrical life. This was the first time the theatre rushed to join the battle, and open its doors for free to everyone, while on the stage appeared famous actors and actresses.[61]

The government took note. Although Egypt never embraced Soviet-style state control of cultural production (Zhdanovism), the Nasser regime actively encouraged and funded art that would "contribute to the objectives of a democratic socialist society."[62] The Ministry of Culture, established as an independent entity in 1958, valued theatre as an appropriately collective and "democratic" art form (i.e., one accessible even to illiterate or untrained viewers).[63] Even after television appeared in 1960, theatre made up a large part of its programming. As socialist-realist playwright Numan Ashur (Nuʿmān ʿĀshūr) recalls with approval, "The revolution embraced theatrical activity" and made it "the primary means of expression."[64] Theatre professionals, in turn, embraced the twin imperatives pursued by the government between 1954 and 1964: dignity abroad and social justice at home.

In foreign policy, Nasser's aspirations became frankly global starting in the mid-1950s. The initial goal was to drive out the king and the British; the Anglo-Egyptian Treaty of 1954 secured the withdrawal of British troops, even at the price of giving up Egypt's claim to Sudan. But the "revolutionary" foreign policy that followed looked beyond Egypt's former colonizer. Nasser sought a glorious role on the pan-Arab and Cold War stages. He accumulated political capital during the Bandung Conference in 1955 and the Suez War in 1956 and spent it on such costly ventures as Egypt's merger with Syria (1958–61) and involvement in Yemen's civil war (1962–67). As early as 1954, Nasser boasted of having brought "pride, dignity, and freedom" to Egyptians.[65]

Domestically, a parallel revolution tackled poverty, inequality, and the power of entrenched rural elites. A first agrarian reform law was enacted within months of the Free Officers' coming to power in 1952. A five-year plan was adopted in 1960, and the "July Laws" of 1961 nationalized many industries.[66] State capitalism shaded into socialism: when private landholders declined to invest their capital in heavy industry, further land reform laws were proclaimed. With Soviet help, construction on the Aswan High Dam, which promised to bring electricity and progress to many Egyptian villages, began in 1960.[67] Free universal primary education was announced in 1953; in 1962, this policy was extended to all education, including universities. As the regime pursued these revolutionary goals, Ashur writes, the theatre served as its "main pulpit" (*al-minbar al-asāsī*) to explain them to the people.[68]

Nasser acknowledged that the foreign and domestic policy revolutions were distinct and sometimes in tension, but he insisted on pursuing both:

> It was not within our power to stand on the road of history like a traffic policeman and hold up the passage of one revolution until the other had passed by in order to prevent a collision. The only thing possible to do was to act as best we could and try to avoid being ground between the millstones.
>
> It was inevitable that we go through the two revolutions at the same time. When we moved along the path of the political revolution and dethroned Farouk, we took a similar step on the path of the social revolution by deciding to limit land ownership.
>
> I continue to believe that the July 23rd revolution must maintain its initiative and ability to move swiftly in order to

2.1. Gamal Abdel Nasser and Nikita Khrushchev celebrate the Soviet-built High Dam in Aswan, May 1964. (AP photo.)

> perform the miracle of traveling through two revolutions at the same time, however contradictory our resulting actions might at times appear.[69]

Playwrights and directors of the period, likewise, balanced two sometimes-conflicting revolutionary goals. The first had an international referent: to bring

Egyptian theatre up to world (i.e., Western and Eastern European) standards. The central impulse was not postcolonial anxiety about British theatre in particular. Instead, the effort mirrored Nasser's nonaligned nationalism: it called for creating a "world-class" (*ʿalā mustawā ʿālamī*) Egyptian theatre that would foster greater respect for Arab culture and greater self-respect among Arabs. The government invested in cultural institutions, funded study-abroad missions for gifted young thespians, and launched a program of literary translations into Arabic. Meanwhile, theatre people strove both to master a canon of translated works (Shakespeare, Molière, Sophocles, Ibsen, Sartre, and Chekhov led the list) and to generate an indigenous canon of high-quality scripts in Arabic.[70]

Parallel to this international cultural conversation about world-class theatre, however, ran a domestic political conversation about how to reorganize and regenerate Egypt's government and society. As the revolution groped for a clearly defined social agenda, playwrights felt they should participate actively in this discussion. Some wanted the revolution to pursue a thoroughgoing socialist agenda; others (including Tawfiq al-Hakim) were more concerned about fighting corruption and encouraging the government to be bound by law. A ban on political parties after January 1953 made the theatre even more attractive as an agora for policy debate. Starting with Ashur's socialist-realist drama *The People Downstairs* (*Al-Nās Illī Taḥt,* 1956), several playwrights focused on themes of poverty and class struggle, seeking a transparent means of dramatic expression that sometimes edged into social comedy or satire.[71]

This open forum was relatively short lived. By the 1960s, with many leftists in prison[72] and the regime showing increasing intolerance of dissent, playwrights and directors began to code their political suggestions in more subtle ways. In performance, actors conveyed political messages by inserting ad-libbed phrases or by directing certain lines or gestures to the president's box. (Some plays worked on both literal and allegorical levels.)[73] In scripts, allegory replaced or channeled the concerns of social realism. Writers adapted foreign plays, deployed elaborate symbols, and pretended to depict ancient Egypt or Greece, Mamluk times, the world of *One Thousand and One Nights,* a science-fiction future, or no particular place at all.[74] These historical, classical, foreign, or fabulistic locales let them frame the stirrings of their still-friendly disagreement with the government. Critics half-ironically dubbed this technique "symbolic realism"[75] or "social symbolism."[76] Writer and critic Louis Awad (Luwīs ʿAwaḍ; 1915–90), himself imprisoned as a leftist in this period, observes: "Those who did not wish to wear the mask of conformity had to wear the mask of the drama, which allowed them to bring to the surface with relative impunity the

2.2. UAR President Gamal Abdel Nasser poses with student actors at a University of Damascus performance of *The Merchant of Venice* (February 27, 1961). Courtesy of the Bibliotheca Alexandrina.

ambivalence of life under the . . . puritan, *petit-bourgeois* Revolution . . . [and] to point out that the inherent contradictions in the Nasser Revolution were denuding it of its revolutionary content."[77]

At this point, the international conversation about world-class theatre began to feed into the domestic one about governance. Avant-garde European theatre trends were brought in by new institutions including *al-Masraḥ* magazine and the Pocket Theatre, an experimental company launched in the 1962–63 season with Samuel Beckett's *Endgame*.[78] As such influences spread, Arab playwrights and directors began to apply a set of avant-garde models ranging from Bertolt Brecht's "epic theatre" (introduced with the Pocket Theatre's production of *The Exception and the Rule* in 1963–64) to Luigi Pirandello's disconcerting farce and the "theatre of the absurd" of Beckett and Ionesco.[79] Many of these styles were well suited to carrying political messages. The theatricality of 1960s Egyptian politics, starting with Nasser's own invocation of Pirandello, made it easy to read theatrical or metatheatrical confusion (*Who is the director here? Does he know what he is doing?*) as political critique. The new approaches quickly became tools with which to critique the growing inhumanity of the totalitarian state.[80]

Shakespeare on the Sidelines

I describe the tradition of allegorical political theatre here in order to emphasize that *Hamlet,* for the moment, remained outside it. (We will catch up with the play's early history in Egypt in the next chapter.) Despite the growing popularity of topical plays in the Nasser years, Hamlet's predicament was not used to represent political or social problems on the Egyptian stage before 1970.

I propose three explanations for this. First, Shakespeare as a whole figured exclusively in the international conversation on "quality" theatre, where he served as a cultural totem: a display item to demonstrate that the Egyptian national theatre was mature enough to handle major world classics. Such use of Shakespeare mirrored that of many emerging states striving to prove their worthiness for international respect and political independence.[81] Domestically, therefore, Shakespeare's main function remained public edification, or what Egyptian theatre critic Nehad Selaiha has called "cultural browbeating":

> Surprisingly, the spirit of experimentation which informed the Egyptian theatre in the 1960s left that stultifying Shakespearean cult untouched. Between 1963 and 1965, three consecutive National Theatre productions of *Macbeth, Othello* and *Hamlet* (the first two starring Hamdi Ghayth, the third, Karam Mutawiʿ) flaunted the old grandiose, pseudo-classical mode in full opulence, with all the clichéd paraphernalia.[82]

As long as Arab theatre people still hoped that showing cultural deservingness would lead to enhanced respect and political recognition in the world's eyes, Shakespeare's tragedies would be reserved for such demonstrative use. Until 1967, therefore, the plastic slipcovers stayed on. For instance, the 1963 production of *Macbeth* (in the 1917 translation by Khalil Mutran [Khalīl Muṭrān]) reportedly used such a high register of classical Arabic that "many members of the audience, including the well-educated Director of the Cinema Institute, simply did not understand the dialog."[83]

The second reason is particular to *Hamlet.* As a political text, the play may be better suited to radical condemnation of a regime than to sympathetic critique.

(A shorthand for this distinction in Arabic might be the two words for criticism: *naqd,* which can be constructive, like literary criticism; and *intiqād,* which carries a sense of stronger condemnation or fundamental opposition.) Once it is read as allegory, the plot leaves little room for compromise: Claudius not only rules like a tyrant but, fundamentally, is a usurper with no legitimate claim to the throne. Perhaps Egyptian and other Arab audiences (and their censors) were simply not ready for such stark positions before Nasser's death in 1970. Most intellectuals still held out hope for Nasser's promise to bring the Arabs "pride, dignity, and freedom." Playwrights in Nasser's lifetime did not publicly question his good intentions or the basic rightness of the revolution. Addressing their allegorical plays to the regime as much as to the audience, they still hoped to correct the revolution's missteps. Mistakes had been made, they implied; the sincere leader had been misled by corrupt or ignorant henchmen or had neglected the rule of law in his rush to implement much-needed reforms. Even their more daring allegories still offered gentle *naqd,* not radical *intiqād.* Tawfiq al-Hakim's 1974 description of his 1960 play *The Sultan's Dilemma* helps measure the distance between the two:

> My confidence in ʿAbd al-Nasir had made me interpret his conduct most optimistically and grope for some reasonable vindication of it. When from time to time certain doubts troubled my mind, and I feared that he had committed some excess or outrage, I would seek refuge in making him understand my view, from a distance and with compassion. I would write something from which he was to understand what I was driving at. One day I was afraid that the sword in the hand of the sultan would encroach on law and liberty, and I wrote 'Al-Sultan al-Ha'ir'. . . . All of these various writings, which were neither harsh nor bitter, constituted simply a warning, not an incitement. I learned that in fact ʿAbd al-Nasir read them and understood what I intended. Obviously, however, he did not accept my views, but rather plunged forward on his own course.[84]

The third, most conjectural reason is even more deeply related to Nasser and his failures. I would suggest that *Hamlet* did not start to articulate political sentiments until it became useful as a requiem for Nasserism. As we will see in chapters 5 and 6, Nasser's death in 1970 provoked strong mixed feelings in Egypt and throughout the Arab world. Along with the posthumous recriminations and exposés came a wave of nostalgia: even today, many Egyptians and other Arabs mourn Nasser as a father figure, saying their dreams of building a just and progressive society died along with him. Perhaps his death finally solved the problem of how to cast Nasser, who never quite fit the part of either a heroic Hamlet or a usurping Claudius. He could play Hamlet's father's ghost: awe-inspiring, betrayed, succeeded by men of lesser talent, and continuing to haunt the Arab political imagination.

But all this was yet to come. Meanwhile, in the 1960s, we can start to trace a gradual shift in Arab audience expectations regarding *Hamlet*. Exposed to the global kaleidoscope of influences discussed in the next chapter, playgoers changed their idea of what dramatists and directors needed to do. The presence of multiple models helped drive up the requirements for world-class status. Many Arab critics concluded that an accurate rendition of a Shakespeare play was not enough; only the ability to provide an *original interpretation* constituted true assimilation (and hence deservingness). The models that stressed Shakespeare's contemporary political relevance were especially exciting—culturally avant-garde and politically vociferous at the same time. These new models would be carefully studied and stored away. Then they would be discreetly tried out in plays that wove strands of Hamlet into Arab Muslim political protagonists. Only later, when the right circumstances arose, would Shakespeare and especially *Hamlet* explicitly join the domestic political conversation in Egypt and other Arab countries.

3

THE GLOBAL KALEIDOSCOPE: HOW EGYPTIANS GOT THEIR *HAMLET*, 1901–64

Ask your friends or students if they can remember their very first *Hamlet* experience. Was it a line someone quoted in conversation, a literary allusion, an excerpt read in school, a theatre production, a film? The play is so culturally ubiquitous that few Shakespeare fans—whether professional scholars, undergraduate students, or casual theatregoers—can pinpoint their earliest encounter with it.

Mahmoud Aboudoma (Maḥmūd Abū Dūmā, b. 1953) claims he can. The Alexandria-based playwright-director has revisited *Hamlet* several times: his *Hamlet*-offshoot play *Dance of the Scorpions* (1989) will be analyzed in chapter 6. To a question about relevant *Hamlet* sources and models, Aboudoma has responded as follows:

> I have not read [the play] in English at all, as my English does not allow me to understand it. But when I was young, I saw a Russian black and white film: it was *Gamlet*, with no Arabic subtitles. I saw this film more than 10 times, like a deaf young man. The first time I read *Hamlet* it was in Mohamed Hassan al-Zayyat's translation, with a big introduction. At that time I had not heard about Tom Stoppard's play [*Rosencrantz and Guildenstern Are Dead*, 1967]. I had no idea about versions [of a play] or [even] what the word means.[1]

Already this raises questions about the standard model of how a writer in a postcolonial society encounters a western classic. The "text" Aboudoma cites as his first Shakespeare exposure is not a British play but a Soviet film, Grigori Kozintsev's *Gamlet* (1964). Aboudoma's stylized description ("more than 10 times," "like a deaf young man") conveys the formative nature of the experience. Aboudoma later understands what versions and interpretations are. He seeks out additional background—a translation, a scholarly introduction, other readings and rewritings—to further mediate his Shakespeare encounter. But Kozintsev's interpretation remains decisive. When the former "deaf young man" contemplates the music of *Hamlet* (as we will see from the offshoot play he eventually writes), he hears a political tune.

Why were two generations of Egyptian intellectuals so impressed—and so perfectly primed to be impressed—by Kozintsev's film? Continuing the work of historical reconstruction begun in the previous chapter, this chapter will explore the "horizon of expectations" of Egyptian theatre-lovers in 1964, asking what kind of *Hamlet*s they would be likely to know or expect.[2] My task here is not to survey all the Arabic translations of *Hamlet*—more than fifteen have survived—or to catalogue all the productions ever seen in Arab capitals. Rather, the point is to reconstruct the most significant and best-remembered interpretations, the ones that have entered popular memory and become the building blocks of the Arab *Hamlet* tradition.

Beyond Caliban

This detailed reconstruction is necessary because the Arab world is not a simply "postcolonial" place. Postcolonial criticism, rooted in the psychoanalytic insights of Franz Fanon, likes to imagine intercultural literary appropriation as a struggle between father and son. The postcolonial writer is forced to grapple with an authoritative metropolitan original. He is a talented latecomer from a less prestigious background; the uneven intercultural playing field heightens his anxiety of influence and inspires him to ever greater creative efforts. This Oedipal dynamic underpins the still-standard trope of postcolonial reception-appropriation-subversion: Caliban's struggle to define himself against Prospero. "You taught me language," says the islander in Shakespeare's *Tempest,* his words brilliantly echoed by Caribbean writers and later by North American scholars of postcolonial literature, "and my profit on't / Is I know how to curse."[3]

However, the binary model is inadequate in the Arab case (and actually, I would suggest, in most cases of non-Anglophone Shakespeare appropriation). Unlike Caliban, twentieth-century Arab intellectuals did not grow up on a cultural island. They were not oppressed/inspired by a single dominant source of cultural literacy. Instead, their belatedness (if the word still serves) has consisted of entering a world already populated with a *multitude* of competing dramatic and literary approaches. Their acquaintance with Shakespeare, as we will see, did not come originally or primarily at British hands. In most cases it did not involve a direct experience of Shakespeare's texts. Less like Caliban and more like Hamlet torn between the claims of competing father figures (Claudius, the Ghost, even the Player and Polonius), Arab interpreters of Shakespeare have been enriched and confused by a multiple inheritance from the start.

Egypt is the most significant example, because it drew waves of talented Arab immigrants in the late nineteenth century and became the major exporter of culture to the rest of the Arab world in the twentieth. Although colonized by the British for seventy years (1882–1952), modern Egypt always hosted a diverse mix of cultural influences. After independence it emerged with an outlook more global than postcolonial. Reminiscing about the Cairo of her youth, Egyptian-British writer Ahdaf Soueif describes a landscape she calls Mezzaterra, a global cultural crossroads precisely the opposite of Caliban's island:

> Growing up Egyptian in the Sixties meant growing up Muslim/Christian/Egyptian/Arab/African/Mediterranean/Non-Aligned/Socialist but happy with small-scale capitalism. . . . In Cairo on any one night you could go to see an Arabic, English, French, Italian or Russian film. One week the Russian *Hamlet* was playing at Cinema Odeon, Christopher Plummer's [BBC film] *Hamlet* at Cinema Qasr el-Nil, and Karam Muṭāwi's *Hamlet* at the Egyptian National Theatre. . . . Looking back, I imagine our Sixties identity as a spacious meeting point, a common ground with avenues into the rich hinterlands of many traditions.[4]

Soueif (b. 1950) is almost exactly Aboudoma's contemporary; her recollection provides an alternative to his single-source, tabula rasa account of encountering Shakespeare's *Hamlet*.[5] Neither of them, however, privileges a postcolonial identity or set of influences.

Two Influential Exceptions: Chahine and Said

Of course, some writers do. For the few Arabs in direct contact with Egypt's British overlords, early knowledge of Shakespeare was indeed conditioned by the Prospero-Caliban dialectic of colonial domination and subversive appropriation. For instance, filmmaker Youssef Chahine (1926–2008) and critic Edward Said (1935–2003) coincide in recalling Shakespeare as a battleground on

3.1. Yahya ignores the transcribed soliloquy behind him in Youssef Chahine's *Alexandria Why* (1978). Courtesy MISR International Films (Youssef Chahine).

which a native identity is asserted and an adult artistic personality begins to develop. Shakespeare arrives in the classroom and invites playful or aggressive "writing back."[6] Both Chahine and Said studied at the elite British-run Victoria College, at its Alexandria and Cairo branches, respectively.[7] Both dramatize their encounter with Shakespeare and power in stories centered on *Hamlet,* namely on the closet scene.

Youssef (then called Joe) Chahine was a Victoria student during World War II. The first film of his autobiographical trilogy, *Iskandariyya Līh? (Alexandria, Why?,* 1978), pivots on the "memorize a Shakespeare speech" assignment.[8] It is 1942. Chahine's young alter ego Yahya (Mohsen Mohiedine) is sitting in English class watching a classmate cheat by "reciting," to general hilarity, from Hamlet's "to be or not to be" soliloquy—which is transcribed in Arabic letters on the chalkboard![9] Yahya then seizes ownership of the assignment. He announces in Egyptian colloquial Arabic that he will recite "without looking at the board" and from a different excerpt than assigned, "the scene of the mother" (the closet scene).[10] Classmates and teacher are rapt.[11]

Yahya's switch replaces a meandering soliloquy with some of Hamlet's most direct and unhesitant lines in the play. Further, he delivers them in passionate literary Arabic rather than accented English.[12] His performance thus transforms the rote classroom task to include a mother figure and his own mother tongue—both strictly banned from the all-male, English-only school.[13] The *Hamlet* speech begins Yahya's coming of age as a (homosexual) man.[14] It also launches his arts career: he is elected president of a student theatre club and is soon sent to study acting at the Pasadena Playhouse in California. The film ends with him gazing at the Statue of Liberty from the deck of a steamer pulling into New York, as though appropriating Shakespeare had freed him to develop his artistic voice in the neutral creative space of the United States rather than in the imperial capital.

A darker version of this story plays out in *Out of Place,* Edward Said's 1999 memoir. As a child, Edward first encounters *Hamlet* through the dour quotations of his father ("Neither a borrower nor a lender be"), a domineering use of Shakespeare that foreshadows Said's classroom encounters. Edward enrolls at Victoria in 1949, just as the loss of Palestine is hitting Egyptian politics and revolutionary tensions are coming to a boil.[15] A brawl over *Twelfth Night* marks his first day: after his classmates explicate a scene with "barely concealed lewdness," the teacher lurches from his chair in Malvolio-like exasperation, "a wide-armed heavy-set man flailing wildly at two pocket-sized boys" who jump "nimbly out of the way."[16] The following year, a similar classroom brawl over Shakespeare (whether to devote the day's lesson to the sonnets or to Walter Scott) gets Edward suspended for two weeks, which, after a "preliminary" whipping with his father's riding crop, precipitates his transfer to the Mt. Hermon School in Massachusetts.[17] The schoolmaster's grotesque late-colonial attempted violence leads to the father's real violence, then to exile.

The liberating counterpoint comes from a childhood *Hamlet* experience. Before John Gielgud's visit to Cairo, Edward's mother suggests they read *Hamlet* aloud together from a one-volume Shakespeare whose "handsome red morocco leather binding and delicate onion-skin paper embod[ies] all that [is] luxurious and exciting in a book."[18] Said singles out the closet scene as a moment of special intimacy. He does not delve into the implications of playing Hamlet to his mother's Gertrude—the violence of the lines and their shift of moral censure, for once, from the never-good-enough son (he speaks of "the sodden delinquency of my life") onto his parent.[19] Instead he describes their "*Hamlet* afternoons" as moments of recognition whose memory would fortify him for years. As a child Edward is shamed by the physical attractiveness of "Gielgud and the blond man who played Laertes . . . they were English heroes, after all,"[20] but in the United States he begins to turn his social awkwardness into intellectual independence. When he finds his critical voice, it will again be through Shakespeare.[21]

Chahine's and Said's strikingly parallel autobiographical accounts show the narrative power of the Oedipal-postcolonial model. They also reveal its specificity to a limited Egyptian (or rather, pan-Arab cosmopolitan) social class at a particular late-colonial historical moment. Both biographically and philosophically, these two towering international cultural figures are the exception, not the rule. Their exposure to Shakespeare, unlike almost everyone else's, came directly at British colonial hands. When decolonization came they were already abroad. Their rhetorical self-constructions aim largely at western audiences (Said's memoir was written in English, and Chahine's trilogy was produced by Misr International Films and premiered in Berlin). Their reminiscences should *not* be taken to represent the paradigmatic Arab experience of Shakespeare.

The Global Kaleidoscope

Overall, we will find it helpful to put the Prospero-and-Caliban paradigm out of mind. Shakespeare in the Arab Near East was generally not treated as a dangerous import to be resisted or subverted.[22] From the beginning, he was perceived as a global author rather than a British one. As happened in many other countries (including Italy, Spain, Holland, Russia, and all over Eastern Europe), early adaptations of *Hamlet* came through French, shaped by the battle between taste and nature still besetting the theatres of nineteenth-century Paris. Later Arab *Hamlet* interpreters were in touch with the Anglo-German tradition of character criticism, with its deep interest in Hamlet's psychology. Even after 1952, variations on *Hamlet* never aimed to "write back" to a British "original"; anxiety about the cultural dominance of the former colonizer was simply not the major concern. More relevant was the larger Cold War political environment and the multiple sets of artistic models (from the Soviet Union, Eastern and Western Europe, the United States, and even Latin America and India) that this turbulent context pulled into dialogue and competition.

This history leads me to a new way of theorizing Shakespeare reception and appropriation. An Arabic rewriting of *Hamlet,* I want to propose, is best thought of as an individual writer's response to a *global kaleidoscope* of sources and models. It is not a one-to-one interaction with Shakespeare's "original" text. Nor is it a simple binary negotiation between a colonizer's "source" culture and the "target" culture of the colonized. Most scholars and teachers have responded to Arab Shakespeare this way—through some combination of comparing Text B to Text A and situating Text B in Context X. These interpretive and pedagogical habits are deeply engrained, and they have yielded many productive readings. But the *Hamlet* rewritings presented in the rest of this book cannot be understood simply in terms of these two forces, Shakespeare's text on one hand and an Arab sociocultural and political environment on the other. A thicker description is needed. Between these two sets of stimuli and in constantly changing relationship with each of them, the Arab rewriter faces a bewildering array of *other* intertexts—shards of interpretation in various colors, shapes, and degrees of clarity. These fragments are brought to light and tumbled into ever-shifting patterns by the contingencies of history and biography, which spin the kaleidoscope. At a given moment, some fragments will appear prominent and others obscure due to variations in international politics, literary traditions, cultural fashions, individual upbringing, and sensibility. The particular kaleidoscopic arrangement of these shards, more directly than any words Shakespeare ever wrote, inspires and delimits an Arab rewriter's creative response.

The power of the global kaleidoscope model, as I hope to show, is that it restores previously hidden intertexts to view. My reconstruction will start with two early French-derived Arabic *Hamlet* adaptations, versions widely recalled (if mocked) by Arab intellectuals even today. It will touch on the influence of English-sourced translations and performances, which delved more into the problem of Hamlet's character and psychology. These various French- and British- derived versions helped shape the Egyptian public's expectations of Shakespeare's play and its protagonist; all centered on Hamlet's "great speeches" and provided ample occasions to declaim. I will then turn to some of the new artistic resources that became available after independence and Gamal Abdel Nasser's mid-1950s rapprochement with the Socialist bloc; this political shift brought in Soviet and East European Shakespeare models whose significance today's post–Cold War viewpoint tends to occlude.[23] Especially influential was the "Russian Hamlet" Aboudoma and Soueif mention above, Grigori Kozintsev's 1964 film. I will close with a look at a high-profile *Hamlet* production that opened in Cairo in December 1964; its critical reception reveals both the early impact of these Soviet and East European influences and the continuing force of other models as Arab interpreters experimented toward developing a distinctive *Hamlet* of their own.

"Bend Again toward France"

Several scholars have surveyed the first seventy years of Arabic Shakespeare. Most compare successive translations; taking a teleological view, they tell of a bumpily asymptotic evolution from the "crude, ridiculous and inaccurate"[24] adaptations of the 1890s toward ever more faithful and readable Arabic translations. Eager to distinguish themselves from their forebears, these literary-minded critics scold Arab translators for "misunderstanding" or "misrepresenting" important points in Shakespeare's original.[25] They either overlook or deplore Shakespeare's earliest function in the Arab world: as script fodder for the Levantine immigrant entrepreneurs seeking to fill seats in Egypt's new theatres.

More recently, a few scholars have begun to apply the sociological insights of Pierre Bourdieu to the appropriation of Shakespeare in Arabic. Their work has highlighted the movement from early, commercially driven uses of Shakespeare to later attempts to foster a hierarchy of aesthetic and political values independent of normal market forces. From this angle, it becomes more interesting to examine the commercial and ideological contexts in which different notions of quality were developed and valorized and less interesting to replicate one such standard in assessing competing translations.[26]

The favorite exemplar for both groups of scholars—whipping boy for the pedants and sociocultural phenomenon for the Bourdeiuseans—is Tanyus ʿAbdu (1869–1926), author of the earliest surviving Arabic *Hamlet* adaptation.[27] Like virtually all "Arabizers" of his generation, ʿAbdu translated from the French. Unfortunately, both groups tend to mention but then disregard these French roots. Yet these roots help explain ʿAbdu's resulting text, the operatic nature of early Arabic Shakespeare, and the style of early Egyptian theatre more generally. Much of the distortion or adaptation attributed to ʿAbdu, it turns out, can be traced to his hitherto-overlooked French source.

Operatic Shakespeare

Well into the nineteenth century, the French stage rewarded beautiful language and "tableaux," not interaction between characters. French acting

> was still of the neoclassical "teapot" or declamatory variety, whereby the actor delivering the speech stood at the front of the stage and declaimed his or her lines to the audience, while the rest of the actors onstage stood behind, in a semicircle. . . . The *sociétaires* at the Academie Française were even known to perform encores, repeating speeches out of context when the audience had applauded their delivery.[28]

Shakespeare's plays provoked ambivalence. Critics from Voltaire onward considered him "a drunken savage," overflowing with genius but lacking in taste.[29] Nonetheless, obsessed with Italian opera, French writers seized on the operatic possibilities of Shakespeare's texts. Stage performance began with the late-eighteenth-century "imitations" of Jean-François Ducis (1733–1816), who bragged of knowing "*point l'anglois*" ("no English at all").[30] Working from excerpts and summaries by Antoine de La Place (1707–93), Ducis labored to produce acceptably decorous yet "Shakespearean" adaptations of *Hamlet* (1769), *Romeo and Juliet, King Lear, Macbeth, Othello,* and *King John*.[31] Introducing extra characters and Neoclassical balance, he turned *Hamlet* into a text on filial piety[32] and a pretext for elaborate visual display. (He also made "Ophélie" a household word in France.)[33] For Ducis and his successors,

> the procedure routinely followed was to reduce and regularise the text, while multiplying the cues for spectacle and ostentation. French Shakespeare was, in a word, operatic, and it entered the theatre through the breach that opera had made. Visual and emotional stimulus were provided by big stages, elaborate and realistic scenery, and supplementary pantomime and ballet. At the time when Shakespeare's name began to circulate in France, fashionable Paris was addicted to the Italian opera, and his work was taken up by theatre because it could be a vehicle for this sort of entertainment.[34]

The operatic trend carried over to Egypt. Italian opera had publicly represented the modernizing drives of Egypt's rulers ever since Giuseppe Verdi's *Aïda* was commissioned to inaugurate Khedive Ismail's Italian-style opera house in the 1870s.[35] Italian and French styles shaped Egyptian acting: dialogue was deemphasized, and soliloquies and other climactic speeches were declaimed like arias, facing the audience, often *fortissimo.*[36]

Leading man Shaykh Salama Higazi (al-Shaykh Salāma Ḥijāzī; 1852–1917) epitomized the trend. One of the first Egyptians in a theatre milieu dominated by mostly Christian Syro-Lebanese immigrants, the wildly popular Qur'ān chanter–turned–singer was nicknamed "the Caruso of the East" after his Italian younger contemporary, tenor Enrico Caruso (1873–1921).[37] His popularity helped secure the place of the musical as a lasting form in Egyptian theatre and eventually also Egyptian cinema. Higazi starred in several Shakespeare plays as well as in versions of *Aïda,* Jean Racine's *Andromaque,* Pierre Corneille's *Horace,* Alexandre Dumas' *La Tour de Nesle,* Victor Hugo's *Angelo* and *Marie-Tudor,* Eugène Scribe's *l'Africaine,* Adolphe d'Ennery's *Les Deux Orphelines*, and *La Dame aux Camélias* by Alexandre Dumas, *fils.* To each he brought his distinctive style:

> In performing a role, Higazi would alternate between declamation and singing; this created a vogue for lyrical theatre. Higazi's contemporaries termed this genre *opera,* the term taken up by Iskandar Fahmy, who observed that "it effectively banished dramatic art." One would be tempted to call these works *operettas,* were they not denatured translations of certain European melodramas, tragedies, dramas, and operas.[38]

ʿAbdu Lifts from Dumas

Against this background, it is easier to understand Tanyus ʿAbdu's *Hamlet,* the earliest surviving[39] Arabic version of the play. It was commissioned in 1901 by Syrian-born theatre manager Iskandar Farah (Iskandar Faraḥ), owner of Cairo's al-Tiyātrū al-Miṣrī (Egyptian Theatre) and director of its troupe. The leading role was tailored for the 49-year-old Higazi, whose mere presence in a cast at that time could guarantee a play's commercial success. Higazi would later break with Farah and form his own Arabic Theatre Company (Dār al-Tamthīl al-ʿArabī) in 1905, taking *Hamlet* with him: his fans were loyal, and they knew what they wanted. It is reported that when Higazi once bowed to high-cultural pressures and tried to perform *Hamlet* without singing, the audience members nearly rioted. To mollify them, a new song with lyrics by respected poet Ahmed Shawqi (1868–1932) was commissioned and integrated into future performances.[40] Higazi later recorded the song, a lament that began "*dahr maṣāʾibī ʿandī bilā ʿadad*" (Fate has afflicted me with innumerable calamities), as part of his successful contract with the German phonograph company Odeon.[41]

No one would call Tanyus ʿAbdu's *Hamlet* a literary masterpiece. A Lebanese immigrant to Egypt, ʿAbdu made his living as a journalist and translator. His political sympathies were socialist,[42] but his genius lay in feeding the tastes of Cairo's emerging middle class. He has accordingly been criticized as a mass producer, a hack whose inartistically simple syntax and naïve use of western sources betrayed traditional Arabo-Islamic standards of literary craftsmanship.[43] Critics have accused him of writing more than 600 "Arabizations" of French and English works of fiction and drama. With obvious pleasure, they repeat and embellish the legend that ʿAbdu

> was perhaps the most irresponsible of all: according to writers and journalists who knew him personally, ʿAbdu did not really translate but Arabicized what he read. He never followed the original or tried to convey its meaning. He translated anywhere and everywhere, regardless of his circumstances—in a coffeeshop, on a sidewalk, on a train, even on the flat roof of his house. ʿAbdu was, if we may believe one contemporary description, a walking library. . . . He carried with him sheets of paper in one pocket and a French novel in the other. He would then read a few lines, put the novel back in his pocket, and begin to scratch in a fine script whatever he could remember of the few lines he had read. He wrote all day long without striking out a word or rereading a line.[44]

ʿAbdu's *Hamlet* was published in 1902 and went into two editions. The title page of the second printing trumpeted a five-act play "authored by Shakespeare, the famous English poet" and "Arabized by the skilled writer Tanyus Effendi ʿAbdu, owner of the well-reputed al-Sharq Newspaper."[45] The translator thus brought all his cultural capital to the printed text, giving himself equal billing with Shakespeare and invoking his success as a journalist as well as his Ottoman title of Effendi ("educated gentleman").[46] Later his literary pretensions would lead him to republish several arias from *Hamlet* as part of a slim 1925 *diwān* (poetry collection) with a glowing preface by fellow Lebanese immigrant poet Khalil Mutran.[47] (Mutran's own 1918 *Hamlet* will be discussed below.) But as a book ʿAbdu's *Hamlet* did not enjoy a prestigious afterlife. Long considered lost, it returned to print only in 2005, after a photocopy turned up in the library of St. Antony's College, Oxford.[48]

Where ʿAbdu's adaptation had an impact was on the stage. It was performed in Egypt at least seventeen times during the years 1901 to 1910. From Cairo it traveled to Alexandria, Tanta, and Mansoura, becoming the second-most-popular Shakespeare adaptation after Najib al-Haddad's (Najīb al-Ḥaddad) 1890s play *Martyrs of Love* (*Shuhadā' al-Gharām*), based on *Romeo and Juliet* and also starring Higazi.[49] In a theatre world dominated by adaptations and knockoffs of French comedy, particularly Molière, al-Haddad's *Martyrs* and ʿAbdu's *Hamlet* showed that Shakespeare, too, could bring real box office success.

Higazi's performance carried ʿAbdu's *Hamlet* into popular memory. More than half a century after the curtain last fell, translator Muhammad Awad Muhammad (Muḥammad ʿAwaḍ Muḥammad; 1895–1972) reminisces about it in the introduction to his own far more scholarly version of *Hamlet*. Quoting from memory (he misidentifies the translator, as no one citing a printed text would do), Awad Muhammad reproduces the opening of Hamlet's first aria verbatim, adding some faint praise for the author:

> Some of us still carry, sticking in our minds from childhood, some traces of that old translation, such as Hamlet's chant [*inshād*] in the first act:
>
> > Father where are you? See what's taken place.
> > A wedding where there used to be a wake,
> > Funerals turned to feast days on the morrow,
> > And on that mouth, a smile instead of sorrow.[50]
>
> And although we, too, could smile at this translation, yet its writer deserves our congratulations for opening the

> door to the translation of this literary monument, and for having no inhibitions about using poetry to beautify his Arabization.[51]

There is indeed reason to smile: ʿAbdu's *Hamlet* is a musical with a happy ending. The text is in simple prose. Hamlet's major speeches (and Ophelia's monologue at the end of the nunnery scene) appear as sections of fairly repetitive verse, more like arias than soliloquies, as in the excerpt above. There are scene and plot changes: Shakespeare's opening scene is omitted; Fortinbras is not mentioned in the council scene and never appears on stage; the closet scene is relocated to the palace's main hall. There are character changes as well. Ophelia becomes a somewhat stronger character, participating in an interpolated early scene where she and Hamlet flirt charmingly (like Romeo and Juliet) in rhyming prose; he calls her a "noble angel."[52] Later he thinks of her with regret when he discovers he has killed Polonius.[53] But the most striking departure from Shakespeare is the closing scene: Hamlet fatally wounds Laertes and Claudius and then receives the Ghost's blessing, taking the throne as the curtain descends slowly and "the ensemble sings offstage."[54]

ʿAbdu's many departures from Shakespeare have made his *Hamlet* an "icon of infidelity" among translation critics.[55] Focused on exciting situations rather than on the characters' deep subjectivity, ʿAbdu's play also offends scholars whose notion of *Hamlet* centers on hesitation or indecision. For instance, Nadia al-Bahar writes:

> One may overlook the various changes and excisions in this adaptation, but the most glaring drawback lies in the protagonist himself. Unlike Shakespeare's Hamlet, he is determined to wreak vengeance; he is one given to action rather than reflection. One is made aware of Hamlet's resolution throughout the adaptation; he is not as reluctant or overmeditative as Shakespeare's Prince. More like Laertes, he assigns great value to honor which furnishes a valid motive for any course of action he is to take. But, unlike Laertes, who in succumbing to the demands of honor becomes its very slave and thereby induc[es] his own destruction, Hamlet retires at the end with victory. Thus, much of the inner struggle in the original *Hamlet* is lost and, alongside with it, much of the dramatic tension is diminished.[56]

What no one has pointed out, to my knowledge, is that ʿAbdu's text very closely follows the French version by Alexandre Dumas, *père* (1802–70).[57]

Dumas' *Hamlet,* written in collaboration with Paul Meurice, premiered in Paris in 1847. It was republished many times, including in 1863 and 1874 as part of Dumas' complete works (of which ʿAbdu the "walking library" surely owned a set). Of course, this *Hamlet* emerged from its own kaleidoscope of influences. Expurgated yet exaggerated, it represents a strange mix of Romantic naturalism with the remnants of Ducis' Neoclassical *bienséance* (propriety).[58]

> Dumas recast what in France was still widely regarded as a ramshackle masterpiece, and pulled and pummelled Shakespeare's imagery to make it fit into rhyming alexandrines. . . . Fortinbras disappeared, and the whole of the opening scene on the battlements of the castle was scrapped because there was no gainsaying old wisdom—it was superfluous to depict what was subsequently narrated. But in the first act a scene was added in which Hamlet courted Ophelia and left her exclaiming, breathless with rapture, *Il m'aime! Il m'aime! Oh! Que je suis heureuse!*[59]

Tanyus ʿAbdu's choice of source makes sense: Dumas was in vogue. *Le Comte de Monte-Cristo* had been translated into Arabic in 1871, its enormous success inspiring ten different translators to tackle fourteen additional Dumas novels by 1910.[60] Stage adaptations based on Dumas, many of them "social critiques calling for class equality," were "among the most popular plays" performed in early twentieth-century Cairo, Alexandria, and Beirut.[61] As a source, Dumas represented the convergence of ʿAbdu's commercial instincts and his leftist sympathies.

ʿAbdu's debt to Dumas explains nearly all the peculiarities of his *Hamlet,* from the apparent padding throughout (the French alexandrine is two syllables longer than Shakespeare's iambic pentameter line) to the cleaned-up plot and added scenes. All the character changes with which Arab critics have reproached ʿAbdu—the decisive Hamlet, the active Ophelia, the unsensual Gertrude, and the prayerless Claudius—can be traced to his peculiar French source.

Dumas also deserves the credit (or blame) for ʿAbdu's ending. Unwounded, Dumas' Hamlet exchanges foils with Laertes in the duel and cuts him.[62] The queen drinks poison and dies, Laertes reveals the plot, and Hamlet stabs and poisons the king. At that moment the Ghost appears, both to "see his murderers die" (as Hamlet says) and to deliver the judgment of God and the dramatist. The Ghost forgives Laertes and Gertrude, telling the impulsive courtier to "pray and die" and the morally weak queen to "hope and die." But Claudius, pleading for pardon, is sent to hell's cruelest fires. The Ghost, echoing the phantoms who torment Shakespeare's Richard III at Bosworth Field,[63] tells him: "Go, incestuous traitor! Go! Despair and die!" Only a shred of ambiguity is reintroduced in the play's last lines: Hamlet, asking the Ghost what punishment awaits him for delaying his revenge and causing four unnecessary deaths, is told: "You will live!"[64]

A textual comparison (with Dumas' *Hamlet* this time, not Shakespeare's) shows that ʿAbdu followed his source closely, with only minor revisions.[65] Only ʿAbdu's songs create a different effect, abandoning Dumas' highly fluid and enjambed alexandrines for jingle-like Arabic verse. And in the last scene, which he renders almost verbatim, ʿAbdu adds one closing line to clarify the happiness of the ending, spoken by the Ghost: "As for you, live happy on earth, forgiven in heaven. Ascend before my eyes to your uncle's place, for this throne was created only for you."[66]

Thus the scripts are similar, but the effect on stage was subtly different. Whereas Dumas' version had aimed in the French context to wrest control from the leading actors and give it to the writer and director, ʿAbdu's version refocused the spotlight on heroic crooner-Hamlet Salama Higazi.

Mutran Sings the Marseillaise

A shift in Arab Shakespeare appropriation came with the next important *Hamlet* translator, the Lebanese-born poet and journalist Khalil Mutran (1872–1949).[67] Mutran came to Egypt as a fervent Arab nationalist grounded in French as well as classical Arabic culture. He had studied Arabic prosody and linguistics at Beirut's Roman Catholic Patriarchate College, and as a young man he had spent two years in exile in Paris (1890–92) after calling too loudly for the liberation of Arab lands from Ottoman rule. This background helps account for Mutran's language politics. Unlike the previous generation of Lebanese immigrants, he translated mainly for cultural and ideological effect rather than money. A Christian immigrant to a predominantly Muslim Arab country, Mutran aspired to forge a pan-Arab identity broader than Egypt but not premised solely on Islam. He disdained the spoken Arabic vernaculars of Egypt and the Levant and invested instead in literary Arabic, the currency of the *nahḍa* (Arab renaissance) literary movement. His Shakespeare versions classicize and archaize, "digging up words from the lexical graveyard" (in Mikhail Naimy's phrase) and sometimes using such recherché Arabic vocables that he needs footnotes to gloss his own translations.[68]

Mutran had frequented the theatre in Paris and then Cairo. He had visited Sarah Bernhardt's salon and admired Shaykh Salama Higazi's performances in

Shakespearean and other plays. He even wrote a twelve-line praise poem for Higazi (first published in 1908), singling out Hamlet and four of Higazi's other famous roles.[69] But as he insists with almost religious fervor in the poem's closing line, Mutran wanted the theatre to provide edification rather than mere entertainment. Because of or despite its lavish costumes and enchanting characters, he writes:

> I see theatre as an exhortation [*baʿthan wāʿiẓan*]
> Couched in a temptation [*fitna*] for eyes and ears.[70]

Mutran's Shakespeare translations aimed for a particular kind of edification: cultural-nationalist rather than moral. These works were commissioned by actor-director George Abyad (Jūrj Abyaḍ), a fellow Lebanese Christian immigrant who had studied acting at the Paris Conservatoire before founding a theatre in Egypt in 1912. Abyad's troupe hoped to present "serious" theatre, with no singing. Among other "classical" plays (starting with *Oedipus Rex*), they performed Mutran's *Othello* (1912), *Macbeth* (1917), *Hamlet* (1918), and *The Merchant of Venice* (1922). The physically huge Abyad, both director and star, "declaimed, ranted and spluttered" his way through Mutran's carefully wrought speeches.[71] In his hands, *Hamlet* resembled the "heroic dramas and melodramas . . . prevalent in Paris at the opening of the century."[72] The commercial and critical response was generally poor. Yet Mutran's reputation for literary artistry has survived; his Shakespeare translations remain in print and are still admired today. Although written for the stage, his translations aspired to—and obtained—the status of Arabic literary classics.

It is not certain whether, as is widely alleged, Mutran's Shakespeare plays "depended mainly on the French translation, perhaps glancing at the original from time to time."[73] No one has pinpointed which French version or versions of *Hamlet* he consulted.[74] His deep cuts and rearrangements appear to be his own. But it is clear that Mutran knew French better than English; French readings certainly mediate his translation of particular words and phrases. For instance, he renders the name Horatio as *hūrāsiyū* (the French pronunciation) rather than *hūrāshiyū* (with the Arabic letter *shīn*) and sometimes gives Laertes as *lāyirt* rather than *lāyirtīs*.[75] In the nunnery scene he translates Ophelia's "I was the more deceived"[76] as "You have increased my disappointment" (*la-qad zidtanī khaybat al-amal*),[77] apparently mistaking the English *deceived* for its false cognate, the French *déçu*.[78] (A more serious such misreading occurs in his *Merchant of Venice*, where he renders "Gentile" as *laṭīf*—"kind, nice"—as though reading the French *gentille*. This of course alters the meaning of the play.)[79]

Such oddities in Mutran's translations may be explained either by a direct French source or by a Francophone reading of Shakespeare's English. Other features, such as his rendering of "To be or not to be" as "Am I, or am I not?" (*a-kā'in anā, aw ghayr kā'in*?") can hardly be explained at all.[80]

More obvious than Mutran's direct source is the French-bred outlook that mediated his overall approach to Shakespeare. All his non-Shakespeare translations are from French: Racine's *Berenice*; Corneille's *Le Cid, Cinna,* and *Polyeuctes*; Victor Hugo's *Hernani*; and Paul Bourget's dramatized novel *L'Émigré*.[81] Mutran's Shakespeare is a French figure too: the cult hero of Victor Hugo (1802–85) and the French Romantic movement. In the introduction to his first Shakespeare effort, the 1912 *Othello,* Mutran invokes Shakespeare's "unbounded genius" (a French cliché) and describes him as "the poet who captivated Victor Hugo with the strangeness of his poetry, and in whose acuity, fluency, and power of concretizing abstractions he found the principle of that free sect [*hādhā al-madhhab al-ḥurr*] which he himself later joined and championed, and which then became the law [*sunna*] of writers in all the world [*al-ʿālamayn*]."[82]

Mutran likely knew the *Complete Works of Shakespeare* translated by Hugo's son, François-Victor (1828–73). Volume I (1858 edition) presents two texts of *Hamlet,* in prose, translated from the first and second quartos. More importantly, it includes the younger Hugo's introduction, which starts with a scholarly reconstruction of Shakespeare's sources and ends with revolutionary fire. Hugo casts Hamlet as an unwavering hero:

> Oh young people, young people! all of you, my companions, my friends . . . I urge you here, in the name of the camaraderie that bound Horatio to Hamlet! Do not let yourselves be disconcerted by the ephemeral reactions of matter against the spirit. You, too, have great things to do. Are there no more wrongs to right? ills to cure? iniquities to destroy? oppressions to combat? souls to emancipate? ideas to realize? Ah, you who are responsible for the future, do not fail in your mission. . . . To tyrannical fate, oppose your tireless will. Remain forever faithful to the holy cause of progress. Be firm, intrepid, and noble-minded. And if you sometimes hesitate before your glorious task, if you have doubts, well! then turn your back on the inane Poloniuses and the treacherous Rosencrantzes, and cast your eyes to the horizon. . . . Look well and, on that cold winter night, against the pale light of the

> starry sky, you will see passing—armed cap-à-pié, the rod of command in his hand—the white-haired spectre called Duty.[83]

Mutran's translations express a similar Romantic commitment to self-realization, both national and individual. In *Othello* this outlook produces the uncomplicated dignity of the title character: rather than a threatened and threatening outsider, ʿUṭayl becomes a fearless soldier serving his state, an articulate leader (though prone to jealousy), and thus a fitting spokesman for Arab cultural nationalism. He never collapses into incoherence. Rather, as Sameh Hanna points out, ʿUṭayl's Arabic remains "stylised, heroic and consistent, even at those moments when Othello, in Shakespeare's text, seems to lose control over his discourse."[84] So well did this "grandiloquent" translation suit the rhetorical goals of Arab nationalism that it was republished under the Arab League's imprimatur as part of its series of Shakespeare's Complete Works in the 1960s, and staged at the National Theatre in 1964.[85]

In *Hamlet,* Mutran's Romanticism takes a different turn. The protagonist's self-expression, again eloquent, is supposed to reveal his psychological depth. Mutran's two-paragraph introduction includes a nod to "Arab acting," but it three times uses the word *lubāb* (pith, kernel, core, essence) to denote the part of Shakespeare's play that he wants to "translate literally." This core consists of Shakespeare's "psychological insight," which causes the play's unique "psychological effect on the audience." Mutran gives no details about this psychology but seems to find it mainly in Hamlet's major speeches. He treats much else as superfluous, choosing to cut "some strange parts of the dialogue, which do not enter into the essence [*lubāb*] of the matter but are there by way of ornamentation . . . the entrances and exits of some characters, or various allusions that add only variety and are not tied to the essence of the lofty psychological meanings [*lubāb al-maʿānī al-nafsiyya al-sāmīya*] which are the greatest characteristic of this play."[86]

Except for the soliloquies, Mutran's cuts are ruthless. For instance, he cuts almost all the intervening action between the "rogue and peasant slave" and "to be or not to be" monologues (both in act 2, scene 1 of his translation), leaving only a brief bustling entrance by Polonius for a bridge. Hamlet's transition from the optimism of "The play is the truthful mirror with which I'll reveal the heart of the king" to the suicidal musing of "Am I, or am I not?" seems abrupt, because much of the surrounding action is told rather than seen.[87] Gone are the Players' entrance and the speech about Priam's death; Hamlet simply mentions that these happened.[88] The King and Queen's debriefing of Rosencrantz and

Guildenstern (opening of Shakespeare's act 3, scene 1) is drastically shortened and moved *before* Hamlet's "rogue and peasant slave" soliloquy (end of Shakespeare's act 2, scene 2).

Mutran's decorous translation also smoothes the violence of Hamlet's moods. There is no "fishmonger" scene in which Hamlet mocks Polonius; the Queen, the King, and Polonius simply exit when Hamlet enters reading, leading directly to the "rogue and peasant slave" speech.[89] The nunnery scene is shortened, Hamlet's cruelest insults to Ophelia edited out.[90] In the *Mousetrap* scene, likewise, there are no "country matters."[91] (When Hamlet attempts a witticism, Ophelia protests: "You are talking too much. Let me hear the play.")[92] The tradeoff for this bowdlerization is that the higher registers are heightened, making full use of the lofty rhetorical figures such as parallel structure and hendiadys[93] in which Arabic stylists delight.

As with *Othello,* Mutran's politics preclude not only vulgarity but irony. This guides how he handles the tragedy's ending. Unlike ʿAbdu, Mutran allows Fortinbras to appear in the final scene and inherit the kingdom. But he grants him few words, reassigning the play's closing lines to Horatio. The loyal courtier, not the brawny conqueror, cites "traits indicating that, had [Hamlet] assumed the crown, he would have been a great king."[94] Horatio then gives the orders for Hamlet's body to be carried off, the musicians to play, and the soldiers to shoot. In the mouth of Shakespeare's Fortinbras these words carry a bitter irony, punctuating the discrepancy between the two young would-be kings and heralding the fall of Hamlet's dynasty. Spoken by Mutran's Horatio, they simply reiterate the protagonist's nobility.[95]

Mutran's claim that he worked to adapt *Hamlet* to "Arab acting" is thus only partly true.[96] His focus on the protagonist's main speeches indeed suited the operatic tradition of Egyptian (and French) stage performance. However, most of his revisions run counter to what Egyptian theatregoers would have preferred, positioning his dignified and heroic translation *against* a culture of musicals and variety shows. To differentiate the French from the Arab elements of his agenda is difficult. In Mutran's mind there was likely no distinction: as a young man in 1890 fighting for Lebanon's liberation from the Ottomans, he had expressed his Arab nationalist commitment by climbing a Beirut hilltop with friends and singing "La Marseillaise."[97]

"Do It, England!"

Even as Mutran's play opened, Egypt was changing. World War I signaled the end of the Ottoman Empire (of which Egypt had been a part since 1517, though a self-ruling part under Muhammad Ali and his descendants after 1805). The British protectorate over Egypt, declared in 1914, formalized an occupation under way since 1882; the war turned Egypt into a reluctant garrison for British and Australian troops. Arab nationalists shifted their ire from the Sublime Porte to the British high commissioner. Britain and France vied for control of the Middle East, attempting to divide up their spheres of influence in the Sykes-Picot Agreement of 1916. An anti-British revolt convulsed Egypt in 1919; nominal independence under a constitutional monarchy in 1922 brought a de facto strengthening, not weakening, of British cultural influence through the 1930s and 40s. British educational institutions began to shape the curriculum of the élite, belatedly and partially eclipsing the French-inspired culture of the pre–World War I years.[98]

British Readings

British elements started to enter and rearrange the Arab Shakespeare kaleidoscope. The first change was the strengthened association between Shakespeare and the English language. In 1922, lawyer and political journalist Sami al-Juraydini (Sāmī al-Juraydīnī) published the first full *Hamlet* translation directly into Arabic from English; he revised and republished it in 1932.[99] Later scholars would accuse al-Juraydini of having poor English and simplifying Shakespeare's vocabulary.[100] As we will see, actors and theatre critics also complained that al-Juraydini's *Hamlet* was too dry and stilted when it was staged in 1964. But al-Juraydini was part of a trend in which fidelity (*amāna*) to the English original became the standard of a good translation.

In a related shift, Shakespeare's works came to be perceived primarily as literature, not stage material. As al-Juraydini wrote in the introduction to his first Shakespeare translation, *Julius Caesar* (1912):

> Only those know the difficulty of translating Shakespeare who have suffered it, and only those have suffered it who love to study Shakespeare seriously, not just to read him. For I do not believe that Shakespeare's plays are made to be acted for the brief pleasure of spectators or for superficial hearing; rather, they are for reading to study the lofty meanings and profound ideas [*al-maʿānī al-sāmīya wa-l-afkar al-ʿamīqa*] therein.[101]

Echoing Khalil Mutran's attention to Shakespeare's "profound" and "lofty" meanings, al-Juraydini took the next logical step, ignoring the stage and pledging allegiance to Shakespeare's written words. For the growing number of Anglophone Arab readers (though not theatregoers or directors), Mutran's euphonious adaptations suddenly seemed obsolete.

Shakespeare at School

British interpretations trickled down through the education system. One widely read distillation, Charles and Mary Lamb's 1807 *Tales from Shakespeare,* portrays Hamlet as a "virtuous prince" and tells the play largely from his point of view, repackaging many of the soliloquies as free indirect discourse.[102] Translated into Arabic by 1900, the Lambs' *Tales* were also studied in the original during English classes at Egyptian schools.[103]

The habit of memorizing Shakespeare's "great speeches" for classroom declamation contributed to many an Arab youth's dramatic awakening. Lebanese-born scholar Suheil Bushrui observed in 1964 that "every Arab school-boy has at one time or other during his school-days studied, at least, one of [Shakespeare's] sonnets or one or two speeches from his plays."[104] Shakespeare's plays—*Julius Caesar, Romeo and Juliet,* but above all *Hamlet*—were staged by dozens of universities, secondary schools, amateur groups, and benevolent societies.[105] Fatma Moussa Mahmoud writes that by midcentury in Egypt,

> Shakespeare was part of the regular curriculum of English in many schools, in the departments of English at the [Cairo] University and in the Institute of Drama. *Hamlet* was a familiar play for most educated Egyptians, and it was a favorite play in school and university theatricals.[106]

British interpretations of *Hamlet* (inspired in turn by German interpretations such as Goethe's and the Schlegel brothers') revised the Arab view of Shakespeare's prince. Building on the operatic and Neoclassical tradition of privileging Hamlet's "great speeches," they deepened the psychological engagement with the protagonist. Arias became soliloquies; for Romantic poets, including several of Mutran's students, profound thought and feeling now outweighed scintillating rhetorical figures. The Royal Shakespeare Company visited Cairo in 1927, occasioning an outpouring of essays on Shakespeare's creative genius and psychological insight; these took inspiration from William Hazlitt and A. W. Schlegel as well as Victor Hugo.[107] Even before its early 1960s publication in Arabic, A. C. Bradley's *Shakespearean Tragedy* (which takes Hamlet's delay as the tragedy's central problem) further sharpened Egyptian intellectuals' focus on Hamlet's psychology and inmost thoughts.[108]

The interwar years also brought several traveling British productions. Following the Royal Shakespeare Company's 1927 visit (with John Laurie as Hamlet[109]), Alec Guinness's *Hamlet* toured to Egypt in 1937[110] and John Gielgud's in 1940 and 1946.[111] Laurence Olivier's film *Hamlet* (1948) offered a different protagonist, "a man who could not make up his mind."[112] Yet Olivier's intensely introspective Hamlet, riven by Oedipal conflict, continued the prince-centric focus. Like the Egyptian and French shows, these were all "star" productions rather than ensemble acting pieces. For example, Gielgud has written that many of *Hamlet*'s minor characters have no motivation of their own but "are just meant to support Hamlet."[113] This approach found ready acceptance in a movie-saturated Egyptian culture accustomed, like Hollywood-schooled America, to venerating "leading men."[114]

A Multiple Inheritance

The British shows (and even Olivier's influential film) enriched an already vibrant *Hamlet* stage tradition. Besides Salama Higazi and George Abyad, several famous actors and actresses had played Hamlet between 1900 and 1930. Syrian-born theatre pioneer Sulayman al-Qaradahi (Sulaymān al-Qaradāhī; d. 1909) performed the role at a 1903 benefit for a Roman Catholic charity in Tanta, among other occasions.[115] Italian-trained theatre and film entrepreneur Youssef Wahbi (Yūsuf Wahbī; 1898–1982) played Hamlet in 1928.[116] Egyptian theatre lore also included two female Hamlets inspired by the famed French actress Sarah Bernhardt (1844–1923), whose production had visited Cairo's Abbas Theatre in 1908.[117] Fatima Rushdi (Fāṭima Rushdī; 1908–96, dubbed "the Sarah Bernhardt of the East") played Hamlet in a famed 1929–30 production directed by her husband Aziz Eid (ʿAzīz ʿĪd). Magazines eagerly followed Rushdi's rehearsals, one noting that she went daily to the Ezbekiya Gardens to practice fencing.[118] Like Bernhardt, Rushdi disdained existing translations; she commissioned a new *Hamlet* from poet Ahmed Rami (Aḥmad Rāmī).[119] Not to be outdone, the competing troupe led by actress Amina Rizk (Amīna Rizq; 1910–2003) cast Rizk as Hamlet in 1936.[120]

The idea of variations on *Hamlet* was familiar not only to those Egyptians who actually went to the theatre but also to the much larger public that read newspapers and magazines (including the leading daily *al-Ahrām*), where theatre criticism was thriving. Media reports and reviews provided a metadiscourse that, even during the period of British colonial rule, constructed Shakespeare as a *global* resource for which Egyptians were as eligible as anyone to compete. The 300th anniversary of Shakespeare's death in April 1916 was a highly publicized event: in a keynote speech published in *al-Ahram,* leading Egyptian nationalist thinker Ahmed Lutfi el-Sayed (Aḥmad Luṭfī al-Sayyid; 1872–1963) asserted that "the English poet does not limit his story to a specific people [*sha'b*] or to a particular instance of the human condition, but treats human beings, whatever their nation [*ayy kān mawṭanuhu*]."[121] The ceremony drew detailed newspaper coverage and prompted many reader letters, some criticizing el-Sayed for devoting so much attention to Shakespeare at the expense of Arab writers.

As early as 1929, readers recognized that each interpretation of Shakespeare was in competition with its predecessors. A critic in *al-Mustaqbal* magazine mocked Aziz Eid, who directed Fatima Rushdi in *Hamlet,* for failing to offer "a fresh interpretation of the play which the world theatre, French, or English, or German, has not yet seen." After the director's opening-night attempt to portray the Ghost as imaginary, "that experiment failed and let down the audience. Then he had to let the Ghost appear on the stage, this time without being different from French or English or German theatres, contradicting what he had claimed."[122]

Twice placing "English" in the middle of the list of theatre traditions rather than the beginning or the end, the reviewer (and presumably also the boasting director) shows a lack of anxiety about the colonial power. Originality matters, but the models to imitate and outdo are "French or English or German." British Shakespeare is available, not authoritative. In fact, what defined *Hamlet* for Egyptians was precisely their multiple inheritance: the *absence* of a single authoritative reading. As one 1928 reviewer (deriding Youssef Wahbi's performance as Hamlet) remarked, incidentally throwing "America" into the mix as yet another source of culture:

> There exists a somewhat ironic view that whoever plays Hamlet is bound to succeed. So long as critics in America and Europe have not come to agreement on the character of Hamlet, his identity, and the true nature of his moral makeup and psychology as intended and depicted by Shakespeare, every production of this famous role will find a sect [*ṭā'ifa*] of critics to applaud it and say, "This is Hamlet as Shakespeare intended him."[123]

We can now see what a peculiar historical parenthesis is reflected in the works by Youssef Chahine and Edward Said discussed above. Experiences both earlier and later (Rushdi's and Wahbi's in the 1920s, Soueif's in the 1960s) differ markedly from Said and Chahine's late-colonial Shakespeare encounters. Both autobiographers envision a binary world divided between Arab and western domains, the better to chronicle a gifted young man's passage from one domain to the other. But the world was not in fact binary, and it was about to grow wider still.

Independence and Soviet Shakespeare

Throughout the colonial period, Shakespeare had been an unselfconsciously enlisted ally in the fight against British rule. A portrait in the 1912 Arabic translation of *Julius Caesar* by Muhammad Hamdi (Muḥammad Ḥamdī) is captioned "William Shakespeare, the democratic English poet and playwright." The cover of Hamdi's third edition (1928) carries the explanatory gloss: "this play represents the eruption of nationalistic pride among the nations aspiring to democracy"—apparently because the translation and a new preface associated the figure of Caesar with the British high commissioner.[124] As we saw in chapter 2, other versions used the opposite reading of *Caesar* to the same effect: the high school production starring Gamal Abdel Nasser in 1935 portrayed Caesar as a hero, "vanquisher of the British."

Rather than decrease after Britain's withdrawal from Egypt, the Arab alliance with Shakespeare grew stronger in the 1950s and 60s. More than ever, the emphasis was on mastering and disseminating Shakespeare as a global cultural icon.

Appropriating the "Global Heritage"

In his short mass-market *Introduction to Shakespeare* (*Al-Taʿrīf bi-Shaksbīr*, 1958), the venerable critic Abbas Mahmud al-Aqqad (ʿAbbās Maḥmūd al-ʿAqqād, 1889–1964)[125] accessibly presents current scholarship on Shakespeare's life and times, the plays and poems, and even the authorship controversy. Al-Aqqad's closing chapter explicitly seeks to reclaim Shakespeare from British literature for the "global heritage" (*turāth ʿālamī*). Britain can no more claim credit for producing Shakespeare than Greece can for Homer, he declares: "If England never had two Shakespeares, and Greece never had two Homers, then these figures' relationship to their respective countries is no stronger than to humanity as such."[126] Al-Aqqad describes Herder, Goethe, Schlegel, and Lessing as "in competition" over Shakespeare with Coleridge, Carlyle, Hazlitt, and Arnold; he delves into the reception of Shakespeare by Pushkin, Tolstoy, and Turgenev; and he stresses the embrace of Shakespeare by French, German, and Russian writers, even while their countries were at war with Britain.[127]

Finally, responding to a 1932 book by an Indian scholar, al-ʿAqqad insists that there is no such thing as "Shakespeare through Eastern eyes."[128] A particular Hindu or Buddhist playgoer might respond to a tragedy differently than an Englishman, al-Aqqad argues—but not because some essential religious fatalism renders him unable to appreciate it.[129] The distance from an "Eastern" to a "British" reaction to *Romeo and Juliet* may be smaller than the shift in British reactions between the mid-eighteenth and mid-nineteenth centuries—a change of weather, not a move to a different planet.[130]

In a more nationalist burst of humanism, the Arab League's Cultural Directorate undertook a complete translation of all Shakespeare's plays between 1955 and 1965. The effort was spearheaded by al-Aqqad's friend, the Egyptian literary giant Taha Hussein (Ṭāhā Ḥusayn, 1889–1973). Leading intellectuals (not all of whom specialized in literature) were chosen as translators; some earlier translations were revised by committee. The "mighty project" (*al-mashrūʿ al-jalīl*), as Egyptian critic Ghali Shukri (Ghālī Shukrī) calls it, did little for *Hamlet, Othello, Macbeth, Julius Caesar,* and *Romeo and Juliet,* all of which were already well known and well translated. However, it introduced some lesser-known comedies and histories into Arabic for the first time.[131]

The Arab League project assigned *Hamlet* to Muhammad Awad Muhammad, a distinguished geographer and past president of Alexandria University (1953–54), who duly produced a competent prose translation. It was published in 1972, after revisions by literature professors Suhayr al-Qalamawi (Suhayr al-Qalamāwī, a member of the Arab League's Shakespeare translation committee) and Hassan Mahmud (Ḥassan Maḥmūd).[132] Awad Muhammad's introduction discusses the play's sources, diverging quarto texts, and previous Arabic versions (including the reminiscence of ʿAbdu's *Hamlet*). Curiously, he claims to know only the Egyptian translations, omitting the inspired and idiosyncratic version published by Jabra Ibrahim Jabra in Beirut in 1960.[133]

Awad Muhammad's footnotes, like Jabra's, explain many of the play's puns, anachronistic allusions (such as Claudius's "Switzers," or Swiss guards), and mythological references. An admirer of Goethe (he had translated *Faust* forty years earlier),[134] Awad Muhammad takes a Wilhelm Meister–type view of Hamlet, calling him "a protagonist still not finished with his university studies, tending to deep reflection, . . . gentle and courteous by nature, the furthest of people from violence and cruelty," thrust by an "irony of fate" into an obligation he cannot bear.[135] This contrasts with Jabra's characterization of Hamlet as a willing martyr, a kind of Christ figure. Both views (but Jabra's to a greater extent) would become part of the Arab *Hamlet* tradition.

Soviet Models

After 1955, Nasser's turn toward the Soviet Union and the Socialist bloc added new facets to the Shakespeare kaleidoscope. It was in the style of both the

Egyptian and Soviet regimes to find a high-cultural expression for their political rapprochement.[136] The Soviet emphasis on cultural diplomacy meant new cultural centers (in Cairo, Alexandria, Damascus, and Baghdad), traveling exhibitions,[137] translations, conference invitations, and scholarships to study in the Soviet Union and Eastern Europe.[138] Vernacular poet Abdel Rahman el-Abnudi (ʿAbd al-Raḥmān al-Abnūdī, b. 1938) recalls the sudden influx of Soviet (and pre-Soviet Russian) culture into Egypt:

> In 1956, a new literary realism began to take shape, a school of writing that devoted itself largely to the poor—the disinherited majority that had been more or less excluded from literature. Already the example of the Soviet Union—as revolution, state and system of thought—had exercised an influence on young writers, or, as they are called, intellectuals. Translations of Soviet books had begun to flood Egyptian bookshops, and the great Russian classics at last became available, to many of us for the first time. The great novelists and poets—Dostoievski, Shulokhov, Gorki, Pushkin, Mayakovski—were, as it were, knocking on our doors. . . . A great wave, you could say, was breaking over the old, established literature, breaking it apart.[139]

Among the Arab Shakespeare directors whose work will be mentioned below, several report being influenced by Socialist bloc models. Egyptian director-critic Kamal Eid (Kamāl ʿĪd) studied in Hungary; Iraqi playwright-director Jawad al-Assadi studied in Bulgaria and did an internship in Russia. Syrian playwright-director-critic Riad Ismat studied in England and Arizona but upon return worked closely with colleagues who had studied in Moscow, Sofia, Berlin, and Prague.[140] Even those with no direct travel experiences became aware of nondeclamatory, nonpsychological options for staging Shakespeare through journals such as the newly founded *al-Masraḥ*. (Readers' letters from as far abroad as Homs, Syria, attest to the magazine's international audience.) Among the most widely discussed experiments were Bertolt Brecht's "epic" Shakespeare rewritings (chiefly his 1950s *Coriolanus*) and Nikolai Okhlopkov's post-Stalin *Hamlet* (1954), a bitter loss-of-innocence story.

So by April 1964, as enthusiasts worldwide celebrated the 400th anniversary of Shakespeare's birth,[141] Egyptians and other Arabs could draw on a truly global set of models. However, although most of these competing ideas were available, there is evidence that the dominant Egyptian view of *Hamlet* had not yet metabolized them. For instance, issue number 4 of *al-Masraḥ* (the special quadricentennial Shakespeare issue of April 1964) includes a detailed article by Ramzi Mustafa (Ramzī Muṣṭafā) comparing the set design of *Hamlet* productions in czarist Russia, the Soviet Union, Switzerland, and the United States. Among others he cites Moscow productions directed by Gordon Craig (1911), Nikolai Akimov (1932), and Nikolai Okhlopkov, as well as American open-air Shakespeare.[142] Mustafa's readers in Egypt and the wider Arab world needed no special introduction to the idea that different contexts and directorial aims produce different performance styles.

Yet these performance-based interpretations had not affected mainstream textual criticism. In the same issue, for instance, an article on "Shakespeare's Tragic Heroes" by scholar and playwright Samir Sarhan (Samīr Sarḥān; 1941–2006) sticks to a single idea of Hamlet, the hesitant contemplator most familiar to British-educated readers: "Hamlet turns away from effective revenge for his father's death to a long contemplation of the idea of revenge, then the idea of life and death, and by this he places himself into a situation from which there is no exit, and his fate is sealed, like that of a traveler who lost his way in the desert."[143]

Even more telling, because less scholarly, is an interview with playwright Tawfiq al-Hakim in the same issue of *al-Masraḥ*. Al-Hakim, in a Shakespeare-themed chat with a *Masraḥ* writer, discusses the "opposite" characters of Hamlet and Othello in highly stereotyped, apolitical terms. Uninterrupted by the interviewer, he indulges in a lengthy thought experiment about geography as destiny: what if the valiant but naïve "Black Moroccan" Othello were the son of the murdered king, while the cold Nordic Hamlet were the husband of the accused Desdemona? The swap, he believes, would vitiate both tragedies. In the latter case, Desdemona would have time to exonerate herself while Hamlet delayed and investigated; in the former, the play would end with Othello's successful revenge in act 1! Al-Hakim describes the response of a hypothetical spectator watching *Othello*: "He almost shouts at him, 'You idiot, take the time to get to the bottom of it!' Meanwhile, the spectator of *Hamlet* would be exploding, 'Why all this thinking and contemplation? Go ahead! Avenge!'"[144]

It is notable that al-Hakim, whose own novels and plays are so preoccupied with justice and rule of law, gives neither *Hamlet* nor *Othello* any political spin. He sees no "perplexed sultan" here, no problem hinging on the relationship between political power, individual conscience, and the quest for certainty. Instead al-Hakim caricatures Hamlet in terms that would be familiar to a Victoria College schoolmaster: Nordic coldness, hesitation, excessive contemplation.

1964: Kozintsev's Political Turn

Amid the profusion of *Hamlets* available to Arab audiences and scholars by the mid-1960s, one made a lasting impression: Grigori Kozintsev's film *Gamlet.*[145] First screened at Cairo's Odeon movie theatre in 1964 (it is "the Russian *Hamlet*" mentioned by Ahdaf Soueif above), Kozintsev's film was also shown on television, with subtitles eventually pirated from the Jabra translation.[146]

We have seen Aboudoma's memory of watching Kozintsev's film "more than 10 times, like a deaf young man." Such claims of viewing the film ten times or more are not uncommon. Actor-director Mohamed Sobhi (Muḥammad Ṣubḥī, b. 1948), then a student at Cairo's newly founded Higher Institute of Dramatic Arts, recalls that Kozintsev's *Gamlet* had him running all over Cairo: "I saw it seventeen times. First at the Odeon, even though I was a student and had no money. Then I would go see it at the Soviet Cultural Center, the Italian Cultural Center. Then I would hear that it was playing at the Czech Cultural Center and run and see it there."[147]

Kozintsev's film became an integral part of the Egyptian intellectual landscape of the 1960s. A January 1965 meeting of Cairo's Theatre Club where it was discussed drew an astonishing 700 attendees.[148] A recent reminiscence by Egyptian literary critic Gaber Asfour (Jābir ʿAṣfūr, b. 1944) confirms its impact on the Egyptian intelligentsia of the day. Asfour's choice of pronouns shows that viewing *Gamlet* was not only a private revelation (as Aboudoma and Sobhi describe) but also a widely discussed communal experience:

> I cannot forget to mention the Russian film based on *Hamlet,* which joined exceptional direction with splendid music and riveting performances, especially the genius Russian actor who played Hamlet, as well as the actress who played Ophelia, who captured the delicacy and innocence and then the madness that led to her suicide. And I have not forgotten *how much I enjoyed* the rhythms of the poetic sentences pronounced by the actors in the Russian film—and no wonder, as the film depended on the poetic translation by Russian poet and novelist Boris Pasternak, author of the famous *Doctor Zhivago* and winner of the Nobel Prize, who translated several Shakespearean tragedies. Therefore *we appreciatively enjoyed* [*kunnā nastamtiʿ bi-tadhawwuq*] the poetic rhythm of the Russian language in the actors' mouths, despite *our* lack of comprehension of it.[149]

3.2. A discussion of *Hamlet* draws seven hundred attendees. From *Al-Masraḥ Magazine* (February 1965).

Unlike younger viewers, Asfour had been exposed to other *Hamlet* versions before he saw *Gamlet*. He refers to "several translations" (he was unable to recall which he read first) and mentions earlier and later films, including Laurence Olivier's 1948 version and Franco Zeffirelli's 1990 version starring Mel Gibson. Yet he vividly recalls, more than thirty years later, how he and his peers responded to the Pasternak translation and the Kozintsev film.

Kozintsev's *Gamlet* was produced in response to a uniquely Soviet set of factors. The Lenfilm studio undertook the project in honor of Shakespeare's quadricentennial. All the film's major contributors had suffered under Stalin. The need for a livelihood and an artistic outlet had driven Pasternak to become a Shakespeare translator. Director Kozintsev had been denounced as a "formalist" by the Soviet Communist Party's Central Committee in 1946, and his career had suffered. Composer Dmitri Shostakovich, whose haunting score was integral to the film's impact, had also been attacked for "formalism" in 1936 and 1948, but he had joined the Communist Party (perhaps under duress) in 1960. Innokenti Smoktunovsky, who played Hamlet, had been imprisoned in a labor camp in Norilsk, Siberia, after World War II.[150] Epitomizing Soviet society's loss of innocence after the bitter revelations of the Khrushchevian "thaw," the film became "a symbol for the decade" of the Soviet 1960s.[151]

The film's presence in Cairo was due to international politics, mainly the growing closeness between Nasser and the Soviet Union after 1956. But those

3.3. Innokenti Smoktunovsky in Grigori Kozintsev's *Gamlet* (1964). Courtesy of Lenfilm Studios.

international ties had a particular local resonance. Aboudoma (the playwright-director mentioned above) explores the historical moment in a 2006 short story titled "Gamlet Is Russian for Hamlet,"[152] a semi-autobiographical story about a young boy's very first exposure to Shakespeare set against the backdrop of Khrushchev's May 1964 visit to Cairo:

> It was the time of the socialist extension, the great nationalist dream, justice, the alliance of working people's forces, the fight against colonialism, the Egyptianization of culture, and the rockets pointed toward Israel. Half the country wanted their children to become army officers. . . . [There were] Russian officers and their families in the streets and the cafes and stores, the ironing-man wrote on his store sign in Russian, the gold-sellers wrote in Russian, and even the vegetable vendors would say good morning and good evening in Russian. To us in school they also taught the greetings, and gave us little Russian flags on the day that we went out into the street to welcome Khrushchev and Gamal Abdel Nasser; the

> open car came from the airport road, Abdel Nasser and Khrushchev were holding hands, and pictures of the High Dam filled the country.

From 1964, the story jumps to the aftermath of the June War in 1967. The young protagonist stumbles into the Russian Club in Heliopolis during what he believes will be a showing of *Stalingrad.* Instead he catches the end of Kozintsev's *Gamlet.* Fascinated, he returns the next night to see it in full. The politics of the moment condition how he reads the film and what he perceives as its central line:

> They turned out the lights and the show began; this time I saw the film from the beginning. It was about revenge for the father whom death had taken from the world. The mother was corrupt and the uncle was corrupt, and the minister was corrupt, and maybe the absent father was corrupt too, but his son was confused as a prophet, though one without a scripture. As I sat there . . . I read on the screen the most beautiful phrase, which stuck in my heart from then on: "Something is rotten in the state of Denmark."

As Aboudoma's reading suggests, the film's local impact owed more to Egyptian political and cultural history than to international politics as such. Some communist-leaning intellectuals saw the film soon after their release from literal prisons, where they had spent several years (together with Islamists) after a crackdown on political opposition in the late 1950s.[153] Others were prepared by the visual traditions of 1950s agitprop and 1960s political allegory described in chapter 2, which put all films and plays about power immediately in dialogue with the regime. This audience could not have missed the film's police-state iconography: iron bars, eavesdroppers, armed guards, ubiquitous portraits and statues of Claudius. It was prepared to note the concrete sociological reality (fawning courtiers, toiling peasants, war-torn villages) underlying the film's intricate webs of visual symbols and musical motifs.[154] All this combined with heartrending performances by Innokenti Smoktunovsky (Hamlet) and Anastasia Vertinskaya (Ophelia) to make the film an instant sensation in Egypt.

For perhaps the first time, Kozintsev gave the Cairo public a Hamlet not constituted by declamation. As we have seen, Arab readers and theatregoers by 1964 had access to a variety of Hamlets from French, British, German, and American backgrounds. But most of these diverse influences ultimately reinforced each other: they conspired with the local theatre environment to emphasize Hamlet's "great speeches" and to isolate the prince from the events and other characters of the play. The French versions favored Shakespeare's most "eloquent" verse passages, while the British productions that came to Cairo tended to be star vehicles, nearly one-man shows.

By contrast, Kozintsev's film focuses on the relationship between humanity and power. It minimizes Hamlet's fraught relationship with Gertrude and his questions about the Ghost.[155] It also arguably downplays Shakespeare's references to a religious or providential outlook.[156] Hesitation is barely an issue.[157] Noticeably for Egyptian audiences, several of the most self-searching soliloquies are omitted entirely; those that remain show not Hamlet's inner confusion but the conflict between him and his society.[158] The first soliloquy ("O that this too too sullied flesh would melt"[159]) is sharply cut (especially the talk of incest) and played in voice-over, with Hamlet walking silently through a crowded room as a steady stream of conformists rushes past in the opposite direction. Kozintsev has said the film aims to "emphasize man's essential dignity in a world representing his indignity."[160] Hamlet's all-consuming moral and political struggle to resist the prison of Denmark and the "Pharisean" Claudius dictatorship leaves little room for doubt.[161]

In the Soviet Union, the film, with its attractive humanist hero, was officially received as a denunciation of dictatorship (Stalinism) and potentially a call to reinvigorate the revolution (Leninism). For example, a review by leading Soviet Shakespeare scholar and critic Alexander Anikst

> pitied Ophelia as a symbol of all victims of absolute despotism, and praised Hamlet as a genuine freedom-loving "warrior," neither indecisive nor threatened by madness. In this reading of the film, Hamlet is courageous and strong, motivated by righteous anger at the prison Claudius has made of Denmark; his life-or-death struggle with Claudius acts as a crucible in which to forge and mature his intellect.[162]

This is not radically unlike Kozintsev's own view of *Hamlet*. The difference lies in the degree of optimism: where the semi-official critic sees the forging of a "mature intellect" that will presumably go on to confront and defeat the oppressor, the director sees a mind violently torn from its delusions, abandoned to its own resources, thrust headlong into the awareness that the whole world is rigged and justice is unattainable. Immediately after Stalin's death (1953), Kozintsev had seen *Hamlet* as a chance to show that "the force of poetry which refuses to make peace with the baseness and degradation of the era . . . will outlive the emblems of potentates and the thrones of tsars."[163] But a decade later, and after staging *King Lear,* his reading of Shakespeare's tragedies had taken a more existentialist line:

> In the lives of almost all Shakespeare's heroes there is a moment when each begins to realize that the sufferings which he himself is undergoing have been brought about not by some one malevolent person nor yet by a concurrence of circumstances but are a part of some great evil which threatens the majority of people, the causes of which are hidden in the depths of the social structure. From this moment onwards a new passion appears in the hero's life. All that has happened up till this moment, all the agonizing thoughts and flare-ups of emotion have been nothing but a prologue to the birth of this passion. The violated trustfulness of Othello, the shock Hamlet received on learning of his father's murder, and the despair of Lear on realizing how mistakenly he had judged his daughters—are all but the beginning, the first steps taken by these heroes on the road to their destiny.
>
> Now they are all possessed by one sole passion—one and the same, common to all, devouring them in its white heat. This is—the passion for cognition. The aspiration to discover the meaning behind what is happening. Man begins to think not only of himself, but of mankind. He sees before him not one villain but the evils of society. The sword is useless against this enemy. Claudius may die, but his death will not mend the disjointed time [*smert' ego ne vosstanovit sviazi vremën*], the death of one criminal will not put an end to social injustice. Injustice will not cease to be when it sees Iago subjected to terrible torments, nor will Desdemona come to life again, nor is it possible to resurrect the belief that such feelings as Romeo's love for Juliet, Othello's for Desdemona can exist and prosper in such a time.[164]

The sudden insight does not drive Kozintsev's Hamlet to inaction or suicide. Committed to his sense of his own humanity, he does what a decent man must. There is even something heroic in his grim resolve. But already as he acts he is aware that his actions, while *morally* right, are *politically* futile—they "will not mend the disjointed time."

As I suggested in the previous chapter, the Arab public in 1964 did not yet need to appropriate this insight. In that year it was difficult to imagine Nasser as a righteous Hamlet, but it was still unthinkable to cast him as a remorseless Claudius. It was even harder to imagine either of those roles for Nasser's weak Baʿthist military-ruler counterparts in Syria and Iraq, whom Nasser had just humiliated at unification talks in 1963.[165] Whatever the disappointments of his rule, Nasser was still "the only conceivable leader."[166]

It is possible that many Arab intellectuals simply could not have imagined the speed with which the June War of 1967 would eviscerate their political certainties. A trickle of discontent would begin even before that defeat—including such novels as *The Smell of It* (1966) by Sonallah Ibrahim (Ṣunʿ Allāh Ibrāhīm), *Chatter on the Nile* (1966) and *Miramar* (1967) by Naguib Mahfouz (Najīb Maḥfūẓ), and short stories by Syrian writers Zakaria Tamer (Zakariyā Tāmir) and Walid Ikhlasi (Walīd Ikhlāṣī)—but broader Arab publics (and censors) in 1964 would not have accepted a wholesale critique. The public conversation was more focused on Arab countries' dignity and stature than on their domestic policies. Dozens of top leftist intellectuals had been newly released from prison and were striving to work with the regime. Others, as Tawfiq al-Hakim claims, still served as "instruments of the broad propaganda apparatus with its drums, its horns, its odes, its songs and its films."[167] It would be a few years before they would refuse, like Hamlet, to be played upon like a pipe.[168] More than an immediate revelation, therefore, Kozintsev's *Gamlet* offered Arab audiences food for later thought. The seed of a political Hamlet had been planted; when needed, it would be harvested.

Bidayr's "Cruel Text"

Capping the 1964 celebrations of Shakespeare's quadricentennial, director al-Sayyid Bidayr received permission to stage *Hamlet* with the World Theatre Company at Cairo's Opera House Theatre.[169] Bidayr's production, which opened in December 1964 and played for much of 1965, is still "perhaps the best known Arabic professional stage production of *Hamlet.*"[170] As we have seen, however, Bidayr did not have the luxury of a tabula rasa. His *Hamlet* came into a world already populated with rival interpretations including studies and translations, British and Soviet films, and reports of stage productions worldwide. In this crowded company, Bidayr, whose prior stage and film reputation was mainly for comedy, had to defend not only his own standing but also that of the Egyptian theatre as a whole.[171] A look at the daunting expectations his production faced and the ways it navigated them will help underscore the situation in 1964–65 and set the stage for the remarkable few years that followed.[172]

Bidayr's undertaking was treated, first of all, as a purely technical feat. It followed on the heels of productions of *Othello, Macbeth,* and *The Merchant of Venice* by state theatres during the period 1962 to 1964.[173] After this preparation the Egyptian theatre was deemed ready to tackle *Hamlet,* considered Shakespeare's most grueling play. Karam Mutawi (Karam Muṭāwiʿ), an Italian-trained theatre director and rising film star, took on the challenge of playing Hamlet.[174] Other film actors were recruited: Zouzou Nabil (Zūzū Nabīl) as Gertrude and screen beauty Zizi al-Badrawi (Zīzī al-Badrāwī) as Ophelia.[175] Still, none of the critics fails to emphasize the difficulties of the task. The number of highly qualified actors was insufficient to cover any but the leading roles; experienced theatre technicians were also scarce.[176] Not all the actors were able to project their voices in a large theatre.[177] The sound system was erratic.[178] Against this background, the critics all laud the "daring" of Bidayr's undertaking. Even the harshest reviewer, Kamal Eid, closes his thirteen-page vivisection of the show with a salute to "the great effort that was put into directing this cruel text [*hādhā al-naṣṣ al-qāsī*], *Hamlet,* on the Egyptian stage."[179]

An unforeseen obstacle was Sami al-Juraydini's translation (1922, revised 1932), which now showed its age. Heavy on paraphrase, it introduced gratuitous Arabic clichés and failed to distinguish among different characters' registers of speech. Reviewer Mohamed Enani (Muḥammad al-ʿAnānī), who later retranslated *Hamlet* himself, says the al-Juraydini translation "could have ruined the show completely were it not for the actors' struggle (no other word will do) against the superficial, unpoetic language." Fatma Moussa Mahmoud, who would later translate *King Lear,* reports that the actors' complaints about the "stilted and dry" translation forced Bidayr to call in a modern poet to rewrite the soliloquies.[180]

Besides the technical challenges, Bidayr faced an ideological one. Olivier's film was well known, and Kozintsev's was still playing at the *Odeon* as Bidayr's play opened.[181] In a Cairo familiar with both the British and Soviet lines of *Hamlet* interpretation and in an Egypt carefully balanced on the Cold War fence, on which side would Bidayr's production come down? Critics were not shy about framing this dilemma as almost a foreign policy decision. Some praised Bidayr's neutral solution, which refused to endorse either reading fully. But several others lamented Bidayr's failure to put forward a viable *third* reading to compete with the Soviet and British versions. At stake was not only Bidayr's originality as a director but also the potentially world-class status of "our Egyptian stage" or even "our Arab theatre."[182] Why, they implied, had Bidayr failed to propose an innovation in theatre as ingenious as Nasser and Nehru's Non-Aligned Movement in politics? Marxist literary critic Mahmud Amin al-Alim (Maḥmūd Amīn al-ʿĀlim),[183] who had emerged after his release from the Kharga prison camp the previous year to edit the state-run literary-political journal *al-Muṣawwar,* tried to qualify his disappointment:

> The Egyptian director avoided both the completely emotional stamp that overshadowed the English interpretation, as well as the active determined stamp that overshadowed the Soviet interpretation. Therefore the Egyptian *Hamlet* was more objective than the English *Hamlet* and more emotional than the Soviet *Hamlet.* Does this mean that the Egyptian director added a new interpretation of *Hamlet* besides the two interpretations offered by the Soviet and English films? In fact, no. He did not add a new interpretation. However, he brought a special flavor to some of the play's topics.[184]

Bidayr's "special flavor" relied heavily on darkness, shadows, and colored gel lights. Critics were particularly struck by the use of a red light that suggested both dawn and blood. At times the lights would illuminate Hamlet's back, leaving his face in shadow.[185] The Ghost never appeared on stage but was played as a figment of Hamlet's imagination, its presence signified by a spot of light and its voice piped through a loudspeaker. Bidayr also—in a consciously or unconsciously cinematic touch—used loudspeakers to play back Hamlet's soliloquies, creating a voice-over effect.[186] The décor and costumes mixed realistic and symbolic elements;[187] in one photo from *al-Masraḥ* magazine, the weeping Hamlet throws himself into the embrace of a golden-robed Gertrude, who reclines on a gilt rococo chaise longue, as Polonius's starched white cuffs and collar glint almost comically in the background.[188]

Whatever Bidayr's reading of the play, he does *not* seem to have staged it as a political parable. Rather than impose an overarching interpretation at all, he seems to have relied on Karam Mutawi's acting to create a multifaceted and sympathetic Hamlet, animated by both grief and playfulness, whose character would carry the production. The audience was held in thrall by Mutawi's lively antics and charisma, but many critics expecting a "concept" play were disappointed. Those who had anticipated a willowy, neurotic protagonist like Olivier's felt jarred.[189] The few who wanted a strong revolutionary hero found that the politics had been played down. For instance, Amr Afifi (ʿAmr ʿAfifi) played Polonius as a funny and good-natured buffoon rather than a sinister court official.[190]

In a rather pedantic "study and review" that invokes many prevailing British and Soviet-bloc readings of *Hamlet,* fellow director Kamal Eid chastises Bidayr for failing to understand that the director's role has "changed, or rather developed" in the twentieth century. It is no longer enough, Eid says, to put on a tasteful performance of a classic play, as Bidayr did. Instead, confronting one of "the classics" (*al-klāsīkiyyāt*) requires studying the text and its most influential critics and stage and film versions. Then one must develop one's own distinctive overarching interpretation (*tafsīr*), which should show "the director's hand" clearly.[191] Eid, who had recently returned from studying in Hungary, was particularly impressed by new Eastern European Hamlets that accord with "the theories of Sartre and Camus":

> Thanks to this concept, a society has swapped the old view that rebuked Hamlet for his continuous hesitation in favor of modern theories. So Hamlet has been directed in the theatre of the socialist countries as a noble fighter striving for salvation from a tyrannical monarchy oppressive of his rights. Hamlet continues fighting and fighting and facing humiliations without letting them stop his fight or slow him down until he wins in the end—even if his victory comes at the moment when he is surrendering his spirit to his Lord. Yet the fact of this victory is big, a victory for humankind rather than a surrender to the course of things.[192]

Although he notes cryptically that "the Arabic text has not neglected this point,"[193] Eid finds no clear message in the show at the Opera House. Instead he sees a tangle of technical details and stage business, unconnected by any coherent reading of the play.

Mahmud Amin al-Alim seems to take just the opposite angle, judging Mutawi's Hamlet as too active rather than too weak. Yet, like Kamal Eid, he finds Bidayr's production a mere spectacle, missing the politics that comprise the play's "essential meaning":

> [Muṭāwiʿ bore] the stamp of sadness, mixed with pride and self-love. The Egyptian Hamlet was active, overflowing with liveliness and heat, his movements graceful and his speech flowing in a brilliant rhythm. He barely expressed any madness, real or feigned. Therefore one could have difficulty defining precisely the features of his character. . . . He lacked a sense of internal contradiction or struggle, of being torn and in crisis between thought and reality. He walked and spoke with a resolution that all but drowned out any hesitation and

> confusion in his lines. Therefore his strongest moments were at times when he played vigorous, positive roles, such as the closet scene, his advice to the Players, and the final fencing match. Often he seemed to me like a character acting on the stage, and this [theatrical] aspect is also part of Hamlet, as we have seen. But does this performance advance an interpretation of Hamlet? At least, it does not put forth the essential meaning [*al-maʿnā al-jawharī*] that I see in Hamlet. Not to detract from Karam Muṭāwiʿ's acting competence or the directing effort of al-Sayyid Bidayr . . . yet I look for the meaning, and do not find it.[194]

Al-Alim's disappointment reflects Bidayr's lack of a political message. His notion of the play's "essential meaning" hinges, like the Soviet and Eastern European readings, on the problem of justice. He is critical of Kozintsev's portrayal of Hamlet but shares the Soviet director's basic reading that justice is the "essence" of the play.[195] For al-Alim, *Hamlet* should provide a political lesson for audiences, showing the tragedy of a nonmilitant intellectual

> suffering from a split between his thought and his will, between his contemplation and his practical positions. Shakespeare's play is a call through events and situations, not through sermons and ringing speeches, to doing, to positive action, to breaking out of the contemplation of the closed-in Middle Ages, to the practical responsibilities of the Renaissance, a call to tie the intellectual to the issues of his age, a call to commitment—not only intellectual, but also militant, a call to the active position toward the evils and oppressions and wrongs and corruption; a call to link thought to practical action.[196]

Like Kamal Eid's critique, this one marks a new impatience, born of a new set of theatrical horizons and standards. Al-Alim's drumbeat about the play's "essence"[197] (*jawhar*) echoes Eid's reverence for "the classics" (*al-klāsīkiyyāt*): both barely mask a call for more purposive, topical stagings. Both critics long for a forceful director who can use Shakespeare's sacred texts to frame the pressing concerns of contemporary Arab society. For Eid, such strong direction is an artistic necessity; for al-Alim, a political one. Both are, in a sense, ahead of their time. Eight to ten years later, they would not have to protest so much, for the type of productions they envisioned would be the Arab norm.

But if Bidayr had no interest in using *Hamlet* as an allegory for Arab politics, this is not to say that his production lacked a political agenda. As we have seen, Bidayr's play was widely taken as emblematic of the Egyptian theatre, itself a synecdoche for the maturity and sophistication of Arab culture. Thus Bidayr's allegory occurred at the level of the production as a whole rather than the content of the play. Part of the point, therefore, was the depth and complexity of Karam Mutawi's portrayal of Hamlet. This complexity had political ramifications in the Egyptian 1960s: a "deep" interiorized subjectivity was seen as the qualification for full moral standing and hence for political agency. The ability to put a fleshed-out, persuasive dramatic character on stage was a political achievement in its own right.

The same priorities help drive the two landmark Arabic plays we will examine in the next chapter, Alfred Farag's *Sulayman of Aleppo* and Salah Abdel Sabur's *The Tragedy of al-Hallaj*. Written in 1964, the same year as Bidayr's production, both plays address the problem of how a thinking (and believing) man should handle earthly injustice. Their homegrown heroes are precisely the "noble fighter striving for salvation from a tyrannical monarchy" that Kamal Eid had so admired in Eastern European Hamlets. Yet they also incorporate recognizable echoes of the familiar British-influenced Hamlet-who-thinks-too-much—his speaking style, his philosophical concerns, and above all his psychological interiority. These plays mark the beginning of Hamlet's incorporation into politically themed Arab drama.

As we will see, this incorporation was hardly caused by any conscious agenda of postcolonial appropriation. Rather, I argue, the underlying motive was less an "Arabization of *Hamlet*"[198] than a "Hamletization" of the Arab Muslim political hero. Such Hamletization was an easy way for Arab playwrights to emulate (and cite) Hamlet's complexity of characterization and to obtain the moral standing and cultural capital it conferred. The critical demand for deep, complex, yet politically topical characters encouraged serious dramatists to weave strands of Hamlet into their heroes—in turn forging a link in the audience's imagination between the character of Hamlet and the theme of earthly justice.

4

HAMLETIZING THE ARAB MUSLIM HERO, 1964–67

We have seen how *Hamlet* became near-ubiquitous among Egyptian intellectuals in the mid-1960s. Surrounded by a kaleidoscope of translations, films, stage productions, public discussions, and Arab and foreign literary criticism, young writers began to deploy these versions of Shakespeare in their own work. Although borrowings from Shakespeare and particularly *Hamlet* had long been part of Arab literary life, these now became more pronounced and purposeful. Writing in 1964, Suheil Bushrui points to several recent Arabic poems that draw on *Hamlet*: "Shakespeare is gradually becoming an important force in shaping the intellectual and artistic life of some of the most talented Arabic poets."[1] However, although Hamlet was everywhere, he was not yet part of the conversation about domestic politics. The Soviet and other models had been absorbed, but they were not immediately applied. When Hamlet first approached Arab political drama, it was by another door.

As the Egyptian theatre entered what is usually considered its "golden age," playwrights sought to dramatize models of authentic Arab political action. Authentic political action, in turn, required characters whose capacity for introspection qualified them as fully fledged moral and political subjects. The need for these convincing protagonists, I will argue, is what first led playwrights to borrow from Shakespeare's hitherto-untouchable "classics." *Hamlet,* in particular, became central to the construction of dramatic heroism.

This chapter will consider two landmark Egyptian plays produced between

Table 4.1
Hamletizing the Arab Muslim Protagonist, 1964–67

Play	Author	First director	Year	Where produced
Sulayman of Aleppo	Alfrīd Faraj	ʿAbd al-Raḥīm al-Zarqānī	Produced November 1965; revived in 2004	National Theatre, Cairo
The Tragedy of Al-Hallaj	Ṣalāḥ ʿAbd al-Ṣabūr	Samīr al-ʿAṣfūrī	Published 1964; staged 1966–67; revived in 1984 and 2002	Opera House, Cairo (Modern Theatre), previously in Alexandria

1964 and 1967: Alfred Farag's *Sulayman of Aleppo* (*Sulaymān al-Ḥalabī*) and Salah Abdel Sabur's *Tragedy of al-Hallaj* (*Maʾsāt al-Ḥallāj*) (see table 4.1). Hailed as major literary events, these two tragedies both won the Ministry of Culture's State Incentive Award for 1965.[2] Although set in Arab Muslim contexts and drawn in part from classical Arabic sources, both featured heroes in whom critics recognized "strands of Hamlet."[3] This borrowing was neither subversive in spirit nor driven by any desire to seize mastery of a colonizer's text. Neither writer had a project to "Arabize *Hamlet*";[4] as we will see, Abdel Sabur explicitly rejected such an aim. What happened, rather, was a Hamletization of the Arab Muslim political hero.[5] The two playwrights used elements of *Hamlet* mainly to lend psychological depth to their own protagonists. They did so, I will argue, not to send any message about Shakespeare but to turn their heroes into credible political agents.

In thus appropriating elements of *Hamlet*, Farag and Abdel Sabur continued to balance the twin 1960s imperatives of "world-class" aesthetic standards and political relevance that we saw in chapter 2. On one hand, each sought to offer an Arab Muslim model of political heroism. On the other hand, each sought to advance Arab drama by creating a character as complex and self-aware as the best exemplars of Greek and European tragedy. In this regard, Shakespeare's Hamlet was still the gold standard. Moreover, these topical and aesthetic aspirations could converge. Because his psychological depth and self-awareness qualified him to bid for recognition as a moral subject and political agent, a protagonist modeled on Hamlet promised a political payoff as well.

In a way, therefore, we can consider these two tragedies to be the first political appropriations of *Hamlet* in Arab theatre. They did not succeed perfectly, to be sure; reviewers of both plays perceived an awkward fit between the protagonists' heroic resistance to tyranny and their Hamlet-like doubts. Critics tended to resolve it by reabsorbing both plays into the tradition of regime-directed allegorical drama that dominated Egyptian theatre at that time. Farag's *Sulayman of Aleppo,* a celebration of (violent) resistance against oppressive colonial rule, was interpreted as addressing Nasser's homegrown tyranny. Although it was less transparently allegorical, Abdel Sabur's *Tragedy of Al-Hallaj* nonetheless struck some critics as an appeal to Nasser's regime to give its intellectuals greater freedom of speech. Both protagonists were read as fighters for justice, brave opponents of a tyrannical regime. Thus two Muslim heroes, a seminarian and a Sufi, present intriguing early versions of the Arab Hero Hamlet.

In Search of Social Justice

Alfred Farag (1929–2005) and Salah Abdel Sabur (1931–81) both typified and dominated the generation that came to prominence in the 1960s.[6] The two Egyptian writers were colleagues: they worked together as editors on the Ministry of Culture's *al-Masraḥ* magazine in the late 1960s and wrote warm reviews of each other's work. They shared many interests: ancient Greek tragedy and philosophy, English literature (Shakespeare, George Bernard Shaw, T. S. Eliot), and the development of a modern Arabic idiom that could express the deepest truths of human experience with elegance but without fussy nineteenth-century Neoclassicism.

Like many Arab writers of this generation, they also shared a commitment to social justice defined in broadly socialist terms; their works take care to include "ordinary" characters, highlighting the living conditions, aspirations, and relationships with power of these peasants or struggling urbanites. Farag experimented with "documentary" drama; Abdel Sabur's poetry of the 1950s is known for its *dunyawiyya* (earthiness, worldliness), meaning its incorporation of common people and places "of this world."

The two writers' work set new standards for Arabic drama and poetry, respectively. Farag's plays often drew on stories from *One Thousand and One Nights,* historical sources, or current events. A disciple of master dramatist Tawfiq al-Hakim, he sought to bring serious political and philosophical issues to the stage.[7] Particularly fruitful was Farag's engagement with the problem of earthly justice, a theme that recurs in many of his plays.[8] This and other social concerns led him to a playful, provocative theatrical style heavily indebted to Bertolt Brecht's "epic theatre."[9] Salah Abdel Sabur, meanwhile, came to theatre as one of the leading poets of his day and the pioneer of a newly flexible, limpid poetic style. As we will see, he understood the process of writing poetry as a spiritual illumination akin to the mystical experience of Sufism. Drawn by the artistic possibilities of verse drama and perhaps by baser incentives that favored writing for the stage,[10] he dramatized characters who, like him, sought to balance political/worldly engagement with higher artistic/spiritual truth.

The plays these two men published in 1964 illustrate both how they differed and what they shared. Farag's *Sulayman of Aleppo,* characterized by clean prose, a timely topic, and psychologistic style, was staged immediately at Egypt's National Theatre; Abdel Sabur's *Tragedy of al-Hallaj,* a highly stylized verse drama with a more ambiguous message, sat on the shelf for two years before finding a director.[11] Yet a distance of nearly half a century reveals some similarities of approach, characterization, and theme. In each of these plays, a Hamlet-influenced protagonist chooses between political action and inaction. Both Sulayman and al-Hallaj confront the question "What should I do about earthly injustice?" Although they reach different answers, both become martyrs as those answers lead them into inexorable confrontation with an unjust regime. Yet in each case the martyr wins in the end, his winged words outliving the inarticulate oppressor.

Although neither Farag nor Abdel Sabur was a devout Muslim, their plays couch political agency in Islamic terms. Farag was of Coptic Christian origin; Abdel Sabur seems to have espoused an eclectic, quasi-Sufi mysticism influenced by European Romanticism and existentialism. Their protagonists' visions of Islam are fiercely idiosyncratic and political, coming into tension with orthodox religious centers where the worship of God is kept separate from the pursuit of social justice. Further, both Sulayman and al-Hallaj are self-aware, holding the kind of faith commitment deliberately embraced by a fully self-conscious rational agent. This is important to the dramatic goal of making them plausibly complex characters, capable of independent thought and thus political decisionmaking.

Critics were quick to associate *Sulayman of Aleppo* with Shakespeare's *Hamlet. The Tragedy of al-Hallaj,* more eclectic in its influences, has also been linked to *Hamlet* (as well as other models). Both plays include some *Hamlet*-like phrases and situations. The two protagonists echo Hamlet's verbal style: heavy on riddles, soliloquies, and quick juxtapositions of opposites. Above all, they mirror Hamlet's aloneness, his inwardness, and the acuity with which he understands his moral situation. For Egyptian critics and audiences accustomed to venerating Shakespeare's play and its psychologically deep hero, such resonances helped establish the moral (not just psychological) fullness of the Arab protagonists. Both Sulayman and al-Hallaj, like Hamlet, acquired a stature out of proportion to their objective circumstances.

Psychological Interiority as a Ground for Political Agency

The link I am drawing between psychological interiority and political freedom can be theorized in various ways. From an existentialist point of view, which at times Abdel Sabur shared, the ability to become an authentic individual entails a certain depth of thought: one must grasp both the surrounding world's meaninglessness and one's own ultimate freedom and responsibility to will one's choices in it. This account of meaningful life hinges on a deeper assumption about the value of human rationality. As Charles Taylor has shown, the modern West has built its "ethics of authenticity" on a notion of individual psychological "inwardness."[12] It is taken for granted that self-consciousness (Harold Bloom calls it self-overhearing) is what "creates the human."[13] Self-consciousness also allows for self-control, which in turn creates the political agency that gives a title to self-rule. It is no surprise that postcolonial intellectuals, working to earn their society admission to the modern West, would imagine such self-conscious selves and seek to present them on stage.

In both *Sulayman of Aleppo* and *The Tragedy of al-Hallaj,* the protagonist's psychological inwardness (with the moral stature it confers) is integral to the author's political message. As we will see, Farag set out to reclaim the dignity and political agency of a protagonist who had been radically objectified by the colonial apparatus of law courts and museum exhibits. Abdel Sabur, making a bid for political agency on another level, sought to define a central role for the poet in a sullied world: poetic insight, he argued, can purify or redeem worldly politics. Both writers sought to forge characters whose very inwardness—their ability to hesitate, to deliberate about justice and injustice, to soliloquize about action and inaction, and to overhear themselves thinking—made them credible moral subjects with the standing to contest their political fate.

However, this inwardness could not just be described, as in a novel. It also needed to be shown to the audience somehow. *Hamlet* provided a readymade and widely recognized set of conventions and techniques. Both authors turned to it for the elements of dramatic characterization they needed.

Sulayman: "Justice or Oppression? That Is the Puzzle"

Alfred Farag's play *Sulaymān al-Ḥalabī* (*Sulayman of Aleppo*) celebrates the young man who "offered, in the blink of an eye, a fitting response to European colonialism's first challenge to the East in modern times."[14] The historical Sulayman was a 24-year-old Syrian man, a former student at the al-Azhar Islamic seminary in Cairo, who stabbed to death General Jean-Baptiste Kléber, the leader of Napoleon's army in Egypt, in June 1800. Structured as a sequence of forty-five vignettes, Farag's play shows the young seminarian gradually reaching his decision to kill Kléber over a period of about a month, as Cairo seethes under a cruel and stifling French occupation. The style is nonlinear and classical, not realistic. Character is revealed through neatly orchestrated set-piece dialogue rather than action. The most audacious formal element is a Chorus: part Brechtian narrator addressing the audience, part tragic chorus interrogating the characters (as in Sophocles' *Antigone*).

Farag's ambitious architecture serves two sometimes-competing goals. The first is didactic: to expose the effects of colonial occupation on Egyptian student militants, religious scholars at al-Azhar, helpless civilians, opportunistic bandits, and the occupiers themselves. Thus the reader is treated to the Chorus's introductory narration of the brutally suppressed Cairo rebellion against the French (March–April 1800), followed by passionate arguments among demoralized student leaders, French military brass, al-Azhar clergymen, the highway robber Hiddaya the Lame and his victims, and so on. In its eagerness to show the problem from many sides, the play is crowded with minor characters and scene changes; the published script carries an Author's Note suggesting scenes to omit.[15]

The second goal is psychological: Farag takes an intense interest in the character of his young Syrian protagonist. Introduced as a "nervous, bright, articulate" 20-year-old who "appears younger than his real age,"[16] Sulayman gradually matures or reveals himself through dialogues with his mother and his childhood friend, a dream sequence about judging Kléber, some awkward Robin Hood–like attempts to save Hiddaya's unnamed daughter, arguments with colleagues and shaykhs at al-Azhar, a surreal exchange with a mask-maker, and a monologue about justice. After all this and a climactic debate with the Chorus, he finally kills Kléber. (In an interview shortly before his death in 2005, Farag told Dina Amin that his portrayal of Sulayman was an effort to study the character of a freedom fighter that was inspired by an "arrogant and selfless" college friend who had died as part of a patriotic movement to liberate the Suez region in 1951.)[17]

"The Head of the Killer"

Both the political and psychological agendas require Farag to transform his classical source. The outlines of Sulayman's case come from a sprawling history of Egypt, *ʿAjā'ib al-Āthār fī al-Tarājim wa-l-Akhbār*, by Abd al-Rahman al-Jabarti (ʿAbd al-Raḥmān al-Jabartī, 1753–1825), a leading Egyptian Muslim scholar who served in the administration of Kléber's successor. Al-Jabarti, relying mainly on French sources, uses Sulayman's case to illustrate the French adherence to the rule of law.[18] Farag inverts the perspective. He sets out to recover Sulayman's own story, which he feels the occupier has silenced. He wants to probe the motivations and doubts leading up to the attack. He explains in his introduction that seeing Sulayman's embalmed head in a Paris museum display case, labeled only "The head of the killer: Sulayman of Aleppo," has stirred his sympathetic curiosity:

> So who was this obscure, bold youth? What blood ran in his veins, and what feverish or reasonable thoughts followed him the length of the road from Giza to Ezbekiyya that memorable day? . . . What motives filled his heart when the handle of the fateful knife filled his hand?[19]

Al-Jabarti is silent about Sulayman's motives, describing the murder only as "an amazing event" (*nādira ʿajība*); his account of the interrogation and trial reproduces a long propaganda pamphlet circulated by the French. Farag steps into this void with a powerful reinterpretation. He strives to reclaim Sulayman's political agency by turning him from an object—a head in a display case—back into a subject. His play thus reimagines the Syrian killer as the hero of an Arab nationalist struggle against imperialism: "Egyptian in sympathy, Azhari in culture, and Arab in origin."[20] Farag disregards Sulayman's confession, obtained under torture, that Napoleon's Ottoman rivals had paid him to kill Kléber.[21] He ends the play before Sulayman's trial, the most overtly "dramatic" scene in al-Jabarti's account. Instead Kléber becomes the defendant, Sulayman the judge, and the audience almost an extension of Sulayman. In the play's closing words, the Chorus breaks the theatrical fourth wall to urge the audience: "O judges of this court, do not judge by law! Judge by justice!"[22]

The evidence against Kléber is overwhelming. He is an unmitigated villain, almost a caricature. At his first entrance, he boasts that only systematic humiliation can subdue the Egyptians: the way to disarm an enemy is to destroy his pride. Kléber's stated policy is to reduce the colonized Egyptian to abjection through crippling fines that make him sell his house, prostitute his wife, abandon his religious leaders, and still remain in debt. Later, Kléber is furious when a student named ʿAlī, arrested for posting anti-French pamphlets, accidentally dies under torture—but only because he could have lived to incriminate more comrades.[23] These scenes ignore the historical General Kléber's desire to withdraw from Egypt quickly and safely,[24] instead portraying him as a brutal aspirant to be "the man after the battle, i.e., the strong ruler of the colony."[25]

Against Kléber's policy of cruelty, nothing but assassination could work. A citywide insurgency has been brutally suppressed just before the play begins, bringing mass slaughter and punitive fines. Nonviolent resistance such as pamphleteering is shown to fail—it carries the same cost as militancy but accomplishes nothing. "Partial justice" (submission to the occupier's justice) is shown as useless too, even for securing law and order: when the gangster Hiddaya is turned over to French authorities for prosecution, they instead hire him as a tax collector. ("Long live justice!" the thief shouts on learning the news.)[26] Through Sulayman's eyes we see that Egypt has sold its integrity for a momentary respite—and received nothing in return.

In this sullied world, Sulayman bristles with the certainty of a revolutionary hero. "Partial justice is worse than injustice," he proclaims.[27] Farag portrays him as naïve, socially inconsiderate, sexually puritan, and self-righteous—but correct. Sulayman resolves to kill Kléber. Unlike his al-Azhar colleagues (who call him "mad"), he is willing to accept the violent reprisals likely to rain down on his comrades, his teachers, and Cairo's innocent civilians, including children.[28] His ethics are absolute and deontological (indifferent to consequences). He distinguishes impartial justice from mere revenge, seeing himself as an embodiment of the former:

> Chorus: Why did you come this long way from Aleppo to kill an occupier here when you had Turks there who are just as greedy and oppressive?
> Sulayman: The Turks oppressed my father. . . .
> Chorus: [So then w]hy would you kill the French military commander instead of the Pasha of Aleppo?
> Sulayman: I cannot kill out of revenge.
> Chorus: And killing a military commander? What do you call that?
> Sulayman: Justice.
> Chorus: Do you know what you're saying and what you're doing?
> Sulayman: Yes. I am killing in a pure and just way, without vengefulness.
> Chorus: Oh God! This is madness!
> Sulayman: But it's a cool and rational killing.
> Chorus: But that's how a murderer would put it.
> Sulayman: They're the murderers. I am the judge.
> Chorus: Do you have a sense of the paradox in your words?
> Sulayman: Yes: Life itself is the paradox. The judge wears

> the clothes of the murderer and the murderer wears the clothes of the judge, and both of them are Sulaymān al-Ḥalabī.[29]

Rather than show a decision process, Sulayman's long debate with the Chorus underlines his moral certainty. Couched in the balanced phrases of a scholar (or a fanatic), his conviction is quiet and firm.[30] The device of the Chorus lets the play, not the character, simultaneously entertain conflicting moral arguments.

However, the play's didactic setup competes with its artistic and political need for a suitably deep protagonist. Sulayman cannot be a mere fanatic; he must be as psychologically complex as any western man. Seeking to rehabilitate Sulayman's psychological interiority as a ground for his political agency, Farag weaves in "several strands of Hamlet."[31] Here Sulayman's certainty wavers. He indulges in monologues and dialogues that delay the plot, including some Hamlet-like mood swings, meditations on the world's corruption, and episodes of clowning. These moments are unmistakable echoes—even citations—of *Hamlet*.

Above all, Sulayman's resolve must flow from genuine self-conscious deliberation, not blind belief. He must reason. Farag employs the soliloquy, a form he has studied carefully, to show Sulayman's mind at work.[32] No blind believer, the assassin will not lift his dagger until he is convinced that the necessity of killing Kléber outweighs the terrible consequences. Looking down from a high hill, he addresses his adopted city:

> Oh Cairo! Oh most great and most wretched! My homeland, the cradle of my thoughts and my hopes and the beating heart of the Arabs. I hate you now, Cairo. You make me sick. I don't care what happens to you anymore . . . It is despicable to sell your honor for your life, instead of trading your life for your honor. Mercy! [*Pause*] And even so, I'm not certain. Where is certainty? Maybe I pronounce the words with my tongue but it is Satan who speaks in my mouth?[33]

Later, sitting in front of Kléber's palace, Sulayman interrogates his conscience again in a speech that critics have unanimously flagged as an echo of Hamlet's "to be or not to be" soliloquy:

> To kill . . . that is the simple part. One blow in mid-chest with the right hand while the left holds his neck. And if the first blow misses, those that follow it will not. [But then,] justice or oppression? That is the puzzle. . . .

> Will the lightning bolts pour down on the minaret of Al-Azhar, and innocent blood run in the canals that were first dug to give water to the thirsty? Will the believers' hearts be frightened to bursting, and will the covers be viciously torn away behind which the women, children, old people, and men gather their breath, which was cut off behind the door-latches, and dry their tears? Yes, one stab in the dike, and all that flows out of it will be a little weak stream to fill a cup from, but then, "the earth will quake with its quaking."[34] And the deluge! And the lightning bolts will pour down!
>
> But—whom will the waters engulf? The murderer or the victim? Will the spirit of the soldiers break down like the houses of the people? Which spirit will collapse under its burden?
>
> Justice, or the price of justice?
>
> And yet I know that the judge judges without regard for his pay. And lays down justice without heed for the consequences. His function is limited. That is proper justice within proper limits.[35]

Sulayman's Qur'ān-quoting dialectics pit justice against its unfair consequences: although certain that killing Kléber is just, he hesitates to expose Cairo's innocent population to the apocalyptic savagery that will follow. This is not Hamlet's dilemma: Shakespeare's Hamlet does not deliberate about the effects of his actions on the innocent.[36] But the dialectical style of thought, modeled on Hamlet's, confers the impression that Sulayman has Hamlet-like interiority. And the basic moral stance—reluctant heroism—was quickly recognized as Hamlet's. As fellow playwright Salah Abdel Sabur observes: "Sulaymān al-Ḥalabī . . . looks at the killing of Kléber as the realization of justice, the establishment of legality, and fixing the balance of the out-of-joint world [*iqrār li-mīzān al-kawn al-muḍṭarib*]."[37]

"The Authentic Arab Copy"

Staged at the National Theatre in November 1965, Farag's *Sulayman of Aleppo* was immediately and widely hailed as a landmark of Egyptian theatre. Critics praised its convincing portrayal of a protagonist torn by an "inner struggle" (the recurring phrase is *ṣirāʿ dākhilī*) yet obsessed with justice.[38] Some, especially among the recently released leftist intellectuals now working for the state publishing sector, went further. Critic Louis Awad (1915–90), who had been imprisoned together with Farag in the 1959–63 crackdown, questioned some aspects of the play's plot and characterization but called it the finest Egyptian drama of the season and a step forward for modern Egyptian drama as a whole.[39] Another former prison-mate, Mahmud Amin al-Alim (the same Marxist critic who had been so disappointed in al-Sayyid Bidayr's apolitical *Hamlet* one year earlier), seized on Sulayman as "an authentic tragic character on the Arab stage, based on our intellectual, social, and historical heritage all at once."[40]

The play's strengths were widely traced to *Hamlet.* Novelist and journalist Bahaa Taher (Bahā' Ṭāhir, b. 1935) wrote a review comparing "the Aleppo Man and the Prince of Denmark."[41] Critic Ali al-Rai (ʿAlī al-Rāʿī; 1920–99) called Sulayman "a Middle Eastern Hamlet [*un Hamlet oriental*] . . . no ordinary political murderer, but an intellectual and patriot on whom falls a task that he does not relish, but which he believes is his duty."[42] Many observers shared the enthusiasm of theatre critic Raga al-Naqqash (Rajā' al-Naqqāsh; 1934–2008):

> This character as depicted by Alfred can be considered one of the finest and deepest characters to appear on the Arab stage from [theatre pioneer] Yaʿqūb Ṣanūʿ to this day. For the character of Sulaymān al-Ḥalabī, besides its historical features, shows us something else: the deep human struggle that goes on inside him. For Sulaymān al-Ḥalabī is an "intellectual" accustomed to living the life of thought, observation, contemplation, and dreams. Yet he is suddenly struck in a fateful moment with the necessity of moving from thought to action, from dreams and imagination and theory to entering into the heart of practical life and taking a position that will have grave results. . . . Sulaymān al-Ḥalabī as Alfred Farag has depicted him is the authentic Arab copy [*al-nuskha al-ʿarabiyya al-aṣīla*] of Shakespeare's character, Hamlet.[43]

For the 1965 Cairo audience, Sulayman's dilemma had immediate political relevance. Critics disagreed only on precisely whom, given the abundance of foreign and domestic tyrants in the region, Kléber was supposed to represent. Most read the play as an attack on western imperialism in the Middle East, whether recently ended (French and British) or ongoing (Zionist). For them, Sulayman's ideals and personality recalled the Algerian freedom fighters who had liberated their land from foreign occupation just three years earlier.[44] Several later critics detected a darker, more local message: a cri de coeur to Nasser about the evils of autocracy and military rule. (As Sāmī Munīr Ḥusayn Amīr asked in 1978: "Are Sulaymān's circumstances so different from the ones our society was living through?")[45] Still others read the play as targeting both western imperialism and the local despots who enable it.

One curious contemporary parallel was *not* invoked in print. By 1964, Egypt's Islamist opposition, the Muslim Brotherhood, was already waging a tumultuous battle against Nasser's government. The role of religious ideology in postcolonial politics was obvious to all who cared to look. Many top drama critics had personally met Islamists in prison between 1959 and 1963, if not at university before that. Nasser had survived a 1954 assassination attempt by a Muslim Brother, which had ended his own flirtation with the movement and provoked the first of many violent crackdowns. Islamist thinker Sayyid Qutb (Sayyid Quṭb; 1906–66) had just been imprisoned again in August 1965, a few months before Farag's play went up, after being briefly freed in 1964.[46] The al-Azhar mosque and seminary, where much of Farag's play is set, had been nationalized in 1961, turning it into an arm of the state, just as Sulayman had feared.

But reviewers of *Sulayman of Aleppo* strenuously avoided any reference to contemporary Islam-framed political opposition movements. Religion was approached, if at all, as a problem of dramatic characterization: Louis Awad asked how Sulayman could be a tragic hero and a good "case study of a political killer" if his basic motivation was driven by faith rather than a worldly concept of justice. It is difficult to say whether the critics' reticence on this issue stemmed only from the ban on discussing Islamism in print or also from their own progressive-humanist assumption that all liberationist ideologies were naturally reducible to each other. Salah Abdel Sabur, for instance, argues (in 1969) that Sulayman's religious motives are just anticolonialism by another name:

> [Farag] doesn't cover up Sulaymān's religious motives, but places them in their more general and comprehensive context. . . . Justice is an absolute value, not limited to a particular time or place or a specific society. . . . When Sulaymān told his interrogators he was "waging a holy war in the name of Islam and killing the French infidels," that meant something—it meant, according to the logic of that time, defending the Muslim nation (*umma*) first of all, i.e., defending the people and the country, which is the land. This is no different from the motive for our battles against colonialism and imperialism in this age. The play's lack of mention of these words [holy war, the Muslim nation, unbelievers] opens a

> path for all hearts, minds, and souls to see Sulaymān al-Ḥalabī as a model of a positive battle against colonialism, and a human model that inspires people in every place and of every religion.[47]

"A Beautiful Failure"

Whatever Sulayman's "cue for action"[48], it is remarkable for our purposes to note how poorly his Hamlet-like elements are integrated into Farag's play as a whole. As with Shakespeare's *Hamlet* itself, the rival demands of plot and character produce an unwieldy drama, almost impossible to stage in full. The tension has puzzled some critics, who see Sulayman as a Shakespearean character stuck in a Brechtian play—or, as T. S. Eliot said of Hamlet, a protagonist whose emotions lack an adequate objective correlative.[49] For Louis Awad, Sulayman's character is "a strange mixture of Joan of Arc and Hamlet": a religious militant with a curious introspective bent.[50] The play is thus "an incomplete success and a beautiful failure . . . a tragedy pour[ed] into an epic mold."[51] Others deny that Sulayman, with his lack of character development, can be a tragic hero at all. Nehad Selaiha complains: "All Farag's efforts to invest his hero with Hamletian features—a meditative cast of mind, a rich imagination and a predilection for clowning in moments of crisis—and to develop his obsession with justice into a moral dilemma remain purely verbal, superficial and come to naught."[52]

Such critiques have a point. Surrounded by cardboard-cutout secondary characters and stereotyped events, Sulayman's ruminations on universal justice indeed sound incongruous. But what Selaiha disdains is precisely Farag's deft economy in deploying "verbal" and "superficial" references to *Hamlet.* These citations act as emblems or flags of psychological depth, quick signals that Sulayman is a full-fledged rational moral subject who has "that within which passes show."[53] Onstage, paradoxically, the simplest of external gestures ("actions that a man might play") can suffice to convey psychological interiority, especially to an audience already steeped in readings of *Hamlet.*

Al-Hallaj: "Who Will Give Me a Seeing Sword?"

The moral crisis that disturbs Sulayman is brought to a higher pitch in Salah Abdel Sabur's *Tragedy of al-Hallaj,* a verse drama about the martyrdom of tenth-century Persian mystic Husayn ibn Mansur al-Hallaj (Ḥusayn ibn Manṣūr al-Ḥallāj). The historical al-Hallaj, a poet and preacher as well as spiritual adviser to several top political figures in Abbasid Baghdad, was condemned to death after a judicial process lasting nearly nine years. He was executed—

hung on a gibbet—in 922. The official charge was heresy, specifically "usurpation of the supreme power of God" (*daʿwa ilā al-rubūbiyya*). But al-Hallaj's politics are believed to have played a role as well: his connections and activities brought powerful enemies at a time when the Abbasid Empire was unusually fragile and sensitive to dissent.[54] Abdel Sabur's play draws on al-Hallaj's own writings (collected as *Akhbār al-Ḥallāj* around 991, critical edition published 1957) and early versions of French scholar Louis Massignon's massive study, *La Passion du Hallaj*.[55] The play follows al-Hallaj from his decision to cast off the Sufi cloak and preach in the marketplace through his imprisonment, trial, and crucifixion.

The Islamic art tradition remembers al-Hallaj for his crucifixion and the Christ-like equanimity with which he accepted it.[56] (Rumi, among others, wrote poems inspired by him.) Abdel Sabur turns this beloved religious figure into a metaphor for the artist in the modern state—that is, a self-portrait. His Hallaj feels torn between the political realm on one hand and the intellectual and spiritual realm on the other, between public action and personal salvation. He seeks unity with God through private spiritual practice. Yet he believes in changing the world; disturbed by the sight of injustice and poverty, he corresponds with would-be rulers and preaches to the poor. His ambivalence about the value of action sets him apart from his two best-known literary models: Massignon's Hallaj, who did not hesitate to accept martyrdom, and the doubt-free protagonist of T. S. Eliot's verse drama *Murder in the Cathedral* (1935).[57]

"Under Shakespeare's Cart"

Abdel Sabur never intended to rewrite *Hamlet*. He had read widely; his poetry draws on diverse literary models, both European and Arab. Besides T. S. Eliot, his 1969 memoir, *Ḥayātī fī al-Shiʿr* (*My Life in Poetry*) bristles with quotations from Cavafy, Coleridge, Goethe, Lorca, Jacques Prévert, Rilke, and others, as well as Plato's *Phaedrus* and other works, Aristotle's *Poetics*, and Nietzsche's *Birth of Tragedy*.[58] A graduate of Cairo University's Arabic faculty (rather than English or law like many fellow writers), he also engaged with the Arabic literary tradition. He modeled himself on classical Sufi thinkers such as Abu Nasr al-Tusi (Abu Naṣr ʿAbd Allāh ibn ʿAlī al-Sarrāj al-Ṭūsī, d. 988) and Abu al-Qasim al-Qushayri (Abū al-Qāsim ʿAbd al-Karīm al-Qushayrī, d. 1072), in whose accounts of divine inspiration he saw a prototype of his own creative process.[59]

Yet when Abdel Sabur sat down to write a poetic drama, it was Shakespeare—or rather, the stock political interpretations of Shakespeare—that brought on an almost stifling anxiety of influence.[60] He recalls:

> Poetic drama was an ambition that pursued me for years until I wrote my play, *The Tragedy of Al-Hallaj*. Before that I had made an attempt that was not completed: a play about the Algerian War. I tabled it because I found that I had fallen in thrall to Shakespeare, and created a "Hamletian" character—an Algerian intellectual perplexed [*ḥā'ir*] between a just killing and a contemplative cultural background. I wrote a few scenes of this flawed play, and when I realized I had fallen under the wheels of Shakespeare's cart [*ayqantu min wuqūʿī taḥt ʿarabat shaksbīr*], especially in the scene where the intellectual refuses to kill his adversary while he is praying, I dropped the project.
>
> A second idea came to me, to write the story of Muhalhal ibn Rabīʿa, but I found myself for a second time caught under Shakespeare's cart, for no sooner had I started turning its structure around in my mind than I saw that I was coming fatally close to *Julius Caesar*.[61] For Kulayb is a tyrant, somewhat comparable to Caesar. And Jassās ibn Murra is comparable to Brutus—and therefore it was necessary, since I had made Jassās a seeker of justice, for there to be a man to urge him on to the killing, and here I created a new Cassius, and turned Muhalhal into Marc Antony. . . .
>
> These attempts got me no further than to the boundaries of this domain. And then I left them behind and resolved to write *The Tragedy of Al-Hallaj*. And at that point I strove to escape from under the wheels of Shakespeare's cart, although if I don't know if I've escaped other carts as well.[62]

Abdel Sabur's description suggests that he wanted to escape not only Shakespeare but the thick layer of cliché with which Shakespeare's plays, especially the tragedies, had already grown encrusted. Only a few years into a period of vibrant literary discovery, the sources of inspiration that had recently looked so exciting—decolonization, Arab folklore, and Shakespeare's tragedies—seemed as flat as playing cards to be reshuffled. Hamlet and Brutus each hesitated before justly killing a tyrant, and Abdel Sabur hesitated too, reluctant to surrender his singularity as a writer to the appeal of such banal tropes. Although he shared the socialist beliefs of many of his contemporaries, he had no wish to write propaganda plays or schematic explorations of abstract moral problems.[63] Even while writing for the stage, he felt he was a poet first and foremost: a unique, subjective voice. The aesthetic and spiritual value of the theatrical enterprise for him consisted precisely in its elevation above the sloganized plane of everyday life: "For theatre is not just a slice of life, but an intensified slice."[64] For this reason he expresses fierce scorn for plays which, besides being in prose, are prosaic:

> Ibsen's prose theatre was abused by Ibsenist students. They took his judicious structure, invented a naïve shade of prose theatre, and called it the theatre of "agitprop" [*al-daʿwa*] or "incitement" [*al-taḥrīḍ*]. Its examples are superficial, and its dialogue is unsubtle and easy to process; all the playwright has to do is make good oppose evil and then defeat it, so workers stand against bosses, and peasants against landlords, and the good woman against the cruel man, and then the theatrical events unfold naïvely and simply until they arrive at the desired conclusion.[65]

Rather than escape it, Abdel Sabur's *Tragedy of al-Hallaj* climbs in and redirects "Shakespeare's cart" away from the road of "agitprop or incitement." His Hallaj, despite his concern for the suffering of the poor, does not purvey any simple political message. Strengthened by a passage through radical doubt, he rejects all claims to certainty: his Sufi comrades' complacency, his co-prisoners' radicalism, and the state's arrogance. If he has a lesson to teach, it is precisely about the power of mystical (and poetic) insight to transcend the dictates of the mighty.

The Word or the Sword?

The Tragedy of al-Hallaj opens with the epilogue: the curtain rises on al-Hallaj's hanging corpse ("Look, what's that they've put in our path? A crucified old man!"), and the first scene recounts his trial.[66] The flashback structure precludes plot-driven suspense.[67] Instead, the play draws its momentum from the unfolding of al-Hallaj's spiritual quest and its rhythm from the dialectical confrontation (thesis-antithesis-synthesis) between clashing points of view.

Critics have noted that dialectical patterns of thesis, antithesis, and synthesis pervade much of Abdel Sabur's poetry.[68] Such a design underpins *The Tragedy of al-Hallaj* as well, structuring the three triplet-based scenes of the first act. In scene 1, a trio of curious men (a peasant, a merchant, and a preacher) hears three accounts of al-Hallaj's death: from a group of commoners who testified against him, a group of Sufis who loved him and let him die, and his friend Shiblī, whose personal story makes sense of the other two. Scene 2 also has three parts.

In contrast to the public space and many voices of the first, it shows al-Hallaj in intimate conversation with Shiblī and in private meditation: he is a live subject, not a dead object, and his pity for the poor contrasts with their betrayal of him in scene 1. Scene 3 recapitulates and synthesizes the first two: we see the choruses of gossipers again (in three groups of three), then al-Hallaj shares a sermon with them, and finally a troika of policemen interrogate and arrest al-Hallaj. This culminates the encounter between public and private discourses, lands al-Hallaj in prison, and sets up the main antithesis between spirituality and public engagement to be resolved in the second act.

Al-Hallaj's character, too, is structured by a dialectical confrontation between clashing ideals. He begins the play as Socrates (a gadfly reducing interlocutors to aporia) and ends it as Jesus Christ. The dark antithesis—the dialectic's second term—is Hamlet. Abdel Sabur's reading of *Hamlet* resonates throughout *The Tragedy of al-Hallaj*, expressing the doubt that al-Hallaj must overcome before he can embrace his role as a martyr and potential savior. Key to this reading are the twin tropes of perplexity (*ḥayra*) and the out-of-joint world (*al-kawn al-muḍṭarib* or *al-muʿtall*).

Al-Hallaj's doubt, like that of Alfred Farag's Sulayman, begins with the problem of injustice (*ẓulm*). But it goes deeper, not only weighing the relative importance of consequences ("Justice, or the price of justice?"), but questioning whether human moral judgment can be accurate at all. He begins the play confident of his mission, telling his friend Shibli that God sends illumination to certain people "so that they can give balance to this broken world" (*li-yakūnū mīzān al-kawn al-muʿtall*).[69] This confidence soon fades. The play's climactic prison dialogue, which starts by echoing Plato's *Crito*, ends with al-Hallaj collapsing in tears. He can out-argue the officials who arrest him (and to withstand a savage beating in prison), but he is reduced to Hamlet-like impotence (*ʿajz*) by his own perplexity:

> Hallaj: Why should I escape?
> Second Prisoner: So you can take up your sword and fight
> for humanity.
> Hallaj: Men like myself do not carry swords.
> Second Pr.: Are you afraid to carry a sword?
> Hallaj: I do not fear carrying one,
> But I fear walking with one taken up:
> For a sword in a blind hand becomes the instrument of
> blind death.
> Second Pr.: Couldn't your words guide your sword?

Hallaj: Suppose my words sang for the sword.
The sound of its blows
Would echo their syllables, their commas and their rhymes.
And between one consonant and another
A head that once moved, rolls,
And a heart that once rejoiced, breaks,
And an arm is cut off at the sounds of the letters' poetical rhymes.
How unhappy I would then be: how unhappy!
My words would have killed.
Second Pr.: You'd have killed in the name of the persecuted.
Hallaj: Persecuted!
Where are the persecuted and where are the persecutors?[70]
Has any among the victims not persecuted
A neighbor, a spouse, a child, a maid, or a slave?
Has any among them not wronged the Lord?
Who will give me—a seeing sword?
Who will give me a seeing sword?
[*Tears come to his eyes*]
First Pr.: Are you crying, master?
Don't be sad: things may get better.
Hallaj: I am not crying from sadness but from perplexity [*ḥayra*]
My helplessness [*ʿajz*] makes my tears fall.
My anxiety shows and my sighs pour forth
Because of my perplexity and my doubts.
Is the Lord punishing me in my soul and in my faith,
Concealing His light from my eyes?
Or is He calling me to make my own choice?
Suppose I do make my own choice; what would I choose?
To raise my voice?
Or to raise my sword?
What would I choose?
What would I choose?
[*Lights fade to black.*][71]

Just as shadow in a painting creates the effect of depth, al-Hallaj's episode of Hamlet-like doubt suggests interiority. But here it also allows character development: al-Hallaj emerges from this dark night as a fully fledged moral subject and agent able to take full responsibility for his fate. Although he construes his newfound agency as submission to God, not individual self-assertion,[72] it nonetheless gives him the power to stand up to corrupt earthly authority. He does so for the rest of the second act.

Abdel Sabur's long final scene—the trial—makes brilliant dramatic use of Massignon's research.[73] The three judges' roles closely follow but condense their historical roles and behavior toward al-Hallaj. The defendant is self-assured and serene. He effortlessly upstages Abu Omar (Abū ʿUmar), the pompous and venal chief judge. Casting the court as an object—the instrument of God's will—he claims for himself the status of an authentic moral subject, freely choosing martyrdom.

> Abu Omar: Hey, you, old man with the tangled beard.
> How do you defend yourself?
> Hallaj: You are not my judges.
> Therefore, I do not defend myself.[74]

Yet al-Hallaj testifies. Abdel Sabur gives him a long poetic monologue about his life and faith. He describes the quest for certainty that has animated him since childhood. He tells of pursuing it first through study, which failed, however, to relieve his "terrible perplexity," then through prayer, and finally through love. Having experienced and overcome this "terrible perplexity" [*ḥayra rājifa*])[75] gives al-Hallaj the moral authority to transcend the kangaroo court's jurisdiction. Abu ʿUmar proclaims him a heretic, but the sympathetic judge, Ibn Surayj, declares that al-Hallaj's Sufi practice is "a matter between the servant and his master, of which only God can judge."[76]

The play endorses this view. As the trial turns from religion to politics, al-Hallaj continues to speak over the heads of his onstage judges, sounding more fully human and thus more authoritative than they. He expounds his political views (which are reformist, not revolutionary) in the context of a deeper mystical vision of man's unity with God:

> Ibn Surayj: Let us now question him about his alleged incitement of the people,
> For that is the crime for which the Sultan sent him here.
> (*To Hallaj*) Have you corrupted the people, O Hallaj?

Hallaj: Only a corrupt Sultan who enslaves and starves the people corrupts them.
Ibn Sulayman: What we mean is, have you instigated disobedience to the law?
Hallaj: Rather, I instigated obedience to the God of the law.
God created the world, system and order.
Why did they get disjointed [*iḍṭarabat*]?
Why was the order disrupted?
God created man in His own image:
Why has he fallen to the level of animals?[77]

Here again, echoes of *Hamlet* are helpful. Invoking the *Hamlet*-associated concept of out-of-jointness (*iḍṭirāb*) keeps al-Hallaj from sounding merely arrogant, like Socrates in the *Apology*. It lends depth to his defiance, suggesting that he (unlike the judges) truly understands human pain.

"To Speak . . . and to Die"

Abdel Sabur's 1969 memoir stresses the overlap between himself and his dramatic hero: two visionaries for whom banality is a form of political oppression. Their question is how a poetic visionary should act in an unjust world. Again the key terms are Hamlet's *ḥayra* and *iḍṭirāb*—applied, not surprisingly, to the *Hamlet*-associated problems of justice/injustice and action/inaction:

> As for the issue [*The Tragedy of al-Hallaj*] raises, it was the issue of my personal salvation. I was suffering from a terrible perplexity [*ḥayra*] toward many phenomena of our age. Questions crowded disjointedly [*tazdaḥim izdiḥāman muḍṭariban*] in my mind, and I kept asking myself the question al-Hallaj asks himself: "What do I do?" And here the play took up the issue of the role of the artist in the society, and al-Hallaj's answer was, "To speak . . . and to die." My Hallaj is not only a Sufi, but a poet as well; and the Sufi experience and the artistic experience spring from the same sources and meet at the same goal. This is the return of the world to its purity and harmony after it has been plunged into the torrent of experience. The torment of al-Hallaj was a response to the torment of thinkers in most modern societies, and their confusion [*ḥayra*] between the sword and the word.[78]

Abdel Sabur's word for the "disjointed" crowd of questions in his mind is *muḍṭarib* (literally: disturbed, mixed up), the adjective form of *iḍṭirāb* and the same fairly rare term with which, a few years earlier, he had described the "out-of-joint world" of Alfred Farag's Sulayman.[79] His Hallaj, too, as we have seen, is concerned with restoring the world's balance. Nehad Selaiha, following Abdel Sabur's lead, sees a fusion of writer, literary model, and character: "The dilemma of the historical Hallaj, the poetical persona of Abdul Saboor, unconsciously merged, in the crucible of the imagination, with Hamlet's dilemma. 'O, cursed spite, that I was ever born to set it right' became Abdul Saboor's and his hero's urgent and agonizing cry, as well as Hamlet's."[80]

Like his protagonist, Abdel Sabur demanded the right to care about his society but to approach its brokenness in his own spiritualized, aestheticized, sometimes incomprehensible way. To this end he appropriated Hamlet, reading him as the perplexed hesitator most familiar to Anglo-American critics. However, by grafting this hesitation onto a beloved political martyr, Abdel Sabur's passion play had the effect of reinforcing a different reading, the Arab martyr-hero Hamlet to be discussed in the next chapter.

De-Hamletized Revivals

It is no wonder that Abdel Sabur, the Sufi existentialist, was briefly tempted to depict two tyrant-killer protagonists as Brutus and Hamlet. His milieu drew a link between politically committed art (*al-fann al-multazim*) and the depiction of protagonists who ponder and brood. Correctly understood, these were two sides of the same political problem: the problem of how to achieve authentic existence in the world, which required winning enough recognition of one's agency to make that existence possible.

For Egyptian intellectuals of the mid-1960s, such recognition had to come from the Nasser regime itself—the sponsor and first addressee of all cultural production—before it could come from the wider world. Therefore, in creating al-Hallaj as a character whose spiritual reality lets him transcend his political context, Abdel Sabur may have gone too far. Al-Hallaj was a puzzle: part Socrates, part Hamlet, and part Jesus Christ, and like all three of these figures a semi-willing, semi-detached victim of the political authorities of his day. What was the nationalist theatre to do with a protagonist who saved nobody but achieved only martyrdom? With a verse drama that had no edifying message to impart?[81]

The 1966–67 production was not a great success. Some Egyptian critics accused Abdel Sabur of aestheticism or conservatism, of practicing "art for art's

4.1. Mahmoud El Lozy's revival (2004) turns Farag's *Sulayman of Aleppo* into a "political cabaret." Courtesy of Mahmoud El Lozy.

sake." Others tried to rehabilitate his play as a piece of leftist "art with a message": a cri de coeur begging the Nasser regime to grant more freedom to its intellectuals.[82] On this reading, the play was addressed partly to the audience but mainly to the very "centers of power" it criticized; if Abdel Sabur had already dismissed the regime as an addressee, many critics had not. It would take two soulful revivals by Ahmed Abdel-Aziz (Aḥmad ʿAbd al-ʿAzīz) at Cairo's Vanguard Theatre in 1984 and 2002 for the small audience to appreciate the pathos at the play's core; both culminated in an iconic image of al-Hallaj bound by a cross of ropes or chains spanning the whole stage.[83]

Farag's *Sulayman of Aleppo,* written the same year as *The Tragedy of al-Hallaj,* enjoyed a smoother initial reception but dated faster. The need to claim political agency by demonstrating psychological interiority was peculiar to the mid-1960s context. Perhaps it was most sharply felt among Farag's cohort of leftist writers, wounded by the Nasser regime but not yet ready to forsake its modernizing and dignifying goals. Soon Farag's Shakespearean gestures would look quaint—even his own 1970s and 80s works would abandon them, finding other means to suggest dramatic self-consciousness.[84] The only recent Egyptian production of *Sulayman of Aleppo* (American University in Cairo, May 2004) downplayed interiority altogether, turning the play into a "political cabaret" that likened the French occupation of Egypt to the U.S.-led war in Iraq.[85]

Although they soon became irrelevant, Sulayman al-Halabi's long moments of Hamlet-like introspection were crucial in 1965. They helped rehabilitate Farag's character from a skull in a display case into a worthy political agent. Appropriating Hamlet's dialectical style, they also had the effect of absorbing Shakespeare's prince into the socialist and anticolonial Arab discourse of the struggle for justice.

By borrowing from *Hamlet,* then, Farag and (to a lesser extent) Abdel Sabur helped revise its standard Egyptian reading. Ironically, they helped make Hamlet's inwardness—their reason for appropriating him in the first place—less important. The new reading, stressing the "out-of-joint" time and the heroic political martyr "born to set it right," would come to full bloom in the 1970s Arab Hamlet adaptations discussed in the next chapter. Unlike al-Hallaj and Sulayman, this next generation of martyr-heroes would carry Hamlet's name. However, because earning political recognition was no longer the goal, they would shed the very aspects of Hamlet that Farag and Abdel Sabur had found so useful.

5

TIME OUT OF JOINT, 1967–76

My exploration of 1960s Egyptian drama in chapters 3 and 4 has shown how *Hamlet* was adapted to the political imperatives of the times. Exhibited as a marker of cultural maturity (proof that the Arab theatre could handle "the great world classics"), *Hamlet* also served as a model of dramatic interiority, with Hamlet-like hesitation as a shorthand for psychological depth. Both uses of *Hamlet* appealed for recognition and respect: they attested to a society with real cultural achievements, whose heroes were qualified to be real political agents. Like other areas of post-colonial Egyptian culture, the theatre was eager to show off the psychological fruits of the revolution—and to claim the political rewards.

Such appeals for recognition largely stopped after the Arab defeat in the June War of 1967. (The defeat also ended Egypt's unquestioned dominance of Arab culture; therefore, starting in this period, we will begin to look at plays from Syria, Jordan, and elsewhere.) This chapter will begin with a brief survey of the June War's cultural impact and its epilogue, Gamal Abdel Nasser's death in 1970. As we will see, the 1967 defeat fundamentally altered Arab conceptions of political theatre's role. A well-developed high culture was no longer enough to guarantee the world's respect—indeed, it began to look like an impediment. Psychological interiority was no help: what mattered was not to deserve agentive power, but to seize it. Disappointed in their regimes, dramatists stopped addressing subtly allegorical plays to the government; instead, they appealed directly to audiences, trying to rouse them to participate in political life. But Nasser's death in September 1970 added a dark subtext to such calls: the fear that even the most sincere effort could not bring unity and justice to the Arab world but would kill the hero who attempted it.

This context encouraged directors to read *Hamlet* as a political melodrama. Hamlet, like the protagonists of Farag and Abdel Sabur, became a man facing an urgent ethical and political dilemma. Because his will was pure, the outcome was foreknown: Hamlet's conflict with the overwhelming corruption of his environment destined him for martyrdom. The new consensus on the play's meaning grew popular with audiences, spreading beyond Egypt's state-run drama troupes to reach other Arab countries and venues such as commercial theatres and high schools. Among the many pairs of opposites associated with Hamlet's rhetoric (seems/is, thought/action, noble/base, honesty/doubt, etc.), one gained particular prominence for Arab audiences: justice/oppression (*ʿadl/ẓulm*). Hamlet's famous question—"To be or not to be?"—became conjoined in their minds with his declaration at the close of act 1, after learning the truth from the Ghost.[1] These lines, in various Arabic renderings, became the key to future Arab readings of the play:

> The time is out of joint. O cursèd spite
> That ever I was born to set it right.[2]

The notion of a "time out of joint" informs both the *Hamlet* productions we will examine in this chapter, which opened in 1971 and 1973 in Egypt and Syria respectively (see table 5.1). Both used translations of Shakespeare's text but cut the text drastically and offered frankly political adaptations. Both featured the archetypal Arab Hero Hamlet: a revolutionary martyr for justice who dies confronting a repressive regime. In their angry directness, these plays serve as "abstract and brief chronicles"[3] of a bold period in Arab theatre. They addressed their audiences rather than their regimes; they presented revolutionary purity as a remedy for the rot exposed by the 1967 defeat. These plays advocated action, not contemplation. Yet, as we will see, their calls to arms were tinged with despair, and their political messages were ultimately self-defeating. Their failures help explain the quick obsolescence of the Arab Hero Hamlet and point toward the ironic *Hamlet* appropriations that began in the late 1970s.

As an epitaph for this disillusioned yet still impassioned period, this chapter will end with a look at *Shakespeare Rex,* a 1975 comedy by Egyptian playwright Rafat al-Duwayri (Ra'fat al-Duwayrī; b. 1937). A pastiche about Shakespeare's life and works, *Shakespeare Rex* reflects a deep familiarity with Shakespeare and even a tendency to identify with him. At the same time, the play satirizes the commercialism and government neglect afflicting the Egyptian theatre after Nasser's death. It also expresses skepticism about the efficacy of political the-

TABLE 5.1
Two *Hamlet* Adaptations and a Shakespeare Spoof (1971–78)

Play	Author	First director	Year published/ produced	Where produced
Hamlet	Shakespeare (trans. Khalīl Muṭrān, ʿA. Q. al-Qiṭṭ, and J. I. Jabrā)	Muḥammad Ṣubḥī	1971, 1975, 1977–78	Academy of Arts, Art Studio Theatre, and Galā'a Theatre (all Cairo)
Hamlet	Shakespeare (trans. M. ʿA. Muḥammad)	Riyāḍ 'Iṣmat	1973	Ḥurriyya Institute (formerly Lycée Laïque), Damascus
Shakespeare Rex (Shakespeare in ʿAtaba)	Ra'fat al-Duwayrī	Fahmī al-Khūlī	Published 1975; performed 1976	Ṭalīʿa (Vanguard) Theatre, ʿAtaba, Cairo

atre, whether addressed to the regime or the audience. With its cynical outlook, al-Duwayri's play leaves almost no room for a heroic Hamlet character. Instead it offers a tragicomic requiem for the 1960s and early '70s, when heroism was conceivable and dramatists still hoped to provoke political or at least moral change.

"Something Is Rotten": Theatre and the 1967 Defeat

The June War of 1967 is unanimously considered a turning point in modern Arab consciousness: a traumatizing theft, a brick wall across the road to progress, or (depending on who is talking) a sharp wake-up call. Historian Albert Hourani summarizes the defeat's psychological impact in a way that echoes, perhaps intentionally, Hamlet's shock on learning of his father's murder:

> The events of 1967, and the processes of change which followed them, made more intense *that disturbance of spirits, that sense of a world gone wrong*, which had already been expressed in the poetry of the 1950s and 1960s. The defeat of 1967 was widely regarded as being not only a military setback but a kind of moral judgment. If the Arabs had been defeated so quickly, completely and publicly, might it not be a sign that there was *something rotten in their societies and in the moral system which they expressed?* The heroic age of the struggle for independence was over; that struggle could no longer

> unite the Arab countries, or the people in any one of them, and failures and deficiencies could no longer be blamed so fully as in the past upon the power and intervention of the foreigner.[4]

The war exposed the hollowness of Arab military pretensions. In six days, Israel more than tripled its size, seizing 42,000 square miles of Arab territory: Egypt's Sinai Peninsula, Syria's Golan Heights, and the Palestinian West Bank (including East Jerusalem) formerly held by Jordan. Egypt lost 85 percent of its military hardware and 10,000 to 15,000 troops (another 5,000 were taken prisoner); Jordan and Syria sustained serious losses as well.[5] In the war's aftermath, intra-Arab recriminations grew sharper. Syria struggled through the last in a series of military coups, leaving Hafiz al-Asad's Alawite circle in power.[6] Palestinian militant groups gained new stature, eclipsing Nasser's discredited pan-Arab agenda.[7] Arab heads of state firmly proclaimed "the three no's" in the September 1967 Khartoum Resolution—no peace with Israel, no recognition of Israel, and no negotiation with Israel—but this statement of resolve masked their deep sense of helplessness and confusion about what to do next.

Intellectuals watched the war's aftermath in shock. Scrambling for points of reference, they immediately and persistently interpreted their own predicament through the lens of *Hamlet*. As theatre critic Nehad Selaiha remarked thirty-six years later:

> I think [Hamlet's] "O cursed spite that I was ever born to set it right" and his "the time is out of joint" have touched a raw nerve in all the intellectuals of the 1960s after the horrible 5th of June. . . . I think he [fits] well as a metaphor for their sense of impotence, betrayal, spiritual desolation and psychic dislocation.[8]

The June War shifted the vocabulary and goals of Arab drama. Beyond the military humiliation at Israel's hands, many Syrian and Egyptian writers recorded their sense of outrage at the discovery that their own governments had lied to them. The lack of democratic openness was seen as a key reason for the Arab countries' dismal military performance. Many recalled the extravagant assurances, long after the decisive battles had been lost, that victory was imminent.[9] Even for longtime regime apologists, the defeat was glaring evidence that the governments of Egypt and Syria had ceased to communicate with their own citizens. These governments neither told the truth nor wanted to hear it. What was the point of sending them gently coded messages?

Far from silencing Arab dramatists or causing an artistic "crisis," as has sometimes been claimed, the defeat gave Arab writers both a mission and a new license to speak their minds. In Syria, the defeat angered and galvanized a generation of poets and playwrights.[10] In Egypt, filmmakers (and to some extent dramatists) seized on the government's new willingness to promote thoughtful, critical work.[11] In criticizing their governments' lack of candor, poets and dramatists finally dropped their allegorical masks.[12] Many, giving up on their regimes altogether, began to speak directly to the public. For a few years, their weakened governments did little to stop them.

"By the Logic of the Tabla *and the* Rababa"

Let me briefly invoke three non-*Hamlet* examples to illustrate the post-1967 and post-1970 artistic mood. The first is a much-quoted long poem, *Notes in the Margin of the Defeat,* by Syrian poet Nizar Qabbani (Nizār Qabbānī; 1923–98). In his lifetime, Qabbani was "by far the most popular poet in the Arab world."[13] Better known for his love lyrics and sometimes even criticized as a "bourgeois" poet, he modified his style in 1967 and began to address explicitly political topics. In *Notes,* which poet-critic Salma Khadra Jayyusi has called "the angriest poem in contemporary Arabic,"[14] he writes with remarkable directness of the defeat's origins in domestic politics. Pakistani-British visitor Tariq Ali witnessed the poem's "explosive impact" in Egypt, Jordan, Syria, and the Palestinian territories in the summer of 1967. He recalls that stanza 17, "in particular, outraged the scribes of the state and the secret police in every Arab capital but was recited and sung throughout the Arab world."[15] It pleaded and taunted:

> If someone could grant me safety
> If I could meet the Sultan
> I'd say to him: Mr. Sultan,
> Your fierce dogs have torn my clothes
> And your agents are always following me
> Their eyes follow me
> Their noses follow me
> Their feet follow me
> Like determined fate, like judges
> They interrogate my wife
> And they have my friends' names written down,
> Mr. Sultan,
> Because I have approached your massive walls
> Because I

Tried to reveal my sorrow and distress
I was beaten with shoes
Your soldiers forced me to eat from my shoes
My lord
My lord Sultan
You've lost the war twice
Because half your people
Has no tongue
What's a people worth that
Has no tongue?
Because half our people
Is confined like the ant and the rat
Inside the walls.
If someone could grant me safety
From the troops of the sultan,
I would say to him:
You've lost the war twice
Because you've become cut off from the cause of the people.[16]

Contrary to its surface appearance, Qabbani's poem does not really aim to promote government reform. It does not seek the "sultan's" ear at all. Rather, it addresses his countrymen, bitterly attacking what he calls their shared culture of poetry and empty talk. The critique is part self-serving apology: Arab culture is too rich and complex for such mechanical tasks as winning wars. Still, the poet's frustration is real:

If we lose the war . . . it's no surprise
Because we enter it
With all the easterner's talent for rhetoric
With all the heroics of ʿAntar, which never killed a fly
Because we enter it
By the logic of the *ṭabla* and the *rabāba*[17]

And later, in a stinging (ironically musical) couplet:

With the *nāy* and *mizmār*
You don't win a war.[18]

In the end, however, Qabbani's poem does not give up hope but addresses the next generation. The tone is still angrily paradoxical—a poet condemning poetry, a wise adult (Qabbani was forty-four) telling young people not to listen to their elders. Yet the poem concludes:

> O children
> From the Ocean to the Gulf, you are the shoots of hope
> You are the generation that will break the shackles
> And will kill the opium in our heads
> And kill the delusions
> O children, you are still good,
> Pure, like snow or dew, pure
> Don't read about our defeated generation, children.
> We are failures
> And, like the rind of a watermelon, we are trivial
> And we are rotten . . . rotten as sandals
> Don't read news of us
> Don't follow in our tracks
> Don't accept our ideas
> For we are the retching, coughing, syphilitic generation
> The generation of the trickery and dancing on the rope
> O children
> O spring rain, o shoots of hope
> You are the seeds of fertility in our barren life
> And you are the generation that will defeat the defeat.[19]

For all his pessimism about words, then, Qabbani's poetic narrator keeps talking. All is not lost. The next generation still has a duty it can usefully carry out.

The Audience Fights Back

A second example of post-1967 writing, also from Syria, helps concretize what it might mean for young writers to "defeat the defeat." Damascus-based playwright Saadallah Wannus (Saʿd Allāh Wannūs; 1941–97) was twenty-six years old in 1967. A graduate of Cairo University's literature department, he had written some minor plays by 1967, but the June War set off a decade-long creative streak. His breakthrough work, *Party for June 5* (*Ḥaflat Samar min Ajl Khamsa Ḥuzayrān*), was performed in Damascus and Beirut in 1968.[20] The play "shook the theatre community" with both its style and its message.[21] In his introduction to Wannus's complete works, titled "The Child Who Saw the Emperor Naked," novelist Abdelrahman Munif (ʿAbd al-Raḥmān Munīf) writes that *Party for June 5* "was the first time an Arab playwright confronted, in such difficult times, the truth in all its cruelty and nakedness.... It was necessary that someone would be found, like that child who pointed to the king and said that he was naked . . . and Saʿd Allāh Wannūs was that child who said it."[22]

Wannus's socialist and Arab nationalist critique of Syria's government and society is incendiary enough.[23] More striking than this critique, however, is the way his play enacts and models the process of political participation. Wannus's play (subtitled *With the Participation of the Audience, History, Officials, and Professional Actors*) bulldozes through the fourth wall. Instead of regular acts, scenes, an intermission, and so forth, the performance consists of a long metadramatic argument about how to write a play on the June War. This dialogue involves a theatre director, a playwright, and various ordinary Syrians who share their memories of the events on stage and from their seats in the audience.

The Damascus and Beirut playgoers, unable to read the script in advance as we can do now, must have been bewildered. Actors planted among them jumped up and shouted back at the stuffed shirts on stage. A row of "officials" seated in the front row became visibly nervous; "police" stationed inside and outside the theatre barred the doors and began taking down names. At no time would viewers have been able to distinguish with certainty between the real spectators and the cast members planted among them.[24] As disorienting as this would be for an audience anywhere in the world (even today), the original Damascus audience must have found it terrifying. Rather than breaking the fourth wall in order to puncture a theatrical illusion, Wannus *created* for his audience the momentary theatrical illusion of participating in a real, public political discussion. (At the end of the show, to heighten the realism, the performance was "canceled" and the audience was escorted out to be "arrested.")

This extraordinary format gives the audience a hands-on civics lesson. Rather than mere criticism of the regime, the play offers a tangible alternative. The play's actors show and teach the audience how to behave in a political dialogue. No monolithic mass ("the people," singular) these interrupting voices represent a cacophony of opposing views, interests, and agendas. They tell stories, argue, bring in analogies and new facts to support their points, and disagree about whether or not to let various people voice opposing views. What they share is a refusal to be silenced, either by fancy sloganeering or by a canned folklore show desperately called in by the Theatre Director. Rather than slogans about unity, they are all interested in hearing each other's real experiences of the war.

Inspired by Wannus's example, a new generation of playwrights set out to build, one auditorium at a time, the participatory spirit they had found so lacking in their societies. Like Wannus, these writers endorsed Brecht's core belief that theatre should educate its audience. (They also drew heavily on some of Brecht's techniques, notably the use of character "types" rather than full-fledged characters.)[25] Directors and actors, too, brought a timely political interpretation to the classic plays they staged, deemphasizing the psychological development of the characters and instead stressing the forces of history. For the first time, this trend came even to productions of Shakespeare.

"You Were Our Father"

So far I have sketched a three-part etiology of the Arab Hero Hamlet: postcolonial aspirations to world-class high culture, a mid-1960s kaleidoscope of sources and models (notably Kozintsev's film), the catalyzing shock of the 1967 defeat. However, this story is incomplete: Hamlet the political martyr did not emerge in the immediate aftermath of the June War. As far as I know, the first political Arab *Hamlet* adaptation was not staged until 1971, over three years later. What had to happen first, I believe, was the death of Gamal Abdel Nasser.

Nasser died on September 28, 1970; he was only fifty-two. Although his health problems were known, the fatal heart attack was widely blamed on the stress of recent events, particularly the failure of the Cairo peace talks he had convened to try to stop the "Black September" civil war between the Palestine Liberation Organization and King Hussein's forces in Jordan. Intra-Arab fighting, it was said, had broken Nasser's heart.[26]

Nasser's emotional bond with Egyptians and other Arabs was discussed in chapter 2, but the impact of his death and funeral is hard to describe. The crowds that had taken to the streets begging him not to resign on June 9, 1967, poured out once more; an estimated five million mourners joined his funeral procession, one of the largest in history. Heads of state and foreign television anchors were seen weeping. The BBC reported that "scores" of Egyptians "were battered or crushed to death" as the crowd spontaneously surged forward trying to carry their dead leader's body.[27]

As their bereavement sank in, Arabs all over the region, not only in Egypt, knew an era had ended. Even more than the 1967 defeat, Nasser's death marked the irrevocable passing of the dream of Arab unity. This loss—like Hamlet's loss of his father—occasioned a dilemma: it was disloyal to accept the new reality but impractical to deny it. As in *Hamlet,* the leader's death occasioned guilt and self-doubt as well as sorrow. Certainties gave way to questions. The ideal of "Arabness" (*ʿurūba*) had lost its self-evidence: was it even meaningful to use the term? Instead, the phrase "*ilā ayn*?" ("Where to?") started to crop up frequently in Arab political and cultural debate.

It was again Nizar Qabbani, the Syrian poet whose *Notes in the Margins of the Defeat* had so recently blasted Nasser and other Arab leaders, who captured the mood. In an instantly famous poem, Qabbani absolved the great leader of all blame for his failures. It was rather the Arabs who were unworthy; their selfish infighting had prevented Nasser from realizing his heroic agenda. In five astonishing stanzas, Qabbani compares Nasser to the (Judeo-Christian and) Islamic prophets Moses, Jesus, and Muhammad and to the Shiʿa martyr Ḥusayn ibn ʿAlī. He imagines them all betrayed by their followers, focusing on the golden calf incident, the crucifixion of Jesus, and the schism in the early Muslim community. A relentless rhythm of "we" and "you" casts Nasser as a paternal protector and the Arabs as disloyal children:

> We killed you. . . .
> Oh our love and our longing
> You were the friend, you were the truthteller,
> You were our father.
> And when we washed our hands, we discovered
> That we had killed what we desired
> And that the blood on the pillow
> Was our blood.[28]

The poem's opening line—"We killed you, O last of the prophets"—approaches blasphemy. But although coded in the language of prophetic monotheism rather than Greek myth (cf. "Hyperion to a satyr"[29]), the emotions recall Hamlet's: "after you / all kings are ash." Like Hamlet in act 1, the speaker in Qabbani's poem alternates between intricate sarcasm and apparent despair. He denounces hypocrisy ("pouring out tears over you / With a dagger in his robe"), magnifies the dead father's virtues to the point of comparison with the divine, and accuses of betrayal those who, Gertrude-like, fail to recognize the father's excellence. An accusation of murder (in Hamlet's case, an accurate one) underpins all these claims:[30]

> We killed you with both our hands
> And then said: it is fate.
> Why did you agree to come to us?
> The like of you was too much for us.
> We gave you Arabness to drink till you were full
> We threw you in the fire of Amman till you were burnt[31]
> We showed you the betrayal of Arabness till you lost your
> faith.
> Why did you appear in the land of the hypocrites?

Why did you appear?
We are Jahiliyya peoples[32]
Flip-flopping
And shilly-shallying
We pledge loyalty to our masters in the morning
And eat them when evening comes.[33]

Many of Qabbani's images resemble Hamlet's. He links monstrous eating to fickleness, the last two lines just quoted expressing an irony comparable to Hamlet's "The funeral bak'd meats / Did coldly furnish forth the marriage tables."[34] He contrasts the dead leader's "vigor and pride" with the tawdriness of successor regimes. He even credits the deceased with prophetic powers to elicit language, in a modernist poet's version of Hamlet's Bible-appropriating claim: "His form and cause conjoin'd, preaching to stones, would make them capable"[35]:

Abu Khalid[36] . . . Oh poem:
Spoken aloud,
You greened forth leaves.
Where to?
Oh dream-horseman,
What is the race, when the horse is dead?
Where to?
All the myths died
With your death. . . . And Shahrazad killed herself
Behind the funeral procession.[37]

I am not suggesting that Qabbani had *Hamlet* in mind. Rather, his tone and imagery help explain why and how *Hamlet* would carry a special resonance for Arab audiences after Nasser's death. Already well known and widely available in politicized Eastern-bloc versions, Shakespeare's play provided a dignified language for early 1970s bewilderment and guilt. By identifying with Hamlet and casting the late Nasser as the ghost of Hamlet's father, Arab intellectuals could "play" their mourning (in Walter Benjamin's sense of *Trauerspiel*[38]), redrawing their humiliating recent history in the clear lines of tragedy.

Martyrs for Justice: "Abstract and Brief Chronicles" of the 1970s

Sobhi's "Revolutionary Fighter, Furious and Pure"

The first 1970s adaptation we will consider, Mohamed Sobhi's *Hamlet,* was part mourning rite, part swashbuckling heroic tale.[39] Sobhi (b. 1948) first directed

Hamlet with an amateur cast in 1971, while a student at the recently founded Higher Institute of Theatrical Arts in Giza. (He recalls: "Back then the Academy was in the middle of farmland. There were peasants in the audience, women breastfeeding their babies. Later in the village I saw little kids sword-fighting and quoting Hamlet's words to the Ghost.")[40] He restaged it with his own company in 1975. Late-1970s revivals made a successful crossover from a state-funded to a commercial venue, moving from the Art Studio Theatre (1977) to Cairo's private-sector Galā'a Theatre (1978). There, to critics' amazement, it drew a bigger audience than *It Happened on Pyramids Road,* a kitschy musical staged a few months earlier.[41]

To some critics' surprise, this commercial theatre audience sat still and paid attention. Reviewing the 1978 performance, Nasim Migalli (Nasīm Mijallī) enthused:

> No sooner had the performance of *Hamlet* begun, with that grave funeral scene, than the audience was gripped by a kind of silent concentration, with opened eyes and ears and sharpened hearing and sight, following the play with decorous gravity. One got the impression of sitting in a holy temple surrounded by Sufis intoxicated with the spirit of divine unity. And it stayed that way until the final moment, when the play concluded with the same scene.[42]

Sobhi's production made no explicit allusion to contemporary Arab politics. Aesthetically, it was conservative: ornate doublet-and-hose costuming, a classical European score. The language was laden with archaisms; rather than use the most modern Shakespeare translation available, Sobhi created a painstaking collage of three versions, relying heavily on Khalil Mutran's florid 1918 text.[43] Structurally and visually the play borrowed from the cinema, taking as much from Laurence Olivier's psychological *Hamlet* film (1948) as from Grigori Kozintsev's political one (1964), which Sobhi claims to have seen seventeen times.[44] Yet I believe the production's broad appeal was due in part to its comforting "revolutionary" political resonance. Refashioning both script and role, Sobhi rewrote Olivier's tragedy of psychological paralysis as a simple martyrology or passion play. His prince represents perhaps the first and purest incarnation of the Arab Hero Hamlet.

What critics recall from Sobhi's production, and what most strikes its film viewer today, is the opening scene: Hamlet's funeral. Sobhi, playing Hamlet, lies dead on the black-and-white tiled floor; the other act 5 corpses bestrew the floor as well. The first lines are spoken by Horatio: "Now . . . a noble heart has fallen. The young man has died. Good night, dear prince."[45] Horatio (not Fortinbras, as in Shakespeare) then gives the order for a military funeral. Soldiers enter, some bearing torches. In silence, they drape Hamlet's body with a red cloth, ceremonially draw their swords, and march with exaggerated slowness around the stage. Horatio's wish, "May angels carry your soul to heaven, O Hamlet,"[46] leads into the opening tympani beat of Carl Orff's *Carmina Burana*. Over the music, Horatio's recorded voice intones a blend of his own lines and Hamlet's, each repeated several times with slight variations. The repetition is not a postmodern device to draw ironic attention to the multiplicity of translations used; on the contrary, it accentuates Hamlet's tragic death and Horatio's grief with an impressively varied accumulation of goodnights and farewells. Here and throughout, Hamlet's habit of thrice repeating key lines[47] is exaggerated for melodramatic effect:

> Now a noble heart has stopped. Good night, dear prince. Good night. And flights of angels sing thee to thy rest. Goodbye, my prince. *(He repeats these lines four times, in different versions.)*[48] Give me the man who is not passion's slave and I will hold him in my heart's core. As I do you. *(Pause.)* Death is a sleep. A sleep. A sleep. A sleep. *(Music rises. Funeral procession continues across the stage and exits left.)*[49]

Shakespeare's *Hamlet* famously opens with a question: "Who's there?" So do all three Arabic translations named in Sobhi's credits: those of Mutran, Jabra, and Abdel Qader al-Qitt (ʿAbd al-Qādir al-Qiṭṭ, 1971).[50] But Sobhi's opening provides an answer, alerting viewers to the main themes of the coming story and letting them relax into the expectation of a death foretold. Borrowing and greatly expanding the brief silent glimpse of Hamlet's funeral that opens Olivier's film, Sobhi creates an atmosphere of ritual grief. Like the overture to an opera, this opening signals that Sobhi's *Hamlet* will not be a play built on suspense. Instead, the emotional chords of the funeral scene will continue to resonate through the rest of the action.

Like both Mutran and Olivier, Sobhi reassigns Fortinbras's lines to Horatio. This removes the contrasting outsider's perspective on the Danish empire's self-destruction; Horatio's praise of Hamlet's "most royal" nature and final instructions for his military funeral are spoken and heard without irony. Continuing to omit Fortinbras (and his threat to Denmark) throughout the play eliminates international politics entirely; the ambassadors Voltemand and Cornelius are also excised, along with scene 4.4. Such editing (which follows Olivier's) settles some of what readers or audiences may find unsettling about

Shakespeare's play: its mysterious opening, its ambiguous politics, and its incongruous conclusion.

But even this framing is not enough for Sobhi. Before the action begins, Sobhi also casts Horatio in the role of *rāwī*, or narrator. As though musing to himself, Horatio speaks (again in film-style voiceover) a lengthy monologue:

> How shall I describe that day? The sky full of fog. The people silent. Eyes far away, cheeks streaked with tears. Bells tolling in the distance, carrying the grievous news. *(Deep sigh.)* The mighty king Hamlet the Elder was dead. I urged Hamlet the young prince to let me go with him to Denmark to attend his father's funeral, but he went ahead. And when I arrived here, in Denmark, there was no funeral, and no signs of mourning. I saw Claudius, the uncle of the prince, who had become a king on the throne, and had married the queen, the wife of his dead brother. From here began the tragedy which ended with the death of the young prince, Hamlet. And only I am left: Horatio, alone, lost. I have to set the people straight and tell them the whole story [*khabar*] of the things that took place, including crimes of passion and blood, deaths put on by fate and forced cause.

Horatio's interior monologue offers some exposition for those few audience members who do not remember the story. This function of a *rāwī* would not have surprised Arab audiences. Some playgoers would have seen or heard about western "memory plays" such as Tennessee Williams's *The Glass Menagerie.*[51] At a deeper level of cultural comfort, they would have seen coffeehouse storytellers and play-within-a-play formats inspired by classical Arabic framed-story collections such as *Kalila and Dimna* and especially *One Thousand and One Nights.* Indeed, Tawfiq al-Hakim had proposed in his 1967 book *Our Theatrical Mold* that a *rāwī* and *rāwiya* (male and female narrators) should anchor a new, authentically Arab form of theatre.[52]

Sobhi, however, uses the *rāwī* device mainly to recast *Hamlet* as a hagiography. Horatio's speech turns the whole ensuing drama into his flashback, coopting the audience to his faithful pro-Hamlet point of view. He sets the scene with maximum pathos: tolling bells, tear-streaked faces.[53] The end of the monologue slips into the words of al-Qitt's translation, but even there, Sobhi edits the text meticulously to support his reading.[54] Horatio promises to tell Hamlet's "story" using the word, *khabar,* that usually refers to the life stories of prophets and saints. (Later he will call it a *sīra,* the word used for the biography of the Prophet Muhammad.) He allows no reference to chance, cutting Horatio's lines about "accidental judgments, casual slaughters," and "purposes mistook / fall'n on the inventors' heads."[55] He even modifies the translation of "cunning and forced cause," changing al-Qitt's *al-ghadar wa-l-qahr* ("perfidy and compulsion") to *al-qadar wa-l-qahr* ("fate and compulsion").[56] Altering just one letter, Sobhi not only improves the alliteration but replaces treachery with fate.

Such textual manipulations—using a speech from act 5 as a prologue, removing its audience, adding a contextualizing monologue, combining different translations, cutting several lines, and micro-editing at the single-word level—exemplify Sobhi's editing strategy throughout the play. Egyptian scholar Abdel Qader al-Qitt (1916–2002), the only one of the three credited translators who could have seen the production, reportedly quarreled with Sobhi over the latter's "tampering with the text."[57] But Sobhi's choices add up to a coherent rereading of *Hamlet*: removing the contingency, replacing it with a deterministic tragic irony. The reviewer Migalli writes: "The contemplative, thinking side of the character is obscured here by the plotting, active side, so that he appears to be a revolutionary fighter, furious and pure, seeking justice and freedom with integrity and honor."[58]

Because he was sure that he had (in his words) "uncovered Shakespeare's meaning,"[59] Sobhi felt free to improve on every actual Shakespearean text, rearranging scenes and amalgamating translations in pursuit of the ideal *Hamlet* in his mind's eye. Several major edits reinforce Hamlet's active heroism even as they push viewers to see events from Hamlet's perspective. For instance, Sobhi gives characters other than Hamlet and Horatio no soliloquies and few asides. He moves the "to be or not to be" soliloquy from act 3, scene 1 into the graveyard scene just before the final duel ("I found the soliloquy's correct place, at the beginning of Act 5," Sobhi told me); the speech, begun while holding Yorick's skull, ends with a rousing slogan-like reprise of the line, "To be or not to be!"[60] And Sobhi deletes the prayer scene, in which Claudius tries to repent and Hamlet passes up a chance to kill him. This cut removes the grounds for accusing Hamlet of hesitation, meanwhile destroying any potential audience sympathy for Claudius.[61]

Finally, Sobhi prolongs the duel scene to twenty minutes and adds a second swordfight, between Hamlet and Claudius. This choice, perhaps guided by Sobhi's desire to show off his fencing skill (he practiced the sport for years and even gave lessons), also affects the plot. Rather than execute his revenge on an unarmed man, Sobhi's Hamlet kills in self-defense, dispatching an endlessly resourceful Claudius. Selfless to the end, Hamlet leaves the kingdom to Horatio, "the son of the common people." Again this is motivated by Sobhi's sense of knowing *Hamlet* better than Shakespeare did himself. As he explained (in 2007): "I don't accept that Hamlet would leave the kingdom to Fortinbras, his enemy and the enemy of the kingdom. It's like if Hosni Mubarak would die and say, okay, Israel can come and occupy and rule my country now. I don't accept it. Hamlet would never do that."[62]

Sobhi's performance, too, follows this patriotic reading of the character. Actor-directors around the world have used *Hamlet* as a star vehicle; Sobhi unabashedly does the same. His Hamlet is a dashing young revolutionary, Che Guevara in doublet and hose. His urgency expresses Egypt's situation at the moment of emerging from the Nasser era of anticolonial struggle, or, as critic Galal al-Ashri (Jalāl al-ʿAshrī) put it at the time, "the moment of leaving the battle for liberation and entering the battle for enlightenment,[63] and on the other side of the canal there awaits us a new battle, the battle of civilization, and a new challenge we have no choice but to confront, and either 'to be or not to be,' as Hamlet put it!!!"[64]

There are moments of humor, of course. Adil Saqr (ʿĀdil Ṣaqr) plays Polonius as a wordy buffoon, not a sinister spymaster. Rosencrantz and Guildenstern occasion much comic business. Sobhi, with his reputation as a comic genius, plays for some laughs as well. Perhaps the most notable comes at the end of the nunnery scene: Hamlet reenters as though repenting his cruelty, bends low to raise up the prostrate and sobbing Ophelia (played by Sobhi's wife Nevine Ramiz [Nīfīn Rāmiz]), walks her around the stage to a crescendo of romantic music, cradles her head, prepares to kiss her . . . and then, with slapstick timing, abruptly drops her on the floor, shouting "No marriage! To a nunnery!" The audience's laughter, audible on the videotape, indexes the playgoers' comic expectations of Sobhi as well as their unconditional sympathy for his Hamlet.[65]

Yet Sobhi's clowning does not detract from the seriousness of his cause. His response to the Ghost, in a scene whose blocking echoes Kozintsev's, is awe, then a firm resolution. (The Ghost itself is staged as an oversized armor helmet projected on the wall.) His moments of antic devilry threaten his enemies: Rosencrantz and Guildenstern, Polonius, and especially Claudius. During the *Mousetrap* scene Hamlet interrupts the play-within-a-play, coming to center stage between Claudius and the actors and shouting at the top of his voice: "This is one Lucianus, *nephew* to the king. He poisons him in the garden for his estate." Claudius and Gertrude run from the stage, more shaken by Hamlet's implicit assassination threat than by the play.

As in Kozintsev's version, the audience is meant to identify with Hamlet throughout. Mahmoud Al-Shetawi reports that Sobhi's production used Brecht-inspired "epic theatre tools" such as placards and captions to break the narrative flow and "foreground his political interpretation of the play."[66] The filmed version, however, uses no alienation effect. Sobhi's prologue sets up an emotional structure that precludes suspense but encourages identification with the hero-martyr. The audience is held close by the magnetic force of Hamlet's character, enthralled by grief, transported beyond itself. As a mourning play, Sobhi's *Hamlet* is tighter than Shakespeare's: with the extraneous details removed, attention is refocused on the hero and his fate.

That fate, the production insists, is shared by a whole generation. Just twenty-two years old when Nasser died, Sobhi does not—perhaps cannot—represent the unavenged Ghost as an actual man. Rather, he creates a disembodied Ghost who represents Hamlet's inner sense of mission—something like the "devouring" political insight felt by Kozintsev's Hamlet. This mission cannot be pursued because the characters of his own generation are too weak to help. In thirty years of interviews, Sobhi has consistently stressed his play's focus on the "conflict of generations," and more specifically on the societal sickness that turns members of the younger generation on each other to create figures like Rosencrantz and Laertes. Critics caught the angry allegory pointing to Sobhi's own peers growing up in the shadow of 1967, a generation betrayed and corrupted by its elders.[67]

Ismat's "Furious Political Struggle"

The anguish of a disappointed generation also fueled the pseudo-subversive *Hamlet* staged by Riad Ismat[68] at an elite Damascus high school in 1973. Ismat's theatre-in-the-round production used traditional European sets and costumes[69] but had a contemporary feel, with music by the popular Lebanese singer Fayruz as well as by Tchaikovsky and Mussorgsky.[70] The young director drew on the interpretation of Jan Kott and the demoralized mood of early 1970s Syrian society. As he writes in a later essay, "*Hamlet* As I Directed It":

> I put forward a contemporary interpretation of Shakespeare's famous play, one with an Arab and progressive significance. During the rehearsals I always emphasized, implicitly or explicitly [*talmīḥan aw taṣrīḥan*], the connection between the play's lines and our own times and with people's thoughts and feelings in our current daily lives, and with the political anger boiling in the people's blood without their having any power to take positive action for change. These were the

> thoughts and feelings that dominated this period after the 1967 defeat, known as the "setback."[71]

Like Sobhi's (which he did not see until five years later), Ismat's *Hamlet* stressed the theme of martyrdom. He used Muhammad Awad Muhammad's newly published Arab League translation but made major cuts and some modernizing revisions, "through which I confirmed my political interpretation of the play."[72] He abridged the text to three acts titled Sorrow, Revolution, and Martyrdom. His program notes reinforced this plot, presenting Hamlet as a "new voice rebelling against the world and the falsehood latent in its depths—the voice that is forced to become a martyr in order to speak the truth."[73]

Ismat, who would later rise to become a high-ranking Syrian diplomat and cultural official, undertook his *Hamlet* with the regime's tacit support. A University of Damascus undergraduate at the time of the 1967 defeat, he was now an energetic 26-year-old director. He had staged *Antigone* at Damascus's Ḥurriyya school the year before, winning a directing award from the Syrian Ministry of Education.[74] Invited back, he wanted to do a frankly political play. He thought of Friedrich Dürrenmatt's *Romulus the Great,* deciding against it because he doubted it would clear the censors.[75] Yet he feared no interference in his "revolutionary" *Hamlet* production—and, he says, encountered none from either the school director or government authorities. Both gave him directorial carte blanche to "dictate" the terms of his production.[76]

Two factors may have contributed to this freedom. First, Ḥurriyya (the name means liberty) was a special place. Founded by the French government in 1925 as the Lycée Laïque (also called Lycée Franco-Arabe), it was renamed Maʿhad al-Ḥurriyya [The Liberty Institute] in 1961 and nationalized in 1967. However, it continued to enjoy a reservoir of freedom secured by its French roots and its ties to Syria's cultural and political ruling class.[77] The play capitalized on this tradition in unexpected ways. For instance, Ismat emphasizes that the "dark, heavyset" young actor playing Hamlet was an unusual casting choice, the opposite of "the traditional slim pale dreamy Hamlet—and this too was a feature of my rationalized interpretation of both the character and the play."[78] Yet the unlikely young man also turned out to be the grandson of the last great Syrian actor to play Hamlet at the National Theatre in Damascus. In the event, grandson Tammam al-Aqil (Tammām al-ʿĀqil) performed the part wearing his grandfather's vintage Hamlet costume and sword, which his grandmother had excavated from an old trunk.[79]

Probably more important in guaranteeing Ismat's artistic freedom in 1973, however, was his play's alignment with the official ideology of the still-young

Hafiz al-Asad regime. Far from threatening the military government or exposing any Claudius-like outrages, Ismat's play meshed well with the Baʿthist revolution's core values: ideological purity in the face of an outside threat, prioritization of collective over private interests, and the politicization of all aspects of social life. The play's "revolutionary" perspective matched that of the new leaders who had unseated the discredited government of Nureddin al-Atassi and Salah Jadid in a "corrective revolution" just three years before.[80] This ideological affinity is clear from Ismat's 1973 program notes:

> Between the thought and the action ... between will and hesitation ... we live with Hamlet as he gradually comes to understand not only the crime that was committed but also the widespread corruption and hypocrisy lurking in the structure of the kingdom.
>
> All of this is not new, and does not justify the adventure of putting on *Hamlet* with amateurs, most of whom are facing the audience and even the art of theatre for the first time in their lives. When I chose to stage *Hamlet*, I didn't care at all about the traditional scholarship and its many studies researching and analyzing and interpreting Shakespeare's characters. I didn't care about Hamlet's hesitation or his anxiety or his madness or the tragedy of his doomed love for Ophelia, and I didn't care to probe the psychological motives pushing him to revenge or delay. What I cared about was the play as a whole and not only its hero (this is the question raised by the famous critic C. S. Lewis).[81] Therefore I deemphasized the individual importance of the character [and instead stressed] his fully conscious involvement in the furious political struggle to purify Denmark from within, preparing it to face the danger of Fortinbras's army and its attack on the country's security. The private love in Hamlet's heart pales before this public love, and his sadness for his father dwindles before his love for his nation.
>
> Here begins the new understanding that we propose. So I am forced to request that you erase from your minds any previous image of the play *Hamlet*, for it is not—as I see it—simply a philosophical or psychological play, but a political play first of all. It is a play full of the spirit of the age, full of a wisdom that has made it still influential even in our present day,

> and applicable to today's philosophy be it through existentialism or Marxism, or some mixture between them (just as the Polish critic and interpreter Jan Kott has pointed out in his book, *Shakespeare Our Contemporary*). . . .
>
> Hamlet is an Arab, despite his European clothing, and he is a contemporary despite the swords and castles and ghosts.[82]

Even more regime-friendly than Ismat's propagandistic phrasing ("widespread corruption and hypocrisy," "struggle to purify Denmark from within," "attack on the country's security," "love for his nation") is his lack of irony. Whereas irony implies a doubleness of message, Ismat exemplifies and urges single-mindedness. His production aims to supplant other versions of Shakespeare's *Hamlet,* actually instructing the audience to "erase" these influences from their minds. He seeks to wipe out the past and substitute a single new, correct, and authoritative reading.

Ismat's 1973 outlook resembles that of Hamlet—the adolescent Hamlet of act 1—upon hearing the story told by the Ghost. Hamlet, too, vows single-mindedness. Shocked by his uncle's betrayal and his mother's corruption, he feels anger (perhaps cognate with the "boiling political anger" Ismat describes), but not despair. Action still seems possible. At that moment, Hamlet's loyalty to his father's cause is undivided. Being of two minds would be hypocrisy—a crime comparable to that of Claudius. The urgency of his cause, Hamlet believes, should erase all competing influences from his mind:

> Remember thee?
> Yea, from the table of my memory
> I'll wipe away all trivial fond records,
> All saws of books, all forms, all pressures past
> That youth and observation copied there,
> And thy commandment all alone shall live
> Within the book and volume of my brain,
> Unmix'd with baser matter.[83]

Ismat's production stressed precisely this "unmix'd" quality in Shakespeare's prince. He presented societal lack of integrity as both the chief enemy and the main impediment in facing that enemy.[84] His program notes describe state institutions as "cracked to the foundations" and urge steadfastness (unity, wholeness) in confronting them:

> Therefore, the important thing is *not the inner torment* of our young prince, but his *sincere attempt* to *demolish a structure*

> *cracked to its very foundations,* and hence his *fully conscious* descent from the tower of the nobles to the vanguard of the cavalry where his sword became famous defending the honor of the kingdom. He reminds us in general of the rebellion of young people of this generation against rotten systems, and in particular he reminds us of the need for our generation to face the reactionary powers that are attempting to thwart its resistance.[85]

Ismat's *Hamlet,* therefore, purported to be "revolutionary." The revolution he urged was in the audience, not the regime. Rather than expose the perfidy of Claudius, the play strove to rouse his audience from the temptation of post-1967 passivity and despair and inspire them to noble action. The didactic program notes draw the contemporary parallel explicitly, almost as though afraid his actors and audience might fail to grasp that the Denmark needing to be "purified from within" is Syrian society.

However, unlike Saadallah Wannus's *Party for June 5,* Ismat's call for "rebellion" names no names, offers no specifics, and accommodates no audience participation. The references to "rotten systems" and "reactionary powers" are abstract; viewers are free to interpret them however they wish, in the silence of the dark auditorium. Available sources (the program notes quoted within the director's essay and the essay itself, surely edited to clear the censors in Damascus)[86] suggest that Ismat's approach was basically similar to the other civic education lectures that his students and their families experienced in a self-proclaimed revolutionary state. His program notes display what Michael Urban (in another context) has called the "rhetorical circularity" typical of ideologically spent revolution-based regimes: an appeal to pursue with renewed vigor the very attitudes and actions that have failed to save the system in the past.[87]

As if sensing this ideological dead end, the program notes further insist: "There is a huge difference between senseless death [*al-mawt al-ʿabathī*] and martyrdom for a cause [*al-shahāda min ajl qaḍīya*]!"[88] But the exclamation point protests too much, revealing how the Arab Hero Hamlet archetype contains the seeds of its own obsolescence. Only a few years after Ismat's earnest production, scorching irony would become the order of the day.

Sadat's Open Door: "To Cook or Not to Cook?"

By the mid- to late 1970s, the Arab Hero Hamlet was a stock character, predictable and even a little passé. Mohamed Sobhi's Cairo *Hamlet* is a good example: its revolutionary message, perhaps rousing in a 1971 student show, was safe even for commercial theatre by the late 1970s. His style, didactic through melodrama and comedy in turn, served what Brecht would have called a "culinary" agenda.[89] That is, the didacticism simply made the play more palatable for those who, like Sobhi himself, felt that theatre should edify. The vague political allegory gave audiences a chance to apply the decoding skills they had learned throughout the 1960s and early 70s, enhancing their enjoyment.[90] (Plays that did not feed the audience's preconceptions, including a 1973 *Hamlet* adaptation in Iraq that mixed ethnography with its politics, were less warmly received.)[91]

The culinary trend took over political theatre as a whole. Rather than advising Arab regimes about reform or smuggling out "hidden transcripts" of political oppression,[92] allegorical plays after the mid-1970s simply provided thoughtful high-class entertainment for members of the Egyptian and Syrian intelligentsia. Ostensibly they aimed to motivate Arab audiences to pursue political and social reform. Yet even directors with Brechtian pretensions no longer achieved an alienation effect: the audience knew the story already, and the president had left his box. Instead, political sensationalism became a familiar plot line and a vehicle for theatrical stardom. Recall that commercial theatregoers found Sobhi's play absorbing and mesmerizing—exactly what Brechtian theatre aims *not* to be.

In Egypt, political theatre was commodified partly in response to new commercial pressures.[93] In his early years President Anwar Sadat (r. 1970–81) at times loosened the formal censorship on newspapers and book publishers; the theatre lost its near-monopoly on serious political discussion. Meanwhile, deprived of the state's ear and wallet, makers of "serious" theatre (still defined as political drama) had to compete with commercial rivals offering sexual titillation and slapstick comedy. While the groundlings tittered and guffawed, critics gnashed their teeth in frustration. Talented adapters like Sobhi cashed in. Less entrepreneurial playwrights, no longer hailed as standard-bearers of a more just political order, simply retreated to the pub.

Shakespeare Comes to 'Ataba

One erudite protest against this culinary trend was Egyptian writer Rafat al-Duwayri's comedy *Shakespeare Rex* (*Shaksbīr Malikan*), staged as *Shakespeare in 'Ataba* in December 1976.[94] The latter title is apt: ʿAtaba Square is a crowded shopping district near downtown Cairo, known for its hundreds of shops and street stalls that sell books, music, toiletries, and cheap knockoffs of brand labels.[95] The neighborhood is also home to several state theatres, including the elegant (though in the 1970s somewhat rundown) National Theatre, and a major hub for the buses and minivans that bring several million commuters daily to low-paying jobs in Cairo. ʿAtaba thus captures the intersecting economic and theatrical concerns that frame al-Duwayri's play: in an "age of quick consumption," is it any longer meaningful (or even possible) to produce works like *Hamlet*?

Al-Duwayri (b. 1937) studied English literature at Cairo's ʿAyn Shams University before beginning to direct and then write plays in the 1960s and 70s. *Shakespeare Rex* is his second play. Rather than Hamlet, his protagonist is Shakespeare himself: an aspiring young playwright, author of a few comedies beloved by the capricious Queen Elizabeth. The play, written largely in Egyptian colloquial Arabic (but with Shakespeare quotations in literary Arabic), is bewilderingly intertextual. In the epilogue-as-prologue, for instance, Shakespeare's funeral in Stratford-upon-Avon is attended by mourners including the mad Ophelia (played by a boy) and the suicidal Romeo and Juliet. A priest recites from Ecclesiastes amid much weeping. The funeral is a medley of graveyard scenes from various Shakespeare plays. For instance, Hamlet pulls a skull out of Shakespeare's grave:

> Hamlet: Horatio, do you believe Shakespeare our creator looks like this in his tomb?
> Horatio: Of course, my lord Hamlet.
> Hamlet: And smells thus? Uff!
> Horatio: Of course, my lord Hamlet.[96]

After the prologue, the action proceeds at breakneck speed. The young Shakespeare's life is interwoven with fragments from his plays. His speech echoes that of his own characters, especially Hamlet and Macbeth, but he also converses with them. (At one point he gets an acting lesson from Hamlet, who tells him not to "saw the air with his hands.")[97] The dramatis personae include Falstaff, King Lear and Cordelia, Laertes, Gertrude, Claudius, Hamlet, Horatio, Macbeth and Lady Macbeth, among others, as well as Thomas Kyd, Christopher Marlowe (double-cast as Banquo's Ghost), Queen Elizabeth (who plays Gertrude in a version of the closet scene with Shakespeare as Hamlet), the Earl of Essex, and the Lord Chamberlain. There are long inset pieces in which actors perform excerpts from Shakespeare's plays, including some less-well-known ones such as *The Merry Wives of Windsor*. These are drawn mostly from the translations recently issued by the Arab League, lightly edited by al-Duwayri. In general, the play presupposes a very high level of audience interest in and knowledge about Shakespeare.

Yet under this madhouse collage, the story is simple and sad. The prologue sets a tone of real grief and loss—like Sobhi's opening scene and others of the period, it represents the funeral of the hero.[98] The second scene finds Shakespeare, age twenty-eight, drinking beer at an inn, trying to write and muttering to himself: "To cook or not to cook? [*uṭbukh aw lā uṭbukh?*] That is the problem." He recites the recipe for successful plays: a sprinkling of love scenes, a dash of demons and witches, some laughter, dancing, singing—a good dish for Her Majesty to digest.[99] He has written *Henry IV, Part 1,* but not yet *Hamlet* and the other major tragedies.[100] A bright young writer of comedies and histories, Shakespeare needs a modicum of financial security to undertake the great tragedies of which he knows he is capable. Yet it seems he can gain this security only by selling out further. "Fame, wealth, popularity," he chants; this mantra is then taken up and repeated by three witches who come to tempt him, Macbeth-like, to pursue his ambitions.[101] He resolves his Hamlet-like dilemma by deciding to hesitate no longer: "To write or not to write? To cook or not to cook? That's the problem. No, wait—to write and to cook, and no problem whatsoever!"[102]

Duwayrī angles his reading of British history to critique Egypt's contemporary situation. His Elizabeth is a complex character, imperious but eager to be appreciated. In this and her close attention to the theatre she recalls Gamal Abdel Nasser. She is sensitive enough to understand political allegory, autocratic enough to silence it.[103] Yet it is not Elizabeth's censorship that starts to corrode Shakespeare's art but rather her sincere enjoyment of his comedies. After *The Merry Wives of Windsor* he apologizes to his own creation, the hapless Falstaff, for submitting them both to Her Majesty's poor taste:

> Falstaff: Did I tell you to create me? Did you ask my opinion when you created me? I wish you had never created me, Shaykhspeare.[104]
> Shakespeare: You rebel against your existence, Falstaff?
> Falstaff: My existence? My existence in a laundry basket? My existence buried under a pile of stinking filthy clothes? May God forgive you, Shaykhspeare.
> Shakespeare (*laughing*): So quit your skirt-chasing and your drooling over the respectable women of Windsor.
> Falstaff: But you made me like this! You think I'd run after Mrs. Page just because I felt like it?
> Shakespeare: I didn't feel like it either, Falstaff.
> Falstaff: How's that? Who felt like it then, O creator?
> Shakespeare: Her Majesty felt like it.

> Falstaff: Oh . . . Her Majesty [. . .]
> Shakespeare: Her Majesty Queen Elizabeth.
> Falstaff (*Whispers, after looking around*): Hush, my creator.
> Shakespeare: Her Majesty saw you before, in my play *Henry IV*. You won her heart (*with pride*) and the hearts of all the audiences of London. (*Whistles with his mouth and shouts clamorously, imitating the London audiences. Then:)* Falstaff! Falstaff, I wish I had never created you!
> Falstaff: I'm the one who created you, William Shakespeare, and the money raining down on you.
> Shakespeare: In fourteen days I wrote the play *Merry Wives of Windsor* and made you its hero.
> Falstaff: Like boiling an egg—you cooked up this play the way I was cooking under all that dirty laundry. . . . Oh, it stank . . . God forgive you, Shakespeare. God forgive you. (*Exits, crying*)[105]

Like Falstaff, Shakespeare cannot help himself. His momentary pensiveness is drowned out by a flood of money raining on him from the ceiling. Immediately some criers enter, announcing the *Comedy of Errors*. His moral and artistic compromises continue.[106] A conversation with Christopher Marlowe (a resolute antimonarchist) shows that in betraying his artistic principles, Shakespeare has abdicated his political responsibility as well. Marlowe favors socialist realism:[107]

> Shakespeare: Is it true, Mr. Marlowe? So my first attempt [at play writing] that I wrote back when I was still in Stratford, before coming to London . . . you liked it?
> Marlowe: An authentic work: from the mud and dust of your village. If only, William, you could hold on to your roots. . . .
> Shakespeare: And the *Comedy of Errors*. . . .
> Marlowe (*interrupting*): The beginning of your descent down the slippery slope, William.
> Shakespeare: But the people liked it . . . they laughed. . . . The people also want to rest their minds from their troubles . . . and the court as well.
> Marlowe (*interrupts him*): It's the court that wants the people's minds at ease, William. The same people whom you're underestimating, William. The same people who

welcomed my last play, *The Struggle (Al-Niḍāl)*, a real tragedy.[108] And before this these same people you're underestimating welcomed *Tamburlaine* and *Doctor Faustus* and *Edward II*, and *The Jew of Malta*. . . . And they liked them. . . . And also don't forget Thomas Kyd's *Spanish Tragedy*. . . . What do you say, William?

Shakespeare: But, but Mr. Marlowe, I just need a little fame, a little popularity, a little money.[109]

Things are bad for artists under al-Duwayri's Queen Elizabeth. Yet whatever small space is available for creativity and political integrity under Elizabeth closes totally under her successor. Al-Duwayri's Elizabeth (read Nasser) imposes insipid taste and censorship, sometimes closing the theatres, but at least she is interested in what goes on there. His King James (read Sadat) has no interest in theatre of any kind. He is too busy opening up the economy for profiteering, fostering a quick-consumption society, and making peace with England's longtime enemy, Spain, whose armada Elizabeth so steadfastly opposed.[110] In James's court, frivolous French and Italian clothing prevails. Fast modern music blares. Shakespeare's troupe, now called The King's Men, wears gold-embroidered livery but cannot perform anything Shakespeare considers real theatre. The troupe's most important task is to impress the visiting Spanish ambassador with skits and acrobatics while serving food (again, culinary entertainment) at a banquet in his honor.[111] As Shakespeare and his troupe complain to each other:

Troupe (*in unison*): The audiences of London aren't what they were.

Shakespeare: Plays are written for the court, not the people.

Troupe (*in unison*): The people's taste now is just like the court's.

Shakespeare: It's the age . . . the age of James I.

Troupe (*one after the other*):

—It's an age with a crushed soul.

—An age of quick-grab commercial deals.

—Instant-grab. Grab and run.

—The age of quick consumption.

—The age of light meals.[112]

This state of affairs saps the will of al-Duwayri's Shakespeare entirely. He returns in disgust to Stratford, his "womb." His last line invokes death and recalls the funeral scene with which the play started: "To the belly of the earth from which I came, I will return, I will return, I will return."[113] Thereafter he keeps silent, drinking heavily until his death.

Rafat al-Duwayri's play, then, offers a requiem for the 1960s, usually known as the golden age of Arab drama. Opening with a funeral, it satirizes the contemporary Egyptian situation, an "age of quick-grab commercial deals" no longer conducive to the making of serious art. As a subset of serious art, political theatre, too, has lost its role. Thus the satire addresses the audience rather than the regime—but it is an ironic appeal, one whose failure al-Duwayri expects in advance. Although *Shakespeare in ʿAtaba* played for thirty-five nights at the state-run Ṭalīʿa (Vanguard) Theatre and drew a respectable 6,245 spectators,[114] the play puts no great faith in the mobilizing power of theatre. Some features of al-Duwayri's script, such as elaborate but unstageable stage directions, suggest he was writing more for the page than the stage.[115] "The audiences," as his characters observe, "aren't what they were," because "the people's taste is now just like the court's."

A Dilemma

This chapter has explored several incarnations of the Arab Hero Hamlet. We have seen how this revolutionary hero came into his own as the representative of a betrayed and justice-minded new generation after the 1967 defeat. This Hamlet, driven by the sense that the "time is out of joint" and that he is "born to set it right," is a fighter for justice, brutally martyred by an oppressive regime. Known only in foreign (Soviet-bloc) versions before 1967, he grew to be expected by Arab critics and cultured audiences alike in the 1970s. Versions appeared in Syria and Egypt and in state-run, commercial, and high school productions.

As we have seen, the Arab Hero Hamlet is neither a Nasser nor an anti-Nasser, but he cannot be understood outside the context of the Arab nationalist hopes Nasser first inspired and then disappointed. Nasserism's collapse after 1967 filled young theatre people in Egypt and other Arab countries with something like the white-hot "passion for cognition" that the Soviet director Kozintsev describes in his Hamlet: "the aspiration to discover the meaning behind what is happening."[116] Then Nasser's death in 1970 cast the dead leader as Hamlet's father, a ghost whose moral demands could neither be fulfilled nor ignored. Abandoning previous efforts to reform their regimes, therefore, the dramatists took their anger directly to the public. They posed what they saw as Hamlet's question: how to confront injustice, or what to do with a political structure "cracked to its very foundations."[117] These playwrights and directors worked bravely and idealistically through the post-1967 "thaw." But it was only about a decade before this effort, too, brought them to a dead end.

By 1976, as al-Duwayri's play shows, serious theatre had become largely "culinary," and playwrights and audiences knew it. The theatre was no longer a branch of the government; political leaders neither heeded its advice nor used it as a communication channel with the people. Censorship continued mainly out of old habit or increasingly generalized paranoia. Disappointing, too, were Brechtian efforts to use the theatre for grassroots community mobilization or mass civic education. The audiences, unwilling to mobilize politically, were as disappointing as the regimes.[118] Playgoers mainly wanted entertainment—albeit *politics as* entertainment.

Dismay spread through theatre communities in Egypt, Syria, and elsewhere in the Arab world. Many writers went into exile. Syrian writer Saadallah Wannus, whose *Party for June 5* had opened the floodgates for a frank new strain of drama after 1967, kept silent for thirteen years, from 1977 to 1990.[119] Alfred Farag (author of *Sulayman of Aleppo*; see chapter 4) exiled himself from Egypt (1973–86), writing plays in Egyptian Arabic that were neither produced nor published. He and others blamed the "crisis" or "decline" of Arab theatre on many factors: lack of state funding, emigration of writers and critics, high ticket prices, lack of central planning of theatre seasons, and so forth.[120] Yet beyond these signs of neglect, the lull in production points to playwrights' and directors' basic uncertainty about the purpose of drama. Veiled allegory and direct talk had each run their course, and political justice was no closer. Why should the rest not be silence?

One of the few modes remaining was irony. The next chapter will examine six Arab *Hamlet* offshoot plays produced or published since 1976, at least five of which are written in an ironic mode. Rather than present *Hamlet* as a nationalist allegory or a passion play about justice, these plays adopt a post-allegorical tone; they deploy audience knowledge of Shakespeare's text for dramatic irony, not moral heft. Several of them play intertextual games as dizzying as al-Duwayri's. Identifying more with Shakespeare than with his Hamlet, their authors seek a language still worth speaking in a world where injustice is a permanent fact. They are aware of their Arab predecessors' *Hamlet*s as well as Shakespeare's text and foreign versions. They are latecomers to the Arab nationalist parade, left to improvise among the trampled banners and deflated balloons. Yet they continue to work with Shakespeare, forging a purpose for him and for themselves in light of the elusiveness of their societies' revolutionary dreams.

6

SIX PLAYS IN SEARCH OF A PROTAGONIST, 1976–2002

Early in *Hamlet Wakes Up Late* (1976), a satirical *Hamlet* adaptation by Syrian playwright Mamduh Adwan (1941–2004),[1] the protagonist describes a macabre scene nowhere present in Shakespeare's *Hamlet*. Half-drunk and sobbing, Hamlet confesses that he has just exhumed his father's coffin:

> Horatio: Answer me, Hamlet. What happened?
> Hamlet (*about to cry*): I saw my father.
> Horatio: Have you started imagining him again?
> Hamlet: It's not imagination, Horatio. I saw him. I went to the grave and I saw him.
> Horatio: Why did you go to the grave?
> Hamlet (*tired*): It came over me, Horatio. Wherever I turn I see his picture. I wanted to make sure that he was not leaving his grave and coming out to me. I can't bear it anymore. I was drinking with them and suddenly he appeared in front of me as usual. I got up right away and rushed to the cemetery.
> Horatio: And what's the good of your going to the cemetery?
> Hamlet: I opened the coffin. Oh God, Horatio. A disgusting thing. Is that what happens to dead people? Imagine. . . . My father . . . has become . . . (*He cannot find the words.*)
> Horatio: How could you open the coffin of a man who's been dead a month? Are you mad?

Hamlet: He's my father.
Horatio: Even if he is your father. How could you open the coffin?
Hamlet: I couldn't bear it anymore. Nothing was doing me any good. If I drank I saw him and if I slept I saw him and if I embraced a woman I saw him. Look. (*Takes a book from his pocket.*) I'm even reading the Gospels to escape from him. But Christ himself talks about nothing but his father! What do I do? What do I do? (*Collapses.*) O God, Horatio, if you saw the image in that coffin. My father. My father in his greatness and his might was a heap of bones. (*Shakes his head to chase out the picture.*) I didn't find his clear eyes or his wrinkled brow. I didn't find his dreams or his faith or his pride or his wrath. (*Explodes.*) All I found were bones and maggots![2]

Published in 1976 and staged at the National Theatre in Damascus in January 1978,[3] *Hamlet Wakes Up Late* bitterly spoofs the Arab Hero Hamlet tradition of the early 1970s. The premise alludes transparently to contemporary politics. Elsinore (read: the Arab world) is recovering from a bitter defeat by Fortinbras (Israel/the West), who still occupies a piece of its land (the Golan Heights/Palestine); the new king (Sadat) is treacherously planning to make peace with Fortinbras. In Adwan's Denmark *everything* is rotten. A murderous new regime has empowered a network of traitors, petty crooks, and informers. Laertes is a coward; Ophelia a whore who seeks only to seduce Hamlet and capture the throne; Rosencrantz and Guldenshtern [*sic*][4] work as spies for Polonius, who heads a sinister semi-independent intelligence service. In this nest of vipers, the late-waking Hamlet is helpless but far from blameless. An alcoholic amateur theatre director, he lets personal grudges blind him to the kingdom's deeper rot. As Mahmoud Al-Shetawi puts it, he "embodies the image of the educated Arab in the sense that he is always taken by surprise."[5] His action against the Claudius regime is belated and ineffectual, leading only to a swift show trial and ignominious death.

As the quoted scene with Horatio shows, Adwan's caricature of the post-1967 Arab intellectual has a tragic side. Hamlet is haunted by a ghost he can neither forget nor satisfy. Its repeated silent visitations drive him to the cemetery; there, he confronts the "bones and maggots" that remain of his father and the principles his father represented. In the late 1970s, as Egypt pursued a separate peace with Israel that would destroy the last pretense of Arab unity, Adwan's meaning was clear enough. Hamlet's father was the late Gamal Abdel Nasser, and his pan-Arab ideals had failed to deliver. Now his ghost still appeared but had nothing to say. The new order had arrived; to accept it was treachery, but to resist it would be suicide.

Adwan's is both the earliest and the most politically explicit of the six Arab rewritings of *Hamlet* examined in this chapter, but its approach is typical. The plays analyzed here were performed in the period 1976 to 2002 (see table 6.1). They meet four fairly neutral criteria: 1) Arabic language or an overtly Arab setting; 2) explicit reference to Shakespeare's *Hamlet* in either the title or character names; 3) acknowledged rewriting in the playwright's own words rather than purported translation of Shakespeare's text; and 4) an available manuscript or published text.[6] Aside from these basic features, they vary widely. Their authors are of six different nationalities (Syrian, Jordanian, Egyptian, Iraqi, Tunisian, British/Kuwaiti); two are émigrés. The plays span a quarter-century and were meant for different audiences; one (*Ismail/Hamlet*) is written in Syrian colloquial Arabic, another (*Al-Hamlet Summit*) in English, and the remaining four at various levels of standard Arabic.[7] Predictably, then, these plays differ in plot, verbal register, and visual style. Yet at least five of the six conform, to a striking degree, to a single ironic pattern. (And the sixth, as we will see, is the exception that proves the rule.)

Silencing Hamlet

At the heart of this pattern is a self-conscious belatedness with respect to both Shakespeare's *Hamlet* and Arab political theatre. (It is apparent even in Adwan's title, *Hamlet Wakes Up Late.*) Unlike early 1970s productions such as Sobhi's and Ismat's, the post-1976 rewritings do not aim to be authoritative renditions of Shakespeare's *Hamlet.* They do not seek to "wipe out" or displace Shakespeare's text from the audience's minds. Instead they stake out a new position between Shakespeare and their audience, emphasizing their plays' divergences from an "original" *Hamlet* that remains present in memory as a dialogizing background.[8] They present themselves as commentary, not news. Audiences are forced to watch them with "binocular vision," keeping both the received and new versions in mind.[9]

Our rewriters can play this game because their audiences already know (the stock Arab interpretation of) their "original" rather well. By the mid-1970s, as we have seen, Arab stage tradition had cast Hamlet as a justice-seeking Arab revolutionary hero. A far cry from him are the ineffective, inarticulate, often alcoholic blunderers now shown on stage. Audiences are invited to weigh the new protagonists against the old and to find them wanting: they

Table 6.1
Six Arab Hamlet Offshoot Plays (1976–2004)

Play	Author (nationality)	Year published or produced	First director	City produced	Synopsis
Hamlet Wakes Up Late	Mamdūḥ ʿAdwān (Syrian)	Published 1976; performed January 1978	Mamdūḥ ʿAdwān	Damascus	Drunkard theatre-director prince awakens too late to the political implications of his father's murder, uncle's dictatorship, and kingdom's impending peace deal with Fortinbras; he is condemned in a show trial and executed.
A Theatre Company Found a Theatre. . . and "Theatred" Hamlet	Nādir ʿUmrān (Jordanian)	1984	Khālid al-Ṭarīfī	Rabat, then Amman	An Arab prince hires a troupe to stage *Hamlet* to "catch the conscience" of his usurping stepfather/uncle. It fails; actors overpower director, claiming autonomy of theatre.
The Dance of the Scorpions	Maḥmūd Abū Dūma (Egyptian)	Published 1988, performed 1989 and 1991	Maḥmūd Abū Dūma	Alexandria	Claudius conspires with Fortinbras in a phony war to extort money from nobles and sideline the largely apolitical Hamlet. But domestic opposition ("Crusaders") stage a revolution.
Forget Hamlet/ Ophelia's Window	Jawād al-Asadī (Iraqi)	Performed 1994, published 2000	Jawād al-Asadī	Cairo	Ophelia watches Claudius murder the king and inaugurate a reign of terror unopposed by passive Hamlet; dissident Laertes is liquidated; gravediggers provide sarcastic commentary.
Ismail/Hamlet	ʿAbd al-Hakīm al-Marzūqī (Tunisian)	1999, 2001, 2010–11	Rūlā Fattāl (Syrian)	London and Cairo	Ismail's mother seduced by *hammam* owner Abu Saʿid, who puts Ismail and his mother to work in the baths. Later Ismail (whom a friend nicknames Hamlet) becomes a corpse-washer. Play is his monologue as he washes Abu Sa'id's corpse.
The Al-Hamlet Summit	Sulayman Al-Bassam (Kuwaiti/ British)	2002 (English-language production); 2004 (expanded Arabic version); published 2006	Sulayman Al-Bassam	Edinburgh, Cairo, London. In Arabic: Tokyo, Seoul, Tehran, etc.	Crumbling Arab dictatorship (a collage of real states) convenes government conference amid car bombs in the capital, rebellion in the south, and an international army massed on the borders. Arms dealer sells to all, including Islamist Hamlet and suicide bomber Ophelia.

are Hamlets in name alone. The contrast is flagged explicitly for any audience members who might miss it. In *Forget Hamlet,* by Iraqi playwright/director Jawad al-Assadi, Horatio bursts out: "You are not the Hamlet I know and have lived with." Hamlet responds with infuriating blankness: "Well, maybe I should change my name."[10]

The new Hamlet lacks power—most notably, *verbal* power. One might have expected late-twentieth-century rewritings to deploy Hamlet's eloquence to advance a political message about rotten states and out-of-joint times, or alternatively (like Stoppard's *Rosencrantz and Guildenstern*) to sustain a leap into the nontopical absurd. Instead, the new Hamlets tend not to be eloquent at all. Five of the protagonists analyzed in this chapter experience breakdowns of meaningful human speech: they collapse into incoherence and tears at crucial moments, listen silently as other characters spit their own best lines at them, leave their most famous soliloquies to be parceled out to several actors or read posthumously by gravediggers, or find no hearers but the deaf and the dead.

Non-Arab *Hamlet* plays, on the whole, do not exhibit this pattern. Many post-1975 *Hamlets* from other regions do share some features of the Arab adaptations examined here—Brechtian framing effects, downsized lists of dramatis personae, abbreviated texts, intertextual collages, allusions to contemporary politics, sexual explicitness, absurdism, and so forth—but it is highly unusual in an adaptation from any country for Hamlet to lose his dominant speaking role.[11] Observers have commented on the ideological importance assigned in Arab societies to rhetorical virtuosity: fluent and even artful language use is an index of competence, power, and manly virtue. For the Yemeni tribesman, as Steven Caton puts it, "to wax poetic is honorable, to blather inconsequentially is not."[12] Many nontribal Arabs absorb such values "by descent, by affiliation or by appropriation (through the medium of language and literature) of [the tribal] ideal of human excellence and standards of beauty."[13] In this context it is doubly striking to find such an inarticulate set of Arab protagonists.

Bleeding out from the disappointing Hamlet figure, belatedness marks every aspect of these plays. It underlies several key formal features: foreshortened exposition, a disjointed or circular temporal framework, and explicit intertextual comparisons to Shakespeare's *Hamlet.* The audience's familiarity with (a certain interpretation of) Shakespeare offers instant access to a set of editorializing tricks that would otherwise require great dexterity. The old play is allowed to haunt the new one.[14] As in a nightmare, time runs backward, in circles, or in a flashback structure where Hamlet always seems to "wake up late." The other characters seem already to know the script; Shakespeare's text is often replaced with offstage commentary on itself.

On the thematic level, too, these plays exploit and dash their audiences' expectations. Political art's pretensions are debunked. Claudius is mythified as a beast, able to seduce or devour everyone in his path. Most shocking of all, the dead King Hamlet is unmasked as a weakling or a liar. Thus Hamlet is a failure, but his circumstances are such that even a stronger protagonist would have no chance. The result, heightened by sordid extra-Shakespearean tableaux that include the audience in Hamlet's humiliation (Claudius and Gertrude spitting on the dead king's corpse, Hamlet overhearing his mother's and uncle's bedroom banter, Claudius shaking hands with the foreign enemy Fortinbras, Claudius seducing Ophelia, etc.), is a world where the committed artist or intellectual has no place to stand. The "unweeded garden" of Hamlet's imagination spreads to cover the whole play; heroism is no longer possible. The protagonist is caught in a no-win choice between his impotent ideals (the ghost of Nasserism is never far from view) and a monstrous reality.

"A Play Can't Stab"

Why did the formal trappings of postmodernism—the belated work's circularity and self-reference—become so thematically useful after 1975? As I argued in the previous chapter, Arab drama had reached an impasse. Audiences, trained by two decades of decoding political plays, clamored to use the hermeneutic skills they had developed. Yet allegorical drama had failed to produce concrete political change, instead becoming merely a form of high-class entertainment. Audiences remained as passive and disempowered as ever. Exposing the emperor's nudity in public was not enough: he remained on the throne, his power obscene in its nakedness.[15] To dwell on his abuses would just flatter the regime, reaffirming its power to outlast its brightest critics. It would also pander to the audience's desire to be entertained—a function "serious" Arabic theatre has always tried to avoid.

Let us reframe the artistic problem, as several of our playwrights do, in terms of *Hamlet*'s play-within-a-play. In Shakespeare, Hamlet's political rewriting of the Italian play *The Murder of Gonzago*, which he re-titles *The Mousetrap*,[16] has an intended audience and a purpose. It aims to "catch the conscience of the King" and, by providing "relative" (publicly sharable) evidence of Claudius's guilt, to convince those in the Danish court who might doubt the Ghost's veracity or question Hamlet's fitness to rule a post-Claudius Elsinore:[17]

> Hum—I have heard
> That guilty creatures sitting at a play,
> Have, by the very cunning of the scene,

Been struck so to the soul that presently
They have proclaim'd their malefactions.
For murder, though it have no tongue, will speak
With most miraculous organ. I'll have these players
Play something like the murder of my father
Before mine uncle. I'll observe his looks;
I'll tent him to the quick. If a do blench,
I'll know my course. The spirit that I have seen
May be a devil, and the devil hath power
T'assume a pleasing shape, yea, and perhaps,
Out of my weakness and my melancholy,
As he is very potent with such spirits,
Abuses me to damn me. I'll have grounds
More relative than this. The play's the thing
Wherein I'll catch the conscience of the King. [18]

The Mousetrap is an ingenious mechanism, set up so that the prey himself will trigger it. To end the performance, Claudius must expose that he feels addressed or targeted by the action onstage, making explicit the act of interpretation the actors have only implied.[19] Fortunately for Hamlet, Claudius betrays himself.[20] He loses his composure in part because he is a generally insecure and fearful character (listen to his nervously hypercorrect verse in the council scene) but in part because *The Mousetrap* catches him by surprise. This it could do only once.[21] His apparently involuntary reaction—rising from his chair, calling for more light—marks the success of the play.

By contrast, a variety of failures can be imagined. What if the king *has* no conscience? What if he has seen another *Mousetrap*-like play before and is on his guard? What if he is so powerful that "exposure" as a murderer would only confirm his brute power to marginalize his critics (e.g., as drunkards or madmen) and to dictate which truths are mouthed in his kingdom?[22] What if his confession is useless because there is no court to hear the evidence? All six of our plays take such failure for granted. The earliest three explicitly confront the artist's resulting dilemma.

Hamlet Wakes Up Late

In Adwan's *Hamlet Wakes Up Late,* the protagonist's theatrical pursuits are portrayed as a self-indulgent substitute for action. Hamlet's abortive play-within-a-play, titled *Shahrayar* and loosely based on *One Thousand and One Nights,*[23] accomplishes nothing. The problem is that Hamlet fixates on the personal betrayals of his mother and friends, who stand for the feminine and private realm, but ignores the much greater injustices committed against his father and "the people" in the public, masculine realm. When he finally awakens to politics, it is too late: his brief challenge to the regime's domination of the symbolic sphere is easily silenced.

The play *Shahrayar,* devised long before Hamlet learns that the King has killed his father, is a simple projection screen for Hamlet's moods. For instance, after an angry conversation with the Queen he splices in a scene: a woman fans the dirt on her husband's grave, hoping to make it dry faster, because he had told her not to remarry while it was still wet.[24] When he learns the street rumors of his father's murder, Hamlet impulsively adds it to his play-in-progress. Unlike Shakespeare's prince, he has no plan to obtain evidence and no intent to kill the King. Horatio realizes immediately that Hamlet's play is mere self-expression, not (as it purports to be) political action:

> Hamlet: I have to verify whether they murdered him. (*To himself*) So this is the secret of his [the Ghost's] visits. He wants me to avenge him! (*Aloud*) Listen. We'll change the play again. Shahrayar enters and instead of surprising his wife with the servant, he surprises her with his own brother!
>
> Horatio: What's the use of that?
>
> Hamlet: We'll turn the play into a lure. We'll turn it into a stab.
>
> Horatio: A play can't stab.
>
> Hamlet: Let us work and don't interfere. Listen. Shahrayar enters. No. No. Listen.
>
> Lorenzo: Can I make a suggestion? Shahrayar is visiting his brother. The brother enters and surprises Shahrayar with his wife. Shahrayar kills his brother in order to cover up the scandal and keep the woman.
>
> Guldenshtern: Then the woman doesn't die at the end.
>
> Hamlet (*Angrily, in thought*): No. Not now. Not yet. Not yet.
>
> Guldenshtern: Then we could call it anything at all. Why *Shahrayar*? We have to provide a motivation for why Shahrayar decided to start killing women.

> Rosencrantz: After Shahrayar murders his brother, he repents and feels that the woman was the one who pushed him to this crime.
>
> Hamlet: No, no. Shahrayar has not repented yet. There is no evidence of his repentance. And the woman didn't push him to kill his brother. He, in his baseness and vileness, kills his brother. He kills him out of greed for his wife and his throne.[25]

Hamlet's allegorical script does not "catch the conscience of the King." Instead, Hamlet learns that his friend Rosencrantz is spying for Polonius, who reports to the King—and the one "caught" is Hamlet. Rather than unmask the royal wrongdoer, Hamlet's playmaking simply tips his hand and endangers his friends:

> King: Is it true that you've made changes in the story of Shahrayar?
>
> Hamlet (*looking at Rosencrantz*): Did you hear of this, my lord?
>
> King: You didn't answer my question.
>
> Hamlet: I didn't realize you took such a deep interest in the theatre.
>
> Polonius: His Majesty takes an interest in everything.
>
> Hamlet: It seems there are those who know His Majesty's interests better than I do.
>
> King: I want to know why you are making these adjustments.
>
> Hamlet: As a kind of surprise for the audience. The audience knows the story of Shahrayar, and it would be boring for them to see the story just as they know it. I said to myself, "Let's make some adjustments to suit our time."
>
> Polonius: But this is not acceptable.
>
> Hamlet: It's acceptable, Mr. Polonius. Stories are adjusted in the theatre just as the places to which emergency aid supplies must be sent can be adjusted.
>
> King: I disagree.
>
> Hamlet: Will you perform with us, my lord?
>
> King: I'm not joking, Hamlet.

Hamlet: May I know the reason for your objection?
King: You're talking back to the king too much. Discussion closed: this is an order. I will not allow the chaos that prevailed in your father's day to continue. (*Turns to leave.*) Polonius, you will attend the rehearsals.
Polonius: As you wish, my lord. But wouldn't it be better for Rosencrantz to continue taking care of this matter, so I can be free for my other obligations?
King: The important thing is that you are responsible for the final performance. (*To Hamlet*) You will receive instructions from Polonius (*Exits*).[26]

This round goes to the King. Hamlet's claim that the artist deserves the same discretionary power as the dictator ("Stories are adjusted in the theatre just as the places to which emergency aid supplies must be sent can be adjusted") is summarily dismissed. To the extent that the King makes a counterargument at all, it is to portray censorship as a defense of public order: "I will not allow the chaos that prevailed in your father's day to continue." Hamlet abandons his play after (uselessly) shouting at the informer Rosencrantz: "Isn't your name Brutus? . . . Aren't you playing the part of Brutus? . . . Or Judas? . . . Tell the king I need to make a new change in the play. One friend betrays his friend in the play."[27] Next time he will attack in a more literal vein.

At the beginning of the second act, Adwan's Hamlet mounts another brief symbolic challenge. He chooses a moment when Fortinbras, the enemy-turned-investor who promises to revive the economy, is visiting the kingdom. Whereas some issues of domestic politics can be handled with brutal literalness (bribing allies, intimidating or jailing opponents), foreign investors respond to symbols. Hamlet and the King both understand this. The King therefore orders Polonius to organize "demonstrations of joy" (*maẓāhir al-saʿāda*)[28] to show Fortinbras that the kingdom is stable—that is, that its rulers are at least powerful enough to compel such displays.[29] Inside the palace, too, he stages what Horatio wryly calls "a really exciting scene" ("*kān al-mashhad muthīran ḥaqqan*"):[30] the King welcomes Fortinbras as "a brother and a friend," Fortinbras responds pleasantly, and they toast their plans for joint ventures to spur economic growth. Into this festive moment walks Hamlet, visibly drunk and quoting the Gospel of Matthew:[31]

Hamlet (*appears, sitting on the window*): Beware, my lords. You are drinking blood.
Ophelia: Hamlet!

Queen: Why are you entering from there?
Hamlet: Enter by the narrow gate, for wide is the gate and broad is the way that leads to destruction.[32]
Fortinbras: Splendid! Splendid! He recites the Gospels wonderfully. (*Applauds joyfully.*)
Hamlet (*continues, ignoring his comment and coming down from the window*): Beware of false prophets, who come to you in sheep's clothing, but inwardly they are ravenous wolves. You will know them by their fruits. Do men gather grapes from thornbushes or figs from thistles? (*Reaches the banquet table and takes a piece of bread*) Then he broke bread and said: Take. This is my body.[33]
Queen: No doubt he is drunk. We should not have brought him in.[34]

The drinking and playacting of Adwan's Hamlet serve the same double-edged dramatic purpose as Hamlet's madness in Shakespeare. Licensing Hamlet's free speech, they also provide a convenient rubric the King can use to shunt him aside. For once, however, Hamlet refuses to be dismissed as an actor or a drunk. He overturns the banquet table, physically disrupting the orchestrated display of order and mastery:

Hamlet *(continues, not paying attention to anyone):* So the Lord Christ entered one day into the Temple (*approaches the table*) and saw merchants and money-changers selling doves there, and he was angry.
Queen: Listen, listen. He's acting!
Hamlet: And he raised his voice and beat them, then he overturned their tables (*overturns the table in front of them*) and the chairs of the dove-sellers and he shouted at them (*Hamlet faces them and shouts at the top of his voice*), You have turned my father's house into a den of thieves! (*Shouts even louder*) O sons of adders, you have turned my father's house into a den of thieves, merchants, traitors, and enemies. You have turned my father's house into a shelter for prostitution, trade, and treachery. You have turned my father's blood into a deal to profit from and a throne to sit on. You have extended your hands to shake the hand smeared with your children's blood. (*Fortinbras turns to walk out in protest. Hamlet follows him, shouting.*)

> And when he entered the city, the city trembled, shouting "Who is this?" And the martyrs rose from their graves in disbelief.[35]

Unlike the easily intercepted *Shahrayar* play, Hamlet's banquet performance targets the King and Queen where they are vulnerable. It bypasses their "conscience," instead challenging their symbolic mastery of the sensitive public occasion. Being improvised, the intertextual terrorist attack is difficult to prevent. Embellishing the Gospels, it borrows the Bible's rhetorical authority but adds details ("a deal to profit from and a throne to sit on") calculated to embarrass the King and Queen. Above all, it breaks the fourth wall, physically overturning the table and chasing Fortinbras out of the room. The spilled food and broken dishes are impossible to ignore.

But Hamlet's victory is short lived. The regime's symbolic domination is backed by real political and military power; it can restore its interpretive control at any time. Fortinbras, too, is in a position to demonstrate (and enhance) his power by compelling obedience. He demands, as a guarantee of political stability and a condition of continued economic relations with Denmark, that the King and Polonius have Hamlet killed. "As long as Hamlet is present, the capitalists will hesitate to invest their millions," Fortinbras says. "They informed me of their worries [about Hamlet] before I left for this visit. Are my words clear?"[36] Over his wife's objections, the King helps Polonius and Rosencrantz stage the play's final performance—a sinister, stylized show trial at which Hamlet is convicted of a long list of (mostly trumped-up) charges and condemned to death.

Adwan's Syrian audience immediately grasped that Hamlet's theatrical outbursts should not be viewed as "resistance." For instance, critic Ghassan Ghunaym (Ghassān Ghunaym), in his taxonomy of satirical character types, classifies Adwan's Hamlet as an "exhausted intellectual." Such an intellectual, he says, is distinguishable from an outright "opportunist" only by the guilt he suffers. He

> is acted upon rather than an actor in events, despairing, ruminating on grief or anger that he pours out in dissipation or drunkenness or passivity or hesitation, so that even if someone came to point him the way, he would still stand there hesitating, despite the real loss represented by his hesitation, a loss for the toiling class, but he is like one who drives his car to the right while signaling to the left, a "reftist" [*shamīnī*]. . . . The intellectual should know when and where to shoot his

> arrows, unlike [Adwan's] Hamlet, who shoots them so that the suffering returns to him and his companions. He did not ally with the people, and he did not release his words in their ranks to light the way and expose the truth and incite them to action; instead, he let fly a few words of criticism borrowed from the Gospels, angered the king and his entourage and guests, and nothing more. His words didn't leave a trace; their only effect was to alert the palace and the enemies—not the optimal way to address what was happening.[37]

Both Adwan's play and Ghunaym's study of political theatre were granted publication in Hafiz al-Asad's Syria. This is not surprising: neither work was construed as threatening to the regime. Like Riad Ismat's production at the Ḥurriyya high school, which Adwan had seen, *Hamlet Wakes Up Late* endorses the regime's official revolutionary ideology. In fact, its National Theatre premiere in January 1978 gave voice to Syria's criticism of Egyptian president Anwar Sadat just after his November 1977 peacemaking trip to Israel.[38] Even the second level of meaning—the play's implied critique of Syrian government brutality—is less subversive than it seems. Adwan's dark rewriting can be read as reinforcing the regime's dominance by dwelling on the impotence of its critics. Ghunaym's commentary, of course, does the same.

A Theatre Company Found a Theatre . . . and "Theatred" Hamlet

The failure of topical theatre is the central theme of a more lighthearted *Hamlet* rewriting, the musical *A Theatre Company Found a Theatre . . . and "Theatred"* Hamlet (1984) by Nader Omran (Nādir ʿUmrān; b. 1955).[39] The word I translate as "theatred" is a neologism in the original. It seems to mean "turned into theatre" rather than "staged" or "presented." Omran, a Jordanian playwright who founded and directs the Al-Fawanees Theatre Troupe, says he began writing his adaptation in a mood of protest against the status quo of Arab drama.[40] His troupe was invited to the 1984 Portable Festival of Arab Theatre in Rabat, Morocco; the organizers announced that the theme was to be "For the Sake of Bringing Arab Theatre to Its Roots" (*min ajl taʾṣīl al-masraḥ al-ʿarabī*).[41] This inspired Omran to take up *Hamlet.* As he explains, "The [Fawanees] company wanted to respond to this slogan by taking up a non-Arab play, but from an Arab viewpoint, considering this slogan to be racist and phony."[42]

Omran's "Arab viewpoint" turns Shakespeare inside out. *Hamlet* becomes the play-within-a-play, while the frame story revolves around the Players, their director, and the Arab royal family whose son commissions the *Hamlet* performance to expose his own usurping uncle/stepfather. The outer play's twin tyrants occupy matching platforms at either end of the stage: the King on his throne, the classically trained Director on a pedestal. Both lack imagination. By contrast, the Players (a fairly large chorus and a small musical ensemble) are mischievous and creative. Jordanian critics have emphasized the inside-out quality of Omran's play and its "happy ending"—after the Prince and King kill each other, the Players mutiny against their director and tie him up, refusing to perform didactic theatre any more.[43]

Omran's Hamlet enjoys discoursing about art but is really interested in his play only for political effect. (In this he resembles Shakespeare's prince.) However, *Hamlet* is not staged as he hopes. Although the British-trained classicist director warns his actors not to deviate from the script, the actors and onstage audience conspire to subvert the performance. Only the very first scene follows Shakespeare's text; after this, various controversies interrupt. Soon the King and Queen begin to interfere in the inset play's action (e.g., the real Queen sets out to seduce the Player playing Polonius). As the "inset fourth wall" (the imaginary wall between the inset play and its onstage audience) disappears, it becomes difficult for a viewer to tell what occurs inside the inset play and what in the outer play.[44]

An early scene exposes the weakness of "mousetrap" theatre. As the inset play is about to begin, the young prince played by Marwan Hamarneh (Marwān Ḥamārna) explains to his mother and uncle, played by Muhammad Haroun (Muḥammad Harūn) and Suhair Fahad (Suhayr Fahd), that he has prepared a show to celebrate their first wedding anniversary.[45] His uncle, no admirer of theatre, makes things difficult from the start. Like the Rabat festival organizers, he demands authentically decolonized art (or else belly dancing). He finally agrees to Shakespeare as a dissident Briton but remains suspicious of this poet who criticizes his own society. This king shows no sign of great intelligence. (This may be tactical.) However, he easily frustrates his nephew's trap, refusing the mimetic bait:

> Harūn: And, what will you show us about these . . . (*breaks off sarcastically*)
>
> Marwān: An amusing story by an English poet called Shakespeare. (*Suhayr grabs him.*) [*The actors lower the cloak and line up behind Marwān, laughing.*][46]
>
> Harūn (*in agitation*): What kind of poet?! Maybe, son, you want them to say about us that we are encouraging the colonialists and disseminating their culture? (*In a sing-*

song) No, no, my son, we won't accept this colonialist poet. (*A slogan.*) And also: down with colonialism.

Players: Down with it. . . down. . . down.[47]

Marwān: This Shakespeare, my lord, was a POET who lived hundreds of years ago.[48] He was not a colonialist. And it is said of this poet that he did more than anyone to expose the secrets of the English and display their corruption.

Harūn: If that's the case, then we have no problem with it. (*Lowers Marwān's hand.*) Although usually I dislike these sorts of poets who sing outside the flock. (*The actors line up at the base of the statue.*)

Marwān (*facing the audience*): As for Shakespeare's story, which we shall "theatre" tonight, it's a play called *Hamlet.* He is a prince from the country of Denmark. He returned from abroad to his country . . . to find that his father had been murdered . . . and his uncle . . . (*with an exaggerated wailing expression*) had married his mother. And this treacherous uncle was none other than the murderer of his brother, i.e., Hamlet's father. (*Marwān freezes for a moment in the proscenium, carrying his bottle, and turns toward Harūn.*) Can you think of anyone more treacherous than that, O uncle?

Harūn (*slyly*): It seems to be an amusing story, nephew of ours. Another glass, servant. (*Laughs.*) Continue.

Marwān: Doesn't this story remind you of anything, uncle?

Harūn (*raises his cup in his right hand; the actors move in a single orderly line from the pedestal to the front of the stage*) [*Long moment of silence in which they stare at each other*]: Of course, my son! It reminds me of the country of Denmark. A beautiful country, and famous for its dairy. I saw milk products there like I had never seen before in my life. I returned from there at half my weight and double my age. (*In ecstasy*) What a country. Go on, son. (*Oratorically*) But be SURE TO DERIDE COLONIALISM as much as you can.

Players: DOWN with colonialism . . . down . . . down . . . down with it. (*A sneeze.*)[49]

6.1. *A Theatre Company Found a Theatre and "Theatred"* Hamlet (Jordan, 1984). Courtesy of Nader Omran.

If the tyrant doesn't blink, Omran's play suggests, then public exposure cannot hurt him. By remaining silent (something Shakespeare's Claudius is unable to do), the King retains symbolic control. Political theatre is impotent to accomplish political change.

The only person more ridiculous than the Moustrapper is the censor. Omran shows a royal guard in this role: watching the ramparts scene of *Hamlet,* the Guard is alarmed when Horatio and Marcellus's dialogue strikes too close to home. "A war may ignite that we don't give a mare or camel about," they fret. "How many lives have we got, to lose one of them for the sake of the master of these walls?"[50] With a censor's paranoia, the Guard reads everything that is not explicit praise for the regime as implicit blame. He wants to ban such comments. (Perhaps he is also upset that one of the seditious characters is a guard like himself.) The Prince responds with a mirroring theory: theatre should expose knavery and "stimulate" viewers by showing them their own ugliness.[51] But both arguments are undermined by the troupe's namesake, Abu Fawanees ("Lantern Man"), whose silent presence rebukes both the Guard and the Prince.[52] Abu Fawanees goes everywhere, to royal courts and darkened slums. For the many characters who invoke him, a play is neither a mirror nor a mousetrap; instead it is a lantern, able to illuminate and thus define new kinds of social spaces.

Omran's play itself is no *Mousetrap.* In fact, its strong stance *against* allegorizing risks becoming a didactic "message" in its own right. What saves it is the playful attention to musical and visual detail. Besides the ubiquitous lanterns and other decorative lighting effects, the show also features an onstage musical ensemble with Middle Eastern instruments; several dance/pantomime numbers (these include a stick dance in which the actors, mimicking blind people, stumble around singing, "A ruler is like a blind man—helpless without his stick!"); and outsized costumes and props (for instance, the royal family wears green dunce caps half a meter tall, the Queen's dress has a 30–meter black train, and several onstage funeral processions include meter-high black and white skull masks). The fairly dry excerpts quoted here do not convey the visual and musical appeal of the play.

As the inset fourth wall breaks down, it becomes clear that *A Theatre Company* is also too morally ambiguous to qualify as a *Mousetrap*. Abu Fawanees is the only clearly positive character, upstaging the Prince and replacing the Ghost but offering no moral or political guidance. The Players are imaginative, energetic, and lively, but their interaction with the tyrannical King and Queen produces mixed results. Onstage audience members interfere in the play, bringing in their own habits of arbitrary judgment, impunity, and blackmail. By the end, the inset play blends with the outer play and several characters in the latter (the Guard, the King, the Queen, and the Prince) have apparently been killed. The only survivors are the Players, who take no responsibility for the violence they have provoked. When the dying Prince (by now fully integrated with the role of Hamlet) asks them to live on and tell his story, the troupe refuses his request.[53] The Players have already told him they are indifferent to human consequences, obeying only the joyful and sometimes destructive mandate of their art:

> Marwān [as Prince]: I see now that you are not performing a Shakespeare play.
> Bashīr [as Actor]: Abū Fawanīs says the artist is ahead of his time.
> Marwān: Quit these dumb little sayings. You've moved away from the characters of Shakespeare's story. And the strange thing is they [the King and Queen] have gotten mixed into the dramatic act.
> Bashir: The Fawanīs[54] theatre everything.
> Marwān: And what will you do next? What else will you "theatre"? My uncle didn't make the connection between the events, and he didn't see himself in your theatre.
> Bashīr (*throws a skull*): But we see ourselves.[55]

Although Jordanian critics have described it as a "comedy" and even a "call to revolution against subjection, submission, oppression, and tyranny,"[56] Omran's play is not concerned with the problem of bad government. Instead it presents theatre as an autonomous force that evades both the 1960s-style allegorizer and the censor. Colorful and seductive, art is also self-serving. Like Abu Fawanees, it owes no explanations to anyone.

Dance of the Scorpions

A third rewriting of *Hamlet* also foregrounds an ineffectual prince and an unhelpful Ghost. Mahmoud Aboudoma is the Egyptian playwright and director (born in 1953) whose awakening to the "political tune" of Kozintsev's film was discussed in chapter 3. Aboudoma's 1988 play *Dance of the Scorpions* strips down *Hamlet* to just five scenes and five characters: Hamlet, Horatio, Claudius, Polonius, and the Ghost. There are no Gertrude and Ophelia, no Rosencrantz and Guildenstern, no Players, no metaphysics, and no poetry: only a stark fable of a kingdom collapsing under its own lies. The parable's moral and aesthetic traction comes from the dialogizing background of Shakespeare's *Hamlet*. For instance, here is how Aboudoma's Horatio, a Brechtian narrator-cum-*ḥakawātī* (traditional Arab storyteller), opens the play:

> Horatio [*playing the role of narrator and welcoming the audience*]: Honored ladies and gentlemen, let me introduce myself to you: I am Horatio, Hamlet's friend whom he entrusted to tell you his story. I've been telling it for five centuries, and finally I got bored of telling it the same way every night. Therefore I will try tonight to tell it to you in a different way. For the winds of change have blown on everything and changed everything around. Borders have vanished and walls and checkpoints have fallen, and a single thing now has many names. Descriptions are gone, and we stand before tough riddles.[57]

Aboudoma's hapless prince does not even get as far as directing a *Mousetrap*. Instead, as in Adwan's *Hamlet Wakes Up Late,* the King and Polonius stage a performance of royal power and impose it on Hamlet. Claudius wants to silence his opponents, so he invents a council of nobles and fabricates a foreign war, then bribes his apparent enemy Fortinbras to attack his kingdom.

The only vestige of an inset play in *Dance of the Scorpions* recalls a traditional form of Arab drama: the puppet show. The venue is a royal cabinet meeting, introduced with an unambiguous stage direction: "The lights come up on a long table with the King sitting at the narrow side. Hamlet sits across from him. To the King's right is seated Polonius, and the rest of the chairs are occupied by the nobles, who are not human but are simply paper dummies."[58]

The King conducts the meeting in all seriousness. He berates his vassals for not collecting enough money from their peasants for the impending war against Fortinbras, appoints Hamlet commander-in-chief of the army, and so on. Then Hamlet, much like Adwan's protagonist, interrupts the show with an attack that has religious overtones:

> Hamlet: Enough! What's happening? What's this stupid buffoonery [*al-taḥrīj al-sakhīf*]? Where are these nobles you're talking to, King?
>
> Claudius: What happened to you, Hamlet? Have you gone mad? Here they are, sitting in front of you. If you mean to make light of them, I will not accept this, I warn you.
>
> Hamlet: But they're paper dolls.

> Claudius: Paper. This is something that cannot be overlooked. We have to put a limit to your fantasies. Polonius.
> Polonius: My lord.
> Claudius: Is the King speaking with paper dolls?
> Polonius: God forbid. My lord is speaking with the nobles, and they are of flesh and blood—would it befit my lord to speak with paper dolls?
> Claudius: Then explain to him. I have no more patience. It's no time for games now: the enemy is gathered at the gates, the money has been gathered, the cavalry is prepared, my people are ready, and in comes Hamlet to piss on our cake with his stupid claims.[59]

Hamlet is correct: the "nobles" are indeed oversized puppets. But being correct does not suffice. Aboudoma's next few lines sharpen the sense of futility:

> Hamlet: If these dolls are human, let me hear their voices.
> Polonius: They're polite folk and don't speak in the presence of the king.
> Hamlet: So make them applaud. Show me the red of a blush in their faces if they're alive. Have I lost my mind, that I can't tell the difference anymore between human beings and paper?[60]

Although Aboudoma's play has an explicitly Christian setting, his Muslim audience may recognize a Qur'ānic echo in the exchange, which paraphrases the challenge of a young Prophet Abraham (Ibrāhīm) to his father's idols.[61] Pointedly, however, the scene fails to unfold according to the prophetic pattern. The attempted unmasking falls flat. Hamlet receives a stern warning not to mock the King's cabinet and the meeting continues. Claudius maintains symbolic control for precisely as long as he has military control. This leaves Hamlet at a loss. Without an audience, what good is being a prophet? He begins to break down: "Everything has become fake! A world made of paper. A big lie. A big lie."[62]

Thus Aboudoma's Hamlet resembles those of Adwan and Omran. He considers himself articulate but babbles childishly. He underestimates the very thing he tries to expose: the ruthlessness of the regime. He is too naïve and too quick to confide in those who have betrayed him. He is so unlike his heroic predecessors in the Arab Hamlet tradition that even the Ghost does not immediately recognize him: "Are you Hamlet?" it asks, as though to verify his identity.[63]

But, reflecting the play's post-Nasserist hangover, Aboudoma's Ghost is likewise a disappointment. Hamlet's faith in his father, the one certainty in a treacherous world, turns out to be unwarranted. Hamlet clings to it throughout the play, even as the Ghost is promiscuously appropriated for politics: Claudius and even servants and prostitutes claim that it has appeared to them.[64] But in the closing scene Hamlet can no longer escape the suggestion that his father, the revered late king, was a despot and profiteer who squeezed the peasantry, extorted from the nobles, bribed army commanders, controlled judges and priests, and killed political opponents. Here Hamlet is finally undone:

> Hamlet: Yes! He was more virtuous than all the kings in the world. . . . My father was pure and untouched, but you contaminate everything.
>
> Claudius: Does that make you feel better? Yes, he was pure and clean, and you don't want anyone to tell you the truth. You always went out of your way to find someone who would mislead you. I suppose you haven't heard anything and have not seen fit to follow the news of the war.
>
> Hamlet: What war? If this is true, then the war is over. If this is true, then for whom did I waste those days sitting and planning revenge? Was it for nothing? (*Looks confused.*) Father. Answer me, for the sake of my humiliated pride. Everyone was on the right path except Hamlet. Everyone said, "Do it, Hamlet." Do it. But what should I do when everything has become just words? Revenge is words and war is words. . . . Words, words, words won't heal the wound.
>
> Claudius: Stop it, Hamlet. It isn't fitting for an army commander to cry like a woman.
>
> Hamlet: Because my heart is wounded and my tears are ready. We should all cry. It isn't right for the likes of us to taste sweetness or see flowers or take pleasure in manly council. We are falling, falling to a place with no decision and no end. . . . If I could find the head of this flaccid life, I would cut it off.[65]

Hamlet's belated tears do not redeem him in the eyes of the other characters (notably Horatio, a hard-boiled court insider as well as the narrator) or, presumably, the audience. Both uncle and nephew belong to the same parasitic class. Both depend on the unmerited loyalty of underlings. In the play's rather sudden ending, a band of homegrown populist revolutionaries, "the Crusaders," unseats them both. (This mob, which never appears on stage, is said to have attacked and overwhelmed the palace, blocking all the exits and setting the stage for the final showdown between Hamlet and Claudius. Polonius escapes and apparently survives.) It is clear that Claudius is the doomed "scorpion" of the title.[66] The play further suggests that Hamlet, with his misguided ideals, is no better. The audience is left to decide whether the revolution—which can be read to represent a grassroots democratic movement and/or an Islamist takeover—will bring a more just government or merely another tyranny.[67]

"His Sword Kept Sticking Up"

Our two 1990s rewritings of *Hamlet* exaggerate still further in portraying their own belatedness, the Ghost's weakness, Hamlet's inadequacy, and Claudius's obscene power. In the monodrama *Ismail/Hamlet* by Hakim Marzougui (ʿAbd al-Ḥakīm al-Marzūqī), the protagonist-narrator remains ignorant of Shakespeare's play and its relevance to his life; *Hamlet* is present as the merest of shadows. Jawad al-Assadi's *Forget Hamlet,* subtitled *An Upside-Down Rewriting of Shakespeare's* Hamlet (*iʿādat kitāba muʿākisa li-hāmlit shaksbīr*), scrambles Hamlet's lines and throws them back at him from many sides. As I have argued in more detail elsewhere, these two very different rewritings express the political insight common to post-1975 Arab *Hamlets*: the father's collapse and the son's abdication allow the villain to steal the show.[68]

Ismail/Hamlet

With a domestic setting and a deliberately petty plot, the late-1990s monodrama *Ismail/Hamlet* uses its contrast with Shakespeare's *Hamlet* to create dramatic irony. Staged by the Damascus-based Sidewalk Theatre Company (Masraḥ al-Raṣīf) at several international festivals, the play won the Best Dramatic Text prize at the Carthage Festival of 1998.[69] It features a protagonist whom an Arab audience would not normally associate with Hamlet. Ismail (Ismāʿīl) "a middle-aged man with strange rough features": a bath attendant turned corpse-washer who has no interest in philosophy, no sense of justice, and no capacity for noble action. He shares only a bathhouse version of Hamlet's predicament: Ismail's mother was seduced in his childhood by a wealthy *ḥammām* (Turkish bath) owner, who hounded Ismail's bath-attendant father to death, married Ismail's mother, put Ismail to work in the baths, and later took as a second wife Saadiyya (Saʿdiyya), the girl whom Ismail had coveted for himself. When he grew up, Ismail shifted from washing the living to washing the dead. *Ismail/Hamlet* takes place as the body of his usurping stepfather, dead at last, lies on a table for its pre-burial cleansing. The play, written in Syrian colloquial Arabic, is Ismail's one-sided dialogue with the corpse.

Ismail's opening lines demonstrate his style of speech: clipped and sardonic, repetitive, heavy in clichés and proverbs, and bound to the physical. Whereas the language of Shakespeare's Hamlet leaps constantly between bodies and abstractions (one of his dizzying traits is that he cannot say "dust" without also saying "quintessence"), Ismail does not leave the corporeal even when discussing God and the afterlife:

> Ah, welcome, welcome, Mister Abū Saʿīd. I take care of your neighborhood. Abū Saʿīd whose word is never spoken twice. He decided to marry Umm Luṭfī—sent her husband to prison and married her. Decided to marry my mother before the dirt on my father's grave was dry, and married her. He decided to marry Saʿdiyya, and he married her. They say, "Whoever marries my mother I'll call him Uncle,"[70] well—whoever marries my girl, what do I call him . . . my boy?
>
> Ah, Uncle Abū Saʿīd. Finally you've come to me. God took you to his place so he could bring you to mine. I'm going to wash you, remove your outside dirt, cut your fingernails, pare your talons, shave you. I'll stuff your orifices with cotton and send you there to get clean, to roast properly in hellfire. If only I could have cleaned you from the inside or pared your nails while you were alive, you son of a snake. When I worked at your place as a bath attendant, you wouldn't deign to be washed between one Feast and the next, you filth, too afraid of wasting water! Why didn't you put in your will for them to dig your grave so you could stand up in it, to cost you less? Abū Saʿīd whose bones were gold . . . they're going to rust away under the dirt and be gnawed by slugs and worms. But I'll have a few words with you, before you go there.[71]

Ismail's "few words" reveal no more interiority than this opening speech. His work gives him knowledge of many secrets (a corpse-washer uncovers hidden amulets, strange scars, and anatomical oddities[72]) but little insight into himself. In part, Ismail's development is limited by the blocked orifices that define his life. These are both auditory and sexual. In his job as a traditional Islamic corpse-washer, Ismail blocks the mouth, nose, and ears of the bodies he works on. His adolescent pursuit of Saadiyya (who later becomes his stepfather's wife) fails both physically and verbally: his attempts to sneak into her house are violently stymied, and his requests for a formal engagement are disregarded. His eventual wife, Saadiyya's sister, is deaf and mute. He knows no one listens to him: "Have you heard of anyone telling his worries to his own stepfather? It's that I'm fated to talk either to someone dead or to someone deaf."[73]

Only the theatre audience is captive to Ismail's ramblings. Without interlocutors to challenge him, he remains fixed in a private, wounded world view. He nurses what he pretentiously calls "the truth of my feelings" (*ḥaqīqat mashāʿirī*).[74] He is aware only of his immediate situation: his poverty, his interrupted education, his usurped bride, and his home with a less desirable deaf-mute wife in a graveyard with corpses for neighbors.[75] He is an unreliable narrator, as lacking in self-knowledge as Shakespeare's Hamlet is overendowed with it.

A striking instance is his ignorance about his own name: Ismail does not know why he is called "Hamlet." He explains that he was given the nickname by a young actor, Fawwaz (Fawwāz), who came to study corpse-washing after his father disowned him for his art. But Fawwaz commits suicide without sharing the secret of the name. At the end the bond between the two men is expressed by bodies, not literary allusions:

> The kid talked a little funny, but he was nice, but a while ago he did something that upset me. . . . He killed himself. . . . I washed him and dried him and read a lot of Qur'ān over him. . . . It was Fawwāz who called me "Ismāʿīl Hamlet." I don't know what he meant by it. He died without ever explaining it to me. But I liked it better than "Loofah Man."[76]

Rather than use the other characters to mock the protagonist's ignorance, *Ismail/Hamlet* gathers them all into Ismail's single voice. But the dramatic irony is still present: his mimicry of other characters reveals depths and angles in their words that he does not himself understand. Although Fawwaz never appears on stage, he and the audience share a common intertextual understanding that Ismail does not grasp.

> Fawwāz: Do you know, O Ismāʿīl, O Hamlet, that life is a theatre?
> Ismāʿīl: What's that? Why should I know the theatre to know life?[77]

Ismail's lack of interiority precludes character growth. His sense of time is static or circular, a meaningless nonprogress to be interrupted by an arbitrary death. His favorite half-understood metaphor is a camel walking around a wheel:

> [M]y condition [is] like an animal's. Every day I wait for someone to die so that I can make a living and feed my wife and children. Like camels, each one eating off the back of the next. Speaking of camels, Fawwāz told me a thing he saw in Tunis, but I just now understood it. There's a well, and at the well there's a camel going round in circles bringing up cold water from it, and the people are drinking, they're happy, and they put a wall around the camel and the well, with a little door in it through which they bring in the little camel, who grows up inside, and he can't get out until he's a piece of meat after he gets old and weak and can't pull up the water anymore, and then it's the turn of the other little camel and he said, with my own eyes I saw a little camel crying and moaning and his tears flowing like a human being, not wanting to go in, as they dragged him into the wall.[78]

Ismail recounts the camel's whole life cycle in one long sentence. The sentence uses no syntactic subordination to move from happy people drinking cool water to a pitiable young camel bemoaning its futureless future. Each clause is at the same level as the previous, as if to mimic the walk of an animal wearing blinders who can see only the section of path directly in front of him. The onlookers see what the camel can only intuit: that the repetitive circles around the well also mark a linear progress toward death. Breaking out of the pattern is impossible, because the exit door has been outgrown.[79]

Perhaps Ismail has some trouble understanding the camel's story because it is so close to his own. The opposite of a justice-seeking revolutionary Hamlet, Ismail spends his life enacting eternal return. He "dreams" not of an equitable world but of one where he can replace his stepfather as the despot.

As usual in our post-1975 plays, the "fair and warlike"[80] father figure is not available as a role model. Ismail's father Ibrahim is a lowly bath attendant, coughing to death while his wife, who is flirting with Abu Said, does not bother to bring him a glass of water. Abu Said openly mocks his rival; he twice insults Ismail using the phrase "like your father." When he reappears as a ghost, Ibrahim is a piteous sight, coughing and still carrying his washing-glove and bowl. His sword (when he carries one) is just a priapic appendage, not a weapon. His continuing call for justice is ridiculous. Ismail delivers the ironic facts in his usual flat paratactic way:

> Only the ghost of my father [still appears] but this time without his sponge and bowl, carrying a sword in his right hand and a hose in the left.
>
> —Father, where's your bowl?
>
> —It's lost.
>
> —And where's your sponge?
>
> —It wore away and doesn't clean right anymore.
>
> And he left me and kept walking carrying his sword, with the water coming out of his hose strongly. Unclear if he was cleaning something or watering something, and when the sun came out he went to sleep in his grave, but his sword kept sticking up, raised as high as the tombstones or maybe a little higher. And even when they bombed the cemetery in the war, and a lot of graves collapsed on their owners' heads, and many of the dead met a heroic end, but they weren't compensated with new graves, even then my father's sword stayed raised.[81]

At the end of his monologue, before he finishes with Abu Said's corpse, Ismail at last tries to avenge this pathetic ghost. Pulling an inkwell from his pocket and pressing a forged will to the dead man's fingerprints, Ismail bequeaths himself all his stepfather's wealth. He says:

> All my dreams burned: that one of these days I would be the boss of Abū Saʿīd's store, with a *nargileh* in my hand, shouting at the workers, but now the moment has come that I've been awaiting for years, because God exists, he exists a lot, oh yes, by God.[82]
>
> Now give me your finger. Press down. Yes, press down your other finger.
>
> Don't hold it against me, Uncle Abū Saʿīd: we took what is our right. And now my father can relax in his grave and be rid of his sponge and his bowl and his sword and his hose, and I can become a master. What master—I'm going to open the biggest burial office in the Middle East, and open branches abroad to serve emigrants and patrons of Islam overseas. And my wife from the shock of joy will begin speaking and singing.[83]

Instead of stopping the cycle of usurpation and humiliation, Ismail acts to obtain what he feels is his "right." For possibly the first time in his life he engages in a characteristic Hamletesque behavior: rewriting a document. Like Hamlet substituting a "changeling" text for Rosencrantz and Guildenstern's fatal commission,[84] Ismail forges (in both senses of the word) an identity for himself. But whereas Hamlet's signet-stamped forgery affirms his link to his father, Ismail's binds him to his stepfather. With the thumbprints he becomes an heir to Abu Said. The play's setting is private and domestic, but the presence of Shakespeare's text in the background helps give this moment a political message. As director Roula Fattal (Rūlā Fattāl) has told an interviewer, "Oppression and abuse give birth to a new tyrant: he will be just like his stepfather."[85]

Forget Hamlet/Ophelia's Window

The unheroic Hamlet is most evident—and the Claudius figure most charismatic and brutal—in Iraqi playwright Jawad al-Assadi's play, staged during its author's nearly 30-year exile from Baʿthist Iraq.[86] Al-Assadi's version explicitly instructs his audience: "Forget Hamlet." (It was published under that title in 2000,[87] after being staged as *Ophelia's Window* at Cairo's Hanager Theatre in 1994.)[88] As reviewer Sawsan al-Abtah (Sawsan al-Abṭaḥ) reads the title: "He commands us categorically: Forget the Hamlet you knew before. Here is another Hamlet for you, one who resembles you because he is a child of the current Arab moment with all its vulgarity and ugliness and futility."[89] But al-Abtah also points out the title's irony: anyone who took it literally would lose both al-Assadi's craft and his message. The command to "forget Hamlet" is, of course, an injunction to keep him painfully in mind.

Set in a fictional kingdom that evokes Saddam Hussein's Iraq, the play takes place amid rattling glass and suspended objects. The stage directions call for mirrors, windows, empty picture frames dangling in midair, old masks and chandeliers, creaky chairs and hanging beds.[90] Time is bent into dispiriting shapes: the play opens (like Hamlet's *Mousetrap*) before the old king's death, but it is somehow already too late to take any action to save him or confront his killer.[91] Shrieks are heard, eyewitness testimony is available (Ophelia, through her window, sees Claudius commit the crime), but justice is foreclosed. As the blind dissident Laertes says at the beginning of the play: "Which is blinder, the world or me?"[92]

In a now-familiar intertextual reversal, Hamlet's late father is portrayed as a weakling. We actually see him: a spoiled but harmless hypochondriac wheeled onstage in the first scene, perhaps a version of Shakespeare's gently unimpressive Player King or the "impotent and bedrid" elder Norway.[93] His decency is somehow unimposing. Even before his death, the old king feels cold and complains that Gertrude does not pay him enough attention.

Both before and after the murder, Al-Assadi's Hamlet disappoints. He mainly prattles or sleeps. When Claudius's executioners appear, in a scene recalling the end of Kafka's *The Trial,* he will meekly extend his neck. Other characters try to fill the role he has abdicated. Laertes takes on Hamlet's function as court dissident, exposing the regime's corruption and meeting a sinister end. Shortly before being sent to prison to be tortured to death, he exclaims: "Claudius killed the just king! Which of us does not know that! And Hamlet responds to his father's murder with 'to be or not to be.' Be, just for once *be*, you rat!"[94]

Hamlet's friend Horatio is equally bitter. He chides this forgetful and forgettable Hamlet, invoking his heroic speeches and particularly his pledge to remember:

> Where are your wild cries, where is your madness, where are the words of love and texts of justice you were boasting of, where, O all ye hosts of heaven, O earth! What else? Hold, hold, my heart, and you, my sinews, grow not instant old! I won't forget you, while memory holds a place in this distracted globe, weren't those your words? Didn't you say, I'll wipe all trivial fond records, all saws of books, all forms, all pressures past, your commandment all alone shall live within the book of my brain! Ha! Aren't these your vain texts?[95]

The most interesting Hamlet surrogate is Ophelia. She becomes the moral light of the play, an articulate witness to the Claudius regime's depredations. She speaks or echoes many lines from Shakespeare in confronting first her father, then Hamlet, and finally the king. For instance, her rebuke of Hamlet gets its sting from the background presence of Shakespeare's nunnery scene: "Get yourself to a monastery! There you can rest your mind and body and have leisure to re-pose your question, 'To be or not to be.'"[96] And when she sees that Claudius cannot be brought to justice, her despair echoes that of Shakespeare's Hamlet: "Horatio, everything is collapsing on us at once. . . . Denmark's become a big prison, Horatio."[97]

Ophelia's fearless activism illuminates the genre of contemporary Arab heroine to which she belongs: a truth-teller who bears witness, for the sake of her family and what she calls basic human values, to the damage wrought by an honorless regime on family relationships and especially on the masculinity of her menfolk.[98] "Go search for the cause of your father's death!" she tells Hamlet. "Search for his killer! That will bring back your manliness [*rujūla*]!"[99]

Ophelia is no feminist; she remains committed to a strictly gendered set of values, privileging the private over the political:

Polonius: I hated the dead king.
Ophelia: That's because he never learned how to turn you into a servant. He treated you like a human being.
Polonius: I never liked him for one day—he was stingy and petty, not strong and decisive like Claudius.
Ophelia: I don't care about the dead king or the living king. What bothers me is that you betrayed my brother.
Polonius: And if you follow his example I'll have you banished.
Ophelia: You'd kill your children for a rotten kingdom.[100]

But in defending the safety of her family and community, Ophelia is quickly pushed into a more generalized call for justice. Her reluctant empowerment is not presented as a triumph for womankind but rather as a failure of masculinity in a world that forces men to become either impotent or monstrous.

For the center of gravity in *Forget Hamlet*—as in many of the other post-1975 *Hamlet* rewritings we have considered so far—is the Claudius character. Claudius sits above human politics, like Aristotle's "beast or god."[101] That is because he is impervious to language—a *brute* in the most literal sense. He is referred to not only as a "butcher" and "barbarian" but also as a "bull" and a "dinosaur" (*dīnāṣūr*);[102] at one point Horatio has a vision of him in the guise of Poseidon, as a wild buffalo holding a sword and parting the sea.[103] Like a wild animal or mythological figure, Claudius overruns civilized boundaries; his bestiality gives him an oversized role in the play. Even Al-Assadi's introduction to the published script illustrates this effect:

> I wanted in my dramatic text *Forget Hamlet* to pull the curtain [*uzīḥ al-sitār*] from some characters suffering the edge of madness and to open the door of the text [*aftaḥ bāb al-naṣṣ*] to their desires and their rancor [*raghabātihim wa-ḥaqdihim*], postponed in the face of Claudius, the state barbarian [*barbarī al-dawla*] who swallowed up [*ibtalaʿ*] his brother and sister-in-law both at once to send the former to the gravediggers and the latter to his own bed and his boorish unmanly haste [*ilā firāshihi wa-nazqihi al-niswī al-fazẓ*].[104]

The curtain-pulling and door-opening gestures suggest a liberation or public airing. Yet the "barbarian," rather than the marginalized characters, fills all the air created—he dominates al-Assadi's explanatory sentence, "swallowing up" its second half. Exposing his barbarity makes it no easier to resist. In fact, Al-Assadi's "upside-down rewriting" of Shakespeare makes the "state barbarian" more central than ever.

Claudius invades all conversations in the kingdom, including the earthy gossip of the two gravediggers. Although the diggers are portrayed as women, laborers, and speakers of Egyptian colloquial rather than classical Arabic—three stereotypically subaltern categories[105]— there is nothing subversive or even politically engaged about their bawdy political humor:

> Gravedigger 1: The king's body hadn't even been buried yet when Claudius spilled the news about his marriage to the old hag.
> Gravedigger 2: He not only married the old hag, but he'll marry you too, and me, and he'll marry your mother and my mother. . . . He'll marry all of Denmark![106]

Like the play's other disorienting effects, the gravediggers' banter underscores Hamlet's inadequacy and the regime's power. Even the king's sexual appetites are on a mythical scale. Later the gravediggers cheerfully drink to the dissident Laertes' health, noting that Claudius's reign of terror means good money for the grave-digging business.[107] It is these women, after Hamlet succumbs to Claudius's hired killers, who are left to end the play, reading the "rogue and peasant slave" soliloquy from a yellowing copy of Shakespeare's *Hamlet* at his graveside.[108] They stop reading at the words "fall to cursing like a very drab, a scullion"—well before Hamlet announces his plot to "catch the conscience of the King."

An Unedifying Villain

In *Forget Hamlet*, as in several other plays, Claudius's monstrous omnipotence threatens the whole moral code underlying the Arab Hero Hamlet dramatic tradition. The code criticizes Hamlet for passivity; it calls for awareness of what is wrong in one's world and proper action to "set it right."[109] But how can Hamlet's failures be seen as avoidable (and hence blamable) if the nature of the despot makes it impossible to resist? Like Shakespeare's Iago, the post-1975 Claudius is a gleeful and successful improviser.[110] He adapts smoothly to circumstances; everyone else must adapt to him, like iron filings to a magnet. Not only artistic innuendo but even direct confrontation loses its power; in a truly closed dictatorship, the act of bearing witness is irrelevant. The magnet becomes a black hole, swallowing any attempt at political participation. Martyrdom is impossible too: Hamlet's death is sordid and futile, not glorious as in Sobhi's and Ismat's early-1970s plays.

The moral quandary is perhaps clearest in a scene with no analogue in Shakespeare's *Hamlet*: Claudius's attempted seduction of Ophelia. It begins when Ophelia begs the king to release her brother from prison and agrees to spend an evening drinking with him in exchange. (We will later learn that Laertes by this time has already been tortured to death.) Claudius signs the pardon papers and pours the wine. Then, either drunk or just unable to bear it any longer, she confronts Claudius with the murder of the old king. She is under the spell of the murder scene she has witnessed: "I saw the whole scene [*mashhad*]! I saw it with these two eyes [*bi ʿaynayya hātayn*]!" She recounts it as though reading from a screenplay. Meanwhile Claudius, intent on sex, praises the beauty of those same witnessing eyes ("I've never looked deep into your eyes before. What eyes [*ya laha min ʿaynayn*]!"). A "deaf dialogue" ensues, at one point breaking up into two interlaced monologues:

> Ophelia: The king died an ugly death he didn't deserve. And his son will follow.
> Claudius: "Died" is nicer than "was murdered."
> Ophelia: I mean, he died by being murdered.
> Claudius: The vulgar mob thinks so. But the truth is otherwise.
> Ophelia: The truth is that the king slit his own throat. (*Sarcastically*) Or that a servant went insane and killed him? Are you heading for an excuse like that?
> Claudius: Perhaps, because he was the unhappiest of men. He needed to die. He died, and that's that.
> Ophelia: There is a window in my room looking onto the King's room and close to it. So I saw everything.
> Claudius: Do you want more wine?
> Ophelia: It seems the killer is experienced and knows how to carry out his task with unique skill.
> Claudius: Oh God, your breasts are trembling just like your lips!
> Ophelia: The King was sleeping like a naked child! Gertrude covered him with a light sheet and disappeared! I don't know how he fell asleep and started snoring so quickly! A huge man entered, wrapped in a cloak and

> with a turban on his head, carrying a dagger. He pulled off the sheet and slaughtered the King without a sound! The King died without a sound. He didn't struggle a lot! What a suspicious death. What animal carried out this hideous deed?
>
> Claudius: I issued my order to pardon Laertes in order to drink with you, not so you could tell me bloody tales like this! Don't be afraid. And to get straight to the point, I want you![111]

Finally Claudius attacks her "like a wild buffalo." She escapes only by chance, having achieved no justice and no catharsis. In the Cairo production she was eventually murdered, pushed into the river by Claudius's security forces.

This rewriting pulls *Hamlet* in a disturbing direction. Already in Shakespeare there are hints of Claudius's excessive interest in Ophelia, whether as an attractive woman or as a source of subversive talk ("Pretty Ophelia. . . . Follow her close, give her good watch, I pray you").[112] But nowhere does Shakespeare's Claudius explicitly reach a tentacle across the generation gap. Al-Assadi unpacks and extends these hints, introducing a creepy echo of Angelo's proposition to Isabella in *Measure for Measure.* Marzougui does something similar in *Ismail/Hamlet* by having Abu Said marry his stepson's beloved, Saadiyya. In both cases, the young man finds himself unable to compete with the stepfather, not (as in Freud's triangle) for the mother but for a love object his own age. He cannot grow up and come into his own.

Such villains, I think, prove that these plays do *not* mean to edify. Their presence forecloses the very revolution the plays might otherwise seem to advocate. The tyrant, like the generation of "old men" who have until very recently dominated Arab politics, defines the script.[113] His presence is unendurable, but his absence is unimaginable. As these plays show, his effect on Arab gender relations as well as foreign policy is catastrophic.

A Prodigal Cousin

The five Arabic Hamlet plays we have seen so far emerge from different styles of theatre, but they form a coherent family. To summarize:

All displace their concerns with contemporary Arab politics onto another setting: Adwan, Aboudoma, and al-Assadi onto markedly Christian kingdoms; Omran onto a generic third-world monarchy (whose public royal drinking suggests it is not Muslim); and Marzougui into an Arab Muslim context but a familial space rather than a public one.

All use suspended, circular, or otherwise disjointed temporal frameworks. Adwan and Aboudoma start the narration at the end and proceed in flashback; Omran intermingles two plays with their respective time schemes; al-Assadi starts his action before *Hamlet* begins but has his characters behave as though *Hamlet* had already happened; Marzougui collapses a lifetime into a single monologue of out-of-order flashbacks where change and character development are impossible.

All question the power of words and representations—whether writing, rewriting, speaking, acting, or drama criticism—to achieve political change. Omran's and Adwan's Hamlets stage failed *Mousetraps.* Aboudoma's tries and fails to debunk a royal puppet show. Al-Assadi's dissidents speak out but change nothing because everything is predetermined. Marzougui's protagonist, ill served by words and feelings, at last gets revenge through a bodily signature rather than a written one.

All play on their audiences' prior knowledge of a heroic early-1970s Hamlet to produce dramatic irony. All portray Hamlets who are uninformed, ineffectual, naïve, and either inarticulate or uselessly and diarrhetically articulate. These Hamlets are either disappointing departures from viewers' preconceptions of Hamlet (al-Assadi, Marzougui) or unredeemed exaggerations of his worst traits (Omran, Adwan, Aboudoma).

Finally, all include a creative and nearly self-sufficient power figure. In Omran's play this figure is the slum-haunting, lantern-hanging Abu Fawanees, who looks on as the inset play kills both "real" and fictional characters. In the other four plays the fascinating figure is the stepfather-king Claudius, often presented as grotesquely brutal, or even (in the literal sense of brutality) bestial.

The Al-Hamlet Summit

Our sixth play seems clearly to be a member of the same extended family, but one that grew up overseas. It is by Kuwaiti-British playwright-director Sulayman Al-Bassam, who in recent years has become the Arab adapter of Shakespeare best known in the West, with a 2007–9 *Richard III* commissioned by the Royal Shakespeare Company and a 2011 *Twelfth Night* version.[114] Although he has written non-Shakespearean plays, what made Al-Bassam's reputation was a brisk satire called *The Al-Hamlet Summit* (2002). Originally written in English and premiered in Edinburgh, it was rewritten in Arabic in 2004; Al-Bassam has staged this slightly expanded Arabic version in Tokyo, London, and Tehran, but never in the Arab world.[115]

The Al-Hamlet Summit portrays a tottering Arab dictatorship holding a high-level conference, with nametags and microphones like the Arab League, even as the members secretly plot against each other and international support erodes. There are car bombs in the capital, a Shiʿa rebellion in the south, and Israeli Merkava and British Centurion tanks on the southern border, suggesting a collage of several actual Arab states.[116] Meanwhile the characters of Claudius, Gertrude, Ophelia, Polonius, and Hamlet conspire, declaim, make love, and buy weapons—mostly without leaving their desks in the conference hall.

Al-Bassam's play lacks the first four "family traits" listed above: its setting is explicitly Arab and Muslim; its time is linear; its characters use words that matter; and its Hamlet resembles the active revolutionary of the Arab 1960s and early 70s. It seems to lack the fifth trait as well: Claudius resembles the shreds-and-patches king to whom western audiences are more accustomed. Also absent are many minor features common to the Arabic *Hamlet* plays: pervasive spies and informers, a Horatio figure, any kind of *ḥakawātī* (narrator), open intertextual allusions to Shakespeare, and so on. These intertexts are replaced with a running commentary shown on large video monitors: close-ups of characters as they speak or react, images of current events (burning oil wells, contemporary war footage, etc.), and sometimes scenes from the play that have not yet occurred.[117] Another significant addition is a new character: a polyglot female arms dealer who sells Claudius and Fortinbras their tanks and rockets, Hamlet his phosphorus bombs, and Ophelia her suicide belt.

This play builds on an earlier *Hamlet* adaptation that used Shakespeare's text: *The Arab League Hamlet* (2001), staged by Al-Bassam's British troupe in Kuwait and Tunisia.[118] When rewriting the play for a western audience, Al-Bassam says, he sought to recreate for them the "voyeuristic thrill" and "sense of strangeness in familiarity" felt by a contemporary Arab audience watching "radical political theatre." As Al-Bassam describes it, this alienation effect required him to drop Shakespeare's too-familiar words and take *Hamlet* through the looking glass of a double translation, into a new English text via an imaginary intermediary layer of Arabic:

> My only defense against this paralysis [in the face of rewriting Shakespeare] was to distance myself from the original I knew so well. I imagined myself as one of those Arab spectators in Tunisia: the humble Arab watcher of Shakespeare who knew very little English, and only parts of the plot, but who relied essentially on her own silent translation of the events on stage, using her own experiences and images and words to construct her own distorted, subjective, flawed yet

> entirely whole and true experience of the performance. This imagined Arab spectator was the guide that led me through the rewrite of the play. It was sometimes a man and sometimes a woman, sometimes old and sometimes young, sometimes a Muslim, sometimes a Christian, sometimes Tunisian, sometimes Syrian, sometimes Egyptian . . . and so on. The guide's voice soon multiplied into a concert of voices in which Shakespeare's original got lost and became one voice amongst many. I listened hard to these imaginary Arab guides, I listened hard to their poetry, anger, irony and sorrow and was careful not to lose any of these feelings in writing the play in English.[119]

The resulting five-act script closely follows Shakespeare, with at-times-brilliant trompe-l'oeuil paraphrase. Al-Bassam's English also mimics the bombastic cadences of today's Arab political rhetoric. As in Shakespeare, Hamlet returns from study abroad for his father's funeral. Claudius seizes power: "The dawn has risen upon the people of our nation; the New Democracy begins today."[120] Hamlet, "dazed by the stench of rot"[121] in the kingdom, grief-stricken and disgusted at his mother's remarriage, and then apprised of his father's murder by a People's Liberation Brigade leaflet, gradually becomes an Islamist insurgent and a real threat to the Claudius regime.

In contrast to his impotent, gelded, or cuckolded Arabic-language cousins, this Hamlet's masculinity seems unproblematic. (When he repudiates Ophelia it is for purely political reasons; the Arabic-language rewrite adds back in some of the sexual innuendo absent from Al-Bassam's original.) He is an effective political actor. Nor does he have any trouble with words. He remains a forceful and eloquent speaker even as he rejects politics and declares war:

> I bear witness that there is no God but Allah and that Mohammad is his messenger. The Assembly shall hear my words: I, Hamlet, son of Hamlet, son of Hamlet am the rightful heir to this nation's throne. My rule will crush the fingers of thieving bureaucrats, neutralize the hypocrites, tame the fires of debauchery that engulf our cities and return our noble people to the path of God. Our enemies comprehend only the language of blood for this, the time for the pen has passed and we enter the era of the sword. We crack the skull of falsehood against a rock and lo! Only the Truth re-

> mains. Let it be so and may God raise the profile of His martyrs![122]

In the last scene he is presented as an equal and counterpart to the king: "Hamlet is firing mortars from the Mosque and Claudius is firing from the Palace."[123]

However, the play's real power is bigger than either Hamlet or Claudius. Its representative is the Arms Dealer from whom both men buy their weapons. She goes everywhere and interacts with all the other characters; they compete for her help.[124] Untouched by the action, she is nonetheless central to the play. She introduces herself in the prologue:

> Glimpsed in the corridors of power, blurred in the backdrop of official state photographs, faceless at parties, anonymous at airports, trained as a banker, conversant in Pashtun, Arabic, Farsi, and Hebrew, feeding off desire: I am an Arms Dealer.[125]

As we have seen, at the imaginative center of post-1976 Arabic *Hamlet* plays there is often a self-serving and irresistible force, defined as "The Power" (*al-sulṭa*) and portrayed as protean and all-consuming. Al-Bassam's play fits this pattern, but with a twist. The play's real Power, dwarfing even Claudius, is militarized global capitalism. Its faces include the United States, oil interests, the global arms trade, and so on.

I have alluded to some troubling para-Shakespearean scenes in the Arabic *Hamlet* plays. Like those plays, *The Al-Hamlet Summit* includes a scene in which the central monster's caprice is laid bare and its pattern of domination is vividly, even pornographically evoked. As in some of the other plays (where Claudius, e.g., seduces Ophelia), the tyranny is shown in sexualized terms. However, since *Al-Hamlet Summit*'s mythical villain is bigger than Claudius, its most memorable scene dramatizes Claudius's weakness, not his power.

All five of our other plays omit Shakespeare's "prayer scene," in which Claudius kneels to seek forgiveness for his crimes.[126] That monologue, in which Claudius bows his "stubborn knees"[127] and tries to force his soul to repent, reveals the usurper's anguish and reminds viewers of his human weakness. By omitting the scene, the Arabic plays leave Claudius opaque, adding to the sense of awe that surrounds him. (In this they follow Mohamed Sobhi's early 1970s intuition that "it would not do" for Claudius to have a conscience, as I noted in chapter 3.) Al-Bassam's play does just the opposite. *The Al-Hamlet Summit* turns the prayer scene into a long, delirious monologue. The Saddam Hussein–like Claudius climbs atop his desk, undressing as he talks, until he remains kneeling in his underwear. "Oh God, teach me the meaning of petro dollars," he prays. "I am transparent, so transparent my flesh emerges like calves milk—I beg you, Lord, give me the recognition I need and help me calculate what is good . . .

> Let me not be disagreeable to you, God, I do not compete with you, how could these packets of human flesh compete with your infinity; I am your agent, nor am I an ill partner for your gluttony and endless filth. I do not try to be pure: I have learnt so much filth, I eat filth, I am an artist of filth I make mounds of human bodies, sacrifices to your glory, I adore the stench of rotting peasants gassed with your technology, I am a descendant of the Prophet, Peace be Upon Him, and I have an honorary MA from Oxford University and you, you are God. . . .
>
> In front of your beneficence, I am a naked mortal, full of awe: my ugliness is not unbearable, surely it is not? My nose is not so hooked is it, my eyes so diabolical as when you offered me your Washington virgins and CIA opium. Oh, God, my ugliness does not offend you now, does it?
>
> Your plutonium, your loans, your democratic filth that drips off your ecstatic crowds—I want them all, Oh God; I want your vaseline smiles and I want your pimp ridden plutocracies; I want your world shafting bank; I want it shafting me now—offer me the shafting hand of redemption—Oh God let us be dirty together, won't you?[128]

Claudius's prayer expresses what was only incipient in the other plays: the identification of the monstrous antagonist as a capricious deity. The despot who was all-powerful in several of the other plays appears here completely reduced and transparent. He is as pathetic as an addict pleading with his dealer. Whereas earlier versions of the character govern through puppet shows, this Claudius is a puppet himself. Yet rather than being dissipated, the villain's magical powers are transferred upstairs—to the United States, global capitalism, oil interests, and so forth. The play suggests that these powers are enormous, nearly unlimited. The chameleon Arms Dealer is just a branch of the enterprise. Al-Bassam's audacity lies not in casting an Arab leader as Claudius but in casting the United States as God.

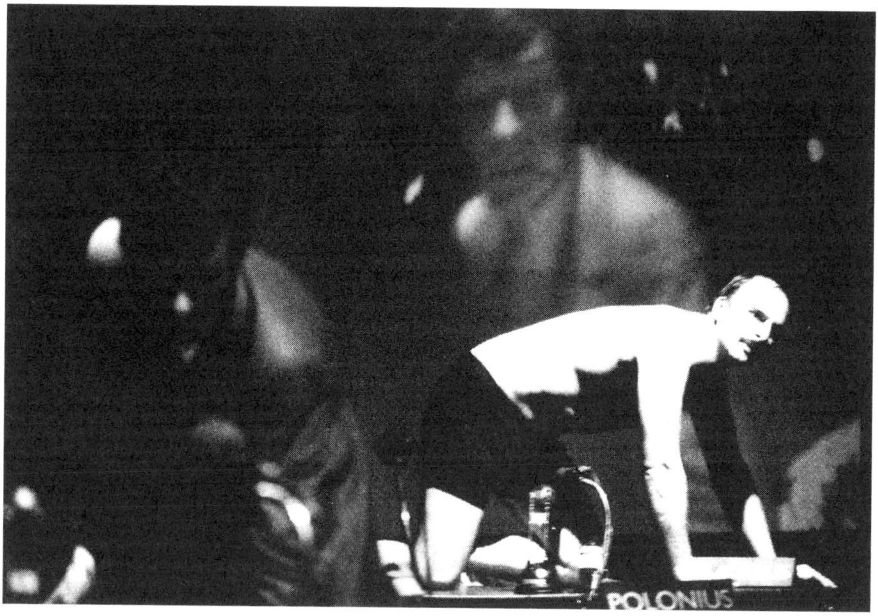

6.2. Nigel Barrett as Claudius in Sulayman Al-Bassam's *The Al-Hamlet Summit* (2002). Courtesy of Sulayman Al-Bassam.

Post-Political Laughs

The borderline case of Al-Bassam's English-language *Al-Hamlet Summit* helps illuminate the reception of some of its Arabic-language cousins. The British play bristles with fragments taken from the contemporary Arab *political* imagination—the imagination of Al-Bassam's fictional "humble watcher." Reflecting a newly globalized Arab public sphere, it offers a channel-flipping mix of Al-Jazeera, CNN, the BBC, democratic rhetoric, TV violence, Umm Kulthūm (1904–75), and Mahmūd Darwīsh (1941–2008).[129] Claudius's last speech, a televised address declaring war on "terrorist positions belonging to Hamlet and his army,"[130] manages to lift from then-current speeches by George W. Bush, Saddam Hussein, Osama bin Laden, *and* Ariel Sharon.[131] However, Al-Bassam's play, designed to appeal to British and American viewers unacquainted with Arab drama, is written from outside the Arabic *theatrical* tradition. This helps explain why it deviates from many of the patterns common to our other Arab *Hamlets*.

To its author's surprised delight, the play was quickly reabsorbed into that theatrical tradition when the English-language version played at the Cairo International Festival of Experimental Theatre in September 2002. A mostly Egyptian crowd had mobbed the venue, complaining that only foreigners seemed to get in. Al-Bassam recalls:

> At midnight we were asked to perform a second "command" performance to placate the angry audiences who were still waiting outside the theatre. The actors were happy to oblige and so at midnight the curtain went up again to a predominantly Arab[ic]-speaking audience. This Arab[ic]-speaking audience (who had access to a live translation) uncovered a strain of comedy in the work that until that night had been completely neglected. The opening scene that had previously been received in silence and solemnity by English-speaking audiences, had the house rolling in laughter. Once over the shock, the actors responded to their house and the work took on entirely new cultural meanings.[132]

This audience's unexpected laughter helps us solve an obvious puzzle: if young Arab dramatists have renounced *Mousetrap* allegories, why do they still write *Hamlet* offshoots at all? I have suggested that Shakespeare's Hamlet needs evidence to convict Claudius in the eyes of the Danish court, "grounds more relative" (relatable, tellable) than a ghost story. As we saw in the previous chapter, 1960s and early 70s Arab political theatre often operated on this model, either addressing friendly criticism to the regime or (later) seeking to expose its shortcomings in the court of public opinion. After this mousetrap model grew obsolete, dramatists switched from allegorical adaptation of *Hamlet* to ironic intertextual rewriting. This rewriting no longer aims to convince or expose anyone. What, then, do playwrights and audiences get from it?

Mamduh Adwan's 1976 play appears to suggest that appropriate political action could still be possible, if only the audience does not "oversleep" like Hamlet. The play at least imparts a notion of what appropriate action might look like. The later Arab *Hamlet* plays considered in this chapter hold out no such hopes. Omran's carnivalesque musical sidesteps Hamlet's dilemma, instead opting to create a spontaneous, temporary community with the audience.[133] But in the three more recent plays (Aboudoma's *Dance of the Scorpions,* al-Asadi's *Forget Hamlet,* and Marzougui's *Ismail/Hamlet*), the time is already too far "out of joint" for constructive action. The dead father's cause cannot be embraced; that would be useless. Nor can it be sold out or ignored; that would be selfish and unprincipled.

Faced with such a dilemma, one reasonable response is to laugh. I do not think such laughter is a form of "resistance" in the political sense. It is not the discharge of a long-simmering fear and anger at the oppressor, the public expression of a "hidden transcript" or semi-private counter-official discourse. As we have seen, the unveiling of power in these plays has no revolutionary effect; on balance it is politically conservative, reaffirming the all-powerful nature of the regime at the play's center. To expose Claudius's monstrosity may actually increase his power. In practice, until events took a surprising turn in early 2011, the authoritarian regimes ruling the nations of these playwrights had proven impossible for internal critics to reform or dislodge.

A better analogue to the audience's laughter might be that of Nietzsche's Dionysian man. In *The Birth of Tragedy,* Nietzsche describes this type in terms of Shakespeare's Hamlet, with the important difference that he gives the Dionysian man the consolation of the artistic. While Hamlet must live his impossible situation, the Dionysian man can transmute it into art:

> The Dionysian man resembles Hamlet: both have once truly looked into the essence of things, they have gained knowledge, and nausea inhibits action *for their action could not change anything in the eternal nature of things*; they feel it to be *ridiculous or humiliating that they should be asked to set right a world that is out of joint*. Knowledge kills action; action requires the veils of illusion: that is the doctrine of Hamlet, not that cheap wisdom of Jack the Dreamer who reflects too much and, as it were, from an excess of possibilities does not get around to action. Not reflection, no—true knowledge, an insight into the horrible truth, outweighs any motive for action, both in Hamlet and in the Dionysian man.... Here, when the danger to his will is greatest, art approaches as a saving sorceress, expert at healing. She alone knows how to turn these nauseous thoughts about the horror or absurdity of existence into notions with which one can live: these are the sublime as the artistic taming of the horrible, *and the comic as the artistic discharge of the nausea of absurdity.*[134]

On this reading, we can conjecture that Al-Bassam's English play, rife with political signifiers, was received *post*-politically by his Arab audience. The sophisticated Cairene theatre festival community (including those spectators who persevered at the Hanager Theatre until midnight, then managed to squeeze into the small auditorium) was certainly familiar with the heroic Hamlets of 1960s and early 70s Arab drama and would likely have known at least one of the post-1975 plays. Such viewers would understand, either through personal experience or inherited theatrical lore, the irrelevance of *Mousetrap*-like performances to President Hosni Mubarak's regime and its counterparts across the Arab world. They would know all too well that their theatre-making and theatre-watching "action could not change anything in the [seemingly] eternal nature of things." Their laughter, then, watching a British cast enact Arab-style political turmoil in a crowded theatre in the middle of the night, would be a genuinely carefree, no longer bitter, Dionysian laughter.

Epilogue

HAMLETS WITHOUT HAMLET

Since I started working on this project in January of 2001, a strange thing has happened: my intended readers have felt the Arab world draw closer. Part of this has happened by choice: many Anglo-American intellectuals feel that the Arab and Muslim worlds can no longer be ignored. Their hunger for fresh insight has spurred not only thoughtful long-form journalism but also new academic positions, literary translations, theatre festivals, collaborative research projects, Arabic language learning, and unprecedented levels of undergraduate study abroad in Arab countries.

Another part of it has happened by misfortune. In the past decade a broad segment of the American intelligentsia, on both the left and right, has tasted the basic experience (not to say pathology) of modern Arab politics: the feeling of being ruled rather than represented by one's own government. We can understand; our time is out of joint, too.

Leaving behind the generalized "power" and "domination" talk of the 1990s, American audiences' political concerns have grown more immediate. Perhaps this started with the contested U.S. presidential election of 2000; surely it has been heightened by the wars in Iraq and Afghanistan and the new millennium's traumas: September 11, Abu Ghraib, Hurricane Katrina, the economic crisis. Bewildered by events beyond their control, intellectuals have turned to theatre for solace and explanation.

So "political theatre," a quaint or problematic term in Anglo-American criticism in the 1980s and 1990s,[1] has returned. In 2003, Aristophanes' *Lysistrata* reappeared on stages as part of a worldwide antiwar protest; in 2004, Michael

Moore's *Fahrenheit 9/11* played to mass audiences. Since then a spate of new British and American plays, using both "verbatim theatre" and traditional drama techniques (e.g., *Stuff Happens,* 2004; *Damascus,* 2007; *Blackwatch,* 2008; *Betrayed,* 2008; *Bengal Tiger at the Baghdad Zoo*, 2009) has confronted the human cost of misinterpreting the Middle East. More broadly, many original and revived plays from *Frost/Nixon* to *Coriolanus* have explored the rhetoric of power and probed the central political questions both ancient ("What is good government?") and modern ("What is legitimate government?"). Theatre critics at the *New York Times* have noticed directors seeking "to be topical in a time out of joint."[2] A discussion in London's *Guardian* has asked: "Can political theatre change the world?"[3]

Even *Hamlet* scholarship has felt the tide. Breaking consciously with academic decorum, Linda Charnes's *Hamlet's Heirs: Shakespeare and the Politics of a New Millennium* (2006) set out to probe "the wormholes between the 'early modern' era and our own."[4] Deeper and more influential, Margreta de Grazia's *"Hamlet" without Hamlet* (2007) has challenged the 200-year western critical tradition that found the paradigm of modern consciousness in Hamlet's "deep and complex inwardness."[5] De Grazia, one of the leading figures in U.S. Shakespeare studies, refocuses attention on the "ground" of Shakespeare's play: "At his father's death, just at the point when an only son in a patrilineal system stands to inherit, Hamlet is dispossessed—and, as far as the court is concerned, legitimately." Mining *Hamlet*'s land-based wordplay, de Grazia emphasizes the territorial "privation" that leads Hamlet to adopt the roles of clown, madman, Vice, and devil:

> The promise of the patronymic is broken: Prince Hamlet does not become King Hamlet; Hamlet II does not step into the place of Hamlet I. . . . Surely the loss of the kingdom affects what Hamlet has within. . . . The play opens with threatened invasion and ends in military occupation. Framed by territorial conflict, it stages one contest over land after another.[6]

De Grazia's argument does not share the ahistorical thrust of the Arab *Hamlet* tradition, yet it joins Arab writers in recognizing the dispossession and political struggle at *Hamlet*'s core.

On Arab stages, too, frank topicality is once again in evidence. As it happens, de Grazia's title, *"Hamlet" without Hamlet,* also belongs to a play by Iraqi writer Khazal al-Majidi (Khazʿal al-Mājidī).[7] First produced in 1992, al-Majidi's short play was revived and adapted for the first production of the Baghdad Iraqi

Theatre Company (founded 2008). Its premise is that Hamlet is shipwrecked and drowns on his way to Denmark for his father's funeral: the other characters muddle along without him. Opening at Elsinore with the report of Hamlet's death (the prince himself is not among the dramatis personae), the play fits clearly into the post-1975 pattern I identified in chapter 6. However, its 2008 revival, titled *This Is Baghdad,* took a more timely turn. Director Monadhil Daood (Munāḍil Dāwūd) emphasized "the violent imagery of Iraq's recent political history" and incorporated stylistic elements of *taʿzīya* theatre in his staging.[8] The use of this traditional Shiʿa dramatic form, specific to passion plays commemorating the death of the Prophet Muhammad's grandsons Hassan and Husayn, carries a political charge: *taʿzīya* was banned in Saddam Hussein's Iraq.

In Egypt, meanwhile, a 2009 *Hamlet* adaptation picked up where Al-Bassam's Anglo-Arab *Al-Hamlet Summit* left off. Hani Afifi (Hānī ʿAfīfī) developed his play *I Am Hamlet* (*Anā Hāmlit*) as a graduation project in directing at the Artistic Creativity Center Studio, a Ministry of Culture initiative then headed by director Khaled Galal (Khālid Jalāl).[9] Afifi used four Arabic translations, further translating most of the dialogue into Egyptian colloquial Arabic.[10] The play was performed at the National Egyptian Theatre Festival in July 2009 and again at the Cairo International Festival of Experimental Theatre that October; Mohamed Fahim (Muḥammad Fahīm) as Hamlet won Best Actor.

Unlike the abstractly located adaptations discussed in chapter 6, Afifi's moves from a "Shakespearean" setting into a recognizable version of contemporary Cairo; the latter foregrounds the city's class disparities and inconveniences. Hamlet rides the metro, getting crushed by the city's commuter nightmare, or broods in his lower-middle-class room (containing only "a mattress on the floor, an old computer, a television on the floor, and many books"). The nunnery scene takes place at the pretentious Café Cilantro next to the American University in Cairo, where Ophelia orders a drink called *hūt shūklat* ("hot chocolate," in an American-style paper cup). At the climactic moment Hamlet exclaims not "Get thee to a nunnery" but: "How can I date someone who has 500 friends on Facebook?"[11] The play includes humor but not irony.

I Am Hamlet's use of twenty-first-century politics is brief but telling. As Hamlet is dying, the audience hears "the sound of helicopters and infantry" and Fortinbras enters, "wearing a full modern suit similar in appearance to the president of a European country or Bush the Son." When he speaks (in blunt colloquial Arabic), the allusion is unmistakable:

EP.1. Nunnery scene at Café Cilantro in Hani Afifi's *I Am Hamlet* (2009). Courtesy of Hani Afifi.

Fortinbras: All this blood. All this violence. This terrorism. We have some interests in this region. We cannot allow one soldier of our armed forces to leave this land until we have secured our interests and laid the foundation for democracy and freedom in this country.

Horatio: Fortinbras!

> Fortinbras: The son. Fortinbras the son. (*He begins to give a speech*) Our interests in this region and our national security require us to fight our enemies abroad rather than wait for them to arrive in our country. We must prevent our enemies from threatening us, our allies, and our friends with weapons of mass destruction. Victory in the war on terror means victory in the war of ideas. It is an ideological war first and foremost. We will not stand by with our hands tied before the issues of human rights and the suppression of freedoms and racial discrimination and the persecution of minorities in this region. We are a nation at war. We have made progress in the war on terror, but we face a long struggle. We have become safer, but we are not yet safe.[12]

As he continues for another three or four cliché-ridden sentences ("with us or against us," "condemn violence," "stop all support for terrorist organizations"), the screen behind him shows George W. Bush making a televised address to the American people.[13] Performed when Bush was no longer president, this closing scene aimed for comic effect. But the comedy was nervous, linking the powerless and futureless Hamlet character with Egypt's unpopular status as a U.S. ally in the Middle East under longtime president Hosni Mubarak.

Afifi's *I Am Hamlet* repeats Al-Bassam's move (at the same festival seven years earlier) of addressing the United States instead of or alongside the local Arab regime. This version of the omnivorous Leviathan/Minotaur figure appeals to Arab and also Anglo-American audiences; it will likely continue to be replayed in Shakespeare adaptations as well as in Arab theatre more broadly. Al-Bassam himself has reprised the trope in his *Richard III: An Arab Tragedy* (2007–9), interpreting the victorious Richmond as a U.S. general or diplomat haplessly entering Iraq. Commissioned by the Royal Shakespeare Company as its first-ever Arabic-language play, *Richard III* also toured widely: Western Europe, Syria, the Gulf, and high-profile festivals in Washington and New York.[14] Deborah Shaw, the company's associate director who commissioned it, has stayed involved in Arab theatre, notably helping to found Monadhil Daood's Baghdad Theatre Company.[15]

Such connections show how the Iraq war has given a new turn to the kaleidoscope in which Arab theatre is received and produced. For the first time in decades, Arab artists are conscious of western eyes upon them; the upheaval has brought new resources and audiences into view. It will be interesting to see whether and how the magnetic pull of European and American grants, theatre festivals, and publications affects the types of work Arab artists produce, especially in expensive arts such as theatre and on the obvious intercultural ground of Shakespeare. Funding attracts; so does the prospect of an audience empowered to make political decisions, even if that audience sits in Washington or London rather than Cairo, Damascus, or Baghdad.

The surprising events of early 2011 (which occurred as this book was in press) seem likely to accelerate all these trends. The postrevolutionary uncertainty in Egypt and Tunisia has energized theatre makers to claim the public sphere lest it disappear again. Meanwhile American television screens and front pages have celebrated the brave public performances of Arab "youth"; Egypt's popular uprising gave CNN's prime-time news shows their highest ratings ever.[16] The images have swirled with increasing speed, appearing to merge Mideast and Midwest (for a few days, the example of Cairo even helped inspire pro-union protesters in Wisconsin) and to fuse political theatre with theatrical politics. When the U.S. government released video of a much diminished Osama bin Laden *watching video footage of himself on television*, the gap between local action and global spectacle seemed to close up entirely.

Amid this apparent convergence between the political concerns of Anglo-American intellectuals and their Arab counterparts, will there continue to be a distinct Arab *Hamlet* tradition? On this question (which only time can answer) let me offer two closing thoughts. First: Arab theatre has been an international phenomenon from the start. As this book has shown, the Arab Hero Hamlet and his ironic successors were born into a world already overpopulated with competing versions and interpretations. In every period there has been a privileged interlocutor (from Alexandre Dumas and Victor Hugo to A. C. Bradley to Grigori Kozintsev), yet these sources have fed a distinct and coherent Arab tradition of Shakespeare interpretation.

Second: today's convergence may be only apparent. Even if different audiences arrive at the same spot, each remains marked by its separate history. They may thirst for the same stories but find different meanings in them. And with all the necessary caveats (global cultural flows on one hand, extreme localization like Afifi's on the other), I do believe that there is such a thing today as an Arab audience. The century of Arab nationalism is spent, but as an imagined community brought together by satellite television, "the Arab world" has more reality than ever. Whatever *Hamlet*s Arab adapters may devise will surely reflect (and reflect on) that reality.

NOTES

Preface and Acknowledgments

[1] Levin, "Shakespeare in the Light of Comparative Literature," 117–18.

[2] Welsh, *Hamlet in His Modern Guises,* 143.

[3] Scofield, *The Ghosts of Hamlet,* 3.

[4] Kott, *Shakespeare Our Contemporary,* 61.

[5] William Shakespeare, *Hamlet,* ed. Harold Jenkins (Walton-on-Thames: Thomas Nelson & Sons Ltd, 1997), 1.2.129. Subsequent *Hamlet* references are to this Arden edition: the one, as Margreta de Grazia has put it, "most saturated with the modern critical tradition." On "sullied" versus "solid," see Jenkins's long note.

[6] The Ghost, perhaps nostalgic for an earlier Elizabethan version of the play, wants to cast Hamlet in an old-fashioned revenge tragedy. Claudius, whose stilted verse and pageantry struggle to stage a believable royal court, needs Hamlet to play "our chiefest courtier, cousin, and our son" (1.2.117). And comic director Polonius would like Hamlet to star in a romantic comedy opposite Ophelia: he echoes the love-as-commerce language of Shakespeare's comedies, sets up overhearing scenes, and plays the obstructing parent role most familiar from the almost-comedy *Romeo and Juliet.* (I am grateful to Matthew Greenfield for comments on an early formulation of this idea.)

[7] Coleridge is quoted in David Farley-Hills, *Critical Responses to Hamlet,* 2:62. See also Nietzsche, *The Birth of Tragedy and the Case of Wagner,* 60.

[8] *Hamlet,* 3.1.71–74.

[9] An excellent introduction to the history and meaning of Russian and Soviet *Hamlet* appropriation, and one of the models for my study, is Rowe, *Hamlet: A Window on Russia.*

[10] "Members of different communities will disagree because from each of their respective positions the other 'simply' cannot see what is obviously and inescapably there. This, then, is the explanation for the stability of interpretation among different readers (they belong to the same community)." Fish, *Is There a Text In This Class?,* 15.

[11] Barbara Everett, *Young Hamlet: Essays on Shakespeare's Tragedies,* quoted in Welsh, *Hamlet in His Modern Guises,* 14.

12 Vysotsky was a popular balladeer and actor at the Taganka Theatre under the direction of Yuri Lyubimov. Known for his unflinching lyrics, hoarse baritone, and heavy drinking, he came to be identified with the character of Hamlet, whom he played throughout the 1970s. See Golub, "Between the Curtain and the Grave"; and Smeliansky, *The Russian Theatre after Stalin,* 94–100.

Introduction

1 Shakespeare, *Hamlet,* 5.1.250.
2 On the welcome but limited opportunities the Royal Shakespeare Company offered to the international shows, see Duncan-Jones, "Complete Works, Essential Year?"
3 Shakespeare, *Hamlet,* 3.2.354–363.
4 Ibid., 1.2.83–85.
5 See, e.g., ibid., 1.3.17–24, 3.1.155, 4.7.134, 5.1.143–44, and 5.2.402–3.
6 He quibbles on *kin-kind, sun-son,* and *common.* Ibid., 1.2.65–74.
7 This book will continue to use the word "appropriation" as the most general term, encompassing translation, adaptation, rewriting, and allusion. I use this term without its sinister subtext (the sense in which, for instance, an authoritarian government might "appropriate" the work of a dissident writer by giving him a prestigious state prize). In this study "appropriation" is neutral as to motive: it simply means taking Shakespeare into oneself, making him one's own.
8 See Berkowitz, *Shakespeare on the American Yiddish Stage,* 92–96.
9 A few I have found particularly inspiring: Taylor, *Reinventing Shakespeare*; Bates, "Shakespeare in Latvia"; Rowe, *Hamlet: A Window on Russia*; and Zimmermann, "Is Hamlet Germany?"
10 The International Shakespeare Association was founded in 1974 in Stratford-upon-Avon. That same year, the journal *Shakespeare Translation,* later called *Shakespeare Worldwide,* was launched in Tokyo. The first World Shakespeare Congress was held in Washington, D.C., in 1976; subsequent congresses in Stratford-upon-Avon (1981), Berlin (1986), Tokyo (1991), Los Angeles (1996), and Valencia (2001) have reinforced in festive style the international character of Shakespeare studies. The published proceedings of the congress have carried such reception-aware titles as *Images of Shakespeare* (1986), *Shakespeare and Cultural Traditions* (1994), *Shakespeare and National Culture* (1997), and *Shakespeare and the Mediterranean* (2004). The 2006 Congress, held in Australia, pluralized the Bard's name for the first time: see Fotheringham, Jansohn, and White, *Shakespeare's World/World Shakespeares.*

It is impossible to summarize the ever-growing body of scholarship on Shakespeare appropriation, but let me cite a sample. On Eastern European Shakespeare, see Hattaway, Sokolova, and Roper, *Shakespeare in the New Europe*; and Stribrny, *Shakespeare and Eastern Europe.* See also Shurbanov and Sokolova, *Painting Shakespeare Red.*

For Japanese Shakespeare, see, e.g., Ueno, *Hamlet and Japan*; Sasayama, Mulryne, and Shewring, *Shakespeare and the Japanese Stage*; Kawachi, *Japanese Studies in Shakespeare and His Contemporaries*; and Anzai, *Shakespeare in Japan.* Also useful is the Shakespeare Performance in Asia project; see their website at http://web.mit.edu/

shakespeare/asia/. On China, see Zhang, *Shakespeare in China*; Li, *Shashbiya: Staging Shakespeare in China*; and especially Huang, *Chinese Shakespeares.*

On Shakespeare in South Africa, see Johnson, *Shakespeare and South Africa*; Quince, *Shakespeare in South Africa*; and Distiller, *South Africa, Shakespeare, and Post-Colonial Culture.*

On Shakespeare in Israel, see Oz, "Transformations of Authenticity: The Merchant of Venice in Israel"; Yogev, "'How Shall We Find the Concord of this Discord?'"; and Oz, *Strands Afar Remote.*

An important addition to the growing world Shakespeare conversation is the series of essay collections International Studies in Shakespeare and His Contemporaries, edited by Jay Halio and published by University of Delaware Press. Other notable recent edited collections have included Loomba and Orkin, *Post-Colonial Shakespeares* (1998); Desmet and Sawyer, *Shakespeare and Appropriation* (1999); Pujante and Hoenselaars, *Four Hundred Years of Shakespeare in Europe* (2003), Hoenselaars, *Shakespeare and the Language of Translation* (2004); and Massai, *World-Wide Shakespeares* (2005).

11 See, e.g, Heylen, *Translation, Poetics, and the Stage.*

12 See Kennedy, *Foreign Shakespeare*; and Pavis, *Theatre at the Crossroads of Culture.*

13 See Dollimore and Sinfield, *Political Shakespeare.*

14 See, e.g, Singh, "Different Shakespeares"; Loomba and Orkin, *Post-Colonial Shakespeares*; and Cartelli, *Repositioning Shakespeare.*

15 Kennedy, "Afterword: Shakespearean Orientalism," 300.

16 An intriguing but simplistic attempt at such a universal theory is Gran, "The Political Economy of Aesthetics."

17 See Alsenad, "Professional Production of Shakespeare in Iraq"; Kanaan, "Shakespeare on the Arab Page and Stage"; Tounsi, "Shakespeare in Arabic": Twaij, "Shakespeare in the Arab World"; and Amel Amin Zaki, "Shakespeare in Arabic." But see also Sameh Fekry Hanna's work on the early translations, cited in chapter 3, note 26, below.

18 See Ṣulayḥa, *Shaksbīriyyāt.*

19 See, however, Bushrui, "Shakespeare and Arabic Drama and Poetry"; Al-Bahar, "Shakespeare in Early Arabic Adaptations"; Moussa Mahmoud, "*Hamlet* in Egypt"; Ghazoul, "The Arabization of *Othello*"; and Al-Shetawi, "*Hamlet* in Arabic."

20 An overly earnest refutation of the legend is Ḥamāda, *'Urūbat Shaksbīr.*

21 An agenda informed by Chakrabarty, "Postcoloniality and the Artifice of History"; and Chakrabarty, *Provincializing Europe.*

22 See Ashcroft, Griffiths, and Tiffin, *The Empire Writes Back.*

23 Shawqī, *Maṣra' Klīyūbātrā.* As Rafik Darragi explains, Shawqi's play pointedly sidesteps Shakespeare's *Antony and Cleopatra.* It reverts instead to sixteenth-century French sources, based in turn on Plutarch's life of Cleopatra, that downplay the affair with Antony and bring Cleopatra's politics to center stage. See Darragi, "Ideological Appropriation and Sexual Politics." See also Al-Khatib, "Rewriting History, Unwriting Literature"; and Soyinka, "Shakespeare and the Living Dramatist." Of Shawqi's anticolonial rewriting, Soyinka remarks, "The emendations are predictable" (152).

[24] Ahmad, *In Theory: Classes, Nations, Literatures.*

[25] Loomba, "'Local-Manufacture Made-in-India Othello Fellows,'" 163.

[26] Makaryk, *Shakespeare in the Undiscovered Bourn,* 5.

[27] Ibid.

[28] For an attempt to theorize "local" Shakespeare appropriation that ultimately returns (albeit via Bourdieu) to "the facts of the matter themselves," see the editor's introduction to Massai, *World-Wide Shakespeares.*

[29] See Bakhtin, *The Dialogic Imagination*; Jauss, *Toward an Aesthetic of Reception*; Friedrich, *The Language Parallax*; and Friedrich, *Language, Context, and the Imagination.*

[30] On social fields that both set parameters for individual action and (to some extent) respond to it, see Bourdieu, *Outline of a Theory of Practice.*

[31] On *Antony and Cleopatra,* see note 23 in this chapter. On postcolonial versions of *Othello,* see Ghazoul, "The Arabization of *Othello.*" Two quite different examples of such appropriations are *Doditello* (2001), Sameh Mahran's farce incorporating the story of Dodi Fayyed and Diana, Princess of Wales; and Salih, *Season of Migration to the North.* On *The Merchant of Venice* see Bayer, "Shylock's Revenge"; and Al-Shetawi, "*The Merchant of Venice* in Arabic."

[32] The first and still dominant interpretation of *Othello* in Arabic emphasizes jealousy and gender violence rather than religion, race, or nation. Badawi notes that the earliest production was subtitled *Ḥiyal al-Rijāl* (The Wiles of Men); see Badawi, "Shakespeare and the Arabs," 195. An anecdote from 1960s Baghdad confirms that this emphasis continued to resonate with viewers in the postcolonial period: "After a production of Othello in Iraq in 1962, one man in the audience wanted to kill the actor who had played Iago when he met him on the street. It seems that the performance had been so real to that man that he thought the actor *was* Iago, the devil who had caused a great love to be destroyed." Alsenad, "Professional Production of Shakespeare in Iraq," 94.

[33] For an argument that the frame stories in *Taming of the Shrew* and *Midsummer Night's Dream* echo the structure of the tales in *One Thousand and One Nights,* see Ḥamāda, *'Urūbat Shaksbīr*; and Ghazoul, *Nocturnal Poetics,* 108–20. For the Sufi resonance of the mystical discourse of love in *Romeo and Juliet*, see Al-Dabbagh, "The Oriental Framework of *Romeo and Juliet.*"

[34] Two exceptions, Tawfiq al-Hakim's brief experiment in *Our Theatrical Mold* and Nader Omran's 1984 *Hamlet* adaptation, are discussed in chapters 5 and 6.

[35] Al-Azm, "Owning the Future." See my lengthy discussion in chapter 1.

[36] Al-Shetawi, "*Hamlet* in Arabic," 49.

[37] The metaphor comes from the way Arabic is written and read. Written as a consonantal skeleton, Arabic words have no definite grammatical function or meaning until "voiced" or "put in motion" (the Arabic word for vowel is *ḥaraka*: movement) by the addition of short vowels. As Brinkley Messick has noted, Arabic thus privileges orality and performance even more than speakers of European languages (and readers of Derrida) are accustomed to think. Every reading must animate the written characters on the page, just as every staging or adaptation of a play must animate the written characters in the script. See Messick, *The Calligraphic State,* 25–27.

[38] Eliot, "The Love Song of J. Alfred Prufrock," 4.

[39] Shakespeare, *Hamlet,* 3.2.16–45.
[40] Ibid., 5.2.29.
[41] Ibid., 3.2.233.

CHAPTER 1. *HAMLET* IN THE DAILY DISCOURSE OF ARAB IDENTITY

[1] Newstrom, "'Step Aside, I'll Show Thee a President': George W. as Henry V?"
[2] Foakes, "Introduction," vii.
[3] "*Lā yazālu shaksbīr kaʿbatan naḥijju īlayhā wa-qiblatan nuṣallī ʿalayhā.*" Quoted in Bushrui, "Shakespeare and Arabic Drama and Poetry," 16. Bushrui remarks that "many Arabs will still feel inclined to agree." Bushrui, "Shakespeare and Arabic Drama and Poetry," 16.
[4] Ṣāghiya, "Yūsuf Zaʿīn, ʿAbd al-Nāṣir, Ṣaddām, wa . . . Jūrj Sūrīl." The word I have translated as "swear by" carries the religious connotation of invoking a text as a scriptural authority. The column itself is about the undead presence of Arab nationalist ideology in contemporary discourse.
[5] On the controversy and its meanings, see Klausen, *The Cartoons That Shook the World.*
[6] See, e.g., Abu-Nasr, "Muslim Leaders Urge Calm over Cartoons" (quoting Lebanese commentator Samir Atallah); Sullivan, "Something Is Rotten . . ."; Stilwell, "Something Is Rotten Outside the State of Denmark"; and Oppenheimer, "Something Rotten in Tehran."
[7] Belien, "Buy Danish: Nothing Rotten in the State of Denmark."
[8] Klausen, "Rotten Judgment in the State of Denmark."
[9] Mishkhas, "Something Is Rotten in the State of Denmark."
[10] Al-Quwayz, "Shukran Bīl Klīntūn wa-Shukran Shaksbīr."
[11] Tarawnah, "Something Is Rotten in the State of Denmark."
[12] An exception, and one of the most sustained engagements with the Shakespeare quotation, was a blog posting by an anthropologist of Islam. See Varisco, "Much Ado about Something Rotten in Denmark."
[13] Google search performed February 19, 2006. Some hits represent duplicate versions of the same articles. On the other hand, articles that allude to the line without using the precise syntax "something is rotten" are not included in the count. Because the phrase can be translated in many different ways in Arabic (and no single translation is standard), it would be difficult to get a corresponding count based on Google searches in Arabic.
[14] However, Shakespeare never visited Denmark; why should his imaginary Dane, some four hundred years later, still shape how we discuss the place?
[15] The uses of *Julius Caesar* and *Merchant of Venice* vary even less than those of *Hamlet.* Briefly: *Julius Caesar* occurs on both sides of debates over dictatorship versus rebellion; Brutus is either a heroic tyrant-slayer or an unleasher of political chaos (or sometimes both). Allusions to *The Merchant of Venice* serve to distinguish principles from interests in a way that parallels the main uses of *Hamlet*: Shylock "with his moneyboxes and his sharp knives" is invoked mainly by Syrian and Iraqi polemicists to warn their readers about the dangers of betraying their (Arab, socialist) principles for (Jewish, capitalist) interests and temptations. The latter could include political

and/or economic modernization, free trade, and normalization with Israel. The invocation of Shylock, sometimes drawing subtly on the Islamic taboo against usury, helps connect the sharp knife to the moneybox, warning readers to be wary of both.

16 The day after the capture, the Lebanese daily *Al-Nahar* wondered in a three-column front-page headline: "To Execute, or Not to Execute? That Is the Question." See "Al-Iʿdām aw Lā Iʿdām Tilka Hiya al-Qaḍīya."

17 Al-Shaḥāt, "Aḥdāth fī al-Akhbār."

18 After the assassination of former Lebanese prime minister Rafiq Hariri, a protester wrote in English on a wall at Beirut's Liberty Square (formerly Martyrs' Square): "To be or not to be, now is the time." Several variations on the phrase occurred on the plaza, along with many other outpourings of grief and anger, mainly at Syria. An op-ed by Yemen's former foreign minister gives the other side of the issue: "So now we Arabs and Muslims are living through difficult hours. Shall we be, or not be? The right response to this question is to say that we will persist, as long as we take a courageous position and announce unambiguously that we categorically reject any aggression against Syria." See Al-Aṣnaj, "Lubnān al-Dars wa-l-Tajriba."

19 A Shiʿa youth group website urged young Iraqis to vote using a short dialogue between Sara and Ahmad. Says Sara: "That's right, Ahmad. As for the question of 'to be or not to be,' if we don't participate in making these elections work, the seats in Parliament will go to those who won't protect the people and the nation, and so the killing and looting will continue." "Ḥubb wasṭ lahīb al-nār" [Love amid the flames], on the website of Nashaṭāt al-hay'a al-shaʿbiyya li-isnād al-intikhābāt [The Popular Youth Organization for Organizing Elections], http://iraqintikhabat.com/public/nashatat/nsha.htm. See also, e.g., Kākhayī, "Nuṣawwit am Lā Nuṣawwit? Dhālika Huwa al-Su'āl" [Do We Vote or Don't We Vote? That Is The Question].

20 For a typical example of the usage of the phrase "a 'to be or not to be' game" see Shobokshi, "The Arab Exorcism."

21 See, e.g., the entry on Ahmed Moustafa's blog for January 21, 2009, entitled "Obama Is the Actual President of the US, Therefore, To Be or Not to Be This Is the Question," http://www.dialogueinaction.net/ar/node/1638.

22 Badr ʿAbd al-Malik, "Ughnīyat al-Ḥurriyya fī Ṭahrān" (The Song of Freedom in Tehran).

23 For instance, a columnist in the Egyptian state daily *Al-Ahram* warns that modernizing Egypt's economy will take a conscious unified effort. She links several themes from *Hamlet*: being versus nonbeing, talk versus action, and dreaming versus conscious awareness: "The idea of modernizing Egypt is among the leading ideas at the opening of the year 2002. Wisdom and philosophy come from the call to this idea, which implies a deep meaning and an important issue called 'To Be or Not to Be.' . . . We stand to realize the most difficult and urgent task Egypt has undertaken since the age of Muhammad Ali. And we should know in advance that we [may have to] dig through stone to be able to modernize Egypt. For the issue is much greater than one of dreams and wishes and words." Al-Burtuqālī, "Taḥdīth Miṣr Yabda' bi-l-ʿIlm wa-l-ʿUlamā.'"

24 E.g., His Royal Highness Prince Khalid bin Faisal (Khālid bin Fayṣal) of Saudi Arabia, president of the Arab Thought Foundation, says of the developing countries who must decide whether (or how) to join the globalized capitalist mainstream: "And

every nation feels now that it is faced with a crossroads . . . or perhaps some [nations] in the developing world particularly are coming up against the famous expression, 'to be or not to be.'" Quoted in Al-Mihnā, "Sumūwuhu Yaftatiḥ al-Yawm al-Ijtimāʿ al-Taʾsīsī li-l-Muʾassasa al-Ahliyya li-l-Fikr al-ʿArabī."

25 A columnist for the socialist newspaper *Al-Ahalī,* commenting on a mixed-gender Friday prayer service led by Dr. Amina Wadud, concludes: "Our dear Shaykh [Jamal] al-Banna, it isn't really a question of "religious authority," but a different civil issue: does a woman have the right to be a whole person, or does she not have it? That is the question, as our friend Hamlet would put it." See Sālim, "Al-Mar'a bayn al-Imāma wa-l-Quwāma."

26 E.g., Muṣṭafā al-Qaradāghi, "Al-ʿIrāq Yakūn aw Lā Yakūn Hadhā Huwa al-Su'āl?"

27 A columnist writes (in English): "[T]o paraphrase Hamlet, democracy is to be or not to be. Either the rules of the game apply to all concerned, or do not apply at all." Sid-Ahmed, "Mohieddin for President."

28 In a religious lesson titled "The Battle of Badr (To Be or Not to Be)," by preacher Hazem Shoman in the Raḥma Channel's "Why Muhammad" series, June 9, 2009. See http://www.way2allah.com/khotab-item-14595.htm. (The decisive Battle of Badr was fought in 624 CE between the early Muslims and their Meccan opponents.)

29 Al-Ḥusaynī, "Filasṭīn Hiya an Nakūn aw Lā Nakūn" [Palestine Is Our "To Be or Not to Be" Issue].

30 The chairman of the Foreign Affairs Committee of Egypt's People's Assembly writes (in English): "There is no doubt that Islam is the object of an increasingly vicious campaign. Rather than rising to that bait, we should draw on our own authentic sources of inspiration. The Prophet and the first Muslims negotiated and coexisted with others. It makes little sense that we should do otherwise as we stand at the threshold of the 15th century on the Islamic calendar, all the more so given how exposed we are and how limited our influence is. When the question is 'to be or not to be,' moderation is the only feasible life raft." El-Feki, "A Faithful Step Forward."

31 Hany, "The Arab System—TO BE OR NOT TO BE."

32 The two met in a celebrated episode of *The Opposite Direction,* a *Crossfire*-type show that airs on the Al-Jazeera satellite channel. The program's host writes: "In one edition, Youssef al-Karadawi, the mufti of Qatar, was put in the position of having to defend his faith to the scorn and derision of [Sadiq Jalal] al-Azm, a professor of philosophy at the University of Damascus. Al-Azm ridiculed religious thought, mocking the prophets, claiming that Islam is a 'backward' religion, and praising Kemal Ataturk for banishing Islam from modern Turkish life. Al-Azm is well known in the Arab world. He has published books and articles that are critical of religion. He is respected by secular Arabs and hated by very religious Muslims. However, never before has he had the chance to go head-to-head with a cleric on television. In fact, it was the first time, al-Azm told me, that he had ever gone on Arab television with his critique. After it aired, cassette tapes of the broadcast sold for up to $100 on the black market." Al-Kasim, "Crossfire: The Arab Version," 95. See also Eickelman, "The Coming Transformation of the Muslim World."

33 One example is *Muslim Extremism in Egypt,* Gilles Kepel's portrait of Sayyid Qutb.

34 *Hamlet,* 1.4.13–38, 1.2.146–56 and 3.1.107–15, and 1.4.36, respectively.
35 Ibid., 1.2.76, 1.2.135, and 3.4.81, respectively.
36 Ibid., 3.3.73–79.
37 Ibid., 1.2.131–32, 5.2.215–20.
38 De Grazia, "*Hamlet*" *without Hamlet.*
39 *Hamlet,* 4.7.16–24, 5.2.65.
40 Ibid., 4.4.61–71.
41 1.5.196–97.
42 Hays, *Shakespearean Tragedy as Chivalric Romance.*
43 E.g., Greenblatt, *Hamlet in Purgatory.*
44 For a seminal early statement of this view, see Smirnov, *Shakespeare: A Marxist Interpretation.*
45 Shapiro, *A Year in the Life of William Shakespeare: 1599,* 276–78.
46 See Welsh, *Hamlet in His Modern Guises*; Prosser, *Hamlet and Revenge.*
47 Polonius promises to "loose" Ophelia to Hamlet (2.2.162); his psychology experiment prefigures the "Mousetrap" one scene later.
48 Claudius's two statements of ambiguous relationship in the council scene—"Our sometime sister, now our queen," and "my cousin Hamlet, and my son" (1.2.8, 64)—are mirrored by Hamlet's retort about "kin" and "kind" (1.2.65); his comment about "my uncle-father and aunt-mother" (2.2.372); and his later jibe that "father and mother are one flesh" (4.4.55).
49 *Hamlet,* 1.4.44–45.
50 Ibid., 1.1.72, 1.4.90.
51 Ibid., 1.2.20.
52 Ibid., 1.2.72–75. Hamlet's offended insistence on particularity in turn offends those around him. With a queen's precision and a mother's annoyance, Gertrude responds: "If it be, / why seems it so *particular* with *thee*?" (1.2.75, emphasis added). She lingers, perhaps derisively, on each syllable of the word "par*tic*ular," and stresses the singular pronoun at the end (at other times, e.g., in parts of the closet scene, she calls him "you").
53 *Hamlet,* 1.2.83.
54 Paul Celafu has suggested that what makes Hamlet seem "at all modern" is not the content of his beliefs about human nature, which are in fact radically conservative (even Augustinian), but simply his freedom to reinterpret the philosophical and theological presuppositions of his time. See Cefalu, "'Damned Custom ... Habits Devil.'"
55 By the crude measure of Google popularity, the exact phrase "*akūn aw la akūn*" (typed in Arabic) turns up 4,310,000 hits; "*nakūn aw lā nakūn*" finds about 9,420,000. Searches performed December 24, 2009.
56 The verbal noun *kawn* ("Being" or "creation" or "cosmos") is not an option. As in Shakespeare, however, the cosmic and scriptural resonance of "Being" casts a shadow on Hamlet's question.
57 Khalil Mutran's classic 1916 translation has "Am I being, or am I not?" (*a-kā'in anā, am ghayr kā'in*). The most scholarly version, published by Jabra Ibrahim Jabra in 1960, has "Shall I be or shall I not be?" (*akūn am lā akūn*). Other translators get around "being" altogether to focus on Hamlet's overall existential drift. Sami al-

Juraydini (1922) has *al-baqā' am al-fanā'* (two terms, familiar from the Sufi religious context, that mean roughly: "Remaining, or dissolution?"); Muhammad Awad Muhammad (1972) has *al-ḥayā am al-halāk* ("Life or destruction?"); and Abdel Qader al-Qitt (1971) has *aḥyā aw lā aḥyā* ("Shall I live, or shall I not live?"). For Muṭrān, Jabrā, ʿAwaḍ Muḥammad, and al-Qiṭṭ, see, respectively, Shakespeare, *Hāmlit,* trans. Khalīl Muṭrān; Jabrā, *Wilyam Shaksbīr*; Shakespeare, *Hāmlit, Amīr Dānimārk,* trans. Muḥammad ʿAwaḍ Muḥammad; Shakespeare, *Hāmlit,* trans. 'Abd al-Qādir al-Qiṭṭ. For Juraydini and a detailed overall comparison, see Zaki, "Shakespeare in Arabic," 230–31.

58 In the contrasting case of Nigeria, for instance, novelist Chinua Achebe portrays a single, abrupt moment of loss or "fall" from a troubled but untraumatized initial state. As he puts it (appropriating not Shakespeare but Yeats and through him the biblical narrative of Revelation), the British come and "things fall apart." Achebe, *Things Fall Apart*, title and epigraph.

59 Badawi, "Perennial Themes in Modern Arabic Literature."

60 The suggestion that modernist Arab writing (fiction and nonfiction) can be considered "a literature of crisis" in another sense is tantalizingly raised, although insufficiently pursued, in Makdisi, "'Postcolonial' Literature in a Neocolonial World." Relying on a typology of repeated historical ruptures similar to the one I outline here, Makdisi claims that "works of Arabic 'modernism' were all produced during or after what these texts themselves helped to define and to understand as a series of calamitous ruptures or breaks with the past." He thus argues that this literature not only reflects but also "contributes to the production of a sense of crisis in the Arab world. And it does so largely by historicizing that sense of crisis—that is, *by producing the very historical categories and concepts, including those of rupture and discontinuity, which enable the critical understanding or interrogation of the contemporary*" (97–98, emphasis in original).

61 Said's bracketed translation.

62 Said, "Arabic Prose and Prose Fiction after 1948," 46–47.

63 Ibid., 47–48, emphasis in original.

64 Ibid., 48.

65 Ibid., 56. Responses to the 1967 defeat will be discussed in more detail in chapter 5.

66 Gräf and Skovgaard-Petersen, "Introduction," ix. "Global mufti" is their term.

67 For photos, speeches, activities, fatwas, biographical information, and other information (in Arabic), see www.qaradawi.net. For his ouster from IslamOnline after he opposed the Qatar-based management's efforts to enforce a more unified conservative tone on the site, see Al-Shalchi, "Moderates Forced Out of Top Islam Web Site."

68 See his book *Priorities of The Islamic Movement in The Coming Phase.*

69 Al-Qaraḍāwī, "Al-Ḥiwār bayn al-Islām wa-l-Naṣrāniyya."

70 The Muslim Brotherhood and al-Qaeda have been at odds almost since the latter's founding, including over the successful participation of Brotherhood-affiliated Hamas in the January 2006 Palestinian legislative elections. In general, al-Qaeda argues for the rejection of national politics.

71 *Hamlet,* 3.1.57, 75.

72 Arafat and Bishara, "Interviews: Yasser Arafat," 6. For more examples of Arafat's "to be or not to be" rhetoric, see Inbari, *The Palestinians between Terror and Statehood,* 42

(on closer ties with Iraq during the First Gulf War); and "Forcing Arafat Out of the P.L.O." (on retaining leadership of the Palestine Liberation Organization).

73 Unlike al-Qaradawi, Mustafa Mahmud lacked serious religious training. He gained influence mainly through his public deployment of Islamic rhetoric. After beginning his career as an agnostic leftist physician in the Nasser period (his vaguely Marxist book *God and Man,* written in the mid-1950s, was banned by a state court in 1957), he experienced a fortuitously timed religious awakening in 1967–68, tied to his disillusionment with Egyptian socialism and its treatment of the poor. He impressed President Sadat, and, with the latter's encouragement, retooled himself as a religious figure in the early 1970s and began hosting a popular show, *Science and Faith,* on Egyptian television. He also collected donations to build a large mosque and to open a Muslim charity organization offering medical services to the poor, both named after himself. With his health organization feeding his credibility and his TV career helping to provide the funds, Mahmud reigned as a kind of charity and media star until he fell afoul of the religious establishment over a theological disagreement and his show was dropped in 1999. But his clinics continue to operate, and he still commands widespread authority as the one who reconciled "science and faith" for many Egyptian Muslims. I am grateful to Said Samir for sharing background notes and interviews for a study he prepared in collaboration with Armando Salvatore. And see Salvatore, "Social Differentiation, Moral Authority and Public Islam in Egypt."

74 I have used the hyphenated noun *Arab-Muslim* to denote the conflated identity Mahmud tries to promote, reserving the open compound *Arab Muslims* to indicate the population that holds both identities (by analogy with Arab Christians).

75 Maḥmūd, "Nakūn aw Lā Nakūn." In the last sentence I have translated *qaḍīya* as "question" rather than "issue" to reinforce the link with *Hamlet* (in Arabic, "that is the question" is often rendered as *tilka hiya al-qaḍīya*).

76 Cf., e.g., Hobbes, *Leviathan,* 3.

77 As mentioned above, analysis of the rhetorical use of other Shakespeare plays, including *The Merchant of Venice,* substantiates this reading. Whether the context is Islamic or Marxist, the cohesion of the group is presented as self-evidently superior to the interests of the individual. Both religious and secular speakers promote this view.

78 Mahmud, a former Marxist turned Sufi-leaning Islamist, plays on readers' sensitivity to both the Marxist and Islamic vocabularies. The term *fitna,* which means both "temptation/captivation/attraction" and "sedition/dissension/civil strife," bridges the concepts of private interest and public harm.

79 Hourani, *Arabic Thought in the Liberal Age.*

80 George Antonius became the historian and spokesman of this movement. See Antonius, *The Arab Awakening.* See also Négib Azoury's *Le Réveil De La Nation Arabe* (Paris, 1905), cited in Hourani, *Arabic Thought in the Liberal Age,* 278.

81 Al-Hakim, *The Return of Consciousness.*

82 Ajami, *The Dream Palace of the Arabs,* xi.

83 *Hamlet,* 3.1.63–64.

84 ʿAdwān, "Hāmlit . . . Yastayqiẓu Mutaʾakhkhiran."

85 For example, Syrian journalist and commentator Anwār Badr begins a column on opponents of the West Bank occupation within the Israeli military with the remark

that "we know Hamlet always wakes up too late." Anwar Badr, "Hāmlit al-Isrā'īlī," *Alhourriah.org*, November 7, 2004. (The publication, a self-described "journal of Arab progressives on the Internet," is no longer online.)

86 His two celebrated books of the post-1967 period are *Al-Naqd al-Dhātī Ba'd al-Hazīma* (Self-Criticism After the Defeat, 1968) and *Naqd al-Fikr al-Dīnī* (Critique of Religious Thought, 1972).

87 Al-Azm quotes from memory. To the familiar complaints about the rotten state and the out-of-joint time, he adduces one more quotation from the end of the play, Hamlet's comment to Horatio: "There's a divinity that shapes our ends, / Rough-hew them how we will" (5.2.10–11). For al-Azm, such sentiments represent the kind of passivity and fatalism he seeks to correct in his Arab audience.

88 Al-Azm, "Owning the Future."

89 Al-ʿAẓm, "Hāmlit wa-l-Ḥadātha al-ʿArabiyya."

90 Al-Azm, "Owning the Future."

91 Ibid.

92 Al-Azm, "Time Out of Joint."

93 "Without finally coming to terms, seriously and in depth, with these painful realities and their paralyzing contradictions . . . there is neither an owning of the future for the Arabs, nor any real responsibility for the present on their part. In other words, either we come to terms critically with this deep-seated, ritualized and stratified complex of highly emotional beliefs, valuations, and images . . . [and] anachronistic but cherished modes of living, thinking, and governing, or, again, the Fortinbrases of this world will win the day and have the final say." Al-Azm, "Owning the Future," 11.

94 First proposed in 2000, al-Azm's Arabs-as-Hamlet analogy was easily updated to account for Osama bin Laden and al-Qaeda: al-Azm simply integrated large-scale terrorism into the familiar list of Arab/Muslim delusional symptoms: see Al-Azm, "Time Out of Joint." Elsewhere, however, al-Azm has credited the Arabs' Hamlet-like cultural confusion as a source of vibrant intellectual and literary production: see Al-Azm, "A Book for a Book Instead [of] an Eye for an Eye."

95 Said, "Arabic Prose and Prose Fiction after 1948," 57.

96 Welsh, *Hamlet in His Modern Guises*, 32, emphasis added.

97 Jabrā, *Al-Baḥth ʿan Walīd Masʿūd*; Jabra, *In Search of Walid Masoud.*

98 See Jabrā, *Al-Safīna*; Jabra, *The Ship.*

99 This is not an isolated use of *Hamlet.* The play performs a similar dark-night-of-the-soul function for the quasi-autobiographical protagonists created by Egyptian novelists Bahaa Taher and Ibrahim Abdel Meguid in *Love in Exile* and *The Other Place,* respectively. In the latter the recollection of *Hamlet* is explicitly connected with the protagonist's uncertainty about whether or not he will be able to be a writer. See Meguid, *The Other Place,* 177–78.

100 Jabra was also a painter, poet, and prominent literary and art critic; his non-Shakespeare translations include James Frazer's *The Golden Bough* and William Faulkner's *The Sound and the Fury.* For background and references, see Boullata, "Living with the Tigress and the Muses." For a remembrance of Jabra's house, which was destroyed by a car bomb in April 2010, see Shadid, "In Baghdad Ruins, Remains of a Cultural Bridge."

101 Jabrā, *Wilyam Shaksbīr*; Shakespeare, *Al-ʿĀṣifa (The Tempest),* trans. Jabrā Ibrāhīm

Jabrā; Shakespeare, *Al-Sūnītāt: Arbaʿūn minhā maʿa al-Naṣṣ al-Injlīzī* [Forty Sonnets], trans. Jabrā Ibrāhīm Jabrā; Shakespeare, *Maʾsāt Kuriyūlānūs* [The Tragedy of Coriolanus], trans. Jabrā Ibrāhīm Jabrā.

102 See Kott, *Shaksbīr Muʿāsirunā*, trans. Jabrā Ibrāhīm Jabrā. His 1981 translation of John Dover Wilson is quoted in Mūsā, *Hāmlit al-Muʿākas*, 30.

103 Jabra, *A Celebration of Life*, 142.

104 Jabrā, *Wilyam Shaksbīr*, 24.

105 The poet Abu al-Ṭayyib al-Mutanabbī (915–965), born in Kufa (now Iraq) as Abu al-Ṭayyib Aḥmad ibn al-Ḥusayn al-Jūfī, is considered one of the most eloquent stylists of classical Arabic verse. He was also known for his political activism and personal arrogance—his nickname means "he who professes to be a prophet."

106 Jabra, *In Search of Walid Masoud*, 200–1; Jabrā, *Al-Baḥth ʿan Walīd Masʿūd*, 267–68.

107 *Kalām*, the Arabic word for speech or speaking, is also the medieval Islamic religious science of dialectical theology, or explaining religious principles by logical/rhetorical means. In contemporary spoken Arabic, *kalām* means both "reason" and "nonsense": e.g., someone who "*lā yasmaʿ kalām*" (doesn't listen to words) is stubbornly refusing reasonable advice, but someone who is full of "*kalām fārigh*" or "*kalām fāḍī*" (empty talk) should not be taken too seriously. Hamlet's phrase "words, words, words" (*kalimāt, kalimāt, kalimāt*) is often used synonymously with "*kalām fārigh*" to signify skepticism or dismissal.

108 *Hamlet*, 2.2.192.

109 Ibid., 2.2.579–83.

110 Jabrā, "Muʿāyashat al-Namira, aw, Mutʿat al-Qirāʾa, Mutʿat al-Kitāba," 10. Similarly phrased paeans to words occur in many of Jabra's nonfiction writings.

111 *Hamlet*, 1.2.85. Called to revenge by the Ghost in Act 1, Hamlet reaches first for an eraser and pen, not a sword: "Yea, from the tables of my memory / I'll wipe away all trivial fond records, / All saws of books, all forms, all pressures past / That youth and observation copied there, / And thy commandment all alone shall live / Within the book and volume of my brain / Unmix'd with baser matter. Yes, by heaven!" (1.5.98–104)

112 Cf. 1.5.104 (quoted above) with 5.2.31–36.

113 At sea in the last act, Hamlet rewrites the death warrant carried by Rosencrantz and Guildenstern. Improvising, he finds his father's signet ring in his bag and seals the commission with it. The ring, a belatedly discovered marker of Hamlet's true royal birth, allows his textual "changeling" to pass undetected. The "yeoman's" skill he had worked to erase from his memory supplies the creative resources to save his life. (The play's other major instance of rewriting, Hamlet's adaptation of the Italian play *The Murder of Gonzago*, will be discussed in chapter 6.)

114 I will return to this idea in chapter 6.

115 For a recent exception, a 2009 adaptation titled *Hamlet-hunna* (Women's Hamlet) by Saʿdaa' Al-Da'aas (Saʿdā' al-Da'ās), see Selaiha, "Hamlet Galore."

Chapter 2. Nasser's Dramatic Imagination, 1952–64

1 Information Department, United Arab Republic Ministry of National Guidance, *Year Book*, 7.

2 Undergraduate enrollment jumped from 34,842 in 1951–52 to 135,462 in 1963–64. At the same time Egypt became both a source of and a destination for international students, accepting 10,727 foreign students into Egyptian universities in 1963–64 and sending 5,685 Egyptians for study abroad. See Qubain, *Education and Science in the Arab World,* 70–72, 184–88, 198.

3 Information Department, United Arab Republic Ministry of National Guidance, *Year Book,* 159–60.

4 By 1964 three national theatre companies coexisted with the experimental Pocket Theatre, a puppet theatre company, and at least ten "television theatre" companies that staged some live performances and recorded plays for broadcasting. This is in addition to various musical, dance, and folklore troupes. See Brown, "The Effervescent Egyptian Theatre."

5 James, *Nasser at War.* (Others give higher figures.) Here, too, Egypt received financial and logistical support from the Soviets. See Ginat, "Nasser and the Soviets."

6 Nasser, "Kalimat al-ra'īs jamāl ʿabd al-nāṣir bi-maydān al-taḥrīr bi-ṣanʿā, 23/04/64 [Remarks of President Gamal Abdel Nasser in Tahrir Square in Sanaa, April 23, 1964]."

7 *Al-Masraḥ* 4 (April 1964). The journal, affiliated with the Tawfiq al-Hakim Theatre and like it sponsored by the Egyptian government, attracted readers (and letters to the editor) from throughout the Arab Near East.

8 Interest in Arab Shakespeare ranged as far as Oxford and Nigeria. See, e.g., Shukrī, "Shaksbīr fī al-ʿArabiyya" (originally printed in the Cairo-based newspaper *al-Ḥiwār*); Badawi, "Shakespeare and the Arabs" (originally a lecture to the Arab Society at Oxford); and Bushrui, "Shakespeare and Arabic Drama and Poetry."

9 Moussa Mahmoud, "*Hamlet* in Egypt," 54.

10 On "horizon of expectations" see Jauss, *Toward an Aesthetic of Reception.*

11 Gordon, *Nasser: Hero of the Arab Nation,* 129–30.

12 Hopwood, *Syria 1945–1986,* 37.

13 Gordon, *Nasser's Blessed Movement,* 52.

14 Ibid., 14.

15 Ibid., 88.

16 Al-Hakim, *The Return of Consciousness,* 13.

17 Mustafa, "Political Theatre in Egypt," 1.

18 Vaucher, *Nasser et Son Équipe,* 56–67. See also Al-Hakim, *The Return of the Spirit.*

19 The best account is by Georges Vaucher, who interviewed the play's director and other classmates: Vaucher, *Nasser et Son Équipe,* 53–56. See also Lacouture, *Nasser,* 34.

20 "*Le type du héros populaire, libérateur des masses, 'vainqueur de la Grande-Bretagne' et assassiné comme par erreur*"; Lacouture, *Nasser,* 34.

21 The playbill is reproduced at "Al-sīra al-dhātīya" [Biography], http://nasser.bibalex.org/Common/pictures01-%20sira.htm.

22 For Nelson Mandela's identification with Brutus, for instance, see Sampson, *Mandela,* 230–31.

23 "*Manqua s'elancer à la rescousse*"; Lacouture, *Nasser,* 34.

24 Gordon, *Nasser: Hero of the Arab Nation,* 16.

25 Nasser, *Egypt's Liberation,* 50.

26 Alexander, *Nasser,* 1.

27 Here he began to read seriously in English for the first time. Some works Nasser devoured at the Royal Military Academy, often with a flashlight under the covers after lights out, are discussed in Vaucher, *Nasser et Son Équipe,* 94–104.

28 Nasser, *Egypt's Liberation,* 45.

29 Ibid., 39, emphasis added.

30 The event is known as "the Manshiya incident" after the plaza in Alexandria where it took place. For text and audio of the speech, see Nasser, "Speech at Manshīya." For its impact, see Gordon, *Nasser's Blessed Movement,* 175–84.

31 For the identification of Julius Caesar with his people, consider Antony's "Even at the base of Pompey's statuë, / Which all the while ran blood, great Caesar fell. / O what a fall was there, my countrymen! / Then I, and you, and all of us fell down, / Whilst bloody treason flourish'd over us." Shakespeare, *Julius Caesar,* 3.2.186–90.

32 ʿAbd al-Nāṣir, *Falsafat al-Thawra.* Two English versions exist: Nasser, *Egypt's Liberation* (1955); and Nasser, *The Philosophy of the Revolution* (1959). I quote from the 1955 edition.

33 Nasser gets Pirandello's name right but misquotes the name of the play, *Six Characters in Search of an Author* (1921). The suggestion that Pirandello is a "great poet" and the play is a "tale" adds a timeless tone to Nasser's comments. See ʿAbd al-Nāṣir, *Falsafat al-Thawra,* 62. Cf. Nasser, *The Philosophy of the Revolution,* 61–62.

34 Nasser, *Egypt's Liberation,* 87–88.

35 For this admission, see Love, *Suez, the Twice-Fought War,* 410–11. "Not for two years did anyone think to liken it to *Mein Kampf*. . . . [French Premier Guy] Mollet was the first to claim to read danger in *The Philosophy of the Revolution,* quoting it out of context to visitors after he became Premier. After ten years of such distortions Nasser told me with a rueful chuckle: 'I don't want to write another book. The first one caused me too much trouble.' I asked him if he had actually read Luigi Pirandello's *Six Characters in Search of an Author,* which he mentioned in his book as the source of his concept of a role in search of a hero. Only the title, he admitted with a grin." (I owe the reference to an online column by Jon Alterman.)

36 See Al-Hakim, *The Return of Consciousness,* 19–20 and 55. The edition of *Falsafat al-Thawra* available to me includes no dedication; it may have been simply an inscription in al-Hakim's copy. However, critics who attacked al-Hakim's memoir did not accuse him of exaggerating Nasser's warm feelings toward him—rather, they asked why he had not spoken up earlier.

37 "What they meant was that it was the officers who had turned Muhammad Najib into a statue [like Galatea] which was being presented to the people as though he were the leader of the movement, whereas in fact they themselves had initiated it. . . . But I wondered whether any one of them had really read my play or whether they had merely known and heard of the name and the title? Whatever the case, in my play Pygmalion threw his statue down after a while, and this is exactly what the officers did with their statue." Al-Hakim, *The Return of Consciousness*, 4.

38 On the "child of the land" phenomenon and the image of Nasser as an authentic, simple, and ordinary Egyptian, see Gordon, *Revolutionary Melodrama,* 43; and Danielson, *The Voice of Egypt.* On the importance of radio in Egyptian daily life, see Danielson, 7–9.

39 Binder, "Gamal ʿAbd al-Nasser," 66.

[40] A spectacular illustration is the comic book biography analyzed in Douglas and Malti-Douglas, *Arab Comic Strips,* 27–45. Several key pages (e.g., the 1956 Suez Canal nationalization speech and the 1967 war) have a sunburst structure, with Nasser's expressive face in a medallion at the center, visually linked to the ordinary Egyptians in the outer panels by the wordless syllables of laughter or despair that flow between them.

[41] Gordon, *Nasser: Hero of the Arab Nation,* 5.

[42] Quoted in Alexander, *Nasser,* 113.

[43] Jawad al-Assadi, commentary in *Haoula'a Al-Akharoun* [*An Artist with a View*].

[44] Information Department, United Arab Republic Ministry of National Guidance, *Year Book,* 165.

[45] James, "Whose Voice? Nasser, the Arabs, and 'Sawt al-Arab' Radio."

[46] Binder, "Gamal ʿAbd al-Nasser," 47–48.

[47] Ibid., 47.

[48] Mansfield, *Nasser's Egypt,* 246.

[49] Alexander, *Nasser,* 78, emphasis added.

[50] Gordon, *Nasser: Hero of the Arab Nation,* 10, emphasis added.

[51] Al-Hakim, *The Return of Consciousness,* 34.

[52] Binder, "Gamal ʿAbd al-Nasser," 53–55.

[53] *ʿAwdat al-Waʿī* was dated July 1972 but first published in June 1974, two months after the announcement of President Sadat's economic about-face, the "open-door" policy. A second edition, incorporating "the most important published attacks on it" and al-Hakim's responses, was printed in December 1974. The English translation includes these "samples of the reaction." Al-Hakim, *The Return of Consciousness,* 62-73.

[54] Al-Hakim, *The Return of Consciousness,* 28. Arabic text in al-Ḥakīm, *ʿAwdat al-Waʿī,* 50.

[55] I would read "as he related" where Winder translates "related." Al-Hakim thus creates a long ungrammatical noun phrase of which the leader's "face" is the subject. The Arabic phrase rendered as "no one argued" is a dependent clause, "without anyone arguing."

[56] For examples, see Awad, "Problems of the Egyptian Theatre."

[57] Danielson, *The Voice of Egypt,* 168.

[58] Gordon, *Revolutionary Melodrama,* 59–60.

[59] Jacob Landau mentions a Syrian actor, Yusuf al-Khayyat (Yūsuf al-Khayyāt), whose troupe received permission to perform at the opera house in Cairo under Khedive Ismail. "Unfortunately the first play was not judiciously chosen, as regards its contents. Probably as a compliment to his friend Salīm Khalīl An-Naqqāsh's abilities, the latter's above-mentioned drama, *The Tyrant,* was chosen for the gala opening in the year 1878. The contents of the play were, naturally enough, interpreted by the Khedive as a reflection on his own personal rule. Al-Khayyat and his troupe were banished from Egypt and had to return to Syria." Landau, *Studies in the Arab Theater and Cinema,* 63–65.

[60] At that time, Hamroush says, there were only two "nationalist plays" to choose from. See ʿAbd al-Qādir, *Izdihār wa-Suqūṭ al-Masraḥ al-Miṣrī*; and Nkrumah, "Ahmed Hamroush: For Corps and Country."

[61] Quoted in ʿAbd al-Qādir, *Izdihār wa-Suqūṭ al-Masraḥ al-Miṣrī,* 51. A *galabiyya* is a

long straight robe, plain or with trim around the neckline, worn by both sexes; a *milaya* (*milāya*; literally: sheet) is a large black shawl typically worn by village women.

62 Wahba, *Cultural Policy in Egypt*, 17.

63 Ibid., 62.

64 ʿĀshūr, *Al-Masraḥ wa-l-Siyāsa*, 49–50.

65 See note 29 in this chapter.

66 Historians have noticed something like a pendulum effect to the two revolutions: the Free Officers' emphasis swung from domestic to international issues in the mid-1950s, and Nasser's domestic policies seem to have swung leftward around the time that Syria withdrew from the United Arab Republic in 1961. See Gordon, *Nasser's Blessed Movement*, 188–90 and 193; and Ansari, *Egypt: The Stalled Society*, 86–89.

67 A vignette retold by Egyptian writer Safinaz Kazem in the documentary film *Four Women of Egypt* (1997) captures the hope and promise associated with the Aswan High Dam: "At the time, whenever we asked for anything, they told us, 'After the High Dam, the country will prosper. After the High Dam, there will be electricity everywhere.' [During a trip to Europe] one man asked us, 'Do you have snow in Egypt?' Without thinking, and in all seriousness, my sister replied, 'After the High Dam, we'll have snow in Egypt!'"

68 ʿĀshūr, *Al-Masraḥ wa-l-Siyāsa*, 51. For a more critical account see ʿAbd al-Qādir, *Izdihār wa-Suqūṭ al-Masraḥ al-Miṣrī*, 61–63 and 121–27.

69 Nasser, *Egypt's Liberation*, 43–44. See also Gordon, *Nasser's Blessed Movement*, 193.

70 To this day, drama critics' terminology reflects Nasser's geopolitical categories: plays are classified into "local" or "Arab" (*maḥallī*, *ʿarabī*) productions on the one hand and "world" or "global" (*ʿālamī*) productions on the other. The distinction is largely linguistic: "local" encompasses anything written in Arabic; "world" means anything translated from any language, including English and French but also Spanish (be it Calderon or Lorca), Italian (Pirandello), Russian (Chekhov, Dostoevsky, Gorky), and even the Bengali of Rabindranath Tagore. The more recent "Arab versus Western" (*ʿarabī/gharbī*) distinction has not fully taken hold in theatre circles.

71 In the heated 1960s debate between "quality theatre" and "theatre in quantity," these two conflicting demands (international respectability and domestic political relevance) both fell on the side of "quality theatre." Both were opposed to "mindless comedy," nationalists' bête noire of the period. Individual playwrights frequently shifted back and forth between political commentary and formal innovation or tried to do both; directors could alternate between canonical highbrow material and more "popular" plays (e.g., written in colloquial Arabic, addressing contemporary social issues, using some traditional Arab storytelling techniques, or devoted to Arab nationalist agitprop). For the quantity versus quality debate, see El-Demerdash, "Dix années de théâtre dans la république arabe unie," 138–40; and Gordon, *Revolutionary Melodrama*, 208–9.

72 Whether Nasser persecuted Egypt's communists or offered them amnesty owed more to international affairs than to any activities of the accused. Many Egyptian Communist Party members (and some unaffiliated leftists) were put in detention camps after a 1959 crackdown provoked by heightened tensions with the USSR. One stress factor was the Iraqi Revolution of 1958; its military leader, Abdel Karim Qasim (ʿAbd al-Karīm al-Qāsim), "raised expectations that Iraq would soon join" with

Egypt and Syria in the United Arab Republic but provoked "bitter disappointment" when his regime instead stayed close to the Iraqi Communist Party and to the USSR; Ginat, "Nasser and the Soviets," 245. Nasser was also preoccupied with the Syrian communists, whom he feared would sabotage Syria's union with Egypt. Just as important, jailing Egyptian communists (while taking increasingly generous Soviet aid) sent a strong signal about Egypt's ideological independence from Moscow. Many of the leftists were freed before or soon after Khrushchev's May 1964 visit to Egypt. A general amnesty was finally declared at the end of 1964, after Khrushchev's ouster; see Binder, *In a Moment of Enthusiasm,* 329–34. Many of the former detainees were immediately put to work at leading newspapers and journals, including the government-founded monthly magazine *al-Ṭalīʿa* (The Vanguard). See Ginat, "Nasser and the Soviets," 237–41; and Dawisha, *Soviet Foreign Policy towards Egypt,* 21–33.

73 For instance, the 1962 play *Smoke* by Mikhail Ruman (Mikhaīl Rūmān) told a realistic story about a desperately poor and disappointed young man named Hamdi (Ḥamdī) who turns to hashish when his education fails to secure him a job; yet audiences also mapped the victim's struggle with his drug dealer onto intellectuals' struggles with the Nasser regime. In the original production, Farouk Mustafa recalls, the actor playing Hamdi would look up at Nasser's box in the theatre (instead of at the Muqaṭṭam hills above Cairo) as he would "rise and shout, 'I spit in your face, King of Muqattam.' In the theatre, nobody believed that he really meant Ramadan the pusher." See Mustafa, "Political Theatre in Egypt." This allegorical resonance grew from the audience's mood and the political context. When *Smoke* was briefly revived in 1986, Mustafa observes, "the audience responded to it as a play about drug addiction only. The political message of struggling against tyranny was almost totally absent" (5).

74 Because they were military rulers, the Mamluk sultans, who ruled Egypt from 1250 until the Ottoman conquest in 1517, provided especially fertile ground for Nasser-era political allegory.

75 Abdel Wahab, *Modern Egyptian Drama,* 27.

76 Awad, "Problems of the Egyptian Theatre," 191; Awad, "Cultural and Intellectual Developments in Egypt since 1952," 159.

77 Awad, "Problems of the Egyptian Theatre," 179.

78 The Pocket Theatre, launched in 1962 with "a budget allotment of $1700 and a 90-seat hall which was outfitted as a theatre for about $2400," introduced Ionesco's *The Chairs* as well as Brecht and Beckett to the Arab theatre; it also hosted the premiere of a landmark Egyptian play, Yusuf Idris's (Yūsuf Idrīs) absurdist *Al-Farāfīr* (The Farfoors, 1964); Brown, "The Effervescent Egyptian Theatre," 333. On Idris, see Abdel Wahab, *Modern Egyptian Drama.*

79 On the arrival and influence of these trends, see El-Demerdash, "Dix années de théâtre dans la république arabe unie," 135–36.

80 One fine example is Mikhail Ruman's mordant farce *al-Wāfid* (*The New Arrival,* 1965), in which a guest arrives at a Kafkaesque "hotel." Humiliated and denied food by the bureaucrats who staff the place, he delivers a long tirade and is eventually liquidated. Ruman's *New Arrival* is translated along with two other allegorical plays of the same period (al-Hakim's *Sultan's Dilemma* and Rashad Rushdi's *Journey Outside the Walls*) in Abdel Wahab, *Modern Egyptian Drama.* See also Al-Raʿi, "Arabic Drama since the Thirties," 379–81 and 387–88.

81 See, e.g., Bates, "Shakespeare in Latvia." A comic send-up of such Shakespeare use appears in *Ali and Nino,* a 1937 novel by Kurban Said (Lev Nussimbaum) set in post–Russian Revolution Baku: the Georgian Christian beauty Nino Kuprava, supporting her Muslim husband Ali's attempt to persuade visiting diplomats that Azerbaijan deserves its independence, assures them that construction of the Azeri national theatre is complete and that *Hamlet* will be performed there "in our Tatar language" starting the next week. See Said, *Ali and Nino,* 218.

82 Selaiha, "Royal Buffoonery." The latter production, directed by al-Sayyid Bidayr and starring Karam Muṭawiʿ, will be discussed in chapter 3.

83 Brown, "The Effervescent Egyptian Theatre," 337.

84 Al-Hakim, *The Return of Consciousness,* 38.

Chapter 3. The Global Kaleidoscope: How Egyptians Got Their *Hamlet,* 1901–64

1 Personal communication from Aboudoma (in English), June 10, 2002. Edited for grammar but otherwise verbatim. To my knowledge, Mohamed Hassan al-Zayyat (Muḥammad Ḥassan al-Zayyāt) never translated *Hamlet*; from a later conversation, I gather Aboudoma was referring to Muhammad Awad Muhammad's translation and introduction, commissioned by the Arab League and published in 1972.

2 For the concept of "horizon of expectations," see Jauss, *Toward an Aesthetic of Reception.*

3 Shakespeare, *The Tempest,* 1.2.364. This literature is descended from Mannoni, *Prospero and Caliban.* See Césaire, *Une Tempête*; and Fanon, *Black Skin, White Masks.* See also Greenblatt, "Learning to Curse"; and Hulme and Sherman, *The Tempest and Its Travels.*

4 See Soueif, *Mezzaterra,* 5.

5 Aboudoma was born in southern Egypt, whereas Soueif, the daughter of Cairo University English literature professor Fatma Moussa Mahmoud, grew up in Cairo.

6 As in Ashcroft, Griffiths, and Tiffin, *The Empire Writes Back.*

7 Victoria College in Alexandria, soon known as "the Eton of Egypt," was founded in 1901 by a group of businessmen with the help of British agent and consul-general (later high commissioner) Lord Cromer. The British-oriented curriculum was taught largely by expatriate English schoolmasters. The student body included many Egyptian minorities (Copts, Jews, Greeks) as well as members of the broader Arab elite. The Cairo branch opened during World War II. The school was nationalized after the 1956 Suez War and renamed Victory College in the early 1960s. See the essays in Hamouda and Clement, *Victoria College,* esp. Sahar Hamouda, "A School Is Born."

8 For a deft postcolonial reading of Chahine's *Hamlet* leitmotif, to which I am indebted here, see Stauffer, "The Politicisation of Shakespeare in Arabic in Youssef Chahine's Film Trilogy."

9 Both the transliteration and the reciting student have an Egyptian accent; for instance, *whether* is spelled ويزر. The schoolmaster is portrayed as able to speak colloquial Egyptian but unable to read literary Arabic. According to Edward Said, many Victoria College teachers could do neither; Said, *Out of Place,* 184.

[10] *Hamlet*, 3.4.53–109.

[11] His performance elides all of Gertrude's lines. Close-ups of the teacher's evidently conflicted facial expression (fascination, anxiety, desire) replace Gertrude's exclamations of "No more" (ibid., 3.4.89, 94, 96, 103). Afterward the teacher seizes Yahya and drags him into the faculty room, as though for punishment, only to make him repeat the performance for his colleagues.

[12] Chahine has him quote Jabra Ibrahim Jabra's translation, which was not published until 1960.

[13] The safe high-cultural vehicle of Shakespeare channels Yahya's edgy homoerotic interaction with his teacher and friends. In an ingenious appropriation, Yahya "speaks daggers" where he can use none (against the colonial education system, whose representative he has seated and silenced just as Hamlet does Gertrude). Meanwhile, the sexually explicit language of Hamlet's verbal assault on his mother both voices and masks the lesser transgressiveness of Yahya's (and the teacher's) emerging desires.

[14] The trilogy repeatedly relates Yahya/Chahine's film career to his homosexual desires and relationships; both hinge on *Hamlet.* In the third film, *Iskandariyya Kamān wa-Kamān* (*Alexandria Again and Forever*, 1990), Chahine tries to cast his love interest, ʿAmr, as Hamlet in a film-within-the-film. Chahine invokes John Gielgud's 1940 Cairo performance as Hamlet. ʿAmr is not interested.

[15] Said, *Out of Place*, 51, 164, and 179.

[16] Ibid., 183.

[17] Ibid., 210.

[18] Ibid., 51.

[19] Perhaps anticipating the smirks of New York reviewers, he protests: "I knew nothing conscious of the inner dynamics that linked desperate prince and adulterous queen at the play's interior, nor did I really take in the fury of the scene between them when Polonius is killed and Gertrude is verbally flayed by Hamlet. We read together through all that, since what mattered to me was that in a curiously un-Hamlet-like way, I could count on her to be someone whose emotions and affections engaged mine without her really being more than an exquisitely maternal, protective, and reassuring person. Far from feeling that she had tampered with her obligations to her son, I felt that these readings confirmed the deepness of our connection to each other; for years I kept [them] in my mind . . . as goods to be held on to at all costs" (Ibid., 52).

[20] Ibid., 53.

[21] Ibid., 230–31.

[22] This is one important difference between the Arab Near East and, for example, North Africa. There has not been much work on the latter. See, however, Amine, "Moroccan Shakespeare and the Celebration of Impasse: Nabil Lahlou's *Ophelia Is Not Dead*"; and Darragi, "The Tunisian Stage: Shakespeare's Part in Question."

[23] See Halliday, "The Unpublished Book of the Cold War."

[24] Bushrui, "Shakespeare and Arabic Drama and Poetry," 6.

[25] For scholarship in this vein, see Ḥabīb's 1927 newspaper article, "Shaksbīr fī Miṣr." See also the later works by al-Bahar, Bushrui, Kanaan, Moussa Mahmoud, Shukrī, Tounsi, Twaij, and Zaki cited in the bibliography.

[26] See Hanna, "Towards a Sociology of Drama Translation"; Hanna, "Hamlet Lives Happily Ever After in Arabic"; Hanna, "Othello in Egypt"; Hanna, "Decommercialising Shakespeare"; and Bayer, "*The Martyrs of Love* and the Emergence of the Arab Cultural Consumer." For the approach more broadly, see Bourdieu, *The Field of Cultural Production*; Jacquemond, *Conscience of the Nation*; and Kendall, *Literature, Journalism, and the Avant-Garde.*

[27] See, e.g., Zaki, "Shakespeare in Arabic," 85–113; and Hanna, "Towards a Sociology of Drama Translation," 125–54.

[28] Heylen, *Translation, Poetics, and the Stage,* 47.

[29] Quoted in Pemble, *Shakespeare Goes to Paris,* 6.

[30] Quoted in Heylen, *Translation, Poetics, and the Stage,* 28.

[31] See Ducis, *Hamlet, tragédie, imitée de l'anglois.*

[32] Dedicating a later edition to his own father in 1812, Ducis explains that in adapting *Hamlet,* "*Mon bût avait été de peindre la tendresse d'un fils pour son père*" (my goal was to depict a son's affection for his father). Ducis, *Hamlet, tragédie en cinq actes, imitée de 'anglois* (1826), 6.

[33] Vest, *The French Face of Ophelia from Belleforest to Baudelaire,* 75–96.

[34] Pemble, *Shakespeare Goes to Paris,* 95.

[35] Cairo's Royal Opera House, designed by Italian architects, was commissioned in 1869 by Khedive Ismail (ruler of Egypt 1863–79) to celebrate the opening of the Suez Canal. Because the Egyptian-themed *Aïda* was not ready for its opening night, Verdi's *Rigoletto* was performed instead; *Aïda* premiered in December 1871. Khedive Ismail's opera house burned down in 1971; a parking garage now stands in its place, and the new Opera House is in another location. For photos, see Hassan, "Not by Bread Alone."

[36] On these "rather melodramatic" signs of French and Italian influence see, e.g., Badawi, "Shakespeare and the Arabs," 195. It is still the case that some Egyptian actors are applauded upon their character's first entrance in a play (which interrupts the action) and that monologues, even those that are not soliloquies but addressed to other characters, are typically recited facing the audience.

[37] Shafik, *Arab Cinema,* 107.

[38] Abul Naga, *Les sources françaises du théatre égyptien,* 214.

[39] Ramses Awad (Ramsīs ʿAwaḍ) cites two earlier translations by Amīn Ḥaddād and George Mirza, now lost. See ʿAwaḍ, *Shaksbīr fī Miṣr,* 84.

[40] Najm, *Al-Masraḥiyya fī al-Adab al-ʿArabī al-Ḥadīth,* 260.

[41] Odeon, which had opened a Cairo office soon after its founding in 1904, signed Higazi in 1906, eventually producing forty-seven of his records. One of the earliest best-sellers was "Peace Be Upon Such a Beauty," a song from the *Romeo and Juliet* adaptation in which Higazi also starred; it sold 20,000 records in one year. See Al-Bahar, "Shakespeare in Early Arabic Adaptations," 20–21; and Lagrange, "Shayk Salama Higazi."

[42] Makdisi, *Theater and Radical Politics in Beirut, Cairo, and Alexandria,* 30.

[43] A criticism analyzed in Hanna, "Towards a Sociology of Drama Translation," 125–154.

[44] Moosa, *The Origins of Modern Arabic Fiction,* 107. He is paraphrasing ʿAbdu's exact contemporary, writer-journalist Salim Sarkis (1869–1926).

45 ʿAbduh, *Riwāyat Hamlit,* title page.

46 See Hanna, "Towards a Sociology of Drama Translation," 51. The title page of the second printing is reproduced in Hanna's dissertation on 305–6.

47 Among the *Hamlet* poems reprinted in ʿAbdu's *dīwān* are "Manājāt Jumjuma" ("Monologue of a Skull," i.e., Hamlet's "Alas, poor Yorick" speech); "Wadāʿ Ḥasnā'" ("Farewell, Beauty," i.e., the words of Laertes and the Queen at Ophelia's grave); "Hāmlit wa-Ummuhu" ("Hamlet and His Mother," partially translated below; cf. *Hamlet,* 1.2.129–59); and "Kalām ʿĀshiq" ("A Lover's Speech," Hamlet's letter to Ophelia; cf. *Hamlet,* 2.2.115ff). They are presented as freestanding poems; only "Hamlet and His Mother" is labeled as coming "From the play *Hamlet* by the author of this *dīwān.*" See ʿAbduh, *Diwān Ṭānyūs ʿAbduh,* 64–65 and 80–81.

48 ʿAbduh, *Hāmlit.*

49 Al-Bahar, "Shakespeare in Early Arabic Adaptations." Al-Bahar also credits ʿAbdu's *Hamlet* with an earlier run in Alexandria (1897–98), but this is contradicted by Hanna ("Hamlet Lives Happily Ever After in Arabic," 170) and not confirmed by the best authority, Najm (*Al-Masraḥiyya fī al-adab al-ʿarabī al-ḥadīth,* 80–81). Perhaps the 1890s performances used one of the two earlier *Hamlet* translations, now lost.

50 أبتي أين أنت تنظر ما تم/صار عرساً ذاك الذي كان مأتم//وغدت بعدك المآتم اعياداً/وذاك الثغر الحزين تبسم.
(This is the opening of the poem reprinted in Tanyus ʿAbdu's *dīwān* under the title "Hamlet and His Mother," in Abduh, *Diwān Ṭānyūs ʿAbduh,* 80. The full twelve-line poem, standing in for Hamlet's first soliloquy, simply laments the fickleness of Hamlet's mother.)

51 Shakespeare, *Hāmlit, Amīr Dānimārk,* trans. Muḥammad ʿAwaḍ Muḥammad, 24.

52 ʿAbduh, *Riwāyat Hamlit* (1902), 13.

53 Ibid., 67.

54 Ibid., 110. In ʿAbdu's 1902 printed text, Ophelia dies. Some later directors, departing from ʿAbdu's script though not his spirit, even made her survive and become Hamlet's queen. Personal communication from Sameh Hanna, April 3, 2009.

55 Hanna, "Towards a Sociology of Drama Translation," 127.

56 Al-Bahar, "Shakespeare in Early Arabic Adaptations," 19.

57 Dumas, *Hamlet.* Nadia al-Bahar points to another French source, the 1769 version by Jean-Francois Ducis ("Shakespeare in Early Arabic Adaptations," 13). However, key features of Ducis' text (Ophélie's status as Claudius's daughter, the added confidant/e characters of Elvire and Norceste, etc.) are absent from ʿAbdu's; ʿAbdu includes scenes absent from Ducis (e.g., the gravediggers); and their endings differ. ʿAbdu's few similarities to Ducis stem from Dumas' own early fascination with the Ducis version. Most other scholars simply note that ʿAbdu used a French source, not inquiring which one.

58 As a child Dumas was awestruck by a performance of Ducis' "imitation"; he claimed to have learned the leading role by heart. As a young man he was inspired by a visiting English production (1827, starring Charles Kemble and Harriet Smithson) that showed "the real flesh and blood passions" of Shakespeare's characters yet deferred to French taste by omitting Fortinbras, Norway, bawdy language, and many subplots and scenes. See Heylen, *Translation, Poetics, and the Stage: Six French Hamlets,* 45. Working from Meurice's literal translation nineteen years later, Dumas sought to recreate this celebrated *Hamlet* in his own rewriting. See Pemble, *Shakespeare Goes to Paris,* 109.

59 Pemble, *Shakespeare Goes to Paris,* 110.

60 Hafez, *The Genesis of Arabic Narrative Discourse,* 279–94.

61 Makdisi, *Theater and Radical Politics in Beirut, Cairo, and Alexandria,* 21.

62 Earlier, Hamlet remarks on the oddity of Laertes participating in such games on the day after his sister's funeral; Dumas, *Hamlet,* 260.

63 Noted in Pemble, *Shakespeare Goes to Paris,* 111.

64 Dumas, *Hamlet,* 268.

65 He appears to have consulted only Dumas' 1848 edition or one of its reprints, not incorporating the later revisions that (at Meurice's insistence) restored Shakespeare's ending. On these, and on Dumas' ambitions in the context of the Parisian theatre scene, see Heylen, *Translation, Poetics, and the Stage,* 45–60.

66 ʿAbduh, *Riwāyat Hamlit,* 110.

67 On Mutran's background and political aspirations, see Saadé, *Halīl Muṭrān*; and Hanna, "Decommercialising Shakespeare."

68 As Seattle-educated Lebanese writer Mikhail Naimy notes in a fierce 1938 essay; see Nuʿayma, *Al-Ghirbāl,* 202.

69 Muṭrān, "Al-Tamthīl" [The Theatre], 299. The characters mentioned in the poem are Othello, Hamlet, Romeo, William (Tell?), and Rodrigue (from Corneille's *Cid*).

70 Ibid. French translation quoted in Saadé, *Halīl Muṭrān,* 240.

71 Selaiha, "Royal Buffoonery." Badawi recounts how Abyaḍ's earlier rendition of Othello terrified his costar: "Abyad, who was playing the title role, raised his stentorian voice so loudly and looked so fearful that the young woman taking the part of Desdemona took fright and, convinced that Abyad was really going to kill her, fled from the stage, and the curtain had to drop, much to the embarrassment of all concerned." Badawi, "Shakespeare and the Arabs," 195.

72 Moussa Mahmoud, "*Hamlet* in Egypt," 28.

73 As Muhammad Awad Muhammad put it. Shakespeare, *Hāmlit, Amīr Dānimārk,* trans. Muḥammad ʿAwaḍ Muḥammad, 24.

74 Badawi names Georges Duval's translation (published in the period 1908–10) as the likely source. But Fatma Moussa Mahmoud, after examining both translations, believes it more likely that Mutran relied on a greatly abbreviated "French *school* edition of *Hamlet*"; Mahmoud, "*Hamlet* in Egypt," 56. At any rate, Duval's clumsily literal complete translation would explain neither Mutran's approach nor his cuts. See Badawi, "Shakespeare and the Arabs," 189; and Duval, *William Shakespeare, Oeuvres Dramatiques.*

75 Mutran is not consistent throughout, sometimes giving "*lāyirt*" and sometimes "*lāyirtīs.*" But see Shakespeare, *Hāmlit,* trans. Khalīl Muṭrān, 9.

76 *Hamlet,* 3.1.120.

77 Shakespeare, *Hāmlit,* trans. Khalīl Muṭrān, 61.

78 Later translators, working directly from English, render "I was deceived" as *kuntu makhdūʿa* ("I was deceived," Awad Muhammad), *khudiʿtu* ("I was betrayed," Jabra and Badawi), or some synonym. In the French versions, Pierre Le Tourneur (first published 1776 and the source for many stage versions) has *déçu* (disappointed); François-Victor Hugo (1859) correctly has *trompée* (deceived).

79 Nuʿayma, *Al-Ghirbāl,* 198. The error could stem either from Mutran or from François-Victor Hugo, who also renders *Gentile* as *gentille*: *Les amis: Les deux gentilshommes de*

Vérone. Le marchand de Venise. Comme il vous plaira, vol. 8 of *Œuvres complètes de W. Shakespeare,* trans. François-Victor Hugo, 205.

80 Muhammad Awad Muhammad has proposed an ingenious but unlikely explanation: Mutran, he suggests, took the wrong literal meaning of the French "*être ou ne pas être,*" reading *être* as "[human] being" and interpreting the question as "Am I a being, or am I not?" Surely Mutran's French was too good to admit such a mistake. See Muḥammad, *Fann al-Tarjama,* 35.

81 Saadé, *Halīl Muṭrān,* 246.

82 Shakespeare, *Riwāyat ʿUṭayl (Awtillū),* trans. Khalīl Muṭrān, 5.

83 *Les deux Hamlet: Le premier Hamlet. Le second Hamlet,* vol. 1 of *Œuvres complètes de W. Shakespeare,* trans. François-Victor Hugo, 67–68.

84 Mutran also removes all references to religion and race: no heathen gods, no Christian oaths, no "as I am a Christian," no "circumcis'ed dog," etc. Perhaps in deference to Egypt's Ottoman rulers (this was 1912), all references to the Turk and the Ottomites as the enemy are deleted too. Hanna, "Decommercialising Shakespeare," 44–45.

85 For a reminiscence of that performance, see Selaiha, "The Moor in Mansoura"; she gives the date as 1962.

86 Shakespeare, *Hāmlit,* trans. Khalīl Muṭrān, 7–8.

87 Ibid., 58.

88 Hamlet says: "Is it not strange that that actor, whom I was examining just now" (ibid., 55).

89 Ibid., 55. Cf. *Hamlet,* 2.2.171–220.

90 Shakespeare, *Hāmlit,* trans. Khalīl Muṭrān, 60–62.

91 Ibid., 65.

92 Ibid., 67.

93 Some of these are already noticeable in Shakespeare's text, as in "book and volume" and "slings and arrows." See Wright, "Hendiadys and Hamlet."

94 Shakespeare, *Hāmlit,* trans. Khalīl Muṭrān, 128.

95 Laurence Olivier's film likewise reassigns Fortinbras's closing lines to Horatio. So does Mohamed Sobhi's 1971 production, which drew on both Mutran and Olivier. Sobhi's *Hamlet* will be discussed in chapter 5.

96 Shakespeare, *Hāmlit,* trans. Khalīl Muṭrān, 7.

97 Saadé, *Halīl Muṭrān,* 111.

98 By 1930, Sabry Hafez notes, there were still no more than fifteen English writers translated into Arabic, compared with more than 150 French writers. Hafez, *The Genesis of Arabic Narrative Discourse,* 90.

99 Al-Juraydini was yet another Syro-Lebanese immigrant to Egypt, a lawyer, and a columnist for *al-Hilāl* newspaper in Cairo. A nation-state nationalist, he opposed the idea of pan-Arab unification; he served as secretary-general of the Cairo-based Moderate Syrian Party, formed in 1919 to advocate for an American mandate over Greater Syria. Al-Juraydini's first Shakespeare translation was *Julius Caesar* (1912), serialized in the newspaper *al-Zuhūr.* The cover of his *Henry V* (1936) identifies him as "translator of *Julius Caesar, Hamlet, King Lear,* and author of *Five in a Car, Lost Messages,* and *Meditations on Law and Literature.*" The cover is reproduced in Hanna, "Towards a Sociology of Drama Translation," 303–4.

100 Najm, *Al-Masraḥiyya fī al-Adab al-ʿArabī al-Ḥadīth: 1847–1914*, 254; Zaki, "Shakespeare in Arabic," 291.
101 Al-Juraydīnī, *Yūlyūs Qayṣar.*
102 Lamb and Lamb, *Tales from Shakespeare*, 320. On the Arabic translation of Lamb's *Tales*, see Ḥabīb, "Shaksbīr fī Miṣr," 201.
103 Personal communication from Farouk Mustafa, January 1, 2006.
104 Bushrui, "Shakespeare and Arabic Drama and Poetry," 15.
105 ʿAwaḍ, *Shaksbīr fī Miṣr*, 83–89.
106 Moussa Mahmoud, "*Hamlet* in Egypt," 54.
107 Abdel Hai, *English Poets in Arabic*, 19–29.
108 Bradley, *Shakespearean Tragedy.* Badawi mentions that the Arabic translation has "just appeared"; see Badawi, "Shakespeare and the Arabs," 194. For Bradley's influence on Egyptian Romantics including poet Ahmad Zaki Abu Shadi (Aḥmad Zakī Abū Shādī, 1892–1955), see Abdel Hai, *English Poets in Arabic*, 26.
109 See records 4/21/1927 (reviews of the *Hamlet* production of April 21, 192, at the Shakespeare Memorial Theatre in Stratford-upon-Avon) and 7/19/1928 (reviews of the *Hamlet* production of July 19, 1928, at the same theatre), Shakespeare Birthplace Trust Library and Archive, Royal Shakespeare Company Performance Database, Shakespeare Centre Library and Archive, Stratford-upon-Avon.
110 See "Theatre," on the website "Sir Alec Guinness, A Man of Many Parts," n.d. [1964], http://www.murphsplace.com/guinness/theatre.html.
111 Gielgud in Cairo is discussed in Said, *Out of Place*, 51–54. See also Youssef Chahine's film *Alexandria Again and Forever* (1990). Gielgud's 1946 Cairo run is cited in Al-Shetawi, "*Hamlet* in Arabic," 46.
112 *Hamlet*, directed by Lawrence Olivier (1948; repr., Janus Films, 2000). On the film's effect in Egypt, see Moussa Mahmoud, "*Hamlet* in Egypt," 54; al-ʿĀlim, "Ma'sāt Hāmlit bayn Shaksbīr wa-l-Sayyid Bidayr," 162.
113 On directing *Hamlet* in the United States many years later, Gielgud remarks: "A lot of my time was wasted by actors who wanted motivation for Shakespeare's supporting parts. If I said, 'You're just meant to support Hamlet,' they were very hurt and cross." Gielgud, *Acting Shakespeare*, 39.
114 Gordon, *Revolutionary Melodrama*, 19–51.
115 ʿAwaḍ, *Shaksbīr fī Miṣr*, 85–86.
116 Ibid., 87.
117 Moussa Mahmoud, "*Hamlet* in Egypt," 54.
118 *Al-ʿArūsa*, November 13, 1929, quoted in ʿAwaḍ, *Shaksbīr fī Miṣr*, 88.
119 ʿAwaḍ, *Shaksbīr fī Miṣr*, 84.
120 Moussa Mahmoud, "*Hamlet* in Egypt," 54. Rizk later became the maternal icon of Egyptian cinema.
121 Quoted in ʿAwaḍ, *Shaksbīr fī Miṣr*, 9.
122 Quoted in Kanaan, "Shakespeare on the Arab Page and Stage," 38.
123 *Rūz al-Yūsuf* magazine, August 21, 1928, quoted in ʿAwaḍ, *Shaksbīr fī Miṣr*, 87.
124 Title page quoted in Hanna, "Towards a Sociology of Drama Translation," 54–55. Shakespeare portrait with caption reproduced on 311.
125 Al-Aqqad, nicknamed "the human encyclopedia," is credited with over 100 books. Publishing his first poems in 1915, he came to dominate the Egyptian literary scene,

hosting a salon and mentoring many writers including the young literary critic (later Islamist thinker) Sayyid Qutb. Perhaps his best-known books are his biographies of religious leaders and thinkers (Benjamin Franklin, Averroes, Saʿd Zaghlūl) and his fourteen-volume "Genius" series written in the 1940s (including *The Genius of Muhammad, The Genius of Christ,* and *The Genius of Abraham*). For his 1927 essays on Shakespeare and *Hamlet,* see al-ʿAqqād, *Sāʿāt bayn al-Kutub,* 228–39.

126 Al-ʿAqqād, *Al-Taʿrīf bi-Shaksbīr,* 207–23.

127 Ibid., 210–14.

128 See Shahani, *Shakespeare through Eastern Eyes* (London: Herbert Joseph, 1932).

129 Al-Aqqad leaves aside the vexed question of whether a Muslim's sense of fate would be closer to a Christian's or a Hindu's. For Taha Hussein's famous 1938 argument that Egypt belongs culturally to "the West" rather than "the East," see Hussein, *The Future of Culture in Egypt.*

130 Al-ʿAqqād, *Al-Taʿrīf bi-Shaksbīr,* 221.

131 Shukri praises the project but objects to the choice of translators, especially on the major plays. See Shukrī, "Shaksbīr fī al-ʿArabiyya," 61–66.

132 Besides *Hamlet,* Awad Muhammad's many books (all in Arabic) include such titles as *The Nile River* (1939), *Colonialism and Its Types* (1953), *Northern Sudan: Its Population and Tribes* (1956), *Africa's Peoples and Races* (1965), and *The Art of Translation* (1969). Educated at the University of London (PhD, 1926), he represented Egypt at the San Francisco Conference at which the United Nations charter was signed (1945) and later served on the Executive Council of UNESCO.

133 Jabra's relationship with Shakespeare and *Hamlet* was discussed in chapter 1.

134 *Fāwst, li-shāʿir almāniya al-kabīr ghūtih* (Cairo: Maṭbaʿat al-iʿtimād, 1929).

135 Shakespeare, *Hāmlit, Amīr Dānimārk,* trans. Muḥammad ʿAwaḍ Muḥammad, 18.

136 See Dawisha, "Soviet Cultural Relations with Iraq, Syria and Egypt 1955–1970"; Dawisha, *Soviet Foreign Policy towards Egypt*; and Laqueur, *The Soviet Union and the Middle East,* 281–93.

137 Cairo hosted exhibitions of painting and sculpture under the title Soviet Art in Egypt in 1956, 1959, and 1966–67.

138 See, e.g., Barghoorn and Friedrich, "Cultural Relations and Soviet Foreign Policy." The authors note: "Current [1956] Soviet interest in Egyptian culture, and the success of Soviet efforts in achieving cultural penetration, are indicated by a growing program of publications, and by the gala opening in Cairo, on September 7, 1955, of a 'permanent' VOKS [All-Union Society for Cultural Relations with Foreign Countries] exposition. This event was attended, apparently, by the cream of the Egyptian opinion-making elite, as well as by the VOKS 'plenipotentiary' for Egypt" (338),

139 Rakha, "Our Revolution."

140 For the importance of these returnees to Syrian theatre, see ʿIṣmat, "Azmat al-Masraḥ al-Sūrī."

141 See, e.g., Marder, "Shakespeare's 400th Anniversary."

142 Muṣṭafā, "Al-Dīkūr al-Masraḥī li-Aʿmāl Shaksbīr."

143 Sarḥān, "Al-Baṭal al-Trājīdī ʿinda Shaksbīr." Sarhan, who later headed the General Egyptian Book Organization, was then a member of *al-Masrah*'s editorial board. The article draws on British critics including E. M. Tillyard and Clifford Leach to distinguish Shakespeare's protagonists from those of Aristotelian tragedy.

144 To Othello: "*Ayyuha al-aḥmaq tamahhal ibḥath ḥaqqiq daqqiq*!" To Hamlet: "*Fīmā kull hādhā al-tafkīr wa-l-ta'ammul . . . aqdim! Intaqim!*" See al-Ḥakīm, "Jalsa maʿa Tawfīq al-Ḥakīm," 9.

145 The film is available on DVD from Ruscico. See also Kozintsev, *Shakespeare: Time and Conscience.*

146 Jabrā later expressed indignation at this piracy, comparing his role as translator to that of Boris Pasternak, who was prominently acknowledged in the film's credits. Jabrā, "Shaksbīr Muḍṭahadan wa-Qaḍāyā Ukhrā," 122.

147 Author's interview with Mohamed Sobhi, Madinat Sonbol, August 9, 2007.

148 The Theatre Club meeting, which also addressed al-Sayyid Bidayr's production, is discussed below. See also "Nādī al-Masraḥ: Hāmlit."

149 ʿAṣfūr, "Hawāmish li-l-Kitāba," emphasis added. Asfour has served as head of Egypt's Supreme Council of Culture, head of Arabic at Cairo University, and editor-in-chief of the literary journal *Fuṣūl.* This reminiscence opens a review of the Royal Shakespeare Company's *Hamlet* production starring Simon Russell Beale, which came to Boston while Asfour was a visiting professor at Harvard in 2001.

150 See Smeliansky, *The Russian Theatre after Stalin,* 15.

151 Woll, *Real Images,* 42.

152 The story is part of Aboudoma's 2006 collection, *Nostalgia,* which has also been performed as a play. See Abū Dūmā, *Nūstāljiyā.* See also Sami, "Remembrance of Things Past," a review of Mahmud Aboudoma's *Nostalgia.* On the performance version, see Selaiha, "Spots of Time."

153 We will return to the comments of one such critic, Mahmud Amin al-Alim, below. He was imprisoned from 1959 to 1964.

154 A useful analysis of these images is Jorgens, "Grigori Kozintsev's Hamlet."

155 Nowhere in the film is the Ghost's authority undermined. Indeed, Shostakovich's score punctuates his entrances with solemn, weighty, even vaguely oppressive theme music.

156 Burke, "'Hidden Games, Cunning Traps, Ambushes.'" But see the bird (a seagull) that appears over Ophelia's death scene and again when Hamlet accepts the fencing challenge.

157 As Pasternak put it: "*Hamlet* is not a drama of weakness, but of duty and self denial." He considered the play "a drama of high calling, of a preordained heroic deed, of entrusted destiny." Quoted in Rowe, *Hamlet: A Window on Russia,* 148.

158 On Hamlet's resulting loss of "interiority," see Burke, "'Hidden Games, Cunning Traps, Ambushes,'" 172.

159 *Hamlet,* 1.2.129ff.

160 Kozintsev's comments at a 1964 conference in Paris, as paraphrased in Manvell, *Shakespeare and the Film,* 80. Manvell's analysis is helpful; see esp. 77–85.

161 By "Phariseeism" Pasternak meant both the aesthetic dreariness and vulgarity typical of a repressive state and its moral rot. The phrase "everything is drowning in Phariseeism" occurs in "Hamlet," the first poem in the poetic appendix to Pasternak's novel *Doctor Zhivago.* An audio recording of an iconic Moscow moment, singer-actor Vladimir Vysotsky performing this poem during the 1971 Taganka Theatre production of *Hamlet,* is at http://www.kulichki.com/vv/ovys/teatr/gul_zatix.html.

162 Woll, *Real Images,* 164. For Anikst's review see *Iskusstvo Kino* 6 (1964): 13–14.

[163] Quoted in Rowe, *Hamlet: A Window on Russia,* 153. Kozintsev produced a stage *Hamlet* in Leningrad using Pasternak's translation in 1953–54, which led to a warm correspondence between the two men. In the letter quoted here, Kozintsev asks permission to modify Shakespeare's final scene, replacing Fortinbras with Sonnet 74 to convey his idealistic vision. Rowe observes that the reference to "baseness and degradation" may be "as close to political commentary as was probably feasible at that time, even in a private letter" (ibid.).

[164] Kozintsev, "King Lear," 232, emphasis added. For the Russian, see Grigori M. Kozintsev, *Nash sovremennik Villiam Shekspir* (Leningrad: Iskusstvo, 1962). Kozintsev's book, whose Russian title translates to *Our Contemporary, Shakespeare*, came out just a few years after Jan Kott's similarly titled and spirited *Shakespeare Our Contemporary*.

[165] Hopwood, *Syria 1945–1986,* 44.

[166] Ibid.

[167] Al-Hakim, *The Return of Consciousness,* 28.

[168] *Hamlet,* 3.2.360–63.

[169] The World Theatre Company was one of several state-sponsored troupes. Although the repertoires of the troupes overlapped, the World Theatre presented mainly foreign and experimental drama.

[170] Al-Shetawi, "*Hamlet* in Arabic," 47.

[171] He had also directed a television *Hamlet* for Channel 2's Tuesday evening World Theatre program in 1959, using Khalil Mutran's translation. Salah Abdel Sabur had mocked the translation and panned the "superficial" show. ʿAbd al-Ṣabūr, "Hāmlit al-Miskīn . . . fī al-Barnāmaj al-Thānī."

[172] A videotape of the production was made and even shown on television but is now lost: Mohamed Sobhi reports that when he looked for it in the 1970s, he found that a soccer match had been accidentally recorded over it; author's interview with Sobhi, August 9, 2007. My reconstruction of the play is based on reviews; see al-ʿAnānī, "Al-Masraḥ al-ʿĀlamī: Hāmlit"; ʿId, "Hāmlit, Amīr al-Dānimārk"; and al-ʿĀlim, "Maʾsāt Hāmlit bayn Shaksbīr wa-l-Sayyid Bidayr," 162–64. See also brief summaries in Moussa Mahmoud, "*Hamlet* in Egypt"; and al-Shetawi, "*Hamlet* in Arabic"; and the transcript of a 1965 meeting of the Theatre Club devoted to *Hamlet,* convened by *al-Masraḥ* magazine ("Nādī al-Masraḥ: Hāmlit"). The panel included Hamdi Ghayth (Ḥamdī Ghayth, who had directed *Othello* the previous year) and critics Abd al-Fattah al-Barudi (ʿAbd al-Fattāḥ al-Bārūdī), Kamal al-Malakh (Kamāl al-Malākh), Shafiq Migalli (Shafīq Mijallī), Ramzi Mustafa, and Aziz Sulayman (ʿAzīz Sulaymān).

[173] *Macbeth,* directed by Nabil al-Alfi (Nabīl al-Alfī) with Khalil Mutran's translation, National Theatre, 1962; *Merchant of Venice,* directed by Futuh Nashati (Futūḥ Nashāṭī) with Khalil Mutran's translation, National Theatre, 1963; *Othello,* directed by Hamdi Ghayth with Khalil Mutran's translation, World Theatre, 1964. See al-Mughāzī, "Shaksbīr fī al-Masraḥ al-Miṣrī," 49.

[174] Mutawi (1933–96) graduated from the Egyptian Institute of Drama before going to Italy to study acting and directing. In the 1960s he was involved in the avant-garde theatre scene, particularly the effort to develop an indigenous Egyptian drama. He directed the premieres of both Naguib Sorour's (Najīb Surūr) *Yāsīn wa-Bahīya* and Yusuf Idris's *al-Farāfīr,* two experimental plays based on traditional Arab storytell-

ing forms. Later he became a renowned television actor and served as director of the state theatre. See Selaiha, "Multiple Ironies."

175 Zouzou Nabil, an older actress (real name Azīza Imām), had been playing "aunt" roles. Zizi al-Badrawi (real name Fadwā al-Baytar) was typically cast as a romantic lead and had starred opposite screen idol Abdel Halim Hafez in 1960. See Gordon, *Revolutionary Melodrama*, 37.

176 Mohamed Enani's supportive review credits the show with "a degree of success for which we could envy ourselves, if we recall the extreme difficulties that accompany the production of a work like this, most importantly the human limitations, i.e., the acting personnel who until now are lacking, limited to only a small number of Arab pioneers of this art"; al-ʿAnānī, "Al-Masraḥ al-ʿĀlamī: Hāmlit," 58.

177 Reviewers complained particularly about an unintelligible Ophelia. See al-Malakh in "Nādī al-Masraḥ: Hāmlit," 74; and al-ʿAnānī, "Al-Masraḥ al-ʿĀlamī: Hāmlit."

178 E.g., Moussa Mahmoud, "*Hamlet* in Egypt," 55.

179 ʿId, "Hāmlit, Amīr al-Dānimārk: Dirāsa wa-Naqd."

180 al-ʿAnānī, "Al-Masraḥ al-ʿĀlamī: Hāmlit," 59; Moussa Mahmoud, "*Hamlet* in Egypt," 54. On al-Juraydini's translation, see also Ḥabīb, "Shaksbīr fī Miṣr," 203–4; and Zaki, "Shakespeare in Arabic," 179–271.

181 See "Nādī al-Masraḥ: Hāmlit"; and Soueif, *Mezzaterra*, 5.

182 Many of the reviews refer to Bidayr simply as "the Arab director" or "the Egyptian director." These critiques echo the attacks on the Aziz Eid–Fatima Rushdi production thirty-six years earlier.

183 Al-Alim (1922–2009), a PhD in philosophy, was coauthor with Abd al-Azim Anis (ʿAbd al-ʿAẓīm Anīs) of the influential *Fī al-Thaqāfa al-Miṣriyya* (*On Egyptian Culture,* 1955), a Marxist tome that took aim at the broadly universalist and humanist approach of earlier-generation critics such as Taha Hussein and Abbas Mahmud al-Aqqad. On cultural life in the prison camp, see Amin, *Alfred Farag and Egyptian Theater,* 10.

184 al-ʿĀlim, "Ma'sāt Hāmlit bayn Shaksbīr wa-l-Sayyid Bidayr," 162–63.

185 In a panel discussion, Aziz Sulayman said this focused the audience's attention on Hamlet's soul rather than his outward appearance, fitting well with the production's overall "impressionistic" (*ta'thīrī*) style; "Nādī al-Masraḥ: Hāmlit," 75.

186 Both Olivier and Kozintsev use voice-over for Hamlet's soliloquies. However, Bidayr's critics unanimously denounced this technique on the stage; it produced a poorly timed and not always intelligible soundtrack to which Mutawi had to mime in silence, leading to an unintended "distancing" or "alienation" of the audience from the character in an otherwise frankly emotional, non-Brechtian production. See Migalli in "Nādī al-Masraḥ: Hāmlit," 74; and al-ʿAnānī, "Al-Masraḥ al-ʿĀlamī: Hāmlit," 59.

187 Décor specialist Ramzi Mustafa criticized this eclecticism at the Theatre Club roundtable. See "Nādī al-Masraḥ: Hāmlit," 74.

188 Photo published with Enani's review; see al-ʿAnānī, "Al-Masraḥ al-ʿĀlamī: Hāmlit," 58. Eid expresses disappointment that Gertrude's closet did not feature a bed or even any silk sheets on the divan to indicate Gertrude's sensuality. ʿId, "Hāmlit, Amīr al-Dānimārk: Dirāsa wa-Naqd."

189 A photo published with Enani's review shows Mutawi in black knee boots and breeches gesticulating forcefully as though about to jump into Ophelia's grave; see al-ʿAnānī, "Al-Masraḥ al-ʿĀlamī: Hāmlit," 59. Moussa Mahmoud says he "seemed too active and decisive for the expectations of many critics, who were familiar with the Olivier film of *Hamlet*"; Moussa Mahmoud, "*Hamlet* in Egypt," 59.

190 al-ʿĀlim, "Ma'sāt Hāmlit bayn Shaksbīr wa-l-Sayyid Bidayr," 163. This use of Polonius as clown required the addition or repetition of some lines. A few critics objected, Hamlet-like, that this was allowed to override "some necessary question[s] of the play," referring to *Hamlet*, 2.2.38ff.

191 ʿId, "Hāmlit, Amīr al-Dānimārk: Dirāsa wa-Naqd," 44–45.

192 Ibid., 47.

193 Ibid. This could be a misprint.

194 al-ʿĀlim, "Ma'sāt Hāmlit bayn Shaksbīr wa-l-Sayyid Bidayr," 163.

195 He objects that Kozintsev's hero is too strong and active, closer to Orestes than to Hamlet, whereas it is Hamlet's very passivity and failure that are meant to goad the audience to action; ibid., 162.

196 Ibid., 161.

197 The word "essence" (*jawhar*) occurs six times on the first page of his review alone.

198 Cf. Ghazoul, "The Arabization of *Othello*."

Chapter 4. Hamletizing the Arab Muslim Hero, 1964–67

1 Bushrui, "Shakespeare and Arabic Drama and Poetry," 14.

2 Jacquemond, *Conscience of the Nation*, 294.

3 Badawi, *Modern Arabic Drama in Egypt*, 173.

4 Cf. Ghazoul, "The Arabization of *Othello*." Focusing on *Othello* and thus identifying the main problem as "the disturbing question of the alien Other undertaking to represent the Self," Ghazoul highlights Arab appropriators' "efforts to repossess a foreign literary product centering around an indigenous hero" (2).

5 It may be a stretch to call the Persian Sufi al-Hallaj an Arab hero. However, he is a hero to millions of Arabs. Further, as we will see, al-Hallaj's Persian origins played little role in Abdel Sabur's adaptation; more relevant were his mystical writings in classical Arabic and his struggle against the (Arab) Abbasid regime.

6 Other common English spellings in use for ʿAbd al-Ṣabūr include Abdel Sabbour, Abdel Saboor, etc.

7 For an introduction to Farag's life and a discussion of his anti-realistic dramatic techniques, including the use of metadrama to create "self-conscious" characters, see Amin, *Alfred Farag and Egyptian Theater*.

8 A helpful discussion in English is El-Enany, "The Quest for Justice in the Theatre of Alfred Farag."

9 For Farag on Brecht, see Selaiha, "Brecht in Egypt."

10 On the economic incentives, see ʿAbd al-Wahhāb, "Ma'sāt al-Ḥallāj," 45.

11 Nehad Selaiha writes: "Given Abdel-Sabour's literary prestige and his wide popularity, one would have expected *The Tragedy of Al Hallag* to be snapped up by the National as soon as it appeared in print. But it was the heyday of realistic prose drama

and the play had to wait two years before director Samir El-Asfouri decided to stage it at El-Masrah El-Hadith (Modern Theatre) where it opened in the 1966/67 season." See Selaiha, "Poet, Rebel, Martyr," Selaiha's review of a 2002 revival.

12 Taylor charts the progression from premodern to modern self-consciousness in the Christian and post-Christian West: Augustine plunges into his own shifting thought processes to better access the unchanging God at their root; Descartes learns to stand "outside" his own thoughts as an impartial observer; and finally John Locke transforms this duality into the modern "punctual self," a fully disengaged reason that offers human beings "the possibility to remake ourselves in a more rational and advantageous fashion." Thus Locke's "punctual self" has implications for politics: it grounds the possibility of self-government, including the right to free oneself from a father or rebel against a tyrant. Taylor, *Sources of the Self,* 111–98, quote on 170. See also Taylor, *The Ethics of Authenticity.*

13 See Bloom, *Shakespeare: The Invention of the Human,* xviii, 383–430.

14 Faraj, *Sulaymān al-Ḥalabī,* 15. In what follows I refer to the play as *Sulayman of Aleppo* and to the character as Sulaymān al-Ḥalabī or simply Sulayman. In Arabic the two are the same: Sulayman's hometown (Ḥalab=Aleppo) becomes his last name.

15 Ibid., 156.

16 Ibid., 29.

17 Amin, *Alfred Farag and Egyptian Theater,* 89.

18 Al-Jabarti compares the French favorably to the Mamluk/Ottoman depredations that followed. Before reproducing the French documents, he comments: "For, indeed, a reckless stranger treacherously attacked their leader and chief; they seized him, interrogated him; yet did not proceed to kill either him or those named by him, on the mere basis of his confession, despite the fact that when they caught him they found on him the deadly weapon spattered with the blood of their commander and leader. Nay, they instituted a court procedure, summoned the assassin, and repeatedly questioned him orally, and under duress; then summoned those named by the assassin, interrogated them individually and collectively, and only then did they institute the court procedure in accordance with what the law prescribed. Yet they released the [alleged accomplice,] calligrapher Muṣṭafā Afandī al-Bursalī, who was not affected by the sentence and was not to be punished; all of which can be learned from the context of the written account. This is quite different from what we saw later of the deeds of the riff-raff of soldiers claiming to be Muslims and fighters of the Holy War who killed people and destroyed human lives merely to satisfy their animal passions, as will be reported below." Al-Jabartī, *ʿAbd al-Raḥmān al-Jabartī's History of Egypt,* 3:182.

19 Faraj, *Sulaymān al-Ḥalabī,* 6.

20 Ibid., 15.

21 The French source notes that Sulayman received a *bastinado,* or beating on the soles of his feet, "in accord with the country's custom" (*ʿalā ṭarīq al-balad*), until he was ready to talk; quoted in al-Jabartī, *ʿAbd al-Raḥmān al-Jabartī's History of Egypt,* 3:185. Farag's introduction quotes this sentence, appending an exclamation mark. Faraj, *Sulaymān al-Ḥalabī,* 11. (The murderer's sentence, execution by impalement following the incineration of the right hand in a fire, was ascribed to local custom as well.)

22 Faraj, *Sulaymān al-Ḥalabī,* 155.

23 Ibid., 59.
24 McGregor, *A Military History of Modern Egypt,* 46–49.
25 Faraj, *Sulaymān al-Ḥalabī,* 27.
26 Ibid., 116.
27 Ibid., 89.
28 Ibid., 147–50. It seems the French did make plans for massive collective retribution but abandoned these as soon as they found out the assassin was Syrian rather than Egyptian and "realized that the people of Cairo were innocent of the crime"; al-Jabartī, *ʿAbd al-Raḥmān al-Jabartī's History of Egypt,* 180–81.
29 Faraj, *Sulaymān al-Ḥalabī,* 147–48.
30 Nada Tomiche comments on the many "balanced periods" and "logical" sentence constructions "that lend themselves to analysis" that mark Sulayman's speech (e.g., "If you believed X, you would do Y"); Tomiche, "Niveaux de langue dans le théâtre égyptien," 120–22.
31 Badawi, *Modern Arabic Drama in Egypt,* 176.
32 For Farag's study of the dramatic monologue, including his translation of the "to be or not to be" soliloquy, see Faraj, "Dirasāt," 100.
33 Faraj, *Sulaymān al-Ḥalabī,* 109.
34 Qur'ān, Sura 99.
35 Faraj, *Sulaymān al-Ḥalabī,* 140–41.
36 His remark about forgetting himself to Laertes (*Hamlet,* 5.2.77–78) may be the only moment of this kind.
37 ʿAbd al-Ṣabūr, "Sulaymān al-Ḥalabī bayn al-Raghba wa-l-ʿAql," 243.
38 For accounts of performance and immediate reception, I have relied more on pre-1967 reviews than on later reconstructions. The former include ʿAwaḍ, "Sulaymān al-Ḥalabī"; al-ʿAyyūṭī, "Al-Masraḥ al-Qawmī"; al-Naqqāsh, "Hāmlit . . . fī al-Azhar al-Sharīf"; Ṭāhir, "Al-Ḥalabī wa Amīr al-Dānimārk." The latter include ʿAbd al-Qādir, *Izdihār wa-Suqūṭ al-Masraḥ al-Miṣrī*; Al-Shetawi, "The Arab-West Conflict as Represented in Arabic Drama"; Selaiha, "Old Tune, New Resonance"; and Amin, *Alfred Farag and Egyptian Theater.*
39 ʿAwaḍ, "Sulaymān al-Ḥalabī." See also El-Enany, "The Quest for Justice in the Theatre of Alfred Farag," 175.
40 Quoted in ʿAbd al-Qādir, *Izdihār wa-Suqūṭ al-Masraḥ al-Miṣrī,* 102. Al-ʿĀlim had played the role of the Vizier in the prison production of Farag's first full-length play, *The Barber of Baghdad.* Originally written on cigarette papers, that play was restaged at the National Theatre in 1964, immediately upon the leftists' release. Amin, *Alfred Farag and Egyptian Theater,* 10.
41 Ṭāhir, "Al-Ḥalabī wa Amīr al-Dānimārk," 32–33.
42 Al-Rai, "Le génie du théâtre arabe des origines à nos jours," 92–93.
43 Al-Naqqāsh, "Hāmlit . . . fī al-Azhar al-Sharīf," 42.
44 See ʿAbd al-Qādir, *Izdihār wa-Suqūṭ al-Masraḥ al-Miṣrī*; Al-Shetawi, "The Arab-West Conflict as Represented in Arabic Drama"; and El-Enany, "The Quest for Justice in the Theatre of Alfred Farag."
45 See Amīr, *Al-Masraḥ al-Miṣrī baʿd al-Ḥarb al-ʿĀlamiyya al-Thāniya,* 2:273–86, cited in El-Enany, "The Quest for Justice in the Theatre of Alfred Farag," 187n45. This view seems to have influenced later critics. Badawi, e.g., finds that "the contemporary rel-

evance of the play is revealed in the description of Egyptian life under the tyrannical rule of the French imperialists in which Egyptians could recognize aspects of life under the dictatorship of Nasser"; Badawi, *Modern Arabic Drama in Egypt,* 175.

46 Qutb's *Milestones on the Road,* the manifesto of modern Egyptian political Islam, had already been published. The following year, after a show trial bearing some resemblance to Sulayman's, Qutb would be hanged on charges of treason.

47 ʿAbd al-Ṣabūr, "Sulaymān al-Ḥalabī bayn al-Fann wa-l-Tārīkh," 8.

48 *Hamlet,* 2.2.555.

49 El-Enany, "The Quest for Justice in the Theatre of Alfred Farag," 188. See Eliot, "Hamlet and His Problems."

50 ʿAwaḍ, "Sulaymān al-Ḥalabī," 373.

51 Ibid., 384. Cf. ʿAbd al-Qādir, *Izdihār wa-Suqūṭ al-Masraḥ al-Miṣrī,* 104–6.

52 Selaiha, "Old Tune, New Resonance."

53 *Hamlet,* 1.2.85.

54 His most famous transgression was to proclaim, "I am the Truth," (*anā al-ḥaqq*), implying that he had become one with God; Sufis had long striven for such mystical union, but without boasting about it in public. Secondary charges against al-Hallaj included proposing a change in the rites of the pilgrimage (*ḥajj*), one of the five basic pillars of Islamic worship. Biographical and historical data on al-Hallaj are drawn from Massignon, *Hallaj: Mystic and Martyr.* On the Abbasid Empire's political instability, see especially pp. 225–27.

55 The study of al-Hallaj was Massignon's life work from 1907 until his death in 1962. He and Paul Kraus co-edited *Akhbar al-Hallaj.* A four-volume expanded edition of *La Passion du Hallaj* appeared posthumously in 1975 and an English translation by Herbert Mason in 1983: Massignon, *The Passion of al-Hallāj.* ʿAbd al-Qādir reports that Abdel Sabur was inspired by a Massignon article on the life of al-Hallaj, originally published in the Christian journal *Dieu Vivant* 4 (1945), which had just been translated in Abdel-Rahman al-Badawi's (ʿAbd al-Raḥmān al-Badawī) book *Shakhṣiyāt Qaliqa fī al-Islām* (*Uneasy Characters in Islam,* 1964). See ʿAbd al-Qādir, *Izdihār wa-Suqūṭ al-Masraḥ al-Miṣrī,* 149.

56 The historical Hallaj did compare himself to Christ, an analogy emphasized in Massignon's work (e.g., in his title *La Passion du Hallaj*). Self-portraits as Jesus Christ were fairly common among Arab modernist poets in the 1950s and 60s. Self-portraits as al-Hallaj include a 1961 elegy by Syrian poet Adonis and a 1965 lyric by Iraqi poet Abdel Wahab al-Bayati (ʿAbd al-Wahhāb al-Bayātī).

57 Abdel Sabur often cited Eliot's criticism; he also translated his play *The Cocktail Party* in 1964. Eliot's *Murder in the Cathedral* is widely recognized as a model for *The Tragedy of al-Hallaj*—to the point that the English translation of Abdel Sabur's play is titled *Murder in Baghdad* in homage. It is reasonable to read Abdel Sabur's comment about escaping from under "other carts," below, as a reference to Eliot. However, Eliot's Archbishop Thomas Becket does not experience the sort of breakdown we will see in Abdel Sabur's al-Hallaj. Although he speaks with four tempters, he never actually appears tempted. The two protagonists share a certainty in God's providence and a resolution to wait for martyrdom—"Now my good angel, whom God appoints / To be my guardian, hover over the swords' points," Becket says. Eliot, *Murder in the Cathedral,* 46.

58 ʿAbd al-Ṣabūr, *Ḥayātī fī al-Shiʿr.* The memoir opens with a discussion of the Delphic Oracle's command, "Know thyself."

59 For instance, Abdel Sabur uses Qushayri's term *wārid* (nonvoluntary praiseworthy feeling) to describe the experience, like an illumination or an intuition that inundates the heart, when a poem first appears to its author. He writes of a poet's holy passion (*ʿishq*) for his art. And he bends Aristotle's notion of catharsis to apply to the artist as much as to the audience, so that artistic creation becomes a moral cleansing of the poet's soul: "The purpose of art is none other than the conquest of the ego." ʿAbd al-Ṣabūr, *Ḥayātī fī al-Shiʿr,* 8–16, quotation on 16. See also al-Qushayrī, *Al-Risāla al-Qushayriyya,* 46.

60 See Bloom, *The Anxiety of Influence.*

61 Muhalhal is another name for Prince Sālim, an Arab legendary hero. Jassās ibn Murra is the cousin who kills Sālim-Muhalhal's brother Kulayb. This killing is provoked by Kulayb's tyrannical power grab after a successful coup in which he and Jassās participated together. Alfred Farag also wrote a play about this feud, *al-Zīr Sālim* (*Prince Salim,* 1967).

62 ʿAbd al-Ṣabūr, *Ḥayātī fī al-Shiʿr,* 114–15.

63 However, he did not reject political relevance as such. *The Tragedy of al-Hallaj* does include significant elements of political satire. So do his later plays: *The Princess Waits* (1969), *Now That the King Is Dead* (1975), and even the absurdist *Night Traveler* (1968).

64 ʿAbd al-Ṣabūr, *Ḥayātī fī al-Shiʿr,* 118.

65 Ibid., 117–18.

66 ʿAbd al-Ṣabūr, "Ma'sāt al-Ḥallāj," 150.

67 As critics noted. See ʿAbd al-Wahhāb, "Ma'sāt al-Ḥallāj," 47–52.

68 See, e.g., ʿIzz al-Dīn Ismāʿīl, paraphrased in Selaiha, "Introduction," 11–12.

69 ʿAbd al-Ṣabūr, "Ma'sāt al-Ḥallāj," 165.

70 "*Ayna al-maẓlūmūn, wa-ayna al-ẓalama?*"

71 Abdel Sabur, *Murder in Baghdad,* 94–96.

72 He welcomes his trial: "This is the best thing God has given me / God has chosen"; ʿAbd al-Ṣabūr, "Ma'sāt al-Ḥallāj," 228. On agency understood as piety rather than individual choice-making, see Mahmood, *Politics of Piety.*

73 Massignon, *Hallaj: Mystic and Martyr,* 208–75. Here I believe Abdel Sabur makes a more fruitful choice than Farag, who omits Sulayman's trial, losing its dramatic potential.

74 Abdel Sabur, *Murder in Baghdad,* 117; and see ʿAbd al-Ṣabūr, "Ma'sāt al-Ḥallāj," 245.

75 ʿAbd al-Ṣabūr, "Ma'sāt al-Ḥallāj," 248.

76 Ibid., 251.

77 Abdel Sabur, *Murder in Baghdad,* 122–23 (slightly amended); and ʿAbd al-Ṣabūr, "Ma'sāt al-Ḥallāj," 252.

78 ʿAbd al-Ṣabūr, *Ḥayātī fī al-Shiʿr,* 119.

79 See note 37 in this chapter.

80 Selaiha, "Introduction," 13.

81 Critic and novelist Bahaa Taher wrote: "I am not making a comparison but simply asking a question. In plays such as *Antigone, St. Joan,* or *Murder in the Cathedral,* martyrdom is always connected with a particular goal: honoring the laws of the gods, saving the nation, defending one's creed, etc. But it is rare for one to find a martyr

[like al-Hallaj] who is martyred so that his words may remain. For this reason the play *The Tragedy of al-Hallaj* remains fascinating and full of promises until the end. And when it ends, a person is beset by feelings of frustration. This is not because the ending is artistically incomplete but because it is intellectually incomplete. The writer does not want us to look at al-Hallaj only as a victim of injustice, but as a martyr—but the curtain falls and we still do not know and cannot guess the impact of this martyrdom or its value." Ṭāhir, "Mīzān al-Kawn," 105.

82 As critic Nasim Migalli wrote: "If we looked at the play in the light of Egypt's objective circumstances at that time, we would find that [the country] was living through one of its most urgent periods. The discussion revolved at that time around the intellectuals and their relationship with the revolution. . . . People saw in this work a call for freedom of conscience and freedom of belief and freedom of speech, at a time when the centers of power had begun to tighten their grip on the reins of power and to try and stifle freedom of opinion in the context of a central call, carried by the media, that urged writers and artists to unity of thought . . . and unity of action in the context of a single system." Mijallī, "Miṣr fī Masraḥiyyāt Ṣalāḥ 'Abd al-Ṣabūr," 172–73.

83 I saw the production at the Ṭalīʿa (Vanguard) Theatre in April 2002. See also Selaiha, "Poet, Rebel, Martyr."

84 See Amin, *Alfred Farag and Egyptian Theater.*

85 Director Mahmoud El Lozy (Maḥmūd al-Lawzī) dropped most of the Chorus scenes, replacing them with vernacular protest poetry by Sheikh Imam (Shaykh Imām) and Ahmad Fouad Nagm (Aḥmad Fuʾād Najm), and cut "many of the passages that critics have seen as reminiscent of Hamlet." Personal communication from Mahmoud El Lozy, December 4, 2005. For a review and photos, see Selaiha, "Old Tune, New Resonance."

Chapter 5. Time Out of Joint, 1967–76

1 *Hamlet,* 1.5.196–97.

2 Arabic translations of "the time [is] out of joint" or "out-of-joint time" include *al-zaman fī iʿtilāl wa-iḥtilāl* (Shakespeare, *Hāmlit,* trans. Khalīl Muṭrān, 50); *al-kawn muḍṭarib* (ʿAbd al-Ṣabūr, "Sulaymān al-Ḥalabī bayn al-Raghba wa-l-ʿAql," 243); *al-kawn al-muʿtall* (ʿAbd al-Ṣabūr, "Ma'sāt al-Ḥallāj," 165); *al-zamān muḍṭarib* (Jabrā, *Wilyam Shaksbīr,* 69); *zamān muḍṭarib wa maʿūj* (Shakespeare, *Hāmlit, Amīr Dānimārk,* trans. Muḥammad 'Awaḍ Muḥammad, 70); *la-qad fusida al-ʿaṣr* (the time has grown corrupted, Shakespeare, *Hāmlit,* trans. 'Abd al-Qādir al-Qiṭṭ); and *al-ʿaṣr al-muhtari'* (Amīn al-ʿAyyūṭī, "Qināʿ Hāmlit").

3 *Hamlet,* 2.2.52.

4 Hourani, *A History of the Arab Peoples,* 442, emphasis added.

5 Oren, *Six Days of War,* 305–12. Syrian losses were much smaller—about 450 dead, 1,800 wounded, and 365 captured.

6 See Hopwood, *Syria 1945–1986,* 47–53.

7 See Al-ʿAẓm, *Al-Naqd al-Dhātī baʿd al-Hazīma*; and Rejwan, *Nasserist Ideology,* 176–91. As we saw in chapter 1, al-Azm's comparison of "modern Arabs" to "Hamlet" is mainly derogatory in tone.

[8] Personal communication (e-mail) from Nehad Selaiha, June 5, 2003.

[9] See Al-Hakim, *The Return of Consciousness.*

[10] Ghassan Ghunaym describes 1967 as the beginning of political theatre in Syria: "The society's masks all came off; we were exposed to ourselves." He sees Syrian political theatre as an interwar phenomenon, basically finished by 1973. Ghunaym, *Al-Masraḥ al-Siyāsī fī Sūriyā,* 190–194 and 301–2; quote on 194.

[11] See Gordon, *Revolutionary Melodrama.*

[12] Egyptian and Syrian theatre critics began using the word "mask" or "veil" (*qināʿ*) with greater frequency, pointing to a new sense that "the masks had fallen" and a strong concern with disguises, hypocrisy, and underlying truth. See, e.g., al-ʿAyyūṭī, "Qināʿ Hāmlit"; al-ʿĀlim, "Maʾsāt Hāmlit bayn Shaksbīr wa-l-Sayyid Bidayr"; and ʿIṣmat, "Azmat al-Masraḥ al-Sūrī." See also note 10 in this chapter.

[13] Jayyusi, "Introduction," x.

[14] Ibid., xv.

[15] Ali, *The Clash of Fundamentalisms,* 117.

[16] Qabbānī, "Hawāmish ʿalā Daftar al-Naksa," 90–93. Cf. Qabbani, "Footnotes to the Book of the Setback," 97–101. An excerpt is also translated as "Notes on the Book of Defeat" in Qabbani, *On Entering the Sea,* 18. The poem was originally published as a small standalone book by Qabbani's own press in Beirut, launched after he left the Syrian diplomatic corps in 1966. Despite his exile and unsparing criticism, Qabbani remained an official hero in his native Syria; there is a street named after him in Damascus.

[17] Qabbānī, "Hawāmish ʿalā Daftar al-Naksa," 75 (part 5). ʿAntar is a hero of Arab legend. The *ṭabla* and *rabāba* are a drum and a one- or two-stringed instrument, respectively, used in Arab music.

[18] Ibid., 78. "*Bi-l-nāy wa-l-mizmār / lā yaḥduth intiṣār*" (part 8). The *nāy* is an Arab flute; the *mizmār* is a reed instrument somewhat similar to an oboe.

[19] Ibid., 96–98 (part 20).

[20] Described in Ofeish, "Gender Challenges to Patriarchy."

[21] "*Jiljila qawiyya fī al-awsāṭ al-masraḥiyya*"; ʿIṣmat, "Azmat al-Masraḥ al-Sūrī," 44.

[22] Wannūs, *Al-Aʿmāl al-Kāmila,* 1:7.

[23] The play blames the government for a failure to educate, inform, and mobilize its people. (The peasant characters, from a village in the Golan, say they have only ever seen government officials at tax collecting time.) Deprived of military help and of any tools to understand their role in the Arab nationalist struggle, these villagers naturally resort to narrow self-interest: trying to save their families and possessions from the occupiers. Their story deflates the government's populist rhetoric and exposes its soldiers as a self-interested and unimpressive lot. Wannūs, *Al-Aʿmāl al-Kāmila,* 21–128.

[24] It would not have been surprising if some actual audience members, confused about what was happening, had succumbed to the illusion and actually jumped up to contribute to the action. Presumably the actors would have rehearsed different ways of incorporating unplanned audience input.

[25] Wannus's stage directions to *Party for June 5* specify that the actors do not play individualized characters but rather "voices and images from a particular historical situation"; Wannūs, *Al-Aʿmāl al-Kāmila,* 23.

[26] Gordon, *Nasser: Hero of the Arab Nation,* 122.

27 See "Mourners Killed as Nasser Is Buried."

28 Qabbānī, "Jamāl ʿAbd al-Nāṣir."

29 *Hamlet,* 1.2.140.

30 Some of his mincing consonants suggest sarcasm (e.g., *taqallub / wa-tadhabdhub,* here "flip-flopping / And shilly-shallying"), but his open vowels ring with despair (e.g., *unādī fī wādī,* "I scream / Into a ravine").

31 Surely an allusion to the civil war in Jordan.

32 *Jāhiliyya,* the Arabic word for "ignorance," is the term used for pre-Islamic culture.

33 Qabbānī, "Jamāl ʿAbd al-Nāṣir."

34 *Hamlet,* 1.2.180–81. Another instance of fickleness as eating is in the closet scene: "Could you on this fair mountain leave to feed / And batten on this moor?" (ibid., 3.4.66–67)

35 Ibid., 3.4.126–27. Hamlet's allusion to Luke 19:40 (noted by Jenkins) means that he, like Qabbani, compares the dead father figure to Jesus Christ.

36 In Arab custom it is respectful to call a man "Abū" (father of) followed by the name of his eldest son. In this poem the appellation also highlights Nasser's paternal role; he was more commonly and intimately called "Gamāl" (by Egyptians) or "Jamāl" (by other Arabs).

37 Qabbānī, "Jamāl ʿAbd al-Nāṣir."

38 See Benjamin, "Trauerspiel and Tragedy," esp. 65–74 and 133–142.

39 My analysis draws on a video of a late-1970s television film provided by Sobhi and my extended interview with Sobhi in his studio at Madinat Sunbul (between Cairo and Alexandria), August 9, 2007. Filming for television was directed by Nour El-Demerdash (Nūr al-Dimirdāsh).

40 Author's interview with Sobhi.

41 Mijallī, "Abū Zayd al-Hilālī . . . wa-Hāmlit," 167. However, Sobhi said his heavy investment in elaborate costumes and sets caused him actually to lose money on the commercial production. Author's interview with Sobhi; see also Kanaan, "Shakespeare on the Arab Page and Stage," 77–78.

42 Mijallī, "Abū Zayd al-Hilālī . . . wa-Hāmlit," 168.

43 Shakespeare, *Hāmlit,* trans. Khalīl Muṭrān; Jabrā, *Wilyam Shaksbīr*; Shakespeare, *Hāmlit*, trans. ʿAbd al- Qādir al-Qiṭṭ.

44 See chapter 3 above. On Sobhi's debt to Olivier, see Kanaan, "Shakespeare on the Arab Page and Stage," 44–83. Kanaan does not mention Kozintsev.

45 From *Hamlet,* 5.2.364–65. (Where it differs substantially from Shakespeare's, I have translated Sobhi's text into English and prefaced the line numbers from the Jenkins edition with "from.")

46 Ibid.

47 E.g., "Except my life, except my life, except my life" (*Hamlet,* 2.2.216–17), and "I humbly thank you, well, well, well" (ibid., 3.1.92; this text occurs only in the first folio of 1623). Perhaps it is a family trait—cf. the Ghost's "List, list, O list" and "Adieu, adieu, adieu" (ibid., 1.5.22, 91).

48 One of the versions included is Mutran's, which asks angels to carry Hamlet's "body" rather than his soul up to heaven (Shakespeare, *Hāmlit,* trans. Khalīl Muṭrān, 125.)

49 To compare it to the translations Sobhi used, I have reconstructed parts of the script

from this video. All subsequent quotations from Sobhi's adaptation are from my transcription.

50 Shakespeare, *Hāmlit,* trans. Khalīl Muṭrān; Jabrā, *Wilyam Shaksbīr*; Shakespeare, *Hāmlit*, trans. ʿAbd al-Qādir al-Qiṭṭ.

51 Mid-1960s performances of *The Glass Menagerie* at Cairo University in Egypt and the Syrian National Theatre in Damascus are attested to in Rubin, *The World Encyclopedia of Contemporary Theatre,* 4:243.

52 Al-Ḥakīm, *Qālabunā al-Masraḥī.*

53 By contrast, Marcellus in Shakespeare's opening scene describes a kingdom more frantic than bereaved: round-the-clock work for guards and shipbuilders, "daily cast of brazen cannon," "foreign mart for implements of war," etc. (*Hamlet,* 1.1.74–82). As we will see in chapter 6, later Arab adapters would make much of this arms race.

54 Shakespeare, *Hāmlit,* trans. ʿAbd al-Qādir al-Qiṭṭ, act 5, scene 2, lines 387–90, pages 278–79; cf. *Hamlet,* 5.2.387–90.

55 These lines are present in the Arabic translations Sobhi used.

56 All transcriptions are based on my viewing of the 1970s video provided by Sobhi. The quality is not optimal. However, the actors enunciate clearly and many of Sobhi's edits are unmistakable. (I have posted several clips from the play on my blog "Shakespeare in the Arab World," arabshakespeare.blogspot.com—search for "Sobhi.")

57 Moussa Mahmoud, "*Hamlet* in Egypt," 59. A longtime professor of Arabic literature at Cairo's Ayn Shams University, al-Qitt (1916-2002, sometimes pronounced and spelled El-Qutt) was known for his own poetry as well as his poetry criticism and his translations of English-language plays, including Shakespeare's *Hamlet, Pericles,* and *Richard III.* See "Obituary: Abdel Qader El-Qutt (1916–2002)."

58 Mijallī, "Abū Zayd al-Hilālī . . . wa-Hāmlit," 168–69.

59 Author's interview with Sobhi.

60 While the soliloquy uses Mutran's translation, presumably for its high-flown eloquence, Sobhi renders "to be or not to be" as "*akūn aw lā akūn,*" the most often quoted singular-pronoun version of the line. He pronounces it in triumphant resolution, not metaphysical speculation or despair.

61 Sobhi said: "I don't believe [Claudius] would say that. Impossible. If he had done that in front of someone—in front of another person—in front of Queen Gertrude—I would believe it. It would be for show. But for him to say that when he's by himself, that would mean he's sincere. Alone? Hmm. For him to have a conscience? It won't do." He added: "And also, I don't want the viewer to be certain that Claudius is the one who murdered the king. This is the scene where Claudius confesses, but I don't want the audience to have confirmation of that. . . . I want the viewer to be in the same position as Hamlet, to merge [*yatawaḥḥad*] with the protagonist, who is not certain." Author's interview with Sobhi.

62 Ibid.

63 In Arabic the words for "liberation" and "enlightenment" rhyme (*taḥrīr* and *tanwīr*), giving the sentence a classical or sloganistic ring.

64 Al-ʿAshrī, "Hāmlit fī al-Masraḥ al-Tijārī . . . wa-Tilka Hiya al-Mushkila" [Hamlet in the Commercial Theatre . . . and That Is The Question], 280.

65 Sobhi's editing all but silences Ophelia. She speaks no lines until the nunnery scene,

and a blackout replaces her monologue ("O what a noble mind is here o'erthrown"; *Hamlet,* 3.1.152ff.) at the end of that scene. Most of her song in the "mad scene" is played in voiceover, with her offstage. With Gertrude, by contrast, Sobhi enjoys an Oedipal confrontation à la Olivier.

66 Al-Shetawi, "*Hamlet* in Arabic," 47. These devices do not appear in the filmed version. In my interview with him (before sharing the video), Sobhi denied any Brechtian intentions. He said he began with Hamlet's funeral in order to eliminate the suspense: "I did not want the audience to be sitting there thinking about what is going to happen, but about *why* it had to happen." But to my remark that this move sounded Brechtian, Sobhi objected: "No, not at all, nothing like that" (*No no no, khāliṣ, mā l-hāsh ʿalāqa*). The video confirms his claim.

67 Author's interview with Sobhi. Cf. Kanaan, "Shakespeare on the Arab Page and Stage," 57–58.

68 Ismat, now Syria's Minister of Culture, studied English literature in Damascus (B.A. 1968) before earning a master's degree in theatre direction from Cardiff University (UK) in 1983 and a Ph.D. in theatre arts from the International University in Arizona in 1989. He is a respected playwright and has also served as deputy minister of culture, head of Syrian radio and television broadcasting, rector of the Higher Academy for Dramatic Arts in Damascus, and Syrian ambassador to Pakistan (2005–10) and Qatar (2010). My analysis of his *Hamlet* draws on his program notes quoted at length within his own later account: ʿIṣmat, "Hāmlit kamā Akhrajtuhu." Al-Shetawi provides a brief English overview: see Al-Shetawi, "*Hamlet* in Arabic," 48.

69 Ismat says he would have preferred modern dress, "Hamlet wearing jeans and a black pullover [*kinza*], for example" (455), as in Yuri Lyubimov's famous 1971 Taganka production in Moscow starring Vladimir Vysotsky; ʿIṣmat, "Hāmlit kamā Akhrajtuhu," 455. He ultimately chose "historic European costumes" to match the hand-me-down set, borrowed from another production designed by his Moscow-trained set designer friend Ali al-Hamid (ʿAlī al-Ḥāmid); ibid., 453. Ismat had wanted an original set for his *Hamlet,* but time limitations prevented it.

70 Fayruz singing "Don't neglect me, don't forget me" was piped in instead of the songs by the mad Ophelia. Ismat says: "I found it able, despite its totally different style from the original, to produce a similar emotional effect." Iṣmat, "Hāmlit kamā Akhrajtuhu," 451.

71 Ibid., 460.

72 Ibid., 449.

73 Ibid., 463.

74 Ibid., 437.

75 Ibid., 448. (*Romulus the Great* tells the story of an emperor who willfully destroys his empire.)

76 Ibid., 454.

77 Marking its continuing connection with the ruling Asad family, the school was later renamed in memory of "The Martyr Basil al-Asad," an alumnus and the elder son of then-president Hafiẓ al-Asad, after Basil's death in a 1994 car crash. As of 2009, the alumni association was chaired by Dr. Bushra al-Asad, Hafiz al-Asad's daughter. (She is the sister of Syrian president Bashar al-Asad and the wife of General Assef

Shawkat [Āṣif Shawkat], the deputy chief of staff of the Syrian army.) Information about the school is available on a Facebook page and two alumni websites, all of which refer to the school by its old French name: http://www.facebook.com/Laique School, http://www.laique78.com/index.htm, and http://www.laique.com.

78 ʿIṣmat, "Hāmlit kamā Akhrajtuhu," 450.

79 Ismat claims to have been surprised by this coincidence. The boy was first cast as an understudy and took the part only after the original Hamlet was deployed to another city for his military service. Ibid., 455.

80 For background on this period, see Hopwood, *Syria 1945–1986.*

81 The reference is to Lewis, "Hamlet: The Prince or the Poem?"

82 The program notes are reproduced in ʿIṣmat, "Hāmlit kamā Akhrajtuhu," 461–64.

83 *Hamlet,* 1.5.97–104.

84 In this he resembles the polemicists discussed in chapter 1, who present disunity or dismemberment of the political community as akin to madness and suicide.

85 ʿIṣmat, "Hāmlit kamā Akhrajtuhu," 463, emphasis added.

86 If there were more subtle political signals in the staging itself (evocative costumes, ad-libbed political allusions, etc.) these sources would not have preserved them, and I have not yet found traces of them.

87 Quoted in Yurchak, *Everything Was Forever, Until It Was No More,* 71–73.

88 ʿIṣmat, "Hāmlit kamā Akhrajtuhu," 463.

89 Cf. Brecht's comments on opera: "Our existing opera is a culinary opera. It was a means of pleasure long before it turned into merchandise. It furthers pleasure even where it requires, or promotes, a certain degree of education, for the education in question is an education of taste. To every object it adopts a hedonistic approach. It 'experiences,' and it ranks as an 'experience.'" Brecht, *Brecht on Theatre,* 35.

90 As an art historian observed in another context: "Much of what we call 'taste' lies in this, the conformity between discriminations demanded by a painting and skills of discrimination possessed by the beholder. We enjoy our own exercise of skill, and we particularly enjoy the playful exercise of skills which we use in normal life very earnestly. If a painting gives us opportunity for exercising a valued skill and rewards our virtuosity with a sense of worthwhile insights about that painting's organization, we tend to enjoy it: it is to our taste." Baxandall, *Painting and Experience in Fifteenth-Century Italy,* 34.

91 For an account of an adaptation by Sami Abd al-Hamid (Sāmī ʿAbd al-Ḥamīd), titled *Hamlet Arabian-Style* (*Hāmlit ʿArabiyyan*) and loosely based on a then-recent succession dispute in Qatar, see Alsenad, "Professional Production of Shakespeare in Iraq," 120–38. Staged at Baghdad's Modern Art Theatre in May 1973, the show combined Arab and Muslim cultural trappings with an indecisive, uncharismatic hero; critics describe it as a highly memorable flop.

92 Scott, *Domination and the Arts of Resistance: Hidden Transcripts.*

93 For a bitter send-up of Egypt's commercialization in this period, see Ibrahim, *Zaat (Dhāt).*

94 Al-Duwayrī, *Al-Aʿmāl al-Kāmila,* 3:5–166. Kanaan reads the play as an earnest indictment of state censorship under both Nasser and Sadat; Kanaan, "Shakespeare on the Arab Page and Stage," 138–87.) See also Ghazoul, "The Arabization of *Othello,*" 27.

95 Walter Armbrust describes 'Ataba Square as "a neighborhood located in a transitional zone between European-built downtown Cairo and more traditional areas. My friends . . . frequently recommended al-ʿAtaba as a place to buy things cheap; the media often denounces it as a wild place where stolen goods are fenced and bad taste runs rampant." Armbrust, *Mass Culture and Modernism in Egypt,* 2.

96 Duwayrī, *Al-Aʿmāl al-Kāmila,* 3:23.

97 Ibid., 121.

98 Other funeral openings: Mohamed Sobhi's is discussed above. Salah Abdel Sabur's *Tragedy of Al-Hallaj* (discussed in chapter 4) also opens with the image of the martyr's body. So does Mamduh Adwan's *Hamlet Wakes Up Late* (discussed in chapter 6). I do not know how many other plays of the 1960s and 70s opened with funerals. It is possible that this structure emerged in imitation of the flashback technique in film.

99 Duwayrī, *Al-Aʿmāl al-Kāmila,* 3:29.

100 An excellent account of this period in Shakespeare's life, albeit not one available to Duwayrī, is Shapiro, *A Year in the Life of William Shakespeare: 1599.*

101 Duwayrī, *Al-Aʿmāl al-Kāmila,* 3:68, 79–80.

102 Ibid., 29.

103 For instance Duwayrī's Queen Elizabeth (like her historical model) sees political incitement in Shakespeare's staging of *Richard II* on the eve of Essex's rebellion. The play challenges divine right and lets the crowd watch a monarch abdicate, she says. "Divine right belongs to the people," Essex responds. A plainly rattled Shakespeare tries his best to stay out of the discussion. He escapes punishment, but Elizabeth rebukes him with an echo of the witches' mantra: why is he so ungrateful as to get involved with the conspirators when she has helped him attain fame, fortune, and popularity? Duwayrī, *Al-Aʿmāl al-Kāmila,* 3:136ff.

104 Perhaps to exploit the assonance with "Shaykh," Falstaff calls Shakespeare "Shaykhspeare" several times. But the stage directions spell his name in the usual Arabic way, *shaksbīr* with a kaf.

105 Duwayrī, *Al-Aʿmāl al-Kāmila,* 3:41–43.

106 Fortunately for the Cairo audience, the play includes long excerpts from both *Merry Wives* and *Comedy of Errors* presented without interruption and with plenty of slapstick. (It is generally a good idea to show audiences whatever one berates them for liking.)

107 In an intertextual comparison that again blends history with fiction, the play calls Marlowe a Don Quixote figure. However, his massive success, of which Shakespeare is very envious, later turns out to be due to a Doctor Faustus–like pact with Satan.

108 It is not certain which Marlowe play Duwayrī refers to. The only one not mentioned in the next sentence is *The Massacre at Paris*; it seems plausible here.

109 Duwayrī, *Al-Aʿmāl al-Kāmila,* 3:68.

110 Given the 1975 publication date of *Shakespeare Rex,* I read this as an indictment of Sadat's post-1973 rapprochement with the West in general, not yet his 1978–79 overtures to Israel in particular.

111 Duwayrī, *Al-Aʿmāl al-Kāmila,* 3:151–53.

112 Ibid., 160.

113 Ibid., 166.

114 Kanaan, "Shakespeare on the Arab Page and Stage," 184.
115 For instance: "A banner with words on it—and what it says, we'll know presently"; Duwayrī, *Al-Aʿmāl al-Kāmila,* 3:8.
116 See chapter 4 on Kozintsev.
117 ʿIṣmat, "Hāmlit kamā Akhrajtuhu," 463.
118 As shown in Wannus's 1976 play *Al-Fīl, Yā Malik al-Zamān,* translated as *The King's Elephant* in Jayyusi, *Short Arabic Plays.* In this parable, Yahya, a self-appointed representative of the people, marshals them to go complain to the king that his pet elephant has been overrunning their neighborhoods and endangering their children. But upon arrival at the palace the people become fearful and tongue-tied; Yahya, in disgust, abandons them and goes to work for the king.
119 When Wannus broke his silence, it was with a series of plays that departed radically from his Brechtian early work. These later plays stressed characterization, portraying characters deeply and sympathetically. They include *The Rape,* which drew controversy for portraying an Israeli character in a positive light. Wannus died of cancer in 1997.
120 See, e.g., Badawi, "Introduction"; and Amin, "Egyptian Playwright Alfred Farag Analyzes Decline of Arab Theatre."

Chapter 6. Six Plays in Search of a Protagonist, 1976–2002

1 Adwan's name is often voweled with a *dumma* in Arabic and written "Mamduh Udwan" in English; I have spelled it with an "A" following the preference of his son, actor Ziad Adwan.
2 ʿAdwān, "Hāmlit . . . Yastayqiẓu Muta'akhkhiran," 186. The play was later reprinted in book form (Beirut: Dar Ibn Rushd, 1980).
3 A detailed analysis of this play is Kanaan, "Shakespeare on the Arab Page and Stage," 84-137; production history on 94.
4 Adwan's script gives no reason for this spelling of Guildenstern.
5 Al-Shetawi, "*Hamlet* in Arabic," 51.
6 I have not been able to see any of these six plays performed live. Where possible, I have supplemented a reading of the script with video recordings of performances, published criticism, correspondence with the authors, and interviews with audience members, performers, and authors.
7 In some cases, such as al-Assadi's, Egyptian colloquial Arabic was also included during performances.
8 Scholars of Shakespeare reception have termed this distinction (in a Bakhtinian vein) "immanent versus dialogic" or (in a Derridian vein) "self-effacing" versus "aware of difference." See, respectively, Ghazoul, "The Arabization of *Othello*"; Modenessi, "'A Double Tongue Within Your Mask.'"
9 On "binocular vision" see Carlson, *The Haunted Stage,* 27.
10 Al-Asadī, *Insū Hāmlit,* 35.
11 See the Shakespeare-reception anthologies cited in note 10 of the introduction as well as Leiter, *Shakespeare around the Globe.* Tom Stoppard's *Rosencrantz and Guildenstern Are Dead* (1966), in which Hamlet is marginal, is the notable exception. More typical is a recent adaptation by the Georgian-influenced Synetic Theater in Wash-

ington, D.C., *Hamlet: The Rest Is Silence* (2002). Performed entirely in pantomime and dance, the Synetic production certainly keeps Paata Tsikurishvili's Hamlet center stage.

12 Caton, *Peaks of Yemen I Summon,* 27–28. Caton further observes that in tribal northern Yemen, "Poetry . . . like a gun, is a weapon by which a man wins and defends his honor" (28). Caton's analysis of talk *as* practice contrasts with some urban Arab intellectuals' derogation of "words, words, words."

13 Hourani, *Arabic Thought in the Liberal Age,* 1.

14 James Shapiro has argued that Shakespeare did something similar with *Hamlet,* playing his new text off audience memories of a 1580s predecessor: "Old certainties were gone, even if new ones had not yet taken hold. The most convincing way of showing this was to ask playgoers to keep both plays in mind at once, to experience a new *Hamlet* while memories of the old one, ghostlike, still lingered." See Shapiro, *A Year in the Life of William Shakespeare: 1599,* 288.

15 Cf. Achille Mbembe's sketch of an African postcolony where obscenity is "an integral part of the stylistics of power." Mbembe, *On the Postcolony,* 115. See also his earlier essay and the surrounding discussion: Mbembe, "The Banality of Power and the Aesthetics of Vulgarity in the Postcolony."

16 *Hamlet,* 2.2.232.

17 Ibid., 2.2.584–601. Jenkins cites Hilda Hulme's (1962) suggestion that "relative" means "relatable (able to be told) to the public" (*Hamlet,* note to 2.2.600). Further, Hamlet's explanation of *The Mousetrap* (some fifty lines after he has commissioned it) is the only context in which he ever uses the word "melancholy" to describe himself; see Jenkins's "Long Note" to 2.2.597, page 484. Arguably, he is ascribing this view of himself to his detractors at court, who could block his access to the throne even after the death of Claudius.

18 *Hamlet,* 2.2.584–601.

19 On the usefulness of this deniability, see Mitchell-Kernan, "Signifying and Marking."

20 On a power figure's taking offense understood as a moment of disempowerment, see Coetzee, *Giving Offense,* 3.

21 Critics therefore refer to the "problem of the dumb show": why, if Claudius had actually glimpsed the "miching malicho" of the dumb-show, did he betray no response and allow the play to continue? Directors' solutions have included gritted-teeth endurance, distracting stage business, and a poker face that leaves the audience guessing whether Claudius saw the show or not.

22 See Wedeen, *Ambiguities of Domination.* Applying experiences from the Soviet Union and Eastern Europe, Wedeen argues that the Asad personality cult served the regime *precisely because* so few people believed in it: the cult crowded out coherent speech, fostered distrust among citizens, and showed skeptical Syrians that it could still force them into the humiliation of compliance.

23 Shahrayar is Scheherazade's husband, the bride-killing king from the *One Thousand and One Nights* frame story.

24 ʿAdwān, "Hāmlit . . . Yastayqiẓu Muta'akhkhiran," 193.

25 Ibid., 196.

26 Ibid., 198–99.

27 Ibid., 199.
28 Ibid., 190.
29 See Wedeen, *Ambiguities of Domination.* It is likely that the play's audience had experienced such required "demonstrations."
30 ʿAdwān, "Hāmlit . . . Yastayqiẓu Muta'akhkhiran," 206.
31 *Hamlet Wakes Up Late* is among the four of our six *Hamlet* plays to be set in a Christian rather than a Muslim context.
32 Matthew 7:13.
33 Matthew 7:15–16 and 26:26.
34 ʿAdwān, "Hāmlit . . . Yastayqiẓu Muta'akhkhiran," 208.
35 Ibid., 210.
36 Ibid., 218.
37 Ghunaym, *Al-Masraḥ al-Siyāsī fī Sūriyā,* 148–51.
38 On this production and reception context, see Kanaan, "Shakespeare on the Arab Page and Stage," 107–24.
39 ʿUmrān, "Firqa Masraḥiyya Wajadat Masraḥan . . . fa-Masraḥat Hāmlit."
40 *Fawanīs* means "lanterns." Since 1994 Omran has been the chief organizer of the Amman International Theatre Festival, co-hosted by his Al-Fawanees Theatre Group.
41 Earlier calls for an originally or authentically Arab theatre included manifestoes by Yusuf Idris and Tawfiq al-Hakim. See Idrīs, *Naḥw Masraḥ ʿArabī*; and al-Ḥakīm, *Qālabunā al-Masraḥī*. Al-Ḥakīm's text actually sketches the beginning of an Arabized *Hamlet* performance: a narrator (*ḥākī*) introduces each scene to the audience; a pair of mimics (*muqallid* and *muqallida*) act out all the male and female parts, respectively. Aside from this formal shift, which adds little to the play, al-Ḥakīm's sketch follows Khalīl Muṭrān's translation precisely. Al-Ḥakīm finds that the most "Arab" theatrical forms are also "modern": a sparse stage, an audience already aware of the storyline, a nonillusionistic acting style. He does not comment on Hamlet's own behavior as *ḥākī* in the *Mousetrap* scene. Al-Hakīm's manifesto proved less influential than that of Idris, which came illustrated with original plays including *al-Farāfīr* (The Farfoors). For subsequent "authenticity" debates see al-Rāʿī, *Al-Masraḥ al-ʿArabī: Bayn al-Naql wa-l-Ta'ṣīl* [*Arab Theatre: Between Adaptation and Authenticity*].
42 Personal communication from Nader Omran, February 2004.
43 Mūsā, *Hāmlit al-Muʿākas,* 19–34. See also Ḥawāmda, "Al-Baḥth ʿan Ṣīgha Masraḥiyya Jadīda."
44 This is foreshadowed as soon as the King and Queen enter: the Players help carry the Queen's 30-meter-long black train, which they later borrow for a stage prop (canopy, sentry tent, etc.). The King, meanwhile, seems able to command the actors—or at least, they eagerly impersonate loyal subjects when he needs to underscore a rhetorical point.
45 Omran's script uses the names of his performers rather than their characters. The performers take on roles only provisionally, at times inhabiting two roles at once or speaking directly to the audience.
46 Stage directions given here in parentheses appear in the manuscript. Those in square brackets are based on the rehearsal video provided by Omran.
47 The actors pronounce this line with much hilarity, deliberately not making clear whether they are agreeing with the king or parroting him mockingly. But the next

time they say these words, it is with the military enthusiasm of soldiers chanting a slogan after a commander.

48 The words I have rendered in uppercase letters are double-underlined in the Arabic manuscript. (Arabic has no capitalization.)

49 ʿUmrān, "Firqa Masraḥiyya Wajadat Masraḥan . . . fa-Masraḥat Hāmlit," 11–12.

50 Ibid., 16.

51 Cf. *Hamlet,* 3.2.22–24.

52 Ḥawāmda calls him "the *ḥakawātī* and the source of light, warmth, and truth"; Ḥawāmda, "Al-Baḥth ʿan Ṣīgha Masraḥiyya Jadīda," 87.

53 ʿUmrān, "Firqa Masraḥiyya Wajadat Masraḥan . . . fa-Masraḥat Hāmlit," 34–35.

54 The word is ambiguous, referring both to the actual lanterns on stage and Omran's Lanterns troupe.

55 ʿUmrān, "Firqa Masraḥiyya Wajadat Masraḥan . . . fa-Masraḥat Hāmlit,"27.

56 See, respectively, Mūsā, *Hāmlit al-Muʿākas,* 31; and Ḥawāmda, "Al-Baḥth ʿan Ṣīgha Masraḥiyya Jadīda," 96.

57 Abū Dūmā, *Raqṣat al-ʿAqārib,* 113.

58 Ibid., 124.

59 Ibid., 125. In Arabic, the sentence starting "It's no time for games now" reads:
الأمر الآن ليس لعبة عدو على الأبواب وأموال جمعت وفرسان يتدربون وشعبي يستعد ثم يأتي هاملت ويبول على كعكتنا بادعاءاته السخيفة.

60 Abū Dūmā, *Raqṣat al-ʿAqārib,* 56.

61 Cf. Qur'ān 21:51–70 and 37:83–98. (Abraham's taunting of his father's idols also occurs in Midrashic Jewish sources.)

62 Abū Dūmā, *Raqṣat al-ʿAqārib,* 129.

63 Ibid., 114.

64 Ibid., 120.

65 Ibid., 139–40.

66 As Aboudoma explains, the play's title refers to an Upper Egyptian game: "In my childhood I saw some people catching a big scorpion and pulling out its tail, which was full of poison, and they put the scorpion beside the fire (a round piece of charcoal). The circumcised scorpion started to turn around the fire, the people were laughing and singing for him, 'Dance, dance, dance.' The scorpion turned faster and faster until it threw itself inside the fire. They call this game 'The Dance of the Scorpion.' This image lived in my memory up till now." Personal e-mail communication, June 10, 2002.

67 Nehad Selaiha's introduction to the play puts aside her usual skepticism of politics: "[T]he revolutionaries here are victorious, or at least the play ends on the hope of their victory, as they advance with determination toward the refuge of the scorpions, from the foot of the mountain to its summit, from the huts to the fortress, to defeat the lies and with them all the wolves, scorpions, and vipers." See Ṣulayḥa, "Muqaddima," 32–33.

68 See Litvin, "When the Villain Steals the Show."

69 It was revived in Christian Siméon's humorous adaptation at the L'étoile du Nord Theatre in Paris in March 2010, with another run scheduled for fall 2011; Jean Macqueron directed. For the text of the French adaptation, see Marzougui, *Ismail-Hamlet ou la vengeance du laveur de cadavre.*

70 A proverb.
71 Al-Marzūqī, *Ismāʿīl Hāmlit,* 1–2. References are to Arabic manuscript pages. The translations are mine but draw on Peter Clark's version.
72 Ibid., 10.
73 Ibid., 12.
74 At first used semi-ironically ("I have to see Saadiyya and tell her 'the truth of my feelings,' as the cultured folks say"), the phrase soon becomes an earnest and obsessively recurring refrain. Al-Marzūqī, *Ismāʿīl Hāmlit,* 6.
75 Ismail's in-laws are in the funeral business. He and his wife live in a house on the cemetery grounds, not in an actual above-ground tomb such as those inhabited by families in Cairo's City of the Dead.
76 Al-Marzūqī, *Ismāʿīl Hāmlit,* 10–11 (ellipses in original). "Loofah Man" was the nickname of Ismail's father, Ibrahim.
77 Ibid., 12.
78 Ibid.
79 The scene may be an actual memory from playwright Hakim Marzougui's native Tunisia or a story he heard there. A camel-pulled water wheel is still in use at the Bir Barrouta in Kairawan.
80 *Hamlet,* 1.1.50.
81 Al-Marzūqī, *Ismāʿīl Hāmlit,* 11–12.
82 في الله في كتير إي والله.
83 Al-Marzūqī, *Ismāʿīl Hāmlit,* 13–14.
84 *Hamlet,* 5.2.27–53.
85 Sulaymān, "Al-Sūriyya Rūlā Fattāl."
86 Born in Karbala in 1947, Al-Assadi graduated from Baghdad's Academy of Theatre Arts in 1974. He fled the country in 1976, earning a PhD in theatre in Bulgaria and continuing to work in Eastern Europe, the United Arab Emirates, and elsewhere. He returned to Iraq after the U.S. invasion in 2003 and founded the Gilgamesh Theatre, which soon closed for security reasons. He now runs the Babel Theatre in Beirut.
87 Al-Asadī, *Insū Hāmlit.*
88 Al-Assadi directed, with Moataza Salah Abdelsabour (Muʿtazza ʿAbd al-Sabūr; daughter of poet Salah Abdel Sabur) as Ophelia and Khaled El Sawy (Khālid al-Ṣāwī) as Claudius. For a review of the Cairo production, see Mahrān, "Shubbāk Ufīliyā aw Hāmlit ʿalā al-Ṭarīqa al-ʿAṣriyya." I am grateful to Muʿtazza Abdel Sabur and Ferial Ghazoul for sharing their personal recollections.
89 Al-Abṭaḥ, "Naṣṣ Masraḥī Yuʿarrib Ru'yat Shaksbīr."
90 Al-Asadī, *Insū Hāmlit,* 15.
91 "The other characters know what has been done and what will be done, as though they had read Shakespeare's text and are now re-enacting it according to a naked, exposed, and clamorous logic, as though al-Assadi's text begins after everything has already happened." Ibn Ḥamza, "Mustaʿīdan Hāmlit fī Ṣīgha Jadīda," 16. Ibn Ḥamza suggests that Hamlet, as well as the other characters, knows Shakespeare's text.
92 Al-Asadī, *Insū Hāmlit,* 16.
93 On the Norwegian king, see *Hamlet,* 1.2.29.
94 Al-Asadī, *Insū Hāmlit,* 29.
95 Ibid., 56. Cf. *Hamlet,* 1.5.92–104.

96 Al-Asadī, *Insū Hāmlit,* 44.

97 Ibid., 61. Cf. *Hamlet,* 2.2.243.

98 This trope occurs in ethnographic and autobiographical as well as literary writings: Palestinian mothers publicly berating Israeli soldiers during arrests and beatings of young men, Lebanese mothers and sisters gathering to protest the disappearance of their relatives imprisoned in Syria, and the many Arab women writers (Salwa Bakr, Nawal El Saadawi, Sahar Khalifeh, etc.) who describe their work as a kind of witnessing. See, e.g., Peteet, "Male Gender and Rituals of Resistance in the Palestinian Intifada"; and Peteet, "Icons and Militants."

99 Al-Asadī, *Insū Hāmlit,* 44.

100 Ibid., 41.

101 Aristotle, *The Politics and The Constitution of Athens,* 14.

102 Al-Asadī, *Insū Hāmlit,* 75, 22, and 32, respectively.

103 Ibid., 34–35.

104 Ibid., 9.

105 That they are women is specified in al-Assadi's script. Played by Hanan Youssef (Ḥanān Yūsuf) and Salwa Muhammad Ali (Salwā Muḥammad ʿAlī) in the Cairo production, they "combined features of *Macbeth*'s witches, the gravediggers in *Hamlet,* old ladies from the popular classes in the Egyptian countryside, silent-film comedy duos, and the Vladimir-Estragon couple from *Waiting for Godot.*" Ṣulayḥa, *Shaksbīriyyāt*, 219.

106 Al-Asadī, *Insū Hāmlit,* 23.

107 Ibid., 47.

108 Al-Asadī, *Insū Hāmlit,* 78. Cf. *Hamlet,* 2.2.544ff.; and Jabrā, *Wilyam Shaksbīr,* 101. Al-Assadi very slightly modifies Jabra's translation.

109 See *Hamlet,* 1.5.197.

110 On Iago, see Greenblatt, "The Improvisation of Power."

111 Al-Asadī, *Insū Hāmlit,* 51–53.

112 *Hamlet,* 4.5.40–74. For a detailed argument, see Ṣulayḥa, *Shaksbīriyyāt,* 168.

113 See, e.g., Mona Eltahawy, "Arab Politics and Society." Eltahawy writes: "A few years ago, I stood in a public square in an Arab capital and watched the funeral procession of an Arab leader. . . . 'It's like eclipse of the sun,' one man told me. 'This is a black day.'"

114 On Al-Bassam's Arab-themed Shakespeare adaptations, including his *Richard III: An Arab Tragedy,* and how they have played to and with his western audiences, see Litvin, "Explosive Signifiers."

115 In the Arabic-language version, only one character, the Arms Dealer, spoke in English. For the text and performance history, see Al-Bassam, *The Al-Hamlet Summit* (edited by Graham Holderness). Al-Bassam's text went through several iterations between 2002 and 2006 as the production developed. My citations are to a 2002 manuscript version Al-Bassam shared with me. A slightly different text was later published as Sulayman Al-Bassam, "The Al-Hamlet Summit: A Political Arabesque." *TheatreForum–International Theatre Journal* 22 (Winter–Spring 2003): 89–107. The Holderness edition incorporates extensive changes introduced during the course of the Arabic-language production. Both the Holderness edition and the manuscript are cited in my bibliography.

116 The allusions to Iraq, Lebanon, and other countries are deliberately ambiguous or contradictory, frustrating viewers' attempts to discern which particular country Al-Bassam has in mind. This amalgamation, different from the very specific allegories we have seen in previous chapters, relies on and reproduces a blurred composite image of Middle East tyranny and violence.

117 The script refers to "contemporary war footage"; Al-Bassam, "The Al-Hamlet Summit," 28. For details see Peter Culshaw, "Shakespeare and Suicide Bombers"; and Ali Jaafar, "Al-Hamlet Daringly Transposes Shakespeare's Classic Play to Modern Middle Eastern Setting."

118 For a review of the first Kuwait incarnation, see Calderbank, "Ẓāhira Masraḥiyya Lāfita."

119 Al-Bassam, "Am I Mad? Creating *The Al-Hamlet Summit.*"

120 Al-Bassam, "The Al-Hamlet Summit," 3.

121 Ibid.

122 Ibid., 28.

123 Ibid., 31.

124 She is thus structurally equivalent to Abu Fawanees, the theatre-spirit in Nader Omran's *A Theatre Company.*

125 Al-Bassam, "The Al-Hamlet Summit," 3.

126 See *Hamlet,* 3.3.36–98.

127 Ibid., line 70.

128 Al-Bassam, "The Al-Hamlet Summit," 22.

129 "Inta Umri," a song by beloved Egyptian singer Umm Kulthūm, is hummed and then played at the end of act 3; Al-Bassam, "The Al-Hamlet Summit," 19. Ophelia's suicide video quotes from a poem by the late Palestinian poet Maḥmūd Darwīsh: "The one who has turned me into a refugee has made a bomb of me." Al-Bassam, *The Al-Hamlet Summit,* edited by Graham Holderness, 78 and 87n8.

130 Al-Bassam, "The Al-Hamlet Summit," 28–29.

131 See Dent, "Interview: Sulayman Al-Bassam."

132 Al-Bassam, "Am I Mad?"

133 The manifesto of Nader Omran's troupe argues that theatre should seek to forge a community, a "we," out of the disparate "I"s of the audience. See Masraḥ al-Fawānīs, "Kalimat Masraḥ al-Fawānīs: al-Masraḥiyya ka-Sharṭ li-Fi'l al-Tanwīr" [A Word from the Fawanees Theatre: The Play as a Condition of Enlightenment].

134 Nietzsche, *The Birth of Tragedy and The Case of Wagner*, 60, emphasis added.

Epilogue: *Hamlets* without Hamlet

1 Kershaw, *The Radical in Performance*; Holderness, *The Politics of Theatre and Drama.*

2 Brantley and Isherwood, "To Be Topical in a Time Out of Joint."

3 Rebellato, "Can Political Theatre Change the World?"

4 Charnes, *Hamlet's Heirs.*

5 De Grazia, *"Hamlet" without Hamlet,* 1, 5.

6 Ibid., 1–2.

7 Al-Mājidī, *"Hāmlit" bilā hāmlit wa-sīrdā.* A scholar of ancient history and a poet, al-

Majidi (b. 1951) emigrated in the 1990s and returned to Iraq after the U.S. invasion in 2003. For details see his page on The al-Nūr Center site, http://www.alnoor.se/author.asp?id=391 (in Arabic).

8 See "*This Is Baghdad*," Baghdad Iraqi Theatre Company website, http://baghdadtheatrecompany.com/id2.html.

9 On Galal's own Shakespeare adaptations, see Selaiha, "Hamlet Galore."

10 ʿAfīfī, "Ana Hāmlit." The title page credits translations by Awad Muhammad, Ghazi Jamal (Ghāzī Jamāl, published in Beirut in 1978), Mohamed Enani (published in Cairo, 2004), and Jabra Ibrahim Jabra.

11 "قولك إيه: أنا مش ممكن أرتبط بواحدة عندها 500 صديق على الفيسبوك."
ʿAfīfī, "Ana Hāmlit," 20. At this writing, Afifi himself has 567.

12 Ibid., 37.

13 Ibid.

14 See Litvin, "Explosive Signifiers."

15 Shaw was director of the Royal Shakespeare Company's Complete Works Festival in 2007. Monadhil Daood acted the part of Catesby in Sulayman Al-Bassam's *Richard III: An Arab Tragedy*; he had also played Polonius in Al-Bassam's Arabic *Al-Hamlet Summit.*

16 As David Bauder of the Associated Press reported on February 11, 2011.

BIBLIOGRAPHY

ʿAbd al-Nāṣir, Jamāl. *Falsafat al-Thawra.* Cairo: Maṣlaḥat al-Istiʿlāmāt, 1966.

———. "Kalimat al-Ra'īs Jamāl ʿAbd al-Nāṣir bi-Maydān al-Taḥrīr bi-Ṣanʿā, 23/04/64 [Remarks of President Gamal Abdel Nasser in Tahrir Square in Sanaa, April 23, 1964]." At "Mawqiʿ al-Ra'īs Jamāl ʿAbd al-Nāṣir" [Website of President Gamal Abdel Nasser], http://nasser.bibalex.org/Speeches/browser.aspx?SID=1074.

———. "Khiṭāb al-Ra'īs Jamāl ʿAbd al-Nāsir fī Maydān al-Manshīya bil-Iskandariyya bi-Munāsibat ʿAyd al-Jalā' (Ḥādithat al-Manshīya) 26/10/1954 [Speech of President Gamal Abdel Nasser in Manshiya Square, Alexandria, on the occasion of Evacuation Day (The Manshiya Incident), 10/26/1954)]. At "Mawqiʿ al-Ra'īs Jamāl ʿAbd al-Nāṣir" [Website of President Gamal Abdel Nasser], http://nasser.bibalex.org/Speeches/browser.aspx?SID =263.

ʿAbd al-Malik, Badr. "Ughnīyat al-Ḥurriyya fī Ṭahrān." (The Song of Freedom in Tehran). *al-Bayān,* November 12, 2009.

ʿAbd al-Qādir, Farūq. *Izdihār wa-Suqūṭ al-Masraḥ al-Miṣrī.* Cairo: Dār al-Fikr al-Muʿāṣir, 1979.

ʿAbd al-Ṣabūr, Ṣalāḥ. "Hāmlit al-Miskīn . . . fī al-Barnāmaj al-Thānī." In *Aqūlu lakum ʿan al-masraḥ wa-al-sīnimā,* vol. 6 of *Al-Aʿmāl al-Kāmila,* ed. Aḥmad Ṣulayha and Maḥmūd ʿAbduh, 52–54. Cairo: al-Hay'a al-Miṣriyya al-ʿĀmma li-l-Kitāb, [1959].

———. *Ḥayātī fī al-Shiʿr.* Beirut: Dār al-ʿAwda, 1969.

———. *Ma'sāt al-Ḥallāj.* In *Al-Aʿmāl al-Kāmila,* 147–271. Cairo: al-Hay'a al-Miṣriyya al-ʿĀmma li-l-Kitāb, 1988.

———. "Sulaymān al-Ḥalabī bayn al-Fann wa-l-Tārīkh." *al-Masraḥ* 68 (1969).

———. "Sulaymān al-Ḥalabī bayn al-Raghba wa-l-ʿAql." In *Aqūlu lakum ʿan al-masraḥ wa-al-sīnimā,* vol. 6 of *Al-Aʿmāl al-Kāmila,* ed. Aḥmad Ṣulayha and Maḥmūd ʿAbduh, 240–45. Cairo: al-Hay'a al-Miṣriyya al-ʿĀmma li-l-Kitāb [1965].

ʿAbd al-Wahhāb, Fārūq. "Ma'sāt al-Ḥallāj." In *Dirāsāt fī al-Masraḥ al-Miṣrī,* 43–65. Cairo: al-Hay'a al-Miṣriyya al-ʿĀmma li-l-Kitāb, 1992.

Abdel Hai, Muhammad. *English Poets in Arabic.* Khartoum: Khartoum University Press, 1980.

Abdel Meguid, Ibrahim. *The Other Place.* Translated by Farouk Abdel Wahab. Cairo: American University in Cairo Press, 1997.

Abdel Sabur, Salah. *Murder in Baghdad.* Translated by Khalil Samaan. Cairo: General Egyptian Book Organization, 1976.

Abdel Wahab, Farouk. *Modern Egyptian Drama.* Minneapolis: Bibliotheca Islamica, 1974.

ʿAbduh, Ṭānyūs. *Diwān Ṭānyūs ʿAbduh.* Cairo: Maṭbaʿat al-Hilāl, 1925.

———. *Hāmlit.* Edited by Sameh Fekry Hanna. Cairo: Supreme Council of Culture of Egypt, 2005.

———. *Riwāyat Hamlit.* 2nd ed. Cairo: al-Maṭbaʿa al-Umamiyya, 1902.

al-Abṭaḥ, Sawsan. "Naṣṣ Masraḥī Yuʿarrib Ru'yat Shaksbīr: Al-Mukhrij al-Masraḥī al-ʿIrāqī Jawād al-Asadī Yadʿūnā fī Kitāb Jadīd la-hu ilā Nisyān Hāmlit." *al-Sharq al-Awsaṭ,* December 18, 2000.

Abu-Nasr, Donna. "Muslim Leaders Urge Calm over Cartoons." Associated Press, February 9, 2006.

Abū Dūmā, Maḥmūd. *Nūstāljiyā: Ḥikāyāt Kharīfiyya.* Cairo: Dār Sharqiyyāt, 2006.

———. *Raqṣat al-ʿAqārib.* In Abū Dūmā, *Jā'ū ilaynā Gharqā; al-Bi'r; Raqṣat al-ʿAqārib.* Cairo: al-Hay'a al-Miṣriyya al-ʿĀmma li-l-Kitāb, 1989.

Abul Naga, el-Saïd Atia. *Les sources françaises du théatre égyptien (1870–1939).* Algiers: SNED, 1972.

Achebe, Chinua. *Things Fall Apart.* New York: Anchor Books, 1994.

ʿAdwān, Mamdūḥ. "Hāmlit . . . Yastayqiẓu Muta'akhkhiran." *al-Mawqif al-Adabī* 65–66 (1976): 178–228.

ʿAfīfī, Hānī. "Ana Hāmlit." 2009. Unpublished manuscript provided by the author.

Ahmad, Aijaz. *In Theory: Classes, Nations, Literatures.* London: Verso, 1992.

Ajami, Fouad. *The Dream Palace of the Arabs: A Generation's Odyssey.* New York: Vintage, 1999.

"Al-Iʿdām aw Lā Iʿdām Tilka Hiya al-Qaḍīya." *al-Nahār,* December 16, 2003, A1.

Alexander, Anne. *Nasser.* London: Haus Publishing, 2005.

Ali, Tariq. *The Clash of Fundamentalisms: Crusades, Jihads, and Modernity.* London: Verso, 2003.

al-ʿĀlim, Maḥmūd Amīn. "Ma'sāt Hāmlit bayn Shaksbīr wa-l-Sayyid Bidayr." In *Al-Wajh wa-l-Qināʿ fī Masraḥinā al-ʿArabī al-Muʿāṣir,* 157–64. Beirut: Dār al-Ādāb, 1973.

Alsenad, Abedalmutalab. "Professional Production of Shakespeare in Iraq: An Exploration of Cultural Adaptation." PhD diss., University of Colorado, 1988.

Amin, Dina. *Alfred Farag and Egyptian Theater: The Poetics of Disguise, with Four Short Plays and a Monologue.* Syracuse, N.Y.: Syracuse University Press, 2008.

———. "Egyptian Playwright Alfred Farag Analyzes Decline of Arab Theatre." *Al Jadid* 5, no. 29 (1999), http://www.aljadid.com/theatre/AlfredFaragAnalyzesDeclineofArabTheater.html.

Amine, Khalid. "Moroccan Shakespeare and the Celebration of Impasse: Nabil Lahlou's *Ophelia Is Not Dead.*" *Critical Survey* 19, no. 3 (2007): 55–73.

Amīr, Sāmī Munīr Ḥusayn. *Al-Masraḥ al-Miṣrī baʿd al-Ḥarb al-ʿĀlamiyya al-Thāniya.* Vol. 2. Alexandria: al-Hay'a al-Miṣriyya al-ʿĀmma li-l-Kitāb, 1978.

al-ʿAnānī, Muḥammad. "Al-Masraḥ al-ʿĀlamī: Hāmlit." *al-Masraḥ* 13 (1965): 58–59.
Ansari, Hamied. *Egypt: The Stalled Society*. Albany: State University of New York Press, 1986.
Antonius, George. *The Arab Awakening: The Story of the Arab National Movement*. Philadelphia: J. B. Lippincott, 1939.
Anzai, Tetsuo, ed. *Shakespeare in Japan*. Shakespeare Yearbook, vol. 9. Lewiston, N.Y.: Edwin Mellen, 1999.
al-ʿAqqād, ʿAbbās Maḥmūd. *Al-Taʿrīf bi-Shaksbīr*. 2nd ed. Cairo: Dār al-Maʿārif, [1967].
———. *Sāʿāt bayn al-Kutub*. 4th ed. Cairo: Maktabat al-Nahḍa al-Miṣriyya, 1968.
Arafat, Yasser, and Ghassan Bishara. "Interviews: Yasser Arafat." *Journal of Palestine Studies* 13, no. 1 (1983): 3–8.
Aristotle. *The Politics and The Constitution of Athens*. Cambridge: Cambridge University Press, 1996.
Armbrust, Walter. *Mass Culture and Modernism in Egypt*. Cambridge: Cambridge University Press, 1996.
al-Asadī, Jawād. *Insū Hāmlit*. Beirut: Dar al-Farābī, 2000.
ʿAṣfūr, Jābir. "Hawāmish li-l-Kitāba: Hāmlit fī Būsṭun." *al-Hayat*, May 30, 2001, 19.
Ashcroft, Bill, Gareth Griffiths, and Helen Tiffin. *The Empire Writes Back: Theory and Practice in Post-Colonial Literatures*. London and New York: Routledge, 1989.
al-ʿAshrī, Jalāl. "Hāmlit fī al-Masraḥ al-Tijārī . . .wa-Tilka Hiya al-Mushkila." In *Tiyātrū fī al-Naqd al-Masraḥī*, 279–87. Cairo: Dār al-Maʿārif, 1984.
ʿĀshūr, Nuʿmān. *Al-Masraḥ wa-l-Siyāsa*. Cairo: al-Hay'a al-Miṣrīyya al-ʿĀmma li-l-Kitāb, 1986.
al-Aṣnaj, ʿAbdallāh. "Lubnān al-Dars wa-l-Tajriba." *al-Sharq al-Awsaṭ*, March 10, 2005.
Awad, Louis. "Problems of the Egyptian Theatre." In *Studies in Modern Arabic Literature*, ed. R. Ostle. Warminster, U.K.: Aris and Phillips, 1975.
——— "Cultural and Intellectual Developments in Egypt since 1952." In *Egypt since the Revolution*, ed. P. J. Vatikiotis, 143–61. London: George Allen and Unwin, Ltd., 1968.
'Awaḍ, Luwīs. "Sulaymān al-Ḥalabī: Najāḥ Nāqiṣ wa-Fashl Jamīl." In *Al-Thawra wa-l-Adab*, 366–384. Cairo: Dār al-Kātib al-ʿArabī li-l-Ṭibāʿa wa-l-Nashr, 1967.
ʿAwaḍ, Ramsīs. *Shakshīr fī Miṣr*. Cairo: al-Hay'a al-Miṣriyya al-ʿĀmma li-l-Kitāb, 1986.
ʿAwaḍ Muḥammad, Muḥammad. *Fann al-Tarjama*. Cairo: Jāmiʿat al-Duwal al-ʿArabiyya: Maʿhad al-Buḥūth wa-l-Dirāsāt al-ʿArabiyya, 1969.
al-ʿAyyūṭī, Amīn. "Al-Masraḥ al-Qawmī: Sulaymān al-Ḥalabī." *al-Masraḥ* 24 (1965): 15–17.
———. "Qināʿ Hāmlit." In *Dirāsāt fī al-Masraḥ*, 165–96. Cairo: Maktabat al-Anglū al-Miṣriyya, 1986.
al-Azm, Sadiq. "A Book for a Book Instead [of] an Eye for an Eye." *al-Qantara*, October 30, 2003.
———. "Owning the Future: Modern Arabs and Hamlet." *ISIM (International Institute for the Study of Islam in the Modern World) Newsletter* 5 (2000): 11.
———. "Time Out of Joint: Western Dominance, Islamist Terror, and the Arab Imagination." *Boston Review* 29, no. 5 (2004), http://bostonreview.net/BR29.5/alazm.php.

al-ʿAẓm, Ṣādiq Jalāl. *Al-Naqd al-Dhātī baʿd al-Hazīma.* Beirut: Dār al-Ṭalīʿa li-l-Ṭibāʿa wa-l-Nashr, 1969.
———. "Hāmlit wa-l-Ḥadātha al-ʿArabiyya." Paper presented at the conference "al-Ḥadātha wa-l-Ḥadātha al-ʿArabiyya," Morocco, 2004. http://www.metransparent.com/old/texts/hamlet_hadatha.htm.
Badawi, M. M. Introduction to *Modern Arabic Drama: An Anthology*, ed. Salma Khadra Jayyusi and Roger Allen. Bloomington: Indiana University Press, 1995.
———. *Modern Arabic Drama in Egypt.* Cambridge: Cambridge University Press, 1987.
———. "Perennial Themes in Modern Arabic Literature." In *Arab Nation, Arab Nationalism,* ed. Derek Hopwood, 129–54. New York: St. Martin's Press, 2000.
———. "Shakespeare and the Arabs." In *Cairo Studies in English* (Cairo: Al-Maktaba al-Anjlū al-Miṣriyya, 1966), 181–96.
Bader, Anwar. "Hāmlit al-Isrāʾīlī." *Alhourriah.org,* November 7, 2004.
al-Bahar, Nadia. "Shakespeare in Early Arabic Adaptations." *Shakespeare Translation* 3, no. 13 (1976): 13–25.
Bakhtin, M. M. *The Dialogic Imagination: Four Essays.* Translated by Caryl Emerson and Michael Holquist. Austin: University of Texas Press, 1981.
Barghoorn, Frederick C., and Paul Friedrich. "Cultural Relations and Soviet Foreign Policy." *World Politics* 8, no. 3 (1956): 323–44.
Al-Bassam, Sulayman. "The Al-Hamlet Summit: A Political Arabesque." Unpublished manuscript shared by the author. September 16, 2002.
———. *The Al-Hamlet Summit: A Political Arabesque.* Edited by Graham Holderness. In Arabic and English. Hatfield: University of Hertfordshire Press, 2006.
———. "Am I Mad? Creating *The Al-Hamlet Summit.*" *Theatre Forum* 22 (2003): 85–88.
Bates, Laura Raidonis. "Shakespeare in Latvia: The Contest for Appropriation during the Nationalist Movement, 1884–1918." PhD diss., University of Chicago, 1998.
Baxandall, Michael. *Painting and Experience in Fifteenth-Century Italy.* Oxford: Oxford University Press, 1972.
Bayer, Mark. "*The Martyrs of Love* and the Emergence of the Arab Cultural Consumer." *Critical Survey* 19, no. 3 (2007): 6–26.
———. "Shylock's Revenge: *The Merchant of Venice* and the Arab-Israeli Conflict." Paper presented at the annual meeting of the Shakespeare Association of America, Bermuda, March 2005.
Belien, Paul. "Buy Danish: Nothing Rotten in the State of Denmark." *Brussels Journal,* January 30, 2006.
Benjamin, Walter. "Trauerspiel and Tragedy." In *The Origin of German Tragic Drama,* translated by John Osborne, 57–158. London: Verso, 1998.
Berkowitz, Joel. *Shakespeare on the American Yiddish Stage.* Iowa City: University of Iowa Press, 2002.
Binder, Leonard. "Gamal ʿAbd al-Nasser: Iconology, Ideology, and Demonology." In *Rethinking Nasserism: Revolution and Historical Memory in Modern Egypt,* ed. Elie Podeh and Onn Winckler, 45–71. Gainesville: University Press of Florida, 2005.
———. *In a Moment of Enthusiasm: Political Power and the Second Stratum in Egypt.* Chicago: University of Chicago Press, 1978.
Bloom, Harold. *The Anxiety of Influence: A Theory of Poetry.* New York: Oxford University Press, 1973.

———. *Shakespeare: The Invention of the Human.* New York: Warner Books, 1999.
Boullata, Issa J. "Living with the Tigress and the Muses: An Essay on Jabra Ibrahim Jabra." *World Literature Today* 75, no. 2 (2001): 214–23.
Bourdieu, Pierre. *The Field of Cultural Production: Essays on Art and Literature.* New York: Columbia University Press, 1993.
———. *Outline of a Theory of Practice.* Translated by Richard Nice. Cambridge: Cambridge University Press, 1992.
Bradley, A. C. *Shakespearean Tragedy: Lectures on Hamlet, Othello, King Lear, Macbeth.* London: Macmillan, 1952.
Brantley, Ben, and Charles Isherwood. "To Be Topical in a Time Out of Joint." *New York Times,* February 21, 2010.
Brecht, Bertolt. *Brecht on Theatre: The Development of an Aesthetic.* Translated by John Willett. New York: Hill and Wang, 1964.
Brown, Irving. "The Effervescent Egyptian Theatre." In *Critical Perspectives on Modern Arabic Literature,* ed. Issa J. Boullata, 332–40. Washington, D.C.: Three Continents Press, 1980.
Burke, Patrick. "'Hidden Games, Cunning Traps, Ambushes': The Russian Hamlet." *Shakespeare Yearbook* 8 (1997): 163–80.
al-Burtuqālī, Tahānī. "Taḥdīth Miṣr Yabda' bi-l-ʿIlm wa-l-ʿUlamā.'" *al-Ahram,* March 12, 2002.
Bushrui, Suheil. "Shakespeare and Arabic Drama and Poetry." *Ibadan* 20 (1964): 5–16.
Calderbank, Anthony. "Ẓāhira Masraḥiyya Lāfita: Mukhrij Kuwaytī li-ʿArḍ Hāmlit al-Inklīzī." *al-Hayāt,* November 11, 2001, 16.
Carlson, Marvin. *The Haunted Stage: The Theatre as Memory Machine.* Ann Arbor: University of Michigan Press, 2001.
Cartelli, Thomas. *Repositioning Shakespeare: National Formations, Postcolonial Appropriations.* London: Routledge, 1999.
Caton, Steven. *Peaks of Yemen I Summon: Poetry as Cultural Practice in a North Yemeni Tribe.* Berkeley: University of California Press, 1990.
Cefalu, Paul. "'Damnéd Custom . . . Habits Devil': Hamlet's Part-Whole Fallacy and the Early Modern Philosophy of Mind." In *Revisionist Shakespeare: Transitional Ideologies in Texts and Contexts,* 145–72. London: Palgrave Macmillan, 2004.
Césaire, Aimé. *Une tempête: d'après "la tempête" de Shakespeare.* Paris: Editions Du Seuil, 1969.
Chakrabarty, Dipesh. "Postcoloniality and the Artifice of History: Who Speaks for 'Indian' Pasts?" *Representations* 37 (Winter 1992): 1–24.
———. *Provincializing Europe: Postcolonial Thought and Historical Difference.* Princeton, N.J.: Princeton University Press, 2000.
Charnes, Linda. *Hamlet's Heirs: Shakespeare and the Politics of a New Millennium.* New York: Routledge, 2006.
Coetzee, J. M. *Giving Offense: Essays on Censorship.* Chicago: University of Chicago Press, 1996.
Culshaw, Peter. "Shakespeare and Suicide Bombers." *London Telegraph,* February 28, 2004.
Al-Dabbagh, Abdulla. "The Oriental Framework of *Romeo and Juliet.*" *Comparatist* 24 (May 2000): 64–82.

Danielson, Virginia. *The Voice of Egypt: Umm Kulthūm, Arabic Song, and Egyptian Society in the Twentieth Century*. Chicago: University of Chicago Press, 1997.

Darragi, Rafik. "Ideological Appropriation and Sexual Politics: Shakespeare's *Antony and Cleopatra* and Ahmed Shawky's *Masra' Cleopatra*." In Fotheringham, Jansohn, and White, *Shakespeare's World/World Shakespeares*, 358–70.

———. "The Tunisian Stage: Shakespeare's Part in Question." *Critical Survey* 19, no. 3 (2007): 95–106.

Dawisha, Karen. "Soviet Cultural Relations with Iraq, Syria and Egypt 1955–1970." *Soviet Studies* 27, no. 3 (1975): 418–42.

———. *Soviet Foreign Policy towards Egypt*. London: Macmillan, 1979.

De Grazia, Margreta. *"Hamlet" without Hamlet*. Cambridge: Cambridge University Press, 2007.

El-Demerdash, Farouk. "Dix années de théâtre dans la république arabe unie." In *Le Théâtre Arabe*, ed. Nada Tomiche and Cherif Khaznadar, 133–40. Paris: UNESCO, 1969.

Dent, Shirley. "Interview: Sulayman Al-Bassam." 2003. Culture Wars website. http://www.culturewars.org.uk/2003–01/albassam.htm.

Desmet, Christy, and Robert Sawyer, eds., *Shakespeare and Appropriation*. New York: Routledge, 1999.

Distiller, Natasha. *South Africa, Shakespeare, and Post-Colonial Culture*. Lewiston, N.Y.: Edwin Mellen Press, 2005.

Dollimore, Jonathan, and Alan Sinfield, eds. *Political Shakespeare: Essays in Cultural Materialism*. Ithaca, N.Y.: Cornell University Press, 1994.

Douglas, Allen, and Fedwa Malti-Douglas. *Arab Comic Strips: Politics of an Emerging Mass Culture*. Bloomington: Indiana University Press, 1994.

Ducis, Jean-François. *Hamlet, tragédie en cinq actes, imitée de l'anglois*. Paris: A. Nepveu, 1826.

———. *Hamlet, tragédie, imitée de l'anglois*. Paris: Chez Gogué, 1770.

Dumas, Alexandre. *Hamlet*. Vol. 11 of *Théâtre Complet de Alex. Dumas*. Paris: Michel Levy Frères, 1874.

Duncan-Jones, Katherine. "Complete Works, Essential Year? (All of) Shakespeare Performed." *Shakespeare Quarterly* 58, no. 3 (2007): 353–66.

Duval, Georges. *William Shakespeare, Oeuvres Dramatiques*. Les Meillieurs Auteurs Classiques. Paris: Flammarion, n.d.

al-Duwayrī, Ra'fat. *Al-Aʿmāl al-Kāmila*. Vol. 3. Cairo: al-Hay'a al-Miṣriyya al-ʿĀmma li-l-Kitāb, 1999.

Eickelman, Dale F. "The Coming Transformation of the Muslim World." *Middle East Review of International Affairs* 3, no. 3 (1999): 78–81.

El-Enany, Rasheed. "The Quest for Justice in the Theatre of Alfred Farag: Different Moulds, One Theme." *Journal of Arabic Literature* 31, no. 2 (2000): 171–202.

El-Feki, Mustafa. "A Faithful Step Forward." *Al-Ahram Weekly On-line* 695 (June 17–23, 2004), http://weekly.ahram.org.eg/2004/695/op2.htm.

Eliot, T. S. "Hamlet and His Problems." In *The Sacred Wood: Essays on Poetry and Criticism*. London: Methune, 1920.

———. "The Love Song of J. Alfred Prufrock." In *Prufrock and Other Observations*.

Reprint of the 1917 London edition. Project Gutenberg, 1998. http://www.gutenberg.org/files/1459/1459-h/1459-h.htm.
———. *Murder in the Cathedral.* San Diego: Harcourt Brace Jovanovich, 1963.
Eltahawy, Mona. "Arab Politics and Society: A Generation's Passing Brings Opportunity." *International Herald Tribune,* November 23, 2004.
Fanon, Frantz. *Black Skin, White Masks.* New York: Grove Press, 2008.
Faraj, Alfrīd. "Dirasāt." In *Dalīl al-Mutafarrij al-Dhakī ilā al-Masraḥ.* Vol. 8 of Mu'allafāt Alfrīd Faraj. Cairo: al-Hay'a al-Miṣriyya al-ʿĀmma li-l-Kitāb, 1988.
———. *Sulaymān al-Ḥalabī.* 2nd ed. Cairo: Dār al-Kitāb al-ʿArabī, 1969.
Farley-Hills, David, ed. *Critical Responses to Hamlet.* Vol. 2. New York: AMS Press, 1996.
Fish, Stanley. *Is There a Text In This Class? The Authority of Interpretive Communities.* Cambridge, Mass.: Harvard University Press, 1980.
Foakes, Reginald. "Introduction." In *The Columbia Dictionary of Quotations from Shakespeare,* ed. Mary and Reginald Foakes. New York: Columbia University Press, 1998.
"Forcing Arafat out of the P.L.O." *Time,* July 26, 1993.
Fotheringham, Richard, Christa Jansohn, and R. S. White, eds. *Shakespeare's World/World Shakespeares: The Selected Proceedings of the International Shakespeare Association World Congress Brisbane, 2006.* Newark: University of Delaware Press, 2008.
Four Women of Egypt. Dir. Tahani Rached. VHS film. New York: Women Make Movies, 1997.
Friedrich, Paul. *The Language Parallax: Linguistic Relativism and Poetic Indeterminacy.* Austin: University of Texas Press, 1986.
———. *Language, Context, and the Imagination: Essays.* Stanford, Calif.: Stanford University Press, 1979.
Ghazoul, Ferial J. "The Arabization of *Othello.*" *Comparative Literature* 50, no. 1 (1998): 1–31.
———. *Nocturnal Poetics: The Arabian Nights in Comparative Context.* Cairo: American University in Cairo Press, 1996.
Ghunaym, Ghassān. *Al-Masraḥ al-Siyāsī fī Sūriyā, 1967–1990.* Damascus: Dār 'Alā' al-Dīn, 1996.
Gielgud, John. *Acting Shakespeare.* New York Charles Scribner's Sons, 1992.
Ginat, Rami. "Nasser and the Soviets: A Reassessment." In *Rethinking Nasserism,* ed. Elie Podeh and Onn Winckler, 230–50. Gainesville: University Press of Florida, 2005.
Golub, Spencer. "Between the Curtain and the Grave: The Taganka in the *Hamlet* Gulag." In Kennedy, *Foreign Shakespeare,* 158–77.
Gordon, Joel. *Nasser: Hero of the Arab Nation.* Oxford: Oneworld Publications, 2006.
———. *Nasser's Blessed Movement: Egypt's Free Officers and the July Revolution.* New York: Oxford University Press, 1992.
Gordon, Joel. *Revolutionary Melodrama: Popular Film and Civic Identity in Nasser's Egypt.* Chicago: Middle East Documentation Center, 2002.
Gräf, Bettina, and Jakob Skovgaard-Petersen. "Introduction." In *Global Mufti: The Phenomenon of Yūsuf al-Qaraḍawī,* ed. Bettina Gräf and Jakob Skovgaard-Petersen. London: Hurst & Company, 2009.

Gran, Peter. "The Political Economy of Aesthetics: Modes of Domination in Modern Nation States Seen through Shakespeare Reception." *Dialectical Anthropology* 17 (1992): 271–88.

Greenblatt, Stephen. *Hamlet in Purgatory.* Princeton, N.J.: Princeton University Press, 2001.

———. "The Improvisation of Power." In *Renaissance Self-Fashioning: From More to Shakespeare.* Chicago: University of Chicago Press, 1980.

———. "Learning to Curse: Aspects of Linguistic Colonialism in the Sixteenth Century." In *Learning to Curse: Essays in Early Modern Culture,* 16–39. New York: Routledge, 1992.

Ḥabīb, Tawfīq. "Shaksbīr fī Miṣr." *al-Hilāl,* December 1, 1927, 201–204.

Hafez, Sabry. *The Genesis of Arabic Narrative Discourse: A Study in the Sociology of Modern Arabic Literature.* London: Saqi Books, 1993.

al-Hakim, Tawfiq. *The Return of Consciousness.* Translated by R. Bayly Winder. New York: New York University Press, 1985.

———. *The Return of the Spirit.* Translated by William M. Hutchins. Washington, D.C.: Three Continents Press, 1990.

———. *ʿAwdat al-Waʿī.* 2nd ed. Cairo: Dār al-Shurūq, 1974.

———. "Jalsa maʿa Tawfīq al-Ḥakīm." *al-Masraḥ* 4 (1964): 8–9.

———. *Qālabunā al-Masraḥī.* Cairo: Maktabat al-Ādāb, 1967.

Halliday, Fred. "The Unpublished Book of the Cold War." *Round Table* 90, no. 358 (2001): 103–10.

Ḥamāda, Ibrāhīm. *ʿUrūbat Shaksbīr: Dirāsāt Ukhrā fī al-Drāmā wa-l-Naqd.* Cairo: al-Markaz al-Qawmī li-l-Ādāb, 1989.

Hamouda, Sahar, and Colin Clement, eds. *Victoria College: A History Revealed.* Cairo: American University in Cairo Press, 2002.

Hanna, Sameh F. "Decommercialising Shakespeare: Mutran's Translation of *Othello.*" *Critical Survey* 19, no. 3 (2007): 27–54.

———. "Hamlet Lives Happily Ever After in Arabic." *Translator* 11, no. 2 (2005): 167–92.

———. "Othello in Egypt: Translation and the (Un)making of National Identity." In *Translation and the Construction of Identity,* ed. Juliane House, M. Rosario Martín Ruano, and Nicole Baumgarten, 109–28. Seoul: IATIS, 2005.

———. "Towards a Sociology of Drama Translation: A Bourdieusian Perspective on Translations of Shakespeare's Great Tragedies in Egypt." PhD diss., University of Manchester, 2006.

Hany, Ahmed. "The Arab System—TO BE OR NOT TO BE." *American Chronicle,* December 17, 2008.

Haoula'a Al-Akharoun [*An Artist with a View*]. Dir. Sawsan Darwaza and Nasser Omar. Beta SP film. 54 mins. Amman: Pioneers Production Company, 2005.

Hassan, Fayza. "Not by Bread Alone." *Al-Ahram Weekly On-line,* November 4–10, 1999, http://weekly.ahram.org.eg/1999/454/feat3.htm.

Hattaway, Michael, Boika Sokolova, and Derek Roper, eds. *Shakespeare in the New Europe.* Sheffield, U.K.: Sheffield Academic Press, 1994.

Ḥawāmda, Mufīd. "Al-Baḥth ʿan Ṣīgha Masraḥiyya Jadīda: Dirāsa li-Iqtibās Nādir

ʿUmrān li-Masrahiyyat Hāmlit." In *Al-Baḥth ʿan al-Masraḥ: Dirāsāt fī al-Masraḥ al-Urdunī.* Irbid: Dar al-Amal Publications, n.d.
Hays, Michael L. *Shakespearean Tragedy as Chivalric Romance: Rethinking Macbeth, Hamlet, Othello, and King Lear.* Cambridge: D. S. Brewer, 2003.
Heylen, Romy. *Translation, Poetics, and the Stage: Six French Hamlets.* London and New York: Routledge, 1993.
Hobbes, Thomas. *Leviathan.* Edited by Edwin Curley. Indianapolis: Hackett, 1994.
Holderness, Graham, ed. *The Politics of Theatre and Drama.* New York: St. Martin's Press, 1992.
Hoenselaars, Ton, ed. *Shakespeare and the Language of Translation.* London: Arden Shakespeare, 2004.
Hopwood, Derek. *Syria 1945–1986: Politics and Society.* London: Unwin Hyman, 1988.
Hourani, Albert. *Arabic Thought in the Liberal Age 1798–1939.* Cambridge: Cambridge University Press, 1983.
———. *A History of the Arab Peoples.* New York: Warner Books, 1992.
Huang, Alexander C. Y. *Chinese Shakespeares : Two Centuries of Cultural Exchange.* New York: Columbia University Press, 2009.
Hulme, Peter, and William H. Sherman, eds. *The Tempest and Its Travels.* London: Reaktion Books, 2000.
al-Ḥusaynī, Muḥammad Ṣādiq. "Filasṭīn Hiya an Nakūn aw Lā Nakūn" *al-Sharq al-Awsaṭ,* June 9, 2002.
Hussein, Taha. *The Future of Culture in Egypt.* Translated by Sidney Glazer. Washington, D.C.: American Council of Learned Societies, 1954.
Ibn Ḥamza, Ḥusayn. "Mustaʿīdan Hāmlit fī Ṣīgha Jadīda: Jawād al-Asadī Yantaqid al-Wila'a li-l-Nuṣūṣ al-Jāhiza." *al-Hayat,* January 29, 2001.
Ibrahim, Sonallah. *Zaat (Dhāt).* Translated by Anthony Calderbank. Cairo: American University in Cairo Press, 2001.
ʿId, Kamāl. "Hāmlit, Amīr al-Dānimārk: Dirāsa wa-Naqd." *al-Masraḥ* 18 (1965): 37–50.
Idrīs, Yūsuf. *Naḥw Masraḥ ʿArabī.* Beirut: s.n., 1974.
Inbari, Pinhas. *The Palestinians between Terror and Statehood.* Brighton, U.K: Sussex Academic Press, 1996.
Information Department, United Arab Republic Ministry of National Guidance. *Year Book.* Cairo: Information Department, United Arab Republic Ministry of National Guidance, 1964.
ʿIṣmat, Riyāḍ. "Azmat al-Masraḥ al-Sūrī." In *Al-Masraḥ al-ʿArabī: Suqūṭ al-Aqniʿa al-Ijtimāʿiyya.* Damascus: Mu'assasat al-Shabība li-l-Iʿlām wa-l-Ṭibaʿa wa-l-Nashr, 1995.
———. "Hāmlit kamā Akhrajtuhu." In *Shayṭān al-Masraḥ,* 445–64. Damascus: Dār Ṭalās, 1986.
Jaafar, Ali. "Al-Hamlet Daringly Transposes Shakespeare's Classic Play to Modern Middle Eastern Setting." *Daily Star,* March 29, 2004.
al-Jabartī, ʿAbd al-Raḥmān. *ʿAbd al-Raḥmān al-Jabartī's History of Egypt, Translation of ʿAjā'ib al-Āthār fī al-Tarājim wa-l-Akhbār.* Edited by Thomas Philipp and Moshe Perlmann. Vol. 3. Stuttgart: Franz Steiner Verlag, 1994.

Jabra, Jabra Ibrahim. *A Celebration of Life: Essays on Literature and Art*. Baghdad: Dār al-Ma'mūn, 1986.

———. *In Search of Walid Masoud*. Translated by Roger Allen and Adnan Haydar. Syracuse, N.Y.: Syracuse University Press, 2000.

———. *The Ship*. Translated by Adnan Haydar and Roger Allen. Washington, D.C.: Three Continents Press, 1985.

Jabrā, Jabrā Ibrāhīm. *Al-Baḥth ʿan Walīd Masʿūd*. Beirut: Dār al-Ādāb, 1978.

———. *Al-Safīna* [*The Tempest*]. Beirut: Dār al-Nahār, 1970.

———. "Muʿāyashat al-Namira, aw, Mutʿat al-Qirā'a, Mutʿat al-Kitāba." In *Muʿāyashat al-Namira wa-Awrāq Ukhra,* 5–10. Beirut: al-Mu'assassa al-ʿArabiyya li-l-Dirāsāt wa-l-Nashr, 1992.

———. "Shaksbīr Muḍṭahadan wa-Qaḍāyā Ukhrā." In *Muʿāyashat al-Namira wa-Awrāq Ukhra,* 117–27. Beirut: al-Mu'assassa al-ʿArabiyya li-l-Dirāsāt wa-l-Nashr, 1992.

———. *Wilyam Shaksbīr: Al-Ma'āsī al-Kubrā*. Beirut: al-Mu'assasa al-ʿArabiyya li-l-Dirāsāt wa-l-Nashr, 1990.

Jacquemond, Richard. *Conscience of the Nation: Writers, State, and Society in Modern Egypt*. Translated by David Tresilian. Cairo: American University in Cairo Press, 2008.

James, Laura. *Nasser at War: Arab Images of the Enemy*. New York: Palgrave Macmillan, 2006.

———. "Whose Voice? Nasser, the Arabs, and 'Sawt al-Arab' Radio." *Transnational Broadcast Studies* 16 (June–December 2006), http://www.tbsjournal.com/James.html.

Jauss, H. R. *Toward an Aesthetic of Reception*. Translated by Timothy Bahti. Minneapolis: University of Minnesota Press, 1982.

Jayyusi, Salma Khadra. "Introduction: A Lover for All Times." In Qabbani, *On Entering the Sea: The Erotic and Other Poetry of Nizar Qabbani,* v–xvii.

———, ed. *Short Arabic Plays: An Anthology*. Northampton, Mass.: Interlink, 2003.

Johnson, David. *Shakespeare and South Africa*. Oxford, UK: Clarendon Press, 1996.

Jorgens, Jack. "Grigori Kozintsev's Hamlet." In *Shakespeare on Film,* 218–34. Bloomington: Indiana University Press, 1977.

al-Juraydīnī, Sāmī. *Yūlyūs Qayṣar*. Cairo: Maṭbaʿat al-Maʿārif, 1912.

Kākhayī, Fahmī. "Nuṣawwit am Lā Nuṣawwit? Dhālika Huwa al-Su'āl" [Do We or Don't We Vote? That Is the Question]. Kurdistan Regional Government website, November 30, 2005.

Kanaan, Falah. "Shakespeare on the Arab Page and Stage." PhD diss., University of Manchester, 1998.

Al-Kasim, Faisal. "Crossfire: The Arab Version." *Harvard International Journal of Press Politics* 4, no. 3 (1999): 93–97.

Kawachi, Yoshiko, ed. *Japanese Studies in Shakespeare and His Contemporaries*. International Studies in Shakespeare and His Contemporaries. Newark: University of Delaware Press, 1998.

Kendall, Elisabeth. *Literature, Journalism, and the Avant-Garde: Intersection in Egypt*. London and New York: Routledge, 2006.

Kennedy, Dennis. "Afterword: Shakespearean Orientalism." In Kennedy, *Foreign Shakespeare,* 290–303.

———, ed. *Foreign Shakespeare: Contemporary Performance.* Cambridge: Cambridge University Press, 1993.

Kepel, Gilles. *Muslim Extremism in Egypt: The Prophet and Pharaoh.* Berkeley and Los Angeles: University of California Press, 1993.

Kershaw, Baz. *The Radical in Performance: Between Brecht and Baudrillard.* London: Routledge, 1999.

Al-Khatib, Waddah. "Rewriting History, Unwriting Literature: Shawqi's Mirror-Image Response to Shakespeare." *Journal of Arabic Literature* 32, no. 3 (2001): 256–83.

Klausen, Jytte. *The Cartoons that Shook the World.* New Haven, Conn.: Yale University Press, 2009.

———. "Rotten Judgment in the State of Denmark." *Salon.com,* February 8, 2006.

Kott, Jan. *Shakespeare Our Contemporary.* Translated by Boleslaw Taborski. New York: Anchor Books, 1966.

———. *Shaksbīr Muʿāsirunā.* Translated by Jabrā Ibrāhīm Jabrā. 2nd ed. Beirut: al-Mu'assasa al-ʿArabiyya li-l-Dirāsāt wa-l-Nashr, 1980.

Kozintsev, Grigori M. "King Lear." In *Shakespeare in the Soviet Union,* ed. R. Samarin and Alexander Nikolyukin, 204–63. Moscow: Progress Publishers, 1966.

———. *Nash sovremennik Villiam Shekspir.* Leningrad: Iskusstvo, 1962.

———. *Shakespeare: Time and Conscience.* Translated by Joyce Vining. New York: Hill and Wang, 1966.

Lacouture, Jean. *Nasser.* Paris: Editions du Seuil, 1971.

Lagrange, Frédéric. "Shayk Salama Higazi (ca. 1852–1917)." Les Archives de la Musique Arabe website, March 1994, http://www.bolingo.org/audio/arab/gudian/higazi.html.

Lamb, Charles and Mary. *Tales from Shakespeare.* Philadelphia: Altemus, [1898].

Landau, Jacob. *Studies in the Arab Theater and Cinema.* Philadelphia: University of Pennsylvania Press, 1958.

Laqueur, Walter Z. *The Soviet Union and the Middle East.* New York: Frederick A. Praeger, 1959.

Leiter, Samuel L., ed. *Shakespeare around the Globe: A Guide to Notable Postwar Revivals.* New York: Greenwood Press, 1986.

Levin, Harry. "Shakespeare in the Light of Comparative Literature." In *Refractions: Essays in Comparative Literature,* 107–27. New York: Oxford University Press, 1966.

Lewis, C. S. "Hamlet: The Prince or the Poem?" In *Proceedings of the British Academy,* vol. 28. London: Oxford University Press, 1942.

Li, Ruru. *Shashbiya: Staging Shakespeare in China.* Aberdeen, Hong Kong: Hong Kong University Press, 2003.

Litvin, Margaret. "Explosive Signifiers: Sulayman Al-Bassam's Post-9/11 Odyssey." Special issue: Shakespeare after 9/11, ed. Matthew Biberman and Julia Lupton. *Shakespeare Yearbook* 18 (2010): 105–39.

———. "When the Villain Steals the Show: The Character of Claudius in Post-1975 Arab(ic) Hamlet Adaptations." *Journal of Arabic Literature* 38, no. 2 (2007): 196–219.

Loomba, Ania. "'Local-Manufacture Made-in-India Othello Fellows': Issues of Race, Hybridity, and Location in Post-Colonial Shakespeares." In Loomba and Orkin, *Post-Colonial Shakespeares,* 143–63.

———, and Martin Orkin, eds. *Post-Colonial Shakespeares.* London: Routledge, 1998.

Love, Kennett. *Suez, the Twice-Fought War: A History.* New York: McGraw-Hill, 1969.

Mahmood, Saba. *Politics of Piety: The Islamic Revival and the Feminist Subject.* Princeton, N.J.: Princeton University Press, 2005.

Maḥmūd, Muṣṭafā. "Nakūn aw Lā Nakūn." 1999. Originally at www.geocities.com/mustafa_mahmood_99/1.html. Reposted in 2002 at http://www.egyptsons.com/misr/showpost.php?p=2156&postcount=2.

Mahrān, Fawziyya. "Shubbāk Ufīliyā aw Hāmlit ʿalā al-Ṭarīqa al-ʿAṣriyya." *al-Hilāl,* May 1994, 154–61.

al-Mājidī, Khazʿal. *"Hāmlit" bilā hāmlit wa-sīrdā.* Amman: Dār al-Shurūq li-l-Nashr wa-l-Tawzīʿ, 2005.

Makaryk, Irena. *Shakespeare in the Undiscovered Bourn: Les Kurbas, Ukrainian Modernism, and Early Soviet Cultural Politics.* Toronto: University of Toronto Press, 2004.

Makdisi, Ilham. "Theater and Radical Politics in Beirut, Cairo, and Alexandria: 1860–1914." Washington, D.C.: Georgetown University Center for Contemporary Arab Studies occasional paper, 2006.

Makdisi, Saree. "'Postcolonial' Literature in a Neocolonial World: Modern Arabic Culture and the End of Modernity." *Boundary 2* 22, no. 1 (1995): 85–115.

Mannoni, Octave. *Prospero and Caliban: The Psychology of Colonization.* 1956; repr., Ann Arbor: University of Michigan Press, 1991.

Mansfield, Peter. *Nasser's Egypt.* Rev. ed. Baltimore: Penguin Books, 1969.

Manvell, Roger. *Shakespeare and the Film.* South Brunswick, N.J.: A. S. Barnes and Co., 1979.

Marder, Louis. "Shakespeare's 400th Anniversary: Suggestions for Commemorative Programs and Activities." *College English* 25, no. 5 (1964): 357–62.

Marzougui, Hakim. *Ismail-Hamlet ou la vengeance du laveur de cadaver.* Translated by Christian Siméon. Paris: Editions Lansman, 2006.

al-Marzūqī, ʿAbd al-Ḥakīm. "Ismāʿīl Hāmlit." Damascus: Masraḥ al-Raṣīf. Unpublished manuscript, 1999.

Massai, Sonia, ed. *World-Wide Shakespeares: Local Appropriations in Film and Performance.* Abingdon, U.K.: Routledge, 2005.

Massignon, Louis. *Hallaj: Mystic and Martyr.* Translated by Herbert Mason. 1st abridged paperback ed. Princeton, N.J.: Princeton University Press, 1994.

———. *The Passion of al-Hallāj: Mystic and Martyr of Islam.* Translated by Herbert Mason. Princeton, N.J.: Princeton University Press, 1982.

———, and Paul Kraus, eds. *Akhbar al-Hallaj: recueil d'oraisons et d'exhortations du martyr mystique de l'Islam Husayn Ibn Mansur Hallaj. Mis en ordre vers 360/991 chez Nasrabadhi et deux fois remanié.* 3rd ed. Paris: Vrin, 1957.

Masraḥ al-Fawānīs. "Kalimat Masraḥ al-Fawānīs: al-Masraḥiyya ka-Sharṭ li-Fiʿl al-Tanwīr" [A Word from the Fawanees Theatre: The Play as a Condition of Enlightenment]. Unpublished manifesto of the Fawanees Theatre, Jordan, 1984.

Mbembe, Achille. "The Banality of Power and the Aesthetics of Vulgarity in the Postcolony." *Public Culture* 4 (1992): 1–30.

———. *On the Postcolony*. Berkeley: University of California Press, 2001.

McGregor, Andrew James. *A Military History of Modern Egypt: From the Ottoman Conquest to the Ramadan War*. Westport, Conn.: Praeger Security International, 2006.

Messick, Brinkley. *The Calligraphic State: Textual Domination and History in a Muslim Society*. Berkeley: University of California Press, 1993.

al-Mihnā, Sāmī. "Sumūwuhu Yaftatiḥ al-Yawm al-Ijtimāʿ al-Ta'sīsī li-l-Mu'assasa al-Ahliyya li-l-Fikr al-ʿArabī." *al-Riyadh*, June 2, 2001.

Mijallī, Nasīm. "Abū Zayd al-Hilālī . . . wa-Hāmlit: Bidāyat Qafza Masraḥiyya." In *Al-Masraḥ wa Qaḍāyat al-Ḥurriyya*, 163–68. Cairo: al-Hay'a al-Miṣriyya al-ʿĀmma li-l-Kitāb, 1984.

———. "Miṣr fī Masraḥiyyāt Ṣalāḥ 'Abd al-Ṣabūr." In *Al-Masraḥ wa Qaḍīyat al-Ḥurriyya*, 170–76 Cairo: al-Hay'a al-Miṣriyya al-ʿĀmma li-l-Kitāb, 1984.

Mishkhas, Tarek. "Something Is Rotten in the State of Denmark." *Arab News*, February 5, 2006.

Mitchell-Kernan, Claudia. "Signifying and Marking: Two Afro-American Speech Acts." In *Directions in Sociolinguistics: The Ethnography of Communication*, ed. J. Gumperz and D. Hymes, 161–79. New York: Holt, Rinehart and Winston, 1972.

Modenessi, Alfredo Michel. "'A Double Tongue Within Your Mask': Translating Shakespeare in/to Spanish-Speaking Latin America." In Hoenselaars, *Shakespeare and the Language of Translation*, 240–54.

Moosa, Matti. *The Origins of Modern Arabic Fiction*. Washington, D.C.: Three Continents Press, 1983.

Moussa Mahmoud, Fatma. "*Hamlet* in Egypt." In *Cairo Studies in English*, 51–61. Giza: University of Cairo Press, 1990.

"Mourners Killed as Nasser Is Buried." BBC: On This Day, October 1, 1970, http://news.bbc.co.uk/onthisday/hi/dates/stories/october/1/newsid_2485000/2485899.stm.

al-Mughāzī, Aḥmad. "Shaksbīr fī al-Masraḥ al-Miṣrī." *al-Masraḥ* 4, no. 40 (1967): 42–52.

Mūsā, Maḥmūd ʿĪsā. *Hāmlit al-Muʿākas: Qirā'āt fī al-Masraḥ al-Urdunī*. Amman: Ministry of Culture, 1995.

Mustafa, Farouk. "Political Theatre in Egypt." Paper presented at the annual meeting of the American Research Center in Egypt, Chicago, 1988.

Muṣṭafā, Ramzī. "Al-Dīkūr al-Masraḥī li-Aʿmāl Shaksbīr." *al-Masraḥ* 4 (1964): 52–54.

Muṭrān, Khalīl. "Al-Tamthīl" [The Theatre]. In *Dīwān al-Khalīl*. Vol. 1. Cairo: Dār al-Hilāl, 1949.

"Nādī al-Masraḥ: Hāmlit." *al-Masraḥ* 14 (1965): 73–75.

Najm, Muḥammad Yūsuf. *Al-Masraḥiyya fī al-Adab al-ʿArabī al-Ḥadīth: 1847–1914*. Beirut: Dār Bayrūt li-l-Ṭibāʿa wa-l-Nashr 1956.

al-Naqqāsh, Rajā'. "Hāmlit . . . fī al-Azhar al-Sharīf." In *Maqʿad Ṣaghīr amām al-Sitār*, 39–54. Cairo: al-Hay'a al-Miṣriyya al-ʿĀmma li-l-Kitāb, 1971.

Nasser, Gamal Abdel. *Egypt's Liberation: The Philosophy of the Revolution*. Washington, D.C.: Public Affairs Press, 1955.

———. *The Philosophy of the Revolution*. Buffalo, N.Y.: Smith Keynes & Marshall, 1959.

Newstrom, Scott. " 'Step Aside, I'll Show Thee a President': George W. as Henry V?" *PopPolitics.com*, May 1, 2003.

Nietzsche, F. W. "*The Birth of Tragedy*" *and* "*The Case of Wagner*." Translated by Walter Kaufmann. New York: Vintage, 1967.

Nkrumah, Gamal. "Ahmed Hamroush: For Corps and Country." *Al-Ahram Weekly Online,* July 26–August 1, 2001, http://weekly.ahram.org.eg/2001/544/profile.htm.

Nuʿayma, Mīkhā'īl. *Al-Ghirbāl.* 12th ed. Beirut: Mu'assasat Nawfal, 1981.

"Obituary: Abdel Qader El-Qutt (1916–2002)." *Al-Ahram Weekly Online,* 20–26 June 2002, http://weekly.ahram.org.eg/2002/591/cu1.htm.

Ofeish, Sami A. "Gender Challenges to Patriarchy: Wannus' Tuqus al-Isharat wa-l-Tahawalat." In *Colors of Enchantment: Theater, Dance, Music, and the Visual Arts of the Middle East,* ed. Sherifa Zuhur, 142–50. Cairo: AUC Press, 2001.

Olivier, Laurence. *Hamlet.* Janus Films, Criterion Collection, 2000 [1948].

Oppenheimer, Mark. "Something Rotten in Tehran." *New Haven Advocate,* February 9, 2006.

Oren, Michael. *Six Days of War: June 1967 and the Making of the Modern Middle East.* New York: Oxford University Press, 2002.

Oz, Avraham. "Transformations of Authenticity: *The Merchant of Venice* in Israel." In Kennedy, *Foreign Shakespeare*, 56–75.

———, ed. *Strands Afar Remote: Israeli Perspectives on Shakespeare.* Newark: University of Delaware Press, 1998.

Pavis, Patrice. *Theatre at the Crossroads of Culture.* London: Routledge, 1992.

Pemble, John. *Shakespeare Goes to Paris: How the Bard Conquered France.* London: Hambledon, 2005.

Peteet, Julie. "Icons and Militants: Mothering in the Danger Zone." *Signs* 23, no. 1 (1997): 103–29.

———. "Male Gender and Rituals of Resistance in the Palestinian Intifada: A Cultural Politics of Violence." *American Ethnologist* 21, no. 1 (1993): 31–49.

Prosser, Eleanor. *Hamlet and Revenge.* Stanford, Calif.: Stanford University Press, 1971.

Pujante, A. Luis, and Ton Hoenselaars, eds. *Four Hundred Years of Shakespeare in Europe.* Newark: University of Delaware Press, 2003.

Qabbani, Nizar. "Footnotes to the Book of the Setback." In *Modern Poetry of the Arab World,* ed. and trans. Abdullah Udhari, 97–101. London: Penguin, 1986.

———. *On Entering the Sea: The Erotic and Other Poetry of Nizar Qabbani.* Translated by Lena Jayyusi and Sharif Elmusa. New York: Interlink Books, 1996.

Qabbānī, Nizār. "Hawāmish ʿalā Daftar al-Naksa." In *al-Aʿmāl al-siyāsīya al-kāmila.* Vol. 3 of *al-Aʿmāl al-shiʿrīya al-kāmila,* 69–98. 2nd. ed. Beirut: Manshūrāt Nizār Qabbānī, 1983.

———. "Jamāl ʿAbd al-Nāṣir." In *al-Aʿmāl al-siyāsīya al-kāmila.* Vol. 3 of *al-Aʿmāl al-shiʿrīya al-kāmila,* 353–64. 2nd. ed. Beirut: Manshūrāt Nizār Qabbānī, 1983.

———. *Hawāmish ʿalā Daftar al-Naksa: Qaṣīda Ṭawīla.* Beirut: Manshūrāt Nizār Qabbānī, 1969.

Qaradāghi, Muṣṭafā, al-. "Al-ʿIrāq Yakūn aw Lā Yakūn Hadhā Huwa al-Su'āl?" *Iraq of Tomorrow,* October 17, 2005.

al-Qaraḍāwī, Yūsuf. "Al-Ḥiwār bayn al-Islām wa-l-Naṣrāniyya." *IslamOnline.net* (December 29, 2001). www.islamonline.net/Arabic/contemporary/arts/2001/article 9.shtml.

———. *Priorities of The Islamic Movement in The Coming Phase.* Cairo: al-Dār, 1992; Swansea: Awakening Publications, 2000. Also available at http://www.witness-pioneer.org/vil/Books/Q_Priorities/index.htm.

Qubain, Fahim Issa. *Education and Science in the Arab World.* Baltimore, Md.: Johns Hopkins University Press, 1966.

Quince, Rohan. *Shakespeare in South Africa: Stage Productions during the Apartheid Era.* New York: Peter Lang, 2000.

al-Qushayrī, Abū al-Qāsim. *Al-Risāla al-Qushayriyya.* Edited by Nawāf al-Jarrāḥ. Beirut: Dār Ṣadr, 2001.

al-Quwayz, Muḥammad. "Shukran Bīl Klīntūn wa-Shukran Shaksbīr." *al-Riyadh,* February 2, 2006.

Al-Rai, Ali. "Le génie du théâtre arabe des origines à nos jours." In *Le Théâtre Arabe,* ed. Nada Tomiche and Cherif Khaznadar, 81–97. Paris: UNESCO, 1969.

———. "Arabic Drama since the Thirties." In *Modern Arabic Literature,* ed. M. M. Badawi. Cambridge: Cambridge University Press, 1992.

al-Raʿī, ʿAlī, ed. *Al-Masraḥ al-ʿArabī: Bayn al-Naql wa-l-Ta'ṣīl.* Kuwait: al-ʿArabī Books, 1998.

Rakha, Youssef. "Our Revolution." *Al-Ahram Weekly,* July 18–24, 2002, http://weekly.ahram.org.eg/2002/595/sc15.htm.

Rebellato, Dan. "Theatre Blog: Can Political Theatre Change the World?" *Guardian,* April 12, 2010.

Rejwan, Nissim. *Nasserist Ideology: Its Exponents and Critics.* Jerusalem: Israel Universities Press, 1974.

Rowe, Eleanor. *Hamlet: A Window on Russia.* New York: New York University Press, 1976.

Rubin, Don, ed. *The Arab World.* Vol. 4 of *The World Encyclopedia of Contemporary Theatre.* London: Routledge, 1994.

Saadé, Nicolas. *Halīl Muṭrān, Héritier du Romantisme Français et Pionnier de la Poésie Arabe Contemporaine.* Beirut: Université Libanaise, 1985.

Ṣāghiya, Ḥāzim. "Yūsuf Zaʿīn, ʿAbd al-Nāṣir, Ṣaddām, wa . . . Jūrj Sūrīl." *al-Hayat,* July 22, 2001, 16.

Said, Edward. "Arabic Prose and Prose Fiction after 1948." In *Reflections on Exile and Other Essays,* 41–60. Cambridge, Mass.: Harvard University Press, 2000.

———. *Out of Place.* New York: Vintage Books, 1999.

Said, Kurban. *Ali and Nino.* Translated by Jenia Graman. New York: Random House, 1970.

Salih, Tayeb. *Season of Migration to the North.* Translated by Denys Johnson-Davies. 1969; repr., London: Heinemann, 1985.

Sālim, Ḥilmī. "Al-Mar'a bayn al-Imāma wa-l-Quwāma." *al-Ahālī,* August 17, 2005.

Salvatore, Armando. "Social Differentiation, Moral Authority and Public Islam in Egypt: The Path of Mustafa Mahmud." *Anthropology Today* 16, no. 2 (2000): 12–15.

Sami, Hala. "Remembrance of Things Past." Review of Mahmud Abu Doma's *Nostalgia. Al-Ahram Weekly On-line,* September 14–20, 2006, http://weekly.ahram.org.eg/2006/812/cu6.htm.

Sampson, Anthony. *Mandela: The Authorized Biography.* New York: Knopf, 1999.

Sarḥān, Samīr. "Al-Baṭal al-Trājīdī ʿinda Shaksbīr." *al-Masraḥ* 4 (1964): 43–44.
Sasayama, Takashi, J. R. Mulryne, and Margaret Shewring, eds. *Shakespeare and the Japanese Stage*. Cambridge: Cambridge University Press, 1998.
Scofield, Martin. *The Ghosts of Hamlet: The Play and Modern Writers*. Cambridge: Cambridge University Press, 1980.
Scott, James C. *Domination and the Arts of Resistance: Hidden Transcripts*. New Haven, Conn.: Yale University Press, 1990.
Selaiha, Nehad. "Brecht in Egypt." *Al-Ahram Weekly On-line*, June 11–17, 1998. http://weekly.ahram.org.eg/1998/381/cu2.htm
———. "Hamlet Galore." *Al-Ahram Weekly On-line*, September 3–9, 2009, http://weekly.ahram.org.eg/2009/963/cu1.htm.
———. "Introduction." In Ṣalāḥ ʿAbd al-Ṣabūr, *Now the King Is Dead*, ed. and trans. Nehad Selaiha, 9–34. Cairo: General Egyptian Book Organization, 1986.
———. "The Moor in Mansoura." *Al-Ahram Weekly On-line*, April 13–19, 2000, http://weekly.ahram.org.eg//2000/477/cu3.htm.
———. "Multiple Ironies." *Al-Ahram Weekly*, May 16–22, 2002, http://weekly.ahram.org.eg/2002/586/cu1.htm.
———. "Old Tune, New Resonance." *Al-Ahram Weekly On-line*, May 13–19, 2004. http://weekly.ahram.org.eg/2004/690/cu1.htm
———. "Poet, Rebel, Martyr." *Al-Ahram Weekly On-line*, April 18–24, 2002, http://weekly.ahram.org.eg/2002/582/cu5.htm.
———. "Royal Buffoonery." *Al-Ahram Weekly On-line*, April 4–10, 2002, http://weekly.ahram.org.eg/2002/580/cu4.htm.
———. "Spots of Time." *Al-Ahram Weekly On-line*, May 19–25, 2005, http://weekly.ahram.org.eg/2005/743/cu4.htm.
Shadid, Anthony. "In Baghdad Ruins, Remains of a Cultural Bridge." *New York Times*, May 22, 2010, A1.
Shafik, Viola. *Arab Cinema: History and Cultural Identity*. Cairo: American University in Cairo Press, 1998.
Shahani, Ranjee J. *Shakespeare through Eastern Eyes*. London: Herbert Joseph, 1932.
al-Shaḥāt, Samīr. "Aḥdāth fī al-Akhbār." *al-Ahram*, November 15, 2004.
Shakespeare, William. *Al-ʿĀṣifa* [The Tempest]. Translated by Jabrā Ibrāhīm Jabrā. Beirut: al-Mu'assasa al-ʿArabiyya li-l-Dirāsāt wa-l-Nashr, 1981.
———. *Al-Sūnītāt: Arbaʿūn minhā maʿa al-Naṣṣ al-Injlīzī* [Forty Sonnets]. Translated by Jabrā Ibrāhīm Jabrā. Beirut: al-Mu'assasa al-ʿArabiyya li-l-Dirāsāt wa-l-Nashr, 1983.
———. *Hamlet*. Edited by Harold Jenkins. Walton-on-Thames: Thomas Nelson & Sons Ltd., 1997.
———. *Hāmlit*. Translated by 'Abd al-Qādir al-Qiṭṭ. Cairo: Dār al-Andalus, 1996.
———. *Hāmlit*. Translated by Khalīl Muṭrān. Beirut: Dar Naẓīr ʿAbbūd, 1997.
———. *Hāmlit, Amīr Dānimārk*. Translated by Muḥammad ʿAwaḍ Muḥammad. 3rd ed. Cairo: Dār al-Maʿārif, 2000.
———. *Julius Caesar*. Arden 3rd series. London: Thomson Learning, 1998.
———. *Maʾsāt Kuriyūlānūs* [The Tragedy of Coriolanus]. Translated by Jabrā Ibrāhīm Jabrā. Kuwait: Wizārat al-Iʿlām, 1983.

———. *Œuvres complètes de W. Shakespeare*. Translated by François-Victor Hugo. 18 vols. Paris: Pagnerre, 1859–72.
———. *Riwāyat ʿUṭayl (Awtillū)*. Translated by Khalīl Muṭrān. Cairo: Maṭbaʿ al-Maʿārif, 1912.
———. *The Tempest*. Arden 3rd series. London: Thomson Learning, 2005.
Al-Shalchi, Hadeel. "Moderates Forced Out of Top Islam Web Site." Associated Press, March 25, 2010.
Shapiro, James S. *A Year in the Life of William Shakespeare: 1599*. New York: HarperCollins, 2005.
Shawqī, Aḥmad. *Maṣraʿ Klīyūbātrā*. Cairo: al-Maktaba al-Tijāriyya al-Kubrā, 1964.
Al-Shetawi, Mahmoud. "The Arab-West Conflict as Represented in Arabic Drama." *World Literature Today* 61 (1987): 46–49.
———. "*Hamlet* in Arabic." *Journal of Intercultural Studies* 20, no. 1 (1999): 43–63.
———. "*The Merchant of Venice* in Arabic." *Journal of Intercultural Studies* 15 (1994): 15–25.
Shobokshi, Hussein. "The Arab Exorcism." *Asharq al-Awsat,* November 22, 2009.
Shukrī, Ghālī. "Shaksbīr fī al-ʿArabiyya." In *Thawrat al-Fikr fī Adabinā al-Ḥadīth,* 54–71. Cairo: Maktabat al-Anglū al-Miṣriyya, 1965.
Shurbanov, Alexander, and Boika Sokolova. *Painting Shakespeare Red: An East-European Appropriation*. Newark: University of Delaware Press, 2001.
Sid-Ahmed, Mohamed. "Mohieddin for President." *Al-Ahram Weekly On-line,* May 5–11, 2005, http://weekly.ahram.org.eg/2005/741/op5.htm.
Singh, Jyotsna. "Different Shakespeares: The Bard in Colonial/Postcolonial India." *Theatre Journal* 41, no. 4 (1989): 445–58.
Smeliansky, Anatoly. *The Russian Theatre after Stalin*. Translated by Patrick Miles. Cambridge: Cambridge University Press, 1999.
Smirnov, A. A. *Shakespeare: A Marxist Interpretation*. Translated by Sonia Volochova. New York: The Critic's Group, 1936.
Soueif, Ahdaf. *Mezzaterra: Fragments from the Common Ground*. New York: Anchor Books, 2005.
Soyinka, Wole. "Shakespeare and the Living Dramatist." In *Art, Dialogue, and Outrage: Essays on Literature and Culture,* 147–62. New York: Pantheon, 1988.
Stauffer, Zahr Said. "The Politicisation of Shakespeare in Arabic in Youssef Chahine's Film Trilogy." *English Studies in Africa* 47, no. 2 (2004): 41–55.
Stilwell, Cinnamon. "Something Is Rotten Outside the State of Denmark." *San Francisco Gate,* February 8, 2006.
Stribrny, Zdenek. *Shakespeare and Eastern Europe*. Oxford: Oxford University Press, 2000.
Ṣulayḥa, Nihād. "Muqaddima." In *Jāʾū ilaynā Gharqā; al-Biʾr; Raqṣat al-ʿAqārib,* by Maḥmūd Abū Dūma, 7–35. Cairo: al-Hayʾa al-Miṣriyya al-ʿĀmma li-l-Kitāb, 1989.
———. *Shaksbīriyyāt*. Cairo: al-Hayʾa al-Miṣriyya al-ʿĀmma li-l-Kitāb, 1999.
Sulaymān, Fawzī. "Al-Sūriyya Rūlā Fattāl: Uqaddim Masraḥan lahu ʿAlāqa bi-l-Shāriʿ al-ʿArabī wa-l-Ḥayā al-Yawmiyya." *al-Bayān,* June 17, 2001.
Sullivan, Andrew. "Something Is Rotten . . ." *Daily Dish,* January 31, 2006.

Taher, Bahaa. *Love in Exile.* Translated by Farouk Abdel Wahab. Cairo: American University in Cairo Press, 2001.

Ṭāhir, Bahā'. "Al-Ḥalabī wa Amīr al-Dānimārk." In *10 Masraḥiyyāt Miṣriyya: 'Arḍ wa-Naqd,* 26–40. Cairo: Dār al-Hilāl, 1985.

———. "Mīzān al-Kawn." In *10 Masraḥiyyāt Miṣriyya: 'Arḍ wa-Naqd,* 96–109. Cairo: Dār al-Hilāl, 1985.

Tarawnah, Naseem. "Something Is Rotten in the State of Denmark." *Black Iris,* January 27, 2006.

Taylor, Charles. *The Ethics of Authenticity.* Cambridge, Mass.: Harvard University Press, 1992.

———. *Sources of the Self: The Making of the Modern Identity.* Cambridge: Cambridge University Press, 1989.

Taylor, Gary. *Reinventing Shakespeare: A Cultural History from the Restoration to the Present.* New York: Weidenfeld & Nicolson, 1989.

Tomiche, Nada. "Niveaux de langue dans le théâtre égyptien." In *Le Theatre Arabe,* ed. Nada Tomiche and Cherif Khaznadar, 117–32. Paris: UNESCO, 1969.

Tounsi, Mohamed M. "Shakespeare in Arabic: A Study of the Translation, Reception, and Influence of Shakespeare's Drama in the Arab World." EdD diss., University of Northern Colorado, 1989.

Twaij, Mohammed Baqir. "Shakespeare in the Arab World." PhD diss., Northwestern University, 1973.

Udhari, Abdullah, ed. and trans. *Modern Poetry of the Arab World.* London: Penguin, 1986.

Ueno, Yoshiko, ed. *Hamlet and Japan.* The Hamlet Collection, no. 2. New York: AMS Press, 1995.

'Umrān, Nādir. "Firqa Masraḥiyya Wajadat Masraḥan . . . fa-Masraḥat Hāmlit." Amman, 1984. Unpublished manuscript provided by the author.

Varisco, Daniel. "Much Ado about Something Rotten in Denmark." *Tabsir,* February 3, 2006.

Vaucher, Georges. *Nasser et Son Équipe.* Paris: Julliard, 1959.

Vest, James M. *The French Face of Ophelia from Belleforest to Baudelaire.* Lanham, Md.: University Press of America, 1989.

Wahba, Magdi. *Cultural Policy in Egypt.* Paris: UNESCO, 1972.

Wannūs, Sa'dallāh. *Al-A'māl al-Kāmila.* Vol. 1. Damascus: al-Ahālī li-l-Ṭibā'a wa-l-Nashr wa-al-Tawzī', 1996.

Wedeen, Lisa. *Ambiguities of Domination: Politics, Rhetoric, and Symbols in Contemporary Syria.* Chicago: University of Chicago Press, 1999.

Welsh, Alexander. *Hamlet in His Modern Guises.* Princeton, N.J.: Princeton University Press, 2001.

Woll, Josephine. *Real Images: Soviet Cinema and the Thaw.* London: I. B. Tauris, 2000.

Wright, George T. "Hendiadys and Hamlet." *PMLA* 96, no. 2 (1981): 168–93.

Yogev, Michael. "'How Shall We Find the Concord of this Discord?' Teaching Shakespeare in Israel, 1994." *Shakespeare Quarterly* 46, no. 2 (1995): 157–164.

Yurchak, Andrei. *Everything Was Forever, Until It Was No More: The Last Soviet Generation.* Princeton, N.J.: Princeton University Press, 2006.

Zaki, Amel Amin. "Shakespeare in Arabic." PhD diss., Indiana University, 1978.
Zhang, Xiaoyang. *Shakespeare in China: A Comparative Study of Two Traditions and Cultures.* Newark: University of Delaware Press, 1996.
Zimmermann, Heiner O. "Is Hamlet Germany? On the Political Reception of Hamlet." In *New Essays on Hamlet,* ed. Mark Thornton Burnett and John Manning, 293–318. New York: AMS Press, 1994.

INDEX

The prefixes al-, Al-, el-, and El have not been taken into account in the alphabetization of Arabic words.

Writing Outside the Nation by Azade Seyhan

The Literary Channel: The Inter-National Invention of the Novel edited by Margaret Cohen and Carolyn Dever

Ambassadors of Culture: The Transamerican Origins of Latino Writing by Kirsten Silva Gruesz

Experimental Nations: Or, the Invention of the Maghreb by Réda Bensmaïa

What Is World Literature? by David Damrosch

The Portable Bunyan: A Transnational History of The Pilgrim's Progress by Isabel Hofmeyr

We the People of Europe? Reflections on Transnational Citizenship by Étienne Balibar

Nation, Language, and the Ethics of Translation edited by Sandra Bermann and Michael Wood

Utopian Generations: The Political Horizon of Twentieth-Century Literature by Nicholas Brown

Guru English: South Asian Religion in a Cosmopolitan Language by Srinivas Aravamudan

Poetry of the Revolution: Marx, Manifestos, and the Avant-Gardes by Martin Puchner

The Translation Zone: A New Comparative Literature by Emily Apter

In Spite of Partition: Jews, Arabs, and the Limits of Separatist Imagination by Gil Z. Hochberg

The Princeton Sourcebook in Comparative Literature: From the European Enlightenment to the Global Present edited by David Damrosch, Natalie Melas, and Mbongiseni Buthelezi

The Spread of Novels: Translation and Prose Fiction in the Eighteenth Century by Mary Helen McMurran

The Event of Postcolonial Shame by Timothy Bewes

Hamlet's Arab Journey: Shakespeare's Prince and Nasser's Ghost by Margaret Litvin